SOUTHERN ILLINOIS
UNIVERSITY PRESS

Carbondale and Edwardsville

Feffer & Simons, Inc.

London and Amsterdam

THE
Poetry
OF
𝕮𝖍𝖆𝖚𝖈𝖊𝖗

John Gardner

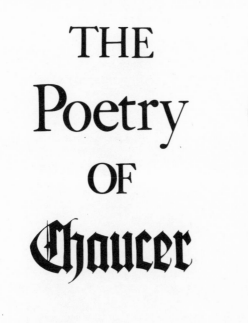

Library of Congress Cataloging in Publication Data

Gardner, John Champlin, 1933–
    The poetry of Chaucer.

    Includes bibliographical references and index.
    1. Chaucer, Geoffrey, d. 1400—Criticism and
interpretation. I. Title.
PR1924.G3   821'.1   76-22713
ISBN 0-8093-0772-3

For Joan, Joel, and Lucy

CONTENTS

Þ

[*vii*]

Preface

THIS BOOK WAS ORIGINALLY DESIGNED as the second half of a two-volume work called *The Life, Times, and Works of Geoffrey Chaucer*, but when I'd finished what I have now published as *The Life and Times of Chaucer*, I saw that my discussion of the poetry couldn't be made to fit with my writing on Chaucer's life. Writing biography, I had felt free to touch up the picture here and there, never altering facts, I hope, but using the tricks of a novelist to heighten their effect a little. Writing about Chaucer's poetry, on the other hand, I use the second side of a novelist's brain — the lobe that calculates and squints, studies older literature in hopes of understanding its methods and purposes with the greatest possible accuracy, perhaps so that someday, when it seems convenient, the novelist can steal them. The result is that this second book is completely different from the first in tone; different, too, in that it's harder to read and will, I'm afraid, appeal to a narrower audience, mainly teachers and college students.

I wish that were not so, in fact. I write about Chaucer because I believe profoundly what he says in his poetry about human life, and believe his ideas are more significant right now, in the twentieth century, than they ever were before, even in his own century. He knew, for instance, about "uncertainty" — knew from having thought about the arguments offered by the philosophical position called nominalism, that quite possibly all truth is relative (if we use "truth" in, say, the moralist's sense), and knew that quite possibly, there can be, in the end, no real communication between human beings. He played with those ideas throughout his career, and toward the end of his life he played even with such particularly, if not exclusively, modern aesthetic problems as the unreliable narrator and the paradox we see in Samuel Beckett and many other writers of the first rank in this century, that is, the paradox of speech denying the validity of speech. Yet to Chaucer, uncertainty was not a cause for panic but, instead, material for comedy and a defense of faith: where there is nothing else one can trust, one had better trust God. He differed from us in that God was a virtually unquestioned assumption in the Middle Ages, whereas for many of us any god now must be an existential assertion. Chaucer had no need to make what Kierkegaard called a leap of faith. His emotional security was established in early childhood — his feeling, below reason, in every situation, that his life was in good hands. Once that emotional security is set, it never much matters what one's intellect may say. We have, in the twentieth century, no such advantage, or at any rate, rather few of us have it. But the leap of faith is always possible; all one needs is a reason for making it. Chaucer's poetry, focusing again and again on doubt and the emotions stirred up by doubt — fear, hostility, despair, and the like — and answering that doubt with affirmative laughter, gives a solid reason for the leap of faith. I do not mean that Chaucer's poetry can make — or should make — every reader a Christian. I doubt that it matters how narrowly or broadly one takes the words of the angel to Dame Juliana of Norwich, that "All shall be well, and all shall be well, and all manner of things shall be well." Whether one achieves selflessness, security, and effectiveness by giving one's life to Jesus, or achieves the same more philosophically, by learning to affirm life's essential goodness, even if indeed there is no God, the result is probably pretty much the same. We live, as Yeats said, in an age when "The best lack all conviction, while the worst / Are filled with passionate intensity." But the principle of uncertainty — the principle, discovered by philosophical thinkers of the fourteenth century (and earlier) that nothing can be known — need not undermine conviction; it should be, on the contrary, the cornerstone of liberalism or, as Chaucer would say, charity. Because we can never be sure of ourselves, we should listen patiently to others' opinions, recognize that we are all clowns, that the world, alas, contains no longer any bareback riders, lion tamers, or acrobats, just us clowns. And having made that discovery, we should settle our restless hearts and get on with the circus.

As I say, because I believe that what Chaucer has to say about life is important, especially in our own century, I wish this book could be a popular one, the kind all well-intentioned people would gladly read. The trouble is that, dealing with difficult philosophical questions, working from a literary tradition now half-forgotten, and employing techniques no longer common in poetry or prose, Chaucer wrote poetry harder to understand — and more brilliant — than a strictly popular book could justly represent. Since one is naturally interested as much in Chaucer's art as in his ideas, if the two can indeed be separated, one has no choice but to work with care at particular poems. And so I've been forced to separate my earlier biographical study from this critical one.

In one way, especially, the separation is unfortunate. In writing on Chaucer's life, I spoke at length of some of the ideas that interested him, what his education entailed, and what kinds of attitudes he found common in the courts for which he worked, especially the royal courts of King Edward III and Richard II. Often matters primarily biographical illuminate the poems. For example, numerous critics have argued, in recent years, that Chaucer was a devout Christian who frowned with angry brows on sexual promiscuity, that in fact he took pretty much Saint Augustine's view of all this world's pleasures. But John of Gaunt was one of Chaucer's faithful patrons and probably his good friend, as well as brother-in-law, and Gaunt was (as an early Chaucerian wrote, and all the evidence supports his opinion) "not very continent." He had a long love affair with Katherine Swynford, whom in the end he married, and probably had several other affairs, one of them, possibly, with Geoffrey Chaucer's wife. Such things were common in the courts Chaucer served. There was, for example, the long and scandalous affair of King Edward III and Alice Perrers. Thus biography throws some light on Chaucer's attitude toward sex. Again, when we read the "marriage group" in the *Canterbury Tales*, that is, the group of tales running from the *Man of Law's Tale* to the *Franklin's Tale*, all dealing in one way or another with political theory as it applies to the home or some other sphere, it is helpful to remember that King Richard, whom Chaucer served, was at exactly this period urgently pursuing his absolutist theory of monarchy, adding to the crown's strength by fair means and foul in such a way that, ultimately, his magnates would rise against him, depose him, and kill him.

Commenting on Chaucer's poetry, here in this book, I cannot repeat all I have said already about Chaucer's life and times but must often leave the reader to make his own connections, in other words, must often assume the reader's knowledge of what I have said before. I do summarize here some of the more important discussions in my earlier book, especially discussions of philosophical ideas dramatized in poems like the *House of Fame*; and I do comment briefly, from time to time, on the social and political background of a given poem. But mainly my purpose here is to describe Chaucer's poetry in a technical and thematic way, showing the purposes and mechanical functions of some of his favorite poetic devices, explaining an occasional joke or allusion, and in general working as best I can toward an overview of the entire canon. Specialists will find much of what I say here familiar, since part of my purpose is to summarize a great heap of scholarly books and articles on Chaucer's poetry. Also, people used to reading the books of specialists may find my book rambling, perhaps, since I am not interested in developing here any one aspect of Chaucer's art, as specialists' studies always do, and rightly. In other words, it is not my purpose to write a book closely examining Chaucer's possible use of the writings of Robert Grosseteste, or Chaucer's relationship to John Gower, or the influence of Livy on Chaucer's aesthetic theory. My purpose is to follow where the poems lead, avoiding presuppositions but turning to ideas popular in Chaucer's day when those ideas seem to illuminate the poem. Anyone who has read much Chaucer criticism will know that one can easily write a full-length book on any one of the major poems, a book like those already published on the *Knight's Tale, Troilus and Criseyde*, the *House of Fame*, and so on. Inevitably, my discussions of the poems are less detailed than the discussions in such books. (Except for some modifications of punctuation, quotations from the poems are from F. N. Robinson's *The Works of Geoffrey Chaucer*, second edition [Boston: Houghton Mifflin Company, 1957].) This book, in short, is an introduction, an attempt to give a fairly accurate impression of the "complete works." I point out, in my Introduction, some of the main positions explored in Chaucer's poetry, and at various points throughout this book I pause for an assessment of how far we have come; but I have no single point to make about Chaucer's poetry, except of course, that it is a joy to read, a magnificent, puzzling, delightful world to move into from time to time, whenever we feel — as Chaucer sometimes felt — that "oure present worldes lyves space / Nis but a maner deth, what wey we trace."

FOR HELP with this book I'm indebted to all the Chaucer students I've had the good luck to teach over the past twenty years, and to the numerous colleagues who have listened patiently to my theories, offering criticism and suggestions, or read drafts of this book and helped me to get rid of some of the things once wrong with it. Since I've been working on this study for a long time, I cannot possibly thank all the people who have significantly modified my way of reading Chaucer, but some of the most important are John Howell, Thomas J. Hatton, Helen Vergette, Carroll Riley, and E. L. Epstein of Southern Illinois University, Neil Snortum and William Dickey of the State University of California at San Francisco, Donald R. Howard, whose book *The Three Temptations* and whose reading of an early draft of the manuscript of this book were an enormous help, and Russell Peck, who generously gave me comments on an almost final draft. My work has been supported by grants and secretarial assistance from the State University of California at San Francisco and Southern Illinois University at Carbondale. On a thousand occasions I've been helped by the advice and brilliant sleuthing of Alan Cohn, Professor of English and librarian at Southern Illinois University. I owe thanks above all, perhaps, to my teacher many years ago, John C. McGalliard, who in the years since I left Iowa has often read drafts of my articles and chapters. It is conventional to remark that any mistakes this book may contain are my fault, but since I have given this book, in early and late drafts, to so many intelligent and sensible readers, I cannot see how any faults my work may contain can be blamed on anyone but my friends.

John Gardner

Carbondale, Illinois
September 1975

Introduction

THE LATE FOURTEENTH CENTURY, the period during which Chaucer wrote, was a time of intense intellectual activity. In the sphere of political theory, scholars were debating the implications of Roman law for Christian Europe, the extent to which monarchy ought to be absolute, the exact meaning of the old phrase *quod principi placuit,* "the king's pleasure" — whether, on grounds of the divine will or some other grounds it ought to mean the king's personal desire or the welfare of the state, at the head of which the king stood as, in Dante's phrase, "the one will which resolves the many." Chaucer must have known the arguments well. He served as a diplomat to the court of Pedro the Cruel of Castile, whose theories on absolutism and divine right would be one of the factors leading to his murder. He was the friend and brother-in-law of Edward III's son John of Gaunt, who married Pedro's daughter and became legitimate pretender to the Spanish throne, and who later became chief supporter of the absolutist theory of Richard II of England — for whom the theory would also prove fatal. He undoubtedly knew the great religious reformer John Wyclif, Oxford scholar and friend of John of Gaunt, whose program of reform included an attack on Church control of secular offices. And he certainly knew all the chief political theorists in Richard's court; he served with several of them on diplomatic missions and served on a commission with another of them as justice of the peace. Chaucer's poetry shows again and again his professional interest, as a public servant, in political theory and practice.

Another matter of great concern among fourteenth-century

intellectuals was accurate translation and understanding of the Latin and, to a lesser extent, Greek classics. (Most of the Greek literature we read today had not yet been recovered in Chaucer's day and was known only at second hand, through writers like Boethius, who flourished in the early sixth century.) For centuries *translatio* had meant retelling, not word-by-word translation. "Translation" in this older sense had elaborate rules — how to shorten the passage in one's source, how to elaborate it for greater emphasis, how to impose allegorical meaning, and so forth — and was rightly considered a noble art; but the purpose of this older form of translation was not understanding of the writer being translated (or at any rate that was a secondary purpose); the purpose was, rather, to create an essentially *new* work, much as Shakespeare made a new work of his source for *Hamlet* or his source for *King Lear*, or as Chaucer made a new work, *Troilus and Criseyde*, out of a poem by Boccaccio. In Paris and then Oxford, a series of great scholars including Robert Grosseteste and Roger Bacon developed the principles of translation as we now understand it, and one result was the great intellectual boom that would open the door to the Renaissance and the Protestant Reformation. Chaucer may have studied at Oxford; he certainly visited there when his son Lewis studied there, and he had several close friends who were Oxford dons — among them Ralph Strode, to whom (along with the poet John Gower) he dedicated *Troilus and Criseyde*. He knew about the new theory of translation and joined the ranks of the new translators by writing several such works, the most important of which is his translation of Boethius' *Consolation of Philosophy*, a superb scholarly work by the standards of the day. His poetry offers abundant evidence that he was also intensely interested in the new kind of scholarship these more accurate translations fostered.

But in the long run perhaps the most important intellectual debate of all in the fourteenth century was the philosophical argument set off by (in effect) the clash between the ideas of Thomas Aquinas and William of Ockham. It would be impossible to treat that argument in detail here (I have summarized its main points briefly in *The Life and Times of Chaucer*), but the upshot was this: after Duns Scotus' proof that Aquinas' harmony of revelation and philosophy (mainly Aristotle's) was illusory, William of Ockham went further, striking at the heart of the Thomistic vision.

Thomas had tried to prove the existence of a single "human nature" and that that nature, which all human beings share, can communicate with the divine nature; in other words, men are capable of understanding each other and God. Ockham disagreed. There are, he said, no *universals,* only *particulars;* in other words, the world contains cows, elephants, anteaters, and gorillas — particular animals — but the universal "animal" is merely a concept, an abstraction; and, more important, while there are particular men, women, and children, there is no universal "nature of man." All ideas, Ockham argues, are abstractions from the concrete; and since this is so, I can neither know that my idea is "right" nor — since you too abstract from concrete particulars (and your experience and mine are not identical) — meaningfully communicate my idea to you. Ockham's view received powerful support later from Roger Bacon of Oxford, when he showed the limitations of both "authority" and "experience" — key words in Chaucer's poetry.

Bacon describes three kinds of authority: 1) divine revelation, 2) the authority of philosophical tradition going back to Plato and Aristotle, and 3) rigorous logic. Of divine authority he says virtually nothing, though he was well aware of the attempts at higher criticism being made in his day and must have wondered where those reassessments of scriptural texts would lead. But he writes at length on the authority of old philosophers and of logic, providing valuable principles for philosophical analysis. In the end he concludes that neither philosophical tradition nor logic can be trusted without the support of "experience," by which he means scientific experimentation, and he lays down what would stand for years as the essential laws of the scientific method. And not even "experience," Bacon discovers, can be trusted absolutely. His experiments in the field of optics revealed to him that no two human eyes are identical — in other words, that there can be no absolute standard of vision. One is left, then, with no absolute but divine revelation — and even that (though Bacon probably never for an instant doubted God's existence and benevolence) must seem here and there a trifle curious. With this support from Bacon, Ockham's nominalism — his denial of universals — became the most attractive and interesting philosophical approach of the day. Chaucer would make it the very heart of his comedy, dramatizing the nominalist position by means of his squinting, dim-witted narrator in the *House of Fame* or such later "unreliable narrators" as the Physician, Prioress, and Manciple in the *Canterbury Tales*. This is not necessarily to say that Chaucer was himself a nominalist. His comedy may have been, at least in his own mind, a way of making fun of the nominalist view of man; and even if he was a nominalist, he was never in his life thrown into self-pity or despair on account of a conviction that nothing can be known for certain. He was a man of faith, profoundly convinced that God had the universe in hand and that Christ had redeemed poor sinful man, so that man's ignorance and confusion need not hurt him much. But whatever Chaucer may have thought of the nominalist way of thinking, it gave him a grip on his experience which allowed him to transform it into successful art.

One might continue at length on the intellectual activity of the late fourteenth century, but since the background of Chaucer's poetry will inevitably come up in the process of our examining particular poems, it may be best to turn to a subject harder to treat than the ideas of Chaucer's age, namely, the emotions or feelings of that age, especially one of prime importance in Chaucer's poetry, love. The matter is of special importance these days since in recent years Chaucerian scholars have made it the center of a heated debate, some claiming that, despite the ribaldry in Chaucer, the poet thought of sex as sinful or, at best, perilous, others claiming that he was a great celebrator of sex, both licit and illicit. The truth no doubt lies between the two extremes. One way of describing Chaucer's attitude, and that of the many fourteenth-century readers and listeners who delighted in his poetry, is through comparison of Chaucer with earlier and later writers.

Consider a poem by Chaucer's late disciple, Edmund Spenser:

> Most glorious Lord of lyfe, that on this day,
> Didst make thy triumph over death and sin:
> And having harrowed hell, didst bring away
> Captivity thence captive us to win:
> This joyous day, deare Lord, with joy begin,
> And grant that we for whom thou diddest dye
> Being with thy deare blood clene washt from sin,
> May live for ever in felicity.
> And that thy love we weighing worthily,
> May likewise love thee for the same againe:

And for thy sake that all lyke deare didst buy,
With love may one another entertayne.
So let us love, deare love, lyke as we ought,
Love is the lesson which the Lord us taught.
[Sonnet 68, from Spenser's *Amoretti*

We call Geoffrey Chaucer a medieval poet, Edmund Spenser, a poet of the Renaissance. Some differences between the two are perfectly apparent, of course. Spenser writes elegant philosophical allegories in which characters function like figures in stained glass, or else writes personal love poems; Chaucer writes more supple allegorical poems, full of comic cartoons, and when he speaks of love he insists that his experience is strictly theoretical. Such differences are trifling, obviously, and the longer we reflect on the matter, the more convinced we become that we need not look with superstitious awe on the categories "Medieval" and "Renaissance." In general, at least, a Renaissance poet is someone who has read the Greeks, and a medieval poet is someone who, according to the Renaissance poet, has not.

Chaucer looks forward to Spenser as surely as Spenser (with his imitation Middle English, his delight in metrical and stanzaic experiment, and his penchant for something like medieval ornamentation) looks backward from the Renaissance to Chaucer. Both poets express an attitude toward love which is grounded on Christian-Neoplatonic ideas on how the soul rises through sensible things to things divine — from the nipple to the virtuous woman to God. Spenser's Platonism is generally recognized, and nothing need be said of it. But it is worth noting that the attitude toward love expressed in Sonnet 68 from the *Amoretti*, quoted above (as also in the *Epithalamion* and elsewhere), is not the fully developed Renaissance attitude tentatively expressed in Sidney or solidly affirmed, from time to time, in Shakespeare. This is not to say that Spenser is really a medieval poet or even one "more medieval" than Shakespeare, and neither is it to say that Chaucer is really a man of the Renaissance. It is to say, merely, that the overlap of the two ages is so broad that unless we resort to certain focal events of history — for instance the battle of Bosworth Field — no distinction between the two can be made except the precarious distinction between subtle inclinations of emotion.

On the basis of Plato's *Symposium*, with Plato's God transformed to the Christian God, Spenser can comfortably affirm the
sensual; he can even write charmingly pagan invitations to love —
Sonnet 70, for example:

> Fresh spring the herald of loves mighty king,
> In whose cote armour richly are displayd
> All sorts of flowers the which on earth do spring
> In goodly colours gloriously arrayd.
> Goe to my love, where she is carelesse layd,
> Yet in her winters bowre not well awake:
> Tell her the joyous time wil not be staid
> Unlesse she doe him by the forelock take.
> Bid her therefore her selfe soone ready make,
> To wayt on love amongst his lovely crew:
> Where every one that misseth then her make,
> Shall be by him amearst with penance dew.
> Make hast therefore sweet love, whilest it is prime,
> For none can call againe the passed time.

For all its happy paganism, Spenser's poem is as medieval in spirit,
and as thoroughly dependent on Christian tradition, as anything in
Chaucer. The love between men and women is finally justified by
its spiritual value, according to Spenser. One may not directly
mention that fact on May Day. But the Cupid of Sonnet 70, "loves
mighty king," is the mighty and angel-like Cupid of the Middle
Ages, a figure sometimes directly emblematic of Christ; if spring is
Cupid's herald, it is also a traditional resurrection symbol, a
foreshadowing "type," like love itself, of the spiritual "joyous time,"
life everlasting. In fact, all the imagery in the sonnet borrows church
decorations. Flowers are always a central detail in the medieval
paradise, earthly or otherwise; winter is a stock emblem of death,
occurring in hundreds of English, French, Italian, and German
religious lyrics; waiting "on love amongst his lovely crew" faintly
suggests (no more faintly in Spenser's day than in the *Pearl*-poet's)
an image of Jesus among his brides; and the love-penance in the
twelfth line is a conventional medieval detail, a further comparison
of Christian religion and the love religion. None of this means that
the poem is really not secular after all, but a satiric "condemnation
of carnality," and neither does it mean that the poem is an ironic

attack on Christendom. Spenser takes frank delight in the sensual, but his style, his music, and the elegance of his imagery all rule out the possibility that he means the love ritual to diminish the dignity of Christian worship. The interpenetration of the physical and the spiritual insists, simply, on relationship between the two. We must love "lyke as we ought." Spenser's justification of human love — by no means merely a poetic device in the sixty-eighth sonnet, quoted earlier — is that it brings people closer to God. Spenser embraces "the World," the sensual, but far as he may be from monkish *contemptus mundi,* he does so cautiously and with ambivalent emotion: like anything else on the Platonic ladder of higher and lower goods, love is of value in itself, but its chief value is that it leads to things higher.

Sir Philip Sidney occasionally goes farther — or plays the love-poet game with more gusto — for instance here in the fifth sonnet from *Astrophel and Stella:*

> It is most true that eyes are formed to serve
> The inward light, and that the heavenly part
> Ought to be king, from whose rules who do swerve,
> Rebels to nature, strive for their own smart.
> It is most true, what we call Cupid's dart
> An image is, which for ourselves we carve,
> And, fools, adore in temple of our heart,
> Till that good god make church and churchmen starve.
> True, that true beauty virtue is indeed,
> Whereof this beauty can be but a shade,
> Which elements with mortal mixture breed.
> True, that on earth we are but pilgrims made,
> And should in soul up to our country move.
> True, and yet true that I must Stella love.

With the appearance of this poem the impalpable turning point from the orthodoxy of the Middle Ages to the usual emotion of the Renaissance — and of modern man — has slipped into the past. One might not guess it from the first thirteen lines. They present, with evident conviction, the orthodox medieval churchman's view of human love, and every detail Sidney has chosen can be matched in the writings of Chaucer or Dante and explicated by reference to the patristic and scholastic writers who taught medieval men, including

Chaucer, the road to heaven. The "eyes" Sidney speaks of recall
Boethian and pulpit imagery of sight versus blindness, light versus
darkness, that is, wisdom versus concern with the things of this
world — an opposition occasionally expressed by patristic writers as
one between the eye of the spirit and the eye of flesh, the former
inclining the soul to charity, the latter miring it in carnality; an
opposition often expressed in medieval poetry as one between
looking inward, as in the dream vision, and looking outward at the
wilderness world. Sidney's image recalls the elaborate imagery of
eyes in Dante; the unblinking eyes of that conventional Christian
and heraldic emblem, thousand-eyed Argus (of whom Chaucer
speaks); the traditional idea of spiritual dim-wittedness that Chaucer
again and again introduces in comic terms with his myopic
characters and narrators. When Sidney confesses that reason ("the
heavenly part"), not passion, ought to be the micro-republic's
king — and that when lower faculties usurp control, perverting the
natural order of man (or of the analogous cosmos), the result must
be anarchy and grief — he is repeating an assertion ubiquitous in
medieval writing — the whole theme of Alanus de Insulis' book, or
in Fabius Fulgentius' analysis of Virgil; a central concern in the
Divine Comedy, and a common theme in Chaucer, who speaks
repeatedly in the *Book of the Duchess* of how all nature turns on the
grieving, unreasonable lover (e.g., *BD*, 509–13). Sidney's claim that
the worship of Cupid is idolatry is equally standard in medieval
writing, though love poets sometimes take the ritual seriously, as
Spenser does, and at times suggest that Cupid is the Christian "God
of Love" imperfectly apprehended. The whole question of how the
love poetry of Italy and France should rightly be understood is still a
battleground for critics, but one need not squint or think in Latin to
recognize the jokes at the expense of love-religion in Chaucer: in the
second stanza of the *Parliament of Birds*, where Chaucer pretends to
be terrified by "swiche a lord" (meaning Cupid), at numerous
points in the *Troilus*, and in the earlier Prologue to the *Legend of
Good Women*. Sidney's statement that true beauty is identical with
virtue and that physical beauty is merely a shadow of the Ideal are of
course both ideas out of Plato, whose thought was virtually
unknown to the Middle Ages except at secondhand; but these two
ideas reflect that side of Neoplatonism which writers like Augustine
found not too objectionable. They were ideas easily translated into

the Christian idiom — virtue meaning, for fallen man, imitation of the model, Christ, and shadow meaning, in effect, substance, "the slime of the earth." The idea in Sidney's sonnet that all men are pilgrims through a wilderness goes back to Paul, gets emphatic restatement from Augustine, informs the opening lines of the *Divine Comedy*, and serves as the climax of Chaucer's short poem to Vache, *Truth: Balade de Bon Conseyl.*

But Sidney's final line, which defies and emotionally over-whelms the rest (though perhaps only because of the ironic role-playing standard in Elizabethan sonnets) is a thoroughly Renaissance affirmation of the beauty of a particular, mortal woman — which is to say, if the traditional metaphor may be imposed upon the poem, the beauty of this world. Sidney does not deny the validity of the Christian and Platonic views of life, one flatly ascetic, one offering a ladder to otherworldliness; they are right, and he claims that may well mean his ruin; but the beauty of the physical, taken for itself, is also right. Sidney stands (or for Stella's sake pretends to stand) with his feet firmly planted in two worlds, and though his heart is uneasy, he will not give way with either foot.

Affirmation of the world glows still more brightly in Shake-speare's Sonnet 130, "My Mistress' Eyes Are Nothing Like the Sun." I need not point out that more than humor — and more than another clever move in the sonnet game — is involved in Shake-speare's so-called anti-Petrarchan lines. For Petrarch's (or any medieval love poet's) characteristic identification of physical and mutable beauty with the spiritual or at any rate immutable beauty it figures forth, Shakespeare substitutes a stubborn double-mindedness, or rather a *wide*-mindedness: the abstracting of a woman's qualities into vaguely Platonic verities belies the real beauties of body as surely as the beauties of body misrepresent those of spirit. The same Renaissance attitude expressed in Sidney's final line appears, but with greater emotional charge, in Shakespeare's final couplet: "And yet, by heaven, I think my love as rare / As any she belied with false compare." No detailed explication of these lines is necessary, I realize. But my point requires me to call attention again to the fact that "rare" functions doubly here, suggesting at once the ineffable ideal (*rare* in the sense of "etherial" or "insubstantial") and also the uniqueness of a particular woman; so that Shakespeare's final statement must be paraphrased in two ways at once. The lady is as uniquely beautiful as any woman whose beauty has been falsely represented through spurious comparison, and, also (ironically) she is as etherial as any other woman — that is to say, *no* woman is etherial (or completely so), but the lady's partly or even mainly physical beauty is worthy of celebration just the same. The shock in the lines comes from the poet's explosive "by heaven," which calls up the spiritual pole of reality, a pole Shakespeare's tone affirms as vigorously as he affirms the physical beauty of his lady. What is involved here is not philosophical dualism but a broadening of emotion, a Protestant wholeness of vision which embraces not polarities but totality. Shakespeare's sonnet sequence, taken as a whole, has its share of Spenserian Platonism as well as its share of traditional attitude and imagery; but sonnets like this one reveal what seems a new security in the affirmation of things physical. Renaissance man inhabits an expanding reality, just as, psychologically at least, an explorer does. When the explorer sets out westward to find the gold and dark-eyed ladies of India, he knows Church-filled Portugal is still there behind him, and so is all the water between Portugal and his ship. Sir Philip Sidney expresses a characteristic Renaissance joy in things physical, a joy which entails no rejection of the spiritual — a joy analogous to the explorer's delight in his discovery that, despite dark warnings, he has not yet fallen off the world. Shakespeare goes further. Where Sidney stood nervously, startled by his luck, Shakespeare stands at his ease, a native of the place. Later, in *Antony and Cleopatra*, he will draw the perhaps inevitable conclusion: in the Platonic ascent, it is this world's beauty which defines the beauty of the next, not the other way around. In that play, love which begins as broadly comic parody of medieval courtly love grows in virtue and significance until it has become — as much of the play's imagery insists — too big for the world and must get out. This is not to deny the fundamental and thoroughly medieval paradox in *Antony and Cleopatra*: love is responsible for Antony's disgrace and tragedy, exactly as it is responsible for the tragedy of Troilus, but love is also, as in the *Troilus*, noble and ennobling.

To see how far Renaissance emotion has come from its point of departure we need only to recall the scene in which Dante speaks with Paolo and Francesca and learns how, while reading about

Lancelot and Guinevere, they lost control of their passions and fell headlong into love and sorrow. For Dante as for the Church Fathers, physical love between a man and a woman is a precious but also dangerous thing. Dante is led to Paradise by a woman, and the poem's Platonism is abundantly clear; but the Platonism is distant from Spenser's and more distant from Shakespeare's. Dante's ennobling love is for a woman long dead, liberated into spirit. The central idea which illuminates the entire *Divine Comedy* is that in the presence (or remembered presence) of a particularly noble woman, Dante knows right from wrong, knows how to think and feel, or, to put it another way, would be ashamed to be anything less than his finest, most godlike self. Her nature is his absolute standard, his only guide back to the right path which, at the start of the poem, he has lost. His love is partly sexual; in the thirtieth canto of the *Purgatorio* he alludes to Virgil's story of the passionate love of Dido and Aeneas and implicitly equates that love with his love for Beatrice; but sex, for Dante, is never the real point. His love poem — the greatest love poem in the world — is a hymn to a soul in heaven, a spirit who becomes, in the poem's last lines, the Trinity itself.

So the question is, what were the causes of this shift in attitude, from Dante to Shakespeare, and where in the process of the change does Chaucer stand?

Even if it is true that the creed of the Middle Ages was fixed — a point not to be granted in haste, since more time passed between Saint Augustine's time and Chaucer's than has passed between Chaucer's time and our own — there was clearly room within it for the expression of a wide range of feelings. No medieval Christian could comfortably deny that the world, though in itself a thing indifferent, was the source of dangerous temptations to the unwary soul. In the fifth century, Saint Jerome had urged an attitude of *contemptus mundi*, by which he meant nothing more than wise indifference. By the twelfth century, for a variety of reasons, recognition of the dangers inherent in the world had solidified into a prevailing attitude, at least among churchmen, of sometimes quite fierce contempt. But admitting that the world was dangerous and that love of a woman could hurl the lover into hell, a medieval poet might still express emotions not strictly orthodox. In certain medieval works, like the *Council of Love at Remiremont*, carnal love produces rowdy comedy; in works like *Parzifal* love is idealized. The extreme represented by the *Council* looks forward to the Renaissance, but only superficially, since there is all the difference in the world between Sidney's serious recognition that he has sailed without harm past what he has been told is the edge of the world, and the comically overconfident glee of the medieval clownish lover. Medieval poetry commonly expresses a tension between an orthodox theory of reality and an unorthodox intuition of reality. Medieval men *knew* the world dangerous when they thought about it (as the troubador poets never stopped to do), because their teachers told them it was; but only part of the time did they *feel* that it was dangerous.

What was required, if thought and feeling — authority and experience, in a sense — were to be harmonized, was a system which could justify man's real, and apparently not always harmful, secular delights. To put it another way, what was needed was a new explanation of the relationship between natural law and divine law. To the extent that classical literature and Near Eastern philosophy celebrated those values which supported medieval's man's emotional apprehension of the world — his unorthodox pleasure and sense of relative safety in making love to his wife or even mistress — the new explanation was required to solve the problem of the pagans. If we leap forward to Spenser the solution seems easy and obvious: Neoplatonism. By defining the beauty of particular loved ones as Socrates does in the *Symposium*, a properly adapted Neoplatonism can open the way to loving them, without embarrassment, for themselves. Neoplatonism was available enough to medieval men, and it was indeed the solution offered by the early writers of chivalry books — numerous and popular in the later Middle Ages — who treated human love as an ennobling force, viewed the beloved as elevated above the lover, and considered love as a never satisfied, ever increasing desire for the Good, that is for bravery in battle, selflessness, courtesy, and so forth. This view of love satisfied those feelings which were left to starve by official Church doctrine, but it could not satisfy those strong emotions attached to doctrine itself. The chivalric view of love, if one stopped to think about it, was bad theology. If the Neoplatonic attitude toward love was to be made comfortable, and not merely through what might be called a willing suspension of belief for the moment (a suspension of the sort we see in the troubadors or in the love affairs of John of Gaunt), non-Christian thought must first be transformed, in one way or another, to something reasonably Christian. This meant working out in acceptable Christian terms a harmonious relationship between the fundamental laws of pagan life and the wider law of salvation revealed in the Incarnation. In philosophy, it meant Aquinas' rehabilitation of Aristotle; in literature it meant the allegorizing of pagan fables — a long and continuous process which runs through the centuries from Fulgentius' commentary on Virgil to fourteenth- or fifteenth-century works like the *Ovide moralisé* and *Gesta Romanorum*: books showing or implying that pagan tales were really Christian allegories inspired by the Holy Ghost. The tradition need not be treated in any detail here. It is the method Chaucer's contemporary Giovanni Boccaccio, among others, borrows from patristic exegesis to apply to pagan literature. Boccaccio writes:

> The first meaning [of poetry] is the superficial, which is called literal. The others are deeper, and are called allegorical. To make the matter easier, I will give an example. According to the poetic fiction, Perseus, son of Jupiter, killed the Gorgon, and flew away victorious into the air. Now, this may be understood superficially in its literal or historical sense. In the moral sense it shows a wise man's triumph over vice and his attainment of virtue. Allegorically it figures the pious man who scorns worldly delight and lifts his mind to heavenly things. It admits also an anagogical sense, since it symbolizes Christ's victory over the Prince of this World, and his Ascension.[1]

Here we are well beyond Bonaventura's idea (in *The Mind's Road to God*) that nature and scripture (the basis of, respectively, pagan experience and Christian experience) are God's two books, both of which are spiritually instructive. For men like Boccaccio, pagan poetry, like the divinely inspired Old Testament, can contain presignifications of New Testament events.

It is mainly the feeling about pagans as human beings, not the basic idea, that is new in Boccaccio's time. In Lactantius' *Divine Institutes* — after a preface treating "Of What Great Value the Knowledge of the Truth Is and Has Always Been" — Lactantius insists that many pagans had insight into Christian truth. He includes Maro, Orpheus, Ovid, and others (Bk. I, Ch. 6). Yet Lactantius is anything but kind to the pagans: they knew about the oneness of God, he says, but they flattered gods they did not believe in and they made stupid mistakes. He gives credit grudgingly ("no one can be so blind as not to see the divine brightness presenting itself to his eyes. The poets, therefore, however much they adorned the gods . . . frequently confess that all things are held together and governed by one spirit or mind" — Bk. I, Ch. 5). We see the same grudging admiration in Augustine when he admits in the *City of God* (XVIII, 14) that the pagans knew about the one true God; despite their knowledge, he says, they fell into confusion or told lies.

In later tradition Fulgentius' *Exposition on the Contents of Virgil* and *Mythology* present Christian interpretations of pagan poetry which place no emphasis on the pagan's mistakes; but Fulgentius cautiously treats only the "simple" levels of allegory. He claims the *Aeneid* has four levels but treats only the first and sidesteps the question of what Aeneas has to do with, for instance, eschatology. (In a later view, Aeneas is Christ establishing the Kingdom of Heaven.) By the time of Dante, Petrarch, and Boccaccio, the feeling and accepted practice have changed. Whereas Augustine allows that pagans may sometimes acknowledge the true God but angrily condemns them for failing to distinguish between the true God and the surrounding false gods, Boccaccio emphatically denies that pagans were polytheists:

> Who is witless enough to suppose that a man deeply versed in philosophy hasn't any more sense than to accept polytheism? As sensible men we must easily admit that the learned have been most devoted investigators of the truth, and have gone as far as the human mind can explore; thus they know beyond any shadow of doubt that there is but one God. As for poets, their works clearly show that they have attained to such knowledge. Read Virgil and you will find the prayer:
> *If any vows, Almighty Jove, can bend Thy will* — an epithet which you will never see applied to another god. The multitude of other gods they looked upon not as gods, but as members or functions of the Divinity; such was Plato's opinion, and we call him a theologian.[2]

By Boccaccio's time, such views are common. Petrarch, one of Boccaccio's sources, argues that pagan poets by intuitive genius outstripped the philosophers in their idea of God, and that both poets and philosophers rejected polytheism.[3] Virgil was generally considered to have possessed something very close to the truth by inspiration; but other poets, together with certain philosophers, were also thought to have "touched on the truth and almost grasped it," as Lactantius says — among them Orpheus, Ovid, Aristotle, Plato, Cicero, and Seneca.[4]

For Chaucer as for his great Italian contemporaries, or for Spenser later, a pagan god can be — though he need not invariably be — identified with the one true God. In the *House of Fame* Jupiter is apparently equivalent to the Boethian Prime Mover, and elsewhere — notably in *Troilus and Criseyde* — the god of love comes to be, at least some of the time, identical with God. (The pagan god of love and the Christian God as Boethius understands him are indivisible, for example, in Troilus' hymn, Book III, lines 1744–71.) The point is not that Troilus' god of love — or the Black Knight's — is "really" Jehovah, or, as one critic thinks, an attempt on Chaucer's part to appease a Christian audience,[5] and neither is he merely Cupid. He is precisely what he *ought* to be in the view of any intelligent Christian from Augustine's day to Edmund Spenser's, the one true God in his pagan, hence slightly obscured, form: the god of men who, lacking revelation, "loved the lawe of kinde." For Augustine the pagan anticipation of Christian verity was feeble and frequently wrong headed; for Boccaccio and Chaucer, it was strong and, as a rule, fairly healthy.

The Christianizing of the pagans came in two stages: first, in an assertion that classical writings and the classical age might be seen as analogous to the Old Testament and the age of the Old Jerusalem; and, second, in an assertion that pagan doctrine at its best was not contradictory to New Testament doctrine but harmonious with it. No medieval critic, as far as I know, flatly asserts that pagan poets and philosophers were directly inspired by the Holy Ghost, but neither do they flatly deny it; and such critics as Boccaccio and Petrarch come as close as possible to making that perhaps heretical assertion. In his *Invective Against the Physician*, Petrarch points out the ways in which the inspiration of pagan poets is parallel to prophetic inspiration (an idea we find echoed in Sidney's *Defense of*

Poesy), and, as we've seen, Boccaccio sometimes follows his master in looking for the exegetical four levels in poetry from the classical age. These adjustments of the traditional Christian attitude toward pagans began early — long before they were spelled out by Renaissance Italians. And of course artists were making these adjustments at the same time critics made them. A few quick examples will suggest the process. In the Irish *Book of Kells*, pagan motifs are put in the service of the new religion. They perhaps retain their old meaning, but they are placed in a new and wider context. In the same way, the *Beowulf*-poet (eighth century) turns Germanic-pagan history and legend to a Christian purpose.[6] The *Beowulf*-poet treats the pagan Danes very much as Chaucer treats the pagan Trojans, as men whose lives illustrated truths not yet fully revealed or understood. Beowulf is, most critics now agree, at least to some extent typic of Christ; and the poet says at lines 697–702, that the God of the Danes was the one true God, whether the Danes were aware of it or not.[7] The Old English elaboration of the earlier *Phoenix* reflects the same mode of thought; and if it is true that the *Wanderer* and *Seafarer* are ancient poems reworked by a Christian, as most critics think, then these too imply a pagan-Christian correspondence.

But Germanic emotion was a far cry from Greek emotion, and though Anglo-Saxon poets draw parallels between pagan experience and Christian, they rarely go so far as to hint that pagans understood or even came close to understanding true theology. The Christianizing of classical antiquity had to wait for the thirteenth and fourteenth centuries, and it would remain, even then, the kind of movement possible only in hot spots of inquiry like Oxford. As for full Renaissance approval of pagan sensualism as a valid segment of total reality, that had to wait for the combined effect of changes in every sphere of medieval activity.

The progress of the Middle Ages shows, then, not so much a change in what Christian men said about pagan thought as a change in men's attitudes toward pagan thinkers. And to complicate matters, it was not just a rejection of stern old-fashioned Christian thought for a more liberal, quasi-pagan idea but partly a rejection of stern old-fashioned pagan thought. *Contemptus mundi* was not, in early Christian times, an exclusively Christian notion. The system of the pagan philosopher Plotinus is shot through with it. For those who find the essence of history in the progress of logic, it may appear that the central reason for the general rise of interest in the conflict of the two "loves" (carnal, spiritual) in Neoplatonic thought (both pagan and Christian) is that later thinkers felt a need to account for what seemed a gap in Plato's system. For Plato it was a matter of fact that material attempts to embody pure form are never quite successful. He gives no reason. Later Neoplatonists introduce the explanation — foreign to Plato's way of thinking — that attempts to embody form fail because of the "recalcitrance" of matter, which is seen as inherently defective, or evil. Whatever the motivations of earlier and later thinkers, gradually systems like that of Plotinus, which took a dark view of substance, came to be adapted to a brighter view of the things of this world. Plotinus' idea of graduated good — the idea that the universe is built of hierarchies, from worms to lions, lead to gold, peasants to kings — provided a means of approving what formerly had been scorned by Christians. Such approval, along with its theoretical grounding, was explicit in the Arabic culture made available to medieval Europe through the crusades, through Cluniac monks, and through pilgrimages like that of Saint James of Compostella, and so could be examined and tested. The fragmentary *Timaeus* known to the Middle Ages, together with such Arabic works as Avicenna's *Treatise on Love*, provided what was for the period a new insight into pagan experience, particularly classical poetry and philosophy. Non-Christian ideas, suspect when they came from stubbornly unreconstructed pagans like Plotinus, could be discovered in or imposed on the writers of classical antiquity, whose virtues and keen insights were already recognized by Christian writers. Those studies Augustine had disapproved (the quadrivium) could be reaffirmed, as they were by Hugh of Saint Victor and others; and pagan poetry could be pursued further than men like Fulgentius dared pursue it. One of Chaucer's favorite books, Macrobius' *Commentary On the Dream of Scipio* is a notable result. Macrobius' misunderstanding of Cicero — his persistent twisting of Cicero's ideas toward later Neoplatonism — rises not from any inability to read intelligently but from full conviction that the Neoplatonic alternative is inherent in classical thought. This same conviction informs every analysis Boccaccio offers of pagan poetry, whatever critical method he happens to employ for a given work.

At the same time, a manipulation of Christian doctrine could, under the influence of Neoplatonism, derive a view of the world which was in spirit close to the Platonic view. I have alluded already to this process in the thought of Bonaventura. The same appears in Hugh of Saint Victor. He writes at one point,

> Concerning tropology I shall not at present say anything more than what was said above, except that it is more the meaning of things than the meaning of words which seem to pertain to it. For in the meaning of things lies natural justice, out of which the discipline of our own morals, that is, positive justice, arises. By contemplating what God has made we realize what we ourselves ought to do. Every nature tells of God; every nature teaches man; every nature reproduces its essential form, and nothing in the universe is unfecund.[8]

We observed earlier, in very general terms, that the driving emotional and intellectual need to make pagans respectable in the Middle Ages, and thus to reinstate what was best in, as Paul said, the "old man" without murdering the new, is at the heart of the medieval feeling for the *Consolation of Philosophy*, a work as important to Hugh of Saint Victor as to Chaucer. Boethius' lesson for man was no different from Saint Augustine's: renounce the things of this world, love God. But in the *Consolation* Boethius did not ordinarily say "God," he said "the Prime Mover," and equally important, both his matter and his manner — the combination of poetry and prose — represent an attempt to synthesize Christian and pagan emotion. As Gareth Dunleavy has shown,[9] Boethius offered traditional medicine for two "wounds," the wound to the body and the wound to the soul, but he did not offer, except indirectly — through his *manner* — medicine for the wound most painful to fourteenth-century middle-class Englishmen like Chaucer: humiliation in a world where getting and spending lay at the heart of everyday existence, inescapable and impossible to scorn. One might deny that peasants had the "natural rights" they clamored for; one might deny, in theory, that the Merciless Parliament of 1389 was of any significance with respect to men's just or unjust deserts; but no tradesman from a family of tradesmen could comfortably deny the importance, both for good and for evil, of money, possessions, and social advancement, that is, of worldly things for the proper management of the world. Humiliation through the loss of power and possessions was a feeling Boethius himself knew well, and in the *Consolation* he frankly admits his pleasure in these things, even now that he has seen that they crumble. The stoic Christianity which Boethius shares with all patristic and scholastic writers is tempered, throughout the *Consolation*, with a trace of nostalgic paganism — in the verse, in the allusions to classical authors, in the play of wit and imagination, in Boethius' quiet evasion of specifically Christian language. And this nostalgia for an age traditionally identified with materialism (as in *The City of God*) opens the door a crack to let in the World. The emotion in Boethius more than any specifically Neoplatonic tendency (though that, too, is present) points toward the Renaissance.

The renewed popularity of Boethius throughout Europe in the thirteenth and fourteenth centuries, and the popularity, among men of letters, of the neo-pagan Boethian style — the greatest imitation of which if Geoffrey Chaucer's *Knight's Tale* — show a change in feeling, after Augustine's time, the same change evinced by Aquinas' veneration of Aristotle, or Dante's admiration of Virgil. In secular spheres of thought — in law, astrology, optics, medicine, and political theory — medieval admiration of the pagans was even less apologetic.

In short, what we find when we look at Chaucer's poetry is that Chaucer's position is close to Spenser's but disguised. Whereas Spenser speaks openly, having nothing to fear from conservative churchmen of the kind who in Chaucer's day closed Oxford, Chaucer speaks from the security of a comic mask. Spenser describes his joy in love; Chaucer disingenuously presents himself as a dim-witted clot who cannot be held responsible and who, in any case, has never personally experienced love, then describes and with comic ardor defends the joy of *other* lovers. He serves Love's servants, he says. Chaucer's comic stance, though it undercuts his Christian-Neoplatonic position, is not to be mistaken for the comic stance taken by the writers of such works as the *Council of Love at Remiremont*; it's new in one very important respect. Chaucer's narrator is not ludicrous because he's a lover, a victim of carnality whom the orthodox Middle Ages (or satirical Ovid) would laugh at;

in poem after poem before the *Canterbury Tales* he is the Christian commentator on lovers, and he is funny because in his unintelligent, pious Christianity he to some extent comes off badly in comparison with the lovers. Chaucer flaunts the comic mask — and that is important. He jokes to say what he means. Needless to say, Chaucer's tone is our record of his personality — his style as a man — and it would be absurd to imagine that he chose his tone for the calculated purpose of insinuating philosophical opinions his age was not ready to hear. The personality of Chaucer, as much as the tone of the poetry, was at least in part a product of his time and place. Perhaps because he was self-effacing and humorous in his personal life, he was able to survive when many of the king's party could not. The same qualities expressed as poetic technique made it possible for Chaucer to lend support to an intellectual movement he might not otherwise have been able to back. His poetic style is not a means of tricking his audience into hearing what it would rather not hear; neither is it a means of getting away with something which, presented openly, might alarm a watchful Church. On the contrary, Chaucer's popularity in his own time shows that his comic mode gave him the ability to say what his audience, too, believed. It was for this reason that ingenious imitators like Sir John Clanvowe began to spring up on every hand while Chaucer's career was still young. Chaucer's style gave art a means of imitating what felt real and whole in fourteenth-century life. He harmonized the best ideas and emotions of his time and place in a way that would suffice.

Exactly where Chaucer found the Neoplatonic ideas developed in his poems — the optimistic position which balances the darker Augustinian strain — need not concern us; and in any case no very adequate answer to the question can be given.[10] The most we can say with certainty is that Chaucer cites writers who might have made Neoplatonism available to him but also cites writers who would have scorned such notions, that Neoplatonism is common in medieval thought, especially in two areas Chaucer knew well, astronomy and music, and that his poetry is full of specific allusions to both the more obvious and the more subtle doctrines of ennobling love, and to ideas of substance and shadow, but it is also full of allusions to the doctrine that all sex is perilous, and conflicting ideas of substance. To discover Chaucer's precise feelings concerning the material he so easily and so frequently made use of — to discover the extent to which his view of love is or is not ironic, liberal or prudish, sympathetic or scornful — we have finally nothing to depend upon but the poems. The same is true in other areas where Chaucer's intent or opinion seems in doubt — his political persuasions, his attitude toward Lollards, women, Jews, or the conflict of experience and authority.

We do have, of course, one fairly dependable check on interpretation — the poet's life, character, and friendships. To his French admirer, the poet Eustache Deschamps, Chaucer was "a Socrates in philosophy, a Seneca in morals, an Ovid in poetry, brief in speech and a master of eloquence." Chaucer inspired in those who knew him not only admiration but personal devotion. John Lydgate praised Chaucer's art again and again, and more than once makes a special point of the older poet's gentleness in looking at the inferior poetry of others. He speaks in the *Troy Book* of his master's kindness, tolerance and encouragement:

> For he þat was gronde of wel seying
> In al hys lyf hyndred no makyng
> My maister Chaucer þat founde ful many spot
> Hym liste not pinche nor gruche at euery blot
>   [wince or complain]
> Nor meue hym sief to perturbe his reste, [disturb himself]
> I have herde telle, but seide alweie þe best
> Suffring goodly of his gentilnes
> Ful many þing embraced with rudnes. [undertaken clumsily]

Another English poet, Thomas Hoccleve, says much the same, praising his master as an eager teacher, the first discoverer of our fair language, a dear master and "fadir reuerent." Such tolerance and generosity does not usually come on men suddenly in old age; we can be sure Chaucer was a kind and generous human being all his life, and any interpretation that flatly denies that gentleness must be suspect.

The Poetry of Chaucer

Repetition, Structure, and Poetic Allusion in the *Book of the Duchess*

An Introduction to Style as Meaning in Chaucer's Poetry

N 1369, WHEN BLANCHE OF LANCAS-
ter died in France, of the pestilence, Chaucer, as well as John of Gaunt, was probably
there. Gaunt loved his duchess, and though
he was notorious for hiding his emotions, or
for showing them only as a policeman shows his badge, staging
anger for the purpose of bullying parliament or the king, he
was, like all his family, a passionate man, and we can be sure
his grief was violent.[1] Chaucer watched it and did for Gaunt
and himself the only thing he could do, began a poem. The
Book of the Duchess can hardly have come flying from
Chaucer's pen. It has the understated, almost frozen pain of
John Crowe Ransom's "Bells for John Whiteside's Daughter"
and the same complexity — but complexity compounded by its
vastly greater length. And it has in addition what no short
lyric can hope to attain, a cumulative power and philosophical
depth that encourage us to rank it with such masterpieces of
the elegaic genre as Milton's *Lycidas.*

All this may not be immediately apparent to the modern reader. If so, one reason is that the poem is medieval and therefore likely to seem crooked, skewbald, even primitive to us. It is written in a style to which we no longer respond automatically, a style that has far more to do with stained-glass windows in ancient cathedrals or those queer, perspectiveless pictures in old books (pictures in which the serious and comic sit comfortably side by side) than with the kinds of art we're used to. And it is written on assumptions we no longer take for granted, for instance the Neoplatonic assumption of the angel that shines inside the man, so that to speak of the death of a beautiful woman is to think, instantly, of religion and art, time and eternity, and to grapple with one's pain not in the concrete, angry modern way but in a way that at first glance may seem to us frigid, cold-blooded, intellectual. That impression passes. Down all the centuries, pain is pain, and though philosophy can help, it is tears, not philosophies, that chiefly relieve it, as Chaucer understood. To appreciate the poem, we must appreciate its antique style.

First a few general remarks about style and the *Book of the Duchess.*

When one speaks of *literary style* one means, or ought to mean, some regular departure from some norm of language. Needless to say, "normal language" no more exists than does the *prima materia* of the alchemists: the sentences which can be made up in, say, Middle English are as numberless as the forms produced by variations in atomic and molecular combination. But it seems self-evident that poetry at any time is in some general way stylistically different from the ordinary speech of that day's people on the street, and that, within any given time and place, poets of a particular school, and poems by any particular poet, will be found to be more like one another stylistically than they are like poems from outside the school or canon. By the words and rhetorical devices he chooses, whether or not the choice is conscious, the poet says what he means.

Since poetic expression may differ from everyday prose expression not only in its choice of ornaments but also in its choice of methods for organizing details — its disposition and amplification of materials — it is useful to consider style in a broad sense embracing not only verbal pattern but also structural design. Not that *style* and *structure* are synonymous; but just as one can speak of a poet's style in handling sentences, one can speak of characteristic styles of organization.

The more artificial a poetic style becomes — that is, the more sharply it diverges in regular ways from "normal speech" — the more style and meaning interpenetrate. In medieval literature generally, style and meaning become virtually one: artifice was the heart's blood of the age. And this holds even for seeming realists like Chaucer. His first long poem, the *Book of the Duchess*, establishes the basic stylistic laws he will hold to all his life. Compared to other dream-vision poems, this one seems incredibly realistic — some early critics went so far as to argue that the poem records an actual dream Chaucer had. But the realistic surface, the seemingly real dream, is sleight of hand: here as in more obviously artificial poetry, the meaning is the manner.

The complex style of the *Book of the Duchess* has fathered considerable critical disagreement,[2] but in fact we can understand the poem in the same way we understand poems in more familiar styles, by careful analysis of the poem's language and design. Partly this involves accounting for the chief distinguishing features of the poem, the devices and qualities which make the poem unique, and partly it involves consideration of the medieval background.

The most obvious peculiarities of the poem are its wealth of allusions or borrowings from French poetry, its concern with something approaching realistic dream psychology, its apparent use of scholastic and exegetical materials, and its Neoplatonic use of threes, from minute triads of detail (as Russell Peck has pointed out) to its overall three-part structure. Another striking feature is Chaucer's use of an extraordinary number of repetitions, or echoes: words, phrases, images, and dramatic situations. The poem is in fact incredibly neat in its construction, so that there is far less room here than in some of Chaucer's later poetry for various interpretation.

Since my discussion of particulars may obscure the point, let me say in advance that the basic scheme of the *Book of the Duchess* is relatively simple: only its ornamentation is complex. Late medieval rhetoric, as everyone knows, is dilatory, giving most of its space to ornamentation. Only in an age when poetry's *statements* are largely conventional can a poet hope that his audience will follow such intricate elaborations as we find in the *Book of the Duchess*. (In later poems, especially the *Canterbury Tales*, we will find Chaucer abandoning this conventional approach.) For his governing theme, Chaucer takes a stock idea, the uplifting force of love — on the Neoplatonic principle, popularized by Augustine in *De Trinitate*, that man's intellect, memory, and love parallel the trinity of faculties in God, in whose image man is made — and he dilates the idea by means of secondary stock ideas: love of a woman is like love of God (the premise of so-called courtly love);[3] pagans are, up to a point, like Christians; and love is a healing force, whether love of a woman or love of God in the form of contemplation. But Chaucer moves beyond the usual medieval method: his juxtaposition of the narrator, Alcyone, and the Knight proves not so much a means of ornamenting as a means of testing the conventional premises.

§ 1

WE MAY BEGIN by observing that the collection of fables (Ovid's *Metamorphoses*) mentioned in lines 52–56 of the *Book of the Duchess* may well be a sort of Bible of natural man, or pagan Old Testament, and that both Chaucer's "clerkes" and his "other poets" may be the pagan counterparts of the inspired writers of scripture. The book is one wherein

> were written fables
> That clerkes had in olde tyme,
> And other poets, put in rime
> To rede, and for to be in minde,
> While men loved the lawe of kinde.
>
> [BD, 52–56

The law of nature is the highest law available to men prior to revelation: it's the law the best of the pagans "loved" — followed or devoted themselves to. The idea of juxtaposing the law of kind and the law of revelation is firmly rooted in medieval thought and, as I've said already, is explicit in the writings of numerous churchmen. Bonaventura frequently speaks of God's two "books," the first, nature, the second, scripture. According to Bonaventura, man was able to read God's message to man directly in nature before the fall; after the fall, man's wit became so dimmed that he needed a second, clearer book by which to interpret his condition.[4] If man works at it and prays, Bonaventura says, he can glimpse even now traces of the divine hand in nature.

The half-blind pagans were not only right as far as they went; they said, perhaps unwittingly, more than natural law alone could have told them.[5] For the Middle Ages, Virgil in his fourth eclogue predicted Christ's birth; Plato, "the theologian," knew about Christ but was sworn to secrecy. (This tradition is reflected in the *Canon's Yeoman's Tale*, lines 1463–71.) More to the present point, Ovid's medieval reputation derived chiefly from the susceptibility of his work to allegorical interpretation. No educated member of Chaucer's audience could fail to understand that, at least in the official view, the greatness of the *Metamorphoses* lay in the allegory. Whether or not Chaucer or anyone in his courtly audience really believed the official view, the official view was that pagan poetry, and especially that of Virgil and Ovid, was like Old Testament writing in that it contained presignifications of New Testament events.

But if the book of fables is a pagan Old Testament of sorts, what are we to make of what follows next:

> This bok ne spak but of such thinges,
> Of quenes lives, and of kinges,
> And many other thinges smale.
>
> [BD, 57–59

It is impossible to take with complete seriousness the narrator's view of queens' lives and kings' lives as "thinges smale." If we adopt the view that Chaucer is himself the Parson of the *Canterbury Tales*, we may grant that kings and queens are trivial, but we must also observe that the language here is out of control, arousing amusement by abruptness and incongruity. On the other hand, the narrator's lack of interest in royalty is wholly appropriate to his psychological state, in which, he tells us, "Al is ylyche good to me — / Joye or sorowe, wherso hyt be" (9–10). Since the lines suit the state of the narrator, they are effective or ineffective depending upon whether we are meant to take him with complete seriousness. To decide this question we may begin by asking once more about his mysterious physician.

Concerning his sleeplessness Chaucer writes:

> But men myght axe me why soo   [ask]
> I may not sleepe, and what me is.
> But natheles, who aske this
> Leseth his asking trewely;
> Myselven can not telle why
> The sothe; but trewly, as I gesse,
> I holde hit be a sicknesse
> That I have suffred this eight yeer,
> And yet my boote is never the ner;   [remedy]
> For there is phisician but oon
> That may me hele; but that is don.
> Passe we over untill eft;
> That wil not be mot nede be left;
> Our first mater is good to kepe.
>
> [BD, 30–43

The usual interpretation is that the physician is the conventional cruel mistress; an alternative view is that the physician is Christ. Those who favor the first opinion point out that in the love-religion, all terms normally applied to Christ are transferred to the lady, and, indeed, numerous poems of courtly love speak of the lady as a physician. (For all their obscurity, Chaucer's lines are in fact so closely imitative of well-known French passages, it seems impossible that anyone in the court for which he composed can have doubted for a moment that they referred to unrequited love.) On the other side it is argued that the identification of the physician as Christ is the more natural, particularly since there is no clear indication elsewhere in the poem that the narrator suffers from unrequited love. Professor Severs adds — more in desperation than in solid conviction, I hope — that in many of the French poems echoed in the *Book of the Duchess* the narrator's melancholy is not from love but from something else; that in those love poems which identify the physician as a lady the identification is explicit; and that Chaucer quite often uses the physician image in connection with Christ or the Virgin.[6]

The truth, as I think most critics now agree, is that the whole debate is academic. Chaucer's original audience came to the poem, as we do, knowing two possible interpretations of this detail — and perhaps also a third, Boethius's image of Philosophy as physician. Having no evidence pointing definitely to one interpretation or the other, the audience had to suspend judgment, that is, carry both (or all three) possibilities in mind, waiting for clarification. It is true that Chaucer had earlier written of the Virgin as the "soules leche" (*ABC*, 134), but that is no evidence of any kind. It is also true that puns, if one happens to notice them, point toward a religious interpretation of the physician: "but that is *don*" and "Our first *mater* [i.e., mother] is good to kepe." But even if the puns are granted to be present, they do not settle the matter. The narrator's long explanation that he does not know what is wrong with him does look, as Kemp Malone pointed out, like the evasion of a comically inept courtly lover who wants to reveal the cause of his suffering but cannot, because of the lover's code, and so hints at what he dare not say.[7] Interestingly enough, the reader who suspends judgment finds that echoes later in the poem serve only to increase the ambiguity: the Black Knight says no physician can save him and names famous medical men (571–72) then later speaks of his lady as "my lyves leche" (920). To complicate matters further, the narrator places himself in the role of physician at lines 553–57. All that we know for certain, both early in the poem and late, is that the narrator's condition is mysterious. On one hand there is evidence that his melancholy is religious: Chaucer insists that he never heard of any god but one (then, in his "game," darts off into a comically materialistic prayer to Morpheus); and the dream he dreams has many religious elements, notably the castle at the end, which — for anyone even slightly acquainted with medieval iconography — is difficult not to associate, at least on one level, with the New Jerusalem. On the other hand, the narrator wakes up, in his dream, in what is, again on one level, a love temple (his chamber transmuted), and alludes repeatedly to love poetry. We can only conclude that the narrator may have two problems, that the two (or three) possible interpretations of the physician are both (or all) relevant, and that his lack of interest in the lives of queens and kings is to be taken as comic. If the narrator is other-worldly, he is by no means completely so, as his prayer to Morpheus shows, and if he is religious, we may suspect he may be religious by default, turning to God because he cannot win his nearer love. He means the forbidden discussion of his lady's cruelty when he says, "but that is don. . . . / That wil not be mot nede be left"; but he seems to mean, too, his bootless love which "wil not be." If one cannot have one's lady, the only physician left is Christ, and the Virgin, our foremost *mater,* is "good to kepe" — both in the sense that she comforts and in the sense that she will do. In his would-be piety the narrator is comic, we gradually discover, because his melancholy disinterest in fables from the age of natural law and his melancholy abandonment of his love suit miss the real significance of pagan fables and human love: both teach spiritual lessons and support true religion, in addition to being of intrinsic worth. The narrator is established as comic in another way as well: though he is sympathetic and adroit in his dealings with the Black Knight, he is literal-minded to the point of stupidity. Concerning his subtle but definitely interpretable dream, he says,

> never yit
> Y trow no man had the wyt
> To konne wel my sweven rede;
> No, not Joseph, withoute drede,
> Of Egipte, he that redde so
> The kynges metynge Pharao,   [dreaming]

No more than koude the lest of us;
Ne nat skarsly Macrobeus,
(He that wrot al th'avysyoun
That he mette, kyng Scipioun,
The noble man, the Affrikan, —
Suche marvayles fortuned than)
I trowe, arede my dremes even.   [I trust, read]

[BD, 277–89

This comic inability to pierce the literal is one of Chaucer's favorite devices,[8] and a variant of the joke here appears in the *House of Fame*, lines 59–65. The same comic literal-mindedness appears in the *Book of the Duchess* when "Chaucer" finishes his reading of Ovid. After intense scrutiny of the tale (222–32), all he learns is a new way of getting to sleep: the traditional allegory, heightened in this retelling, escapes the narrator. This is not to say that the poem is, unknown to the narrator, a "religious meditation," as Huppé thinks. The theme is love, the bulk of the poem a celebration of earthly love, unlike heaven's love only in its mutability.

§ 2

THE INTERPRETATION I've just sketched out accounts both for the "psychological realism" of the poem and for Chaucer's use of verbal repetition to suggest subtle connections within the narrative. It's impossible to separate completely discussion of one from discussion of the other, but let me deal first with how the dream works as a dream and then later examine in more detail those textural elements which make the structure and meaning of the poem clear.

The psychological realism is obvious, though it's in fact a trick, a device for building allegory. Events throughout seem at once significant and mysterious: a horse enters and leaves the dream unaccountably; when the narrator hears that the huntsman is Octovyen, his exclamation is "A Goddes half, in good tyme!" — that is, "By God's side, just in time!" or "By

God's side, in a fortunate time!" — and just as the narrator hears from the Black Knight that "She ys ded!" the huntsmen (apparently) burst back into the poem and gallop away to a high white castle on a hill.

The great difficulty in dream interpretation, as Chaucer himself says repeatedly, is that one can never be sure whether a dream is of one type or another. On the basis of the evidence we are given in the *Nun's Priest's Tale*, we have reason to think Pertelote right in calling Chaunticleer's dream of the fox a *somnium naturale* (the kind of dream one may get from eating pickles before bed) or a *somnium animale* (the kind of dream Freud understood — anxiety, wish-fulfillment, and so forth); yet the fox does in fact arrive, proving that the dream was, as Chaunticleer maintained, a *somnium coeleste*, a dream sent from heaven. Then how are we to classify the dream in the *Book of the Duchess*?

Again, the question is academic. The *somnium naturale* can be dismissed as aesthetically useless; but as for dreams *animale* and *coeleste*, neither type can be ruled out — as we'll see — and so we must understand the dream in one of the following ways: 1) the dream is both *animale* and *coeleste*; 2) the dream is *animale* but has larger implications in the same way life does, if the world is conceived as a "vast array of emblems"; 3) the dream is a *somnium coeleste* in which divine truths are expressed through sexual metaphor. The second and third possibilities here, which come to about the same thing, are the more likely; but as far as interpretation is concerned, whichever theory we adopt, the fact remains that the dream is consistently open to two interpretations, one sexual, one religious. We may therefore speak — loosely — of the dream as being, on one level, *animale*, and on another, *coeleste*.

Not all of what the waking narrator desires must be deduced from the dream. Whatever his romantic or religious desires, his chief desire is comically low-brow: not rest in the arms of his lady or on the bosom of Christ but plain, earthly sleep. He thinks of three possible ways of boring himself into slumber: chess, "tables" (games of chance), and reading — three standard remedies for melancholy, according to Robert Burton in his Renaissance compendium of medieval notions, the *Anatomy of Melancholy.*[9] He chooses the least strenuous, reading, the one cure *not* recommended for melancholy lovers, but also, according to Boccaccio, a valuable springboard to contemplation, and the result is not deeper melancholy but a comic solution to the problem of getting to sleep. This does not mean that the narrator's melancholy is fake. Like the idealism of Sir Thopas, it is real but comic: the man lacks natural refinement.

He might learn both of love and of religion from the story of Alcyone. From Alcyone's behavior he might learn elegant love-suffering carried to its aesthetic perfection, death. She is, like those Good Women whose loyalty Chaucer half-cele-brated, half-burlesqued in his *Legend*, the model of pagan virtue much admired by medieval readers. And in the whole Alcyone story, if he read in the manner of Dante, Petrarch, Boccaccio, or the writers of the *Gesta Romanorum*, he might have seen the Christian scheme of salvation hinted. Nearly mad with sorrow, Alcyone

> koude no reed but oon;
> But doun on knees she sat anoon
> And wepte, that pittee was to here.
> "A! mercy, swete lady dere!"
>
> [BD, 105–9

The word *reed* ("counsel" or "remedy") parallels the narrator's *boote* (38), and the construction at line 105 above echoes line 39, "For there is phisicien but oon." The language of Alcyone's cry to her comforter Juno is that of the Christian's cry to the Virgin: "A! mercy, swete lady dere!" and thus perhaps recalls the narrator's pun: "Our first mater is good to kepe"; at the same time, the cry looks forward to the parallel cry of the Knight for "mercy" to the holy lady of his love religion (1219). Alcyone's request for a *gift* of grace (111) and her pledge to be "hooly youres" (Juno's) looks forward to the Lady's "gift":

> My lady yaf me al hooly
> The noble yifte of hir mercy,

Savynge hir worship, by al weyes

[BD, 1269–71

and the Knight's pledge, which the Lady comes to understand:

> I ne wilned thyng but god,
> And worship, and to kepe hir name
> Over alle thyng, and drede hir shame,
> And was so besy hyr to serve.

[BD, 1262–65

The Black Knight's love, like Alcyone's, is parallel to Christian devotion, as we see in passages like this one:

> As helpe me God, I was as blyve   [quickly]
> Reysed, as fro deth to lyve,
> Of al happes the alderbeste   [fortunes, the best of all]
> The gladdest, and the moste at reste.

[BD, 1277–80

(As God's love raises man from the grave, so does human love, at least metaphorically.) The cave of Morpheus, in the Alcyone story, is a comic "helle-pit" where "somme" sleep as long as "the dayes last" — forever. Juno's messenger wakes the god not, as in Ovid, by his light but by blowing a horn, a comic version of Gabriel's horn. Morpheus looks up with only one eye (allegorically the natural or fleshly eye, since as a pagan he lacks the eye of spirit) and takes Alcyone the dream-message that her husband is dead. Alcyone casts "hir eyen up" — that is, on the level of allegory, looks heavenward, and, because she comes before revelation (again on the level of allegory) "saw noght." Seeing no hope of reunion with her husband, the queen loyally (though perhaps wrongly) dies, like the love martyrs in the *Legend*.

The narrator might be interested to learn all this, since it's relevant to his own dilemma, providing two legitimate solutions, aesthetically admirable death for love (he would be "dampned in this cas" [725]) or pious faith in that spiritual rest which now is visible through revelation; but like the "Chaucer" who tells of Sir Thopas and tedious old Melibee, the

"Chaucer" of the *Book of the Duchess* is comically simple-minded.

Now let us turn to the dream proper. The dream opens with a scene reminiscent of several passages from the *Roman de la Rose*. The music of the birds, in the opening scene, is a "moste solempne servise," comparable to "a thyng of heven," later, a perfect "armonye." The specific basis for this comparison of the music of the birds and the music of religious devotion is the *Roman*, 665–72, but Chaucer avoids the allusion to the sirens, which immediately follows in the *Roman*, apparently not finding it relevant to his purpose. (Sirens were associated with hell, not heaven.) Chaucer also introduces, as Professor Huppé has pointed out, the pun "town of Tewnes," that is, song of songs or town of towns (over the basic "town of Tunis"). King Solomon's "Song of Songs," Huppé writes, "is the song of love between Christ and His Church, or between Christ and the soul of the faithful which seeks union with Him in the New Jersualem. The dreamer's awakening has placed before him the possibility of peace for his unquiet heart." [10]

In dream fashion, the bird music of Chaucer's dream turns into the sound of a hunter's horn — a detail prepared by the messenger's horn in the Alcyone story — and the dreamer, who finds himself on a horse, joyfully rides out to the hunt. The lord of the hunt, he learns, is "Octovyen." Professor Huppé has observed that the name may carry an etymological pun: *octo*, "eight," and *vyen*, "coming." And "the number *eight* signifies [in patristic numerology] Christ's Resurrection." [11] Identification of Christ as chivalric king or knight is of course common in medieval literature — in Hampole's writings, in all the works of the *Gawain*-poet, in *Piers Plowman*, and so forth. Professor Lowes' comparison of this hunt with that of the huntsmen of the god of love in the *Paradys d'Amours* offers support in that it suggests identification of "this kyng" as a god whom Dante or Boccaccio would be quick to allegorize into Christ. The *hart* which Octovyen pursues, then, may reasonably be read as a pun on *heart*, [12] a standard Middle English pun which Chaucer uses on various occasions. But the identity of Octovyen is, like all the dream, ambiguous. Both the romance associations of Octovyen and his association, through the *Paradys d'Amours* allusion, with Cupid, make him as much a figure of the religion of love as a figure of religion.

The narrator's identity is equally veiled:

> Withynne a while the hert yfounde ys,
> Yholowed, and rechased faste   [chased with shouts]
> Longe tyme; and so at the laste
> This hert rused, and stal away
> Fro alle the houndes a privy way.
> The houndes had overshote hym alle,
> And were on a defaute yfalle   [false scent, error]
> Therwyth the hunte wonder faste   [huntsman]
> Blew a forloyn at the laste.   [recall]
>   I was go walked fro my tree . . .   [BD, 378–87

The reason the narrator goes walking from his tree is perhaps not that, having been posted there, he is now free to leave (abandoning his horse), but rather that the narrator has himself turned into the hart who "rused, and stal away." [13] It is the narrator himself who, now that the hounds are called off, can come out. Within the *somnium animale,* the narrator is the hunter (pursuing his lady in company with the god of love) and also the hunted (pursued by the god of love). Within the *somnium coeleste,* the narrator is again the hunter (pursuing peace or rest in God) and the hunted (pursued by God).

Chaucer might have gotten his idea for this queer transformation through close study of his own dreams, but the transformation may also be at least partly an effect of Chaucer's reflection on conventional poetic matter. In Chaucer's translation of the *Roman* we find:

> And thus while I wente in my play,
> The God of Love me folowed ay,
> Right as an hunter can abyde
> The beest, tyl he seeth his tyde
> To shoten at good mes to the der,
> Whan that hym nedeth go no ner.
>   [ROMAUNT, 1449–54

In the episode which follows, the narrator learns of Narcissus, who came from hunting to the well where the huntsman god of love caught him.[14]

In his dream, Chaucer, now on foot, becomes once more the pursuer, his quarry a whelp which after fawning on him changed its mind and fled. The whelp is another borrowed detail (though the realism of the description is Chaucer's); but the relationship between the hart and the whelp is of course original with Chaucer: both represent the source of the dreamer's unrest — on the most obvious level of interpretation, the lady. The identification of lady and deer is ancient and has the support of literary convention;[15] identification of the lady and the whelp Chaucer underscores by verbal repetition.[16] But the identity of the whelp, like that of the hart, is ambiguous. A whelp may be a hunting dog, but if so it is a harmless hunting dog — a puppy — gentle and affectionate. Having "yfolowed," the whelp is in part pursuer, the "hunter" of the narrator-hart: on one level it is a representation of the lady who first encourages, then grows remote; on another it represents the "hound of heaven" of whom the *Gawain*-poet speaks in *Purity*.

Like his pursuit of the lady and of peace in life, the narrator's dream-pursuit is futile, and again the character of the dream changes. The whelp disappears into a mysterious, dark, "floury grene . . . / Ful thickke of gras" (398–99) where small animals scurry about. For the modern reader familiar with Freud, this flowery green must have obvious sexual significance. That significance is convenient for our reading of the dream in that it simultaneously suggests loss of the lady (in that the whelp escapes) and possession of the lady (in that the garden symbolically suggests a consummation of love). If we add that from a modern psychologist's point of view the dark garden also suggests the idea of death, then clearly the garden handsomely prepares for B. H. Bronson's twentieth-century psychoanalytical interpretation of the dream:

> By a wonderful leap of psychological insight, and in strict accord with truth rediscovered in our own century, his

private grief has been renounced by the Dreamer, to reappear externalized and projected upon the figure of the grieving knight. The modern analyst, indeed, would instantly recognize the therapeutic function of this dream as an effort of the psyche to resolve an intolerable emotional situation by repudiating it through this disguise. The knight is the Dreamer's surrogate; and in this view it would be significant that the force which keeps the surrogate from his lady is the far more acceptable, because decisive and final, fact of death. The train of analysis would lead us to assume, of course, a kindred connection between the lady of the dream and the fair but cruel "physician" who refuses to work a cure in the Dreamer's waking life. And here it would be noted that the Knight's long and rapturous eulogy of his lost lady would serve, in the Dreamer's unconscious, to discharge the latter's sense of guilt for the disloyalty of wishing the death of that Merciles Beaute. The disguise is rendered complete by the surrogate's having perfectly enjoyed his love before death severed them.[17]

Bronson's reading is right — or at any rate valuable — less because of a leap on Chaucer's part than because Chaucer understood the psychologically loaded conventions with which he was working. Compare the dreamer's garden with the garden setting of the Narcissus episode in the *Romaunt*, 1391–1438. In both, the trees are thick and of great height, with boughs so tightly interlocked that no sunbeam can break through; in both, winter has been outlawed, and animals and flowers may be seen in abundance; in both we find "thick" grass — in the *Romaunt* grass "On which men mighte his lemman [mistress] leye, / As on a fetherbed, to pleye, / For therthe [the earth] was ful softe and swete." (These details can all be found in a hundred places; but the diction of the two descriptions under consideration is strikingly similar.) The ambiguity is that of the earthly paradise, or of love itself, a thing as beautiful as heaven but mutable. In the garden of the *Romaunt*, the narrator finds a huge pine tree, sits down against it, learns of Narcissus, then comes to be loosely identified with Narcissus by falling into a similar trap: the god of love captures

his heart. In the garden of the *Book of the Duchess* the narrator
finds a huge oak tree (symbolizing the despair which follows
the joys of an earthly paradise, according to Robertson and
Huppé), finds a man sitting against a tree, and speaks of the
man in phrases which repeatedly echo his description of
himself. Both passages involve the death of a lady, one the
death of Echo, murdered by Narcissus' disdain, the other the
death of Lady White, a beloved wife.

If on the psychological level we find the narrator and
Black Knight to be one man, we can look for explanation to
the myth of Narcissus, who loved his reflection. It is another
reflection of himself that the *Book of the Duchess* narrator loves.
The paradox of the hunted hunter comes both from Narcissus'
dual role as lover and beloved and from the explicit contrast in
the *Roman*, where the narrator comes from being hunted by
the god of love and Narcissus "com fro hunting" to be caught
by the hunter god. Chaucer's compression of this material
results from his conscious pursuit of dream distortions, "veils of
ambiguity" which will be interpretable for his audience. (On
the surface of Chaucer's poem the narrator and Knight are two
different people, and their dialogue need not raise any
questions not answered by Kittredge. We can account for the
relationship between them, as established by verbal echo, just
as we account for relationships between the narrator, the
Knight, and Alcyone: they are caught in similar situations
[sorrow through love], and the echoes simply point up the
similarity.)

At all events, the identification of the dreamer and the
Knight and the identification of both with the intermediate
deer and whelp are clear. As the whelp fawned on the narrator
"as [he] stood," the narrator "stood ryght at his [the Knight's]
fet." The puppy "koude no good" (390); the Knight says that
as a young man "ful lytel good y couthe" (800) and tells of
once having been innocently faithless, like the puppy:

> For al my werkes were flyttynge
> That tyme, and al my thought varyinge.
> Al were to me ylyche good   [alike]
> That I knew thoo.   [then]   [BD, 801–4

These lines recall, also, the narrator's state at the start of the poem, when "Al is ylyche good to me" (9) and his thought is "varyinge" because "Suche fantasies ben in myn hede, / So I not what is best to doo" (28–29). (On this, more later.) Again, in language which recalls the hunt, the narrator's pursuit of the whelp, and the narrator's gloomy thoughts of death (16 et seq.), the Knight says,

> The pure deth ys so ful my foo
> That I wolde deye, hyt wolde not soo;
> For whan I folwe hyt, hit wol flee;
> I wolde have hym, hyt nyl nat me.
>
> [BD, 583–86

In one respect the narrator and the puppy contrast: whereas the whelp flees when the narrator wants him (as death flees when the Knight wants death), the narrator remains with the grieving Knight even though, he says, "Unnethe [not easily] myght y lenger dwelle." If the narrator is slow-witted and inept with women, he is as shaken by tragedy as is anyone else, and he has taste enough to lead the Knight through his story of grief without cheapening it. Though he is himself unfit for nature, as he tells us, the narrator is for the Knight, as the Lady White was formerly, life. Like the whelp as harmless hunter of the heart (either as god of love or as God), the narrator acts as pursuer in relation to the Knight, his quarry being the Knight's "thought," his "sorwes smerte" (555); in fact, he is none other than the Knight's *physician*, telling him,

> For, by my trouthe, *to make yow hool*,
> *I wold do al my power hool.*
>
> [BD, 553–54; my italics

And this time the narrator's pursuit is successful, at least within the dream: after much stalling — by means of, for instance, elaborate metaphors like that of his chess game with Fortune — the Knight finally reveals his heart, that is, puts his sorrow into plain, painful words: "She is dead." The narrator responds with compassion — "By God, hyt ys routhe!" — and instantly, "They gan to strake forth; al was doon, / For that tyme, the hert-huntyng." Granting that *straken forth* is a technical hunting term, so that on the dream's literal level the huntsmen have burst into the poem again, galloping home, I think on the poem's psychological level, on which the *heart* is being hunted, it is the Knight's *tears* which streak forth: the psychological probing or "heart hunting" has been successful, stripping away the patient's defenses and putting him, once more, in touch with his emotion: all his artifice is overcome by the plain English of *She is dead* and *By God, hyt ys routhe!* and the heart has been found, or, to borrow another of the narrator's metaphors, has been properly "confessed." The narrator has claimed (1114) that the Knight is presenting "shryfte wythoute repentaunce." True shrift, of course, means tears. This is the point of Chaucer's joke at the Friar in the *General Prologue*:

> He was an esy man to yeve penaunce,
> Ther as he wiste to have a good pitaunce.
> $\qquad$ [expected . . . pittance]
> For unto a povre ordre for to yive
> Is signe that a man is wel yshryve;   [confessed]
> For if he yaf, he dorste make avaunt,   [dared . . . boast]
> He wiste that a man was repentaunt;
> For many a man so hard is of his herte,
> He may nat wepe, althogh hym soore smerte.
> $\qquad$ [CANTERBURY TALES, I, 223–30

Notice what follows the streaking forth:

> With that me thoghte this kyng
> Gan homwardes for to ryde
> Unto a place, was ther besyde,
> Which was from us but a lyte.
> A long castel with walles white,
> By seynt Johan! on a ryche hil
> As me mette; but thus hyt fil.   [dreamed; befell]
> Ryght thus me mette, as I yow telle,
> That in the castell ther was a belle,
> As hyt hadde smyten houres twelve. —

> Therwyth I awook myselve
> And fond me lyinge in my bed;
> And the book that I hadde red,
> Of Alcione and Seys the kyng,
> And of the goddes of slepyng,
> I fond hyt in myn hond ful even.
> Thoghte I, "Thys ys so queynt a sweven   [dream]
> That I wol, be processe of tyme,
> Fonde to put this sweven in ryme   [endeavor]
> As I kan best, and that anoon."
> This was my sweven; now hit ys doon.
>
> [BD, 1314–34

The passage is famous for its punning allusions to Lancaster ("long castel"), Richmond ("ryche hil"), and John of Gaunt ("seynt Johan"). Granting the puns, we need to ask what the final lines have to do with the dream.

Like all the dream, the conclusion is ambiguous. On the literal level, in which the narrator and Knight are two different people, "this kyng" may refer to the Knight. (By a similarly loose use of terms Chaucer calls Scipio a king in the *House of Fame*, and the *Gawain*-poet speaks of Bertilak as a king.)[18] The release of his grief is a kind of joy, an exultation not to be described except by vaguely religious metaphors. Moreover, freed from self-regarding melancholy, his thought really does veer heavenward, looking forward to ultimate reunion with his lady. On deeper levels the conclusion provides the dream-resolution of the narrator-Knight's dilemma: having found through the dream pursuit the nature of his true feelings, the narrator is free of the god of love, for the lady is dead, as far as the narrator is concerned, and the hopeless love-suit is over. On the level of *somnium coeleste,* Christ the King rides home to his castle on its rich hill, Zion. For the narrator-Knight, the castle is a vision of rest to come. His cry "By seynt Johan!" is an open clue to the identity of the castle that John first saw in the *Apocalypse,* the castle identified with the number *twelve,* the number of the mystical body.[19]

With the twelve strokes of the bell the vision is shattered; the narrator is thrown back into the world of men and into paradox as baffling as ever, for him. Earthly love, which he once hoped to put out of his mind, and of which he does momentarily rid himself in his dream, has been revealed as the pattern or grammar school of heavenly love. Ultimately earthly love may be a thing to be left behind (when one's lady dies), but it is by no means a thing to disparage. Comically inept as he is, the narrator can move not a step up the Platonic ladder, he can only stare miserably at the unattainable bottom rung. And insofar as he recognizes his predicament, he can only write of the joys he can understand but not experience. Thus in his first important poem, Chaucer adopts the stance that will serve him in his greatest finished poem, the *Troilus*:

> For I, that God of Loves servantz serve,
> Ne dar to love, for myn unliklynesse,
> Preyen for speed, al sholde I therfore sterve,   [die]
> So fer am I from his help in derknesse.
> But natheles, if this may don gladnesse
> To any lovere, and his cause availle,
> Have he my thonk, and myn be this travaille!   [thanks]
> [TROILUS AND CRISEYDE, I, 15–21

He can serve as physician to the Black Knight, but, for reasons suggested in the poem, no man can be spiritual physician to himself. The physician's work is unselfish expression of love: when the self-regarding Black Knight is reached by sympathy the "hunt" is successful; but as the earlier hunt shows, it is useless to try to "slee the hert with strength" (351), whether the heart is the lady's, the self-pitying (concupiscent) heart, or the bleeding heart in "Goddes half" — the wellspring of divine grace and mercy. Here as elsewhere in Chaucer, self-love — in theological jargon, cupidity — is the way of death.[20]

§ 3

ONE IMPORTANT FEATURE of the *Book of the Duchess*, as I said earlier, is its rhetoric, particularly Chaucer's use here of verbal repetition. Frequently he repeats whole lines with only some minor change; more often he repeats particular phrases, images, or ideas. In some cases the iteration serves to point up structure: for instance, Chaucer begins the dream proper with the line, "loo, thus hyt was, thys was my sweven [dream]" (290), and at the end of the poem he says, "This was my sweven; now hit ys doon" (1334). Again, the beginning of the deer hunt is signaled by " 'A Goddes half, in god tyme,' quod I" (370), and the beginning of the psychological hunt for the Black Knight's heart is signaled by the echo, " 'A Goddes half!' quod he, and began" (758). In other cases iteration underscores thematically important ideas — "slepe," "reste," "blisse," "hert," "thoght," "sorwe" — as Dorothy Everett pointed out.[21] But the most striking kind of iteration is that which establishes connections between seemingly disparate elements—a garden and a lady, three grieving lovers, a man and a dog and Death and a lady, and so forth. Take an example.

With the hart which "rused, and stal away," compare

1) the hound:

> I wolde have kaught hyt, and anoon
> Hyt fledde, and was fro me goon;
>
> [395–96

2) the narrator's statement that

> unnethe myght y lenger dwell
> Hyt dyde myn herte so moche woo
>
> [712–13

3) the Knight's explanation of why he could not leave his lady:

> "She was lady
> of the body; she had the herte,   [i.e., the Knight's heart]
> And who hath that, may not asterte."   [leave]
>
> [1152–54

4) the lady:

> "my lady bryght,
> Which I have loved with al myght

Is fro me ded and ys agoon."

[477–79

5) the Knight's words on death:

"For whan I folwe hyt, hit wol flee."

[585

6) the narrator's remark to the Knight about the hunt:

"this game be done.
I holde that this hert be goon;
These huntes konne hym nowher see."   [huntsmen]

[539–41

7) the Knight's reaction to his lady's "nay":

"I durste no more say thertoo   [dared]
For pure fere, but stal away"   [fear]

[1250–51

Calling up an association between the behavior of the unfaithful whelp and the faithful narrator (quotations 1 and 2 above), Chaucer asserts the value of faithfulness; and the Knight's fear of arousing his lady's wrath and so making her flee with his heart (3) indicates that faithfulness is not only valuable but in some sense vitally necessary. A terrible situation arises, then, when death takes the lady (cf. 4): the Knight becomes the pursuer of death (5), for death, in a sense, has his heart (3, 4, 5). The crux of the situation is summed up in quotation 6 when we read it in the light of a second echo pattern. After the narrator's statement that the hart is gone (6) — a statement referring to the literal hart, since "huntes" pursue it — the Knight answers, "My thought ys theron *never a del*" (my italics). The narrator answers, " 'By oure Lord,' quod I, 'y trow yow wel' " (543–44). Later the Knight says he was "hooly hires and *everydel*." The narrator replies in the same words he used before: " 'By oure Lord,' quod I, 'y trow yow wel' " (1041–42). Chaucer's suggestion is that the Knight's mistake lies in giving his entire commitment to his lady, that is, her earthly part; the Knight has no interest in anything else whatever, either in heaven or on earth. There is significance, then, in his third echo:

"I leve yow wel, [the narrator says] that trewely   [believe]
Yow *thoghte* that she was the beste."

[1048–49; my italics

The Knight's vision of perfection, the lady, is an illusory vision, a mistake of identity in the medieval Christian sense: the Knight has failed to distinguish between an emblem and its meaning, outer form and inner, with the result that the Knight has fallen into defining himself by his lower inclination.

So complex is the system of relationships established by such verbal echoes that at last virtually every element in the poem is somehow identified with every other, and texture itself is the poem's main principle of unity. Needless to say, assigning names to the kinds of iteration found—*repetitio, conversio, complexio, contentio, annominatio, adjunctio, conduplicatio, interpretatio,* and so on—serves no very useful purpose. Chaucer's method is too complex to be described in such a way without distortion; moreover, his object is not simple dilation in the manner of rhetoricians like Vinsauf, for what Vinsauf saw as decorative, Chaucer, like great poets before him, saw as functional.[22]

One important set of repetitions involves concepts of *nature* or *kind.* Early in the poem the narrator tells us he is unfit for nature and may well die:

> And wel ye woot, agaynes kynde
> Hyt were to lyven in thys wyse;
> For nature wolde nat suffyse
> To noon erthly creature
> Nat longe tyme to endure
> Withoute slep and be in sorwe.
> And I ne may, ne nyght ne morwe,
> Slepe; and thus melancolye
> And drede I have for to dye.

[BD, 16–24

When he first sees the Black Knight the narrator says, echoing "nature," "creature," and "sorwe":

> Hit was gret wonder that Nature
> Myght suffre any creature
> To have such sorwe, and be not ded.
>
> [467–69

A moment later he underscores the connection by means of another echoing device:

> For he had wel nygh lost hys mynde,
> Thogh Pan, that men clepe god of kynde,
> Were for hys sorwes never so wroth.
>
> [511–13

The narrator and Knight, unfit for nature (who is "wroth" with them), contrast with Lady White, who is one with nature and whom nature loves:

> For certes, Nature had swich lest
> To make that fair, that trewly she
> Was hir chef patron of beaute
> And chef ensample of al hir werk,
> And moustre. [form]
>
> [908–12

The Black Knight gets the courage to speak to the lady because, as he says,

> I bethoghte me that Nature
> Ne formed never in creature
> So moche beaute, trewely,
> And bounte, wythoute mercy.
>
> [1195–98

Another echo in the *nature-creature* pattern throws light on the concept of nature in the poem. The narrator says to the Knight,

> "A, goode sir . . . say not soo!
> Have som pitee on your nature

That formed yow to creature.
Remember yow of Socrates,
For he ne counted nat thre strees   [three straws]
Of noght that Fortune koude doo."

[714-19

The phrase *your nature,* together with the allusion to Socrates'
indifference to Fortune (mentioned by Boethius) indicates that
here nature is of two kinds, higher and lower.

The inclinations of body and spirit, or the two "laws,"
may at first glance seem antithetical, for the parallel lines on
the earthly paradise and the lady suggest a sharp disparity
between the things of earth and the things of heaven. Of the
garden where he finds the Black Knight the narrator says,

For hit was, on to beholde
As thogh the erthe envye wolde   [vie with]
To be gayer than the heven,
To have moo floures, swiche seven,
As in the welken sterres bee.

[405-9

The idea of earth's implicitly futile rivalry with heaven appears
in the source (*Roman de la Rose,* 8465-68), but Chaucer
expands his source, introducing wind and winter (extremely
common metaphors for physical and spiritual death in both
the secular and the devotional lyrics of the period). Both the
cosmic imagery and the idea of rivalry in the lines on the
garden appear again in the Knight's description of his lady:

For I dar swere, withoute doute,
That as the someres sonne bryght
Ys fairer, clerer, and hath more lyght
Than any other planete in heven,
The moone, or the sterres seven,
For al the worlde so hadde she
Surmounted hem alle of beaute.

[820-26:

Referring to a woman already dead, the lines recall the irony
in the earlier passage. Whether in the form of flowers or in the

form of a lady, nature can never be gayer than heaven — or at all events cannot remain so. A third echo, this time simply the repetition of an image, adds further irony. The Knight says,

> For there nys planete in firmament,
> Ne in ayr ne in erthe noon element,
> That they ne yive me a yifte echone
> Of wepynge whan I am allone.

[693–96

The perfection of the planets, the very continued existence of things lower on the natural ladder, grimly comment on the mutability of the lady who gave a quite different gift, "The noble yifte of hir mercy" (1270).

But despite these contrasts, the opposition between earth and heaven is not absolute. In the *Book of the Duchess* spirit is at once immanent in nature and transcendent, as it is, we recall, for Plato, Bonaventura, and — most important for Chaucer — Boethius. We have seen already one indication that nature is vicegerent of God: according to the Knight, nature would not form a creature with beauty, bounty, and no mercy. In the Knight's eulogy, where the lady becomes the very type and pattern of nature, she is also emblematic of the Neoplatonic-Christian ideal: Beauty, Goodness, and Truth.

Nearly every line of the Knight's eulogy is borrowed, but the organization is Chaucer's, and it is the organization, above all, that counts. The introduction (848–77) treats the neo-Aristotelean theme of measure and proportion.[23] In the next structural blocks of the eulogy, the Knight praises his lady's *beauty*, spiritual and physical (878–948), her *goodness* (985–98), and her *truth* (999–1014).[24] This order is explicit and rhetorically formal. After telling of the lady's beauty, Chaucer provides a formal transition: "To speke of godnesse" (985); then, introducing his next structural block, he provides another formal transition: "And trewly, for to speke of trouth" (999). To the Neoplatonic-Christian ideal he adds, finally, the Christian virtue *charity* and the courtly virtue *honor* (1015–33). The lady is indeed, as the narrator sees, a kind of salvation, an emblem of the Supreme Good. But to the Knight she is no mere emblem; she is paradise itself. In the extremity of his emotion he chooses, again and again, language with a religious flavor:

> "For certes she was, that swete wif,   [certainly]
> My suffisaunce, my lust, my lyf,   [sufficiency; joy]
> Myn hap, myn hele, and al my blesse   [fortune; health]
> My worldes welfare, and my goddesse,
> And I hooly hires and everydel."
>
> [1037–41

She was the Knight's "lyves leche" (920), and he says, drawing on the same imagistic tradition which informs the *Pearl*,

> For wher-so men had pleyd or waked,
> Me thoghte the felawsshyppe as naked
> Withouten hir, that sawgh I oones,
> As a corowne withoute stones.
> Trewly she was, to myn ye,
> The soleyn fenix of Arabye;
> For ther livyth never but oon,
> Ne swich as she ne knowe I noon.
>
> [977–84[25]

Both verbal echo and sense in the last two lines here recall the narrator's remark, "For I ne knew never god but oon" (237) and his earlier statement, "For there is phisicien but oon—/ That may me hele; but that is don" (39–40). The lady is indeed "goddesse" to the Knight.

The Knight's service to his lady — as we noticed already in another connection — parallels religious devotion. This is to be expected in the poetry of courtly love, but Chaucer's echoes make the parallel emphatic. The Knight's plea to his lady parallels Alcyone's prayer to Juno (1221 et seq. and 110 et seq.) and contrasts sharply with the self-centered and comically lowbrow prayer of the narrator to Morpheus (240 et seq.). Later, the Knight's joy with his lady is like the joy of heaven: after she grants "mercy" he is "reysed, as fro deth to lyve" into "Of al happes the alderbeste, / The gladdest, and the moste at reste" (1279–80).[26] Joined with his lady, he finds "joye [is] ever ylyche newe" (1288), contrasting with the narrator's despair at the start ("Al is ylyche good to me — O Joye or sorowe, wherso hyt be — " [9–10]), contrasting with the Knight's meaningless joy in the innocence of youth ("Al were to my ylyche good" [803]), and contrasting, finally, with the Knight's constant misery since his lady's death — a misery associated with hell:

> This ys my peyne wythoute red, [plan or means of escape]
> Alway deynge and be not ded,
> That Cesiphus, that lyeth in helle,
> May not of more sorwe telle,
> And whoso wiste al, by my trouthe,
> My sorwe, but he hadde rowthe
> And pitee of my sorwes smerte,
> That man hath a fendly herte.
>
> [587–94

For the Knight, the perfection of the lady is an article of faith. He tells the narrator that no man ever placed love as well as he did. The narrator replies, "Y trowe hyt, sir," but ordinary trust does not satisfy the Knight, for he says, "Nay, *leve* hyt wel!" (my italics; see 1042 et seq.), asking acceptance of a creed. Later, when the narrator suggests that the Knight is confessing without true repentance (1112 et seq.), the Knight indignantly rejects the idea of repentance, remaining loyal to his love-religion.

The Knight must ultimately come to accept the transience of the happiness or "reste" provided by the love-religion. Nevertheless, it is true that love is paradise, for as long as it lasts. The dead Seys calls Alcyone "my worldes blysse" — and remarks two lines later, "To lytel while oure blysse lasteth" (209 et seq.). The same idea, almost the same language, occurs in the *Man of Law's Tale*:

> And swich a blisse is ther bitwix hem two
> That, save the joye that lasteth everemo,
> Ther is noon lyk.
>
> [CANTERBURY TALES, II, 1075–77

But again joy is brief:

> . . . litel while in joye or in plesance
> Lasteth the blisse of Alla with Custance.
> [CANTERBURY TALES, II, 1140–41

The old knight in the *Merchant's Tale* is another who — this time too hastily — identifies earthly love and heaven:

> ". . . wedlok is so esy and so clene,
> That in this world it is a paradys."
> [CANTERBURY TALES, IV, 1264–65

Love comes to serve, in the *Book of the Duchess*, as a metaphorical summary of all forms of earthly joy; and love's failure comes to represent any failure of earthly hopes. All three focal characters — the narrator, Alcyone, and the Black Knight — are victims of sorrow and sleeplessness, the narrator because he has not yet won his beloved, Alcyone because her beloved is missing, the Knight because his beloved is dead. Isolation and sorrow, after joy or without joy, are sooner or later the inevitable lot of both men and women, both lords and vassals, in short, of all mankind. In their sorrow, the three focal characters are not equipped to live either in this world or the next (discounting for the moment the fact that the pagan Alcyone can't get to heaven anyway). They are in effect, as the Knight says of himself, the walking dead. To die of sorrow for love, according to the narrator, is to be self-murdered, and "Ye sholde be *dampned* [damned] in this cas" (725; my italics); but to live in sorrow, outside the beautiful and good order of nature, is also to be damned. This is the point of the Knight's association of his present mournful state with damnation (587–94, quoted above) — a thoroughly conventional association, seen, for example, in the alliterative *Purity* as well as in Dante's hell.[27] To win true peace, the Knight must see the relationship between, on the one hand, the ritual of courtly love — neo-pagan in that it looks no higher than Pan — and, on the other hand, Christian devotion. The "counsellors" to trust — as Chaucer suggests through another verbal echo — are not the "ferses twelve" (723) of Charlemagne or King Arthur (the douzeperes of the *Alliterative Morte Arthure*) but God's "halwes twelve" (831), the apostles.

The Knight must learn from the narrator; but the narrator can also learn from the Knight. At the beginning of the poem we see the narrator doing nothing, surrendering to "ydel thoght" (4), a condition (sloth) tolerable only in youth (cf. 797 et seq.). When the Black Knight finds himself sorrowfully idle, he turns — in the conventional fashion of the courtly lover — to art:

> But, for to kepe me fro ydelnesse,
> Trewly I dide my besynesse
> To make songes, as I best koude.
>
> [1155–57

After the loss of his lady he returns to this pastime, for when the narrator first sees him he is speaking verse to himself (461 et seq.). Chaucer underscores the importance of this art motif by introducing the Knight's digression on the origin of art (1160–74). The origin may have been within Judeo-Christian tradition, in the songs of Tubal, or may have been within pagan tradition, but at all events its purpose is clear, as the Knight sees it: "songes thus I made / Of my felynge, myn herte to glade" (1171–72). Art is, in this case, one's attempt to heal oneself and is for that reason finally insufficient. Echoing the narrator's statement that "there is phisicien but oon" (39) who can provide his "boote" (38), and echoing, also, the statement that Alcyone "koude no reed but oon" (105), the Knight exclaims, " 'Alas!' thoghte I, 'y kan no red; / And but I telle hir, I nam but ded' " (1187–88). The point is intensified by *conduplicatio* a few lines later: "For nedes, and mawgree my hed, / I most have told hir or be ded" (1201–2).

Higher than art — in the Christian religion, in pagan religion, and in the neo-pagan love religion — stands selfless, sincere, and complete self-surrender through confession. As Alcyone cried "mercy, swete lady dere!" in her pagan faith, the Knight in his first attempt cried "mercy!" to his lady (1219). As Alcyone swears to Juno, "hooly youres become I shal / With good wille, body, herte, and al" (115–16), the

Knight swears, "youres is alle that ever ther ys / For ever-
more, myn herte swete!" (1232–33), and on the occasion of
his second attempt he insists again on his perfect selflessness. It
is not enough merely to find expression for one's feelings, as
one does in writing poetry like that of the Knight. One must
make one's "thought" known to some other. The trouble with
the Knight's secret love-songs was that "she wyste hyt
noght, / Ne telle hir durste I nat my thoght" (1185–86). And
the reason the narrator is able to serve (like Lady White) as
physician to the Black Knight is that the narrator honestly
seeks "knowynge of hys thought" (538) — a matter of great
importance to the Knight, who says at the start of his
narration,

> "I telle the upon a condicioun
> That thou shalt hooly, with al thy wyt
> Doo thyn entente to herkene hit."

[750–52

The reason the Knight is helped by his confession to the
narrator is that the narrator has brought him from artificial and
remote (allegorical) language, the language of *art* (see especially 598–709), to plain speech: "She ys ded!" (It is probably
no accident that Chaucer's allusions in this poem are to the
loftiest of high-style poems, *Le Song Vert*, the Machault
motets, the *Paradys d'Amours*, and so forth.) On the other
hand, the Knight's story has perhaps been instructive to the
narrator, for at the end of the poem the narrator has moved
from idleness to art: he will, "be processe of tyme, / Fonde to
put this sweven in ryme" (1331–32). Ironically, his art is as
obscure as the Knight's allegory of Fortune. Though we
understand his unhappiness in love, just as the narrator
understands the Knight's grief when he first overhears him
lamenting in the woods, Chaucer's narrator has failed to make
the necessary open statement, relinquishing art for self-surrender. The reason he has failed to speak out is that his own
unattainable lady is alive, unlike Lady White: the tragic clown
who speaks the poem is bound, helpless, by the code of courtly
love.

Pursued to this point and no further, the *Book of the Duchess* appears a poet's condemnation of poetry: hope lies in plain talk. That ornamental quality which is poetry's sole excuse for being, in a world of firmly established doctrine, is reduced by Chaucer (as it is by John Wyclif) to "vicious rhetoric" — self-delusion.[28] But in fact the poem condemns only a certain kind of poetry. The narrator, writing to console himself, is not Chaucer but a fiction. Outside the fictional frame, Chaucer is himself writing a poem of consolation — and counsel — for John of Gaunt. The very indirection which invalidates the narrator's effort makes the poet's consolation tactful and effective. Against the aesthetic of *amor cortois*, with its sweetly dying Alcyones, its Medeas and Didos, its narcissistic grief, and against the win-or-lose aesthetic of chess (outlawed in London because it often led to murder), Chaucer sets a healthier art grounded not on love of self but in charitable love of things external — the art of Lady White, singing among her ladies (849), or Lamech's son Tubal, singing to the rhythm of his brothers' hammers (1162–66), or Pictagoras, musician-philosopher (1167–69). True art, to use modern psychological jargon, is art which "relates," that is, art which gives expression to — and celebrates — commitments. These, for a Christian Neoplatonist, are the very structure of the universe. The Black Knight's heart "That semeth ful sek [sick] under [his] syde" (557) is the human counterpart of another heart wounded by love, that of the celestial Bridegroom (and physician), whose death for his beloved is obliquely recalled in the exclamations of the narrator and the Black Knight, "A Goddess half!" (370, 758). True art — poetry, painting, even the rule-filled "art of love" (see 759–804, especially 786 et seq.) — is selfless and purposeful.

§4

THE *BOOK OF THE DUCHESS* is a highly original work of art, but not in modern terms; and since the purpose of this chapter is not only to comment on the *Book of the Duchess* but also to introduce certain basic features of Chaucer's way of working, let me take time here to remind the reader of how heavily dependent Chaucer was on "sources" for plot ideas, scenery, and specific lines. This poem, you may object, is an extreme case, and that is to some extent true. Yet all Chaucer's poetry makes heavy use of other people's writing. About seventy percent of *Troilus and Criseyde* is from Boccaccio, and at least another twenty percent — individual lines, phrases, long paragraphs from Boethius, and so on — can be traced to other sources. Even the most original of the *Canterbury Tales* — the *Miller's Tale*, for instance, which was generated from a short bawdy song and elaborated to its present length and complexity by Chaucer's own imagination — contains hundreds of allusions and borrowed images.

However much or little Chaucer borrowed, his art — as he and his audience saw it — lay in the shuffling, the reworking. His poetry is like that of a modern builder of collages whose main materials are other people's drawings. It is of course quite true (though some recent critics have labored to deny it) that part of Chaucer's genius was his eye for detail — the runny sore on the Cook's shin, the bristles growing from a wart, the Wife's hat. That eye for detail is one of the qualities held up for praise by his earliest admirers, men like Caxton. And it can be added, as his earliest admirers all remarked, that part of his genius was his ear for speech, the rhythms actually used by men, so that he was indeed the first "finder of our fair language." But Chaucer's main business, in all his poetry, was selection and arrangement. His theory of unity was one not spelled out until Coleridge — the unity of associative detail (the method of, notably, James Joyce). A character is described as "naked," and when a second character is described as "naked," the first is subliminally recalled and the reader makes half-unconscious connections of similarity or opposition. So, detail by detail, association by association (symbolic connection by symbolic connection), the whole poem comes together like a drawstring bag.

What is crucial is the drawing together, the form; the pretty colors on the bag and drawstring are secondary, which is one reason Chaucer sees no harm in borrowing them.

Everybody borrowed in Chaucer's day — sermon writers, philosophers, all the best poets. Hence the interminable quoting of Church Fathers, and hence the contemporary veneration of that to-us-(and to Chaucer himself)-tiresome *Tale of Melebius*, a *Bartlett's Familiar Quotations* plus plot. But in most of his poetry Chaucer's borrowings have a virtue unusual in poetry of the time: the borrowed detail drags in its original context and either clarifies or ironically comments on the new context.

The best way to show how little Chaucer "made up" is to summarize a few of his sources for the *Book of the Duchess* and point out how unfreely he translated the lines he borrowed. I will take just two or three of the poems of Machault, though Chaucer made use of many more. If what I am trying to do works, the reader will be surprised to learn how little Chaucer "invented."

Begin with Machault's *Judgment of the King of Bohemia* (*Le Jugement dou Roy de Behaigne*).[29] It's May, when the days are moderate and clear, the sun brightly shining, no trace of a chill. The narrator (Guillaume de Machault in caricature), stands listening to the birds and looking at the trees in a gardenlike place near a tower. He sees, coming down a path toward him, a lady and her little dog, and, from the opposite direction, a handsome knight. Before they can spot him, the narrator hides in some bushes. The knight greets the lady, but she, lost in thought, fails to notice. He greets her again, she apologizes for her absentmindedness, he politely brushes the apology aside and asks to know her troubled thought. She asks to be left alone, but he insists, to which she replies that no one, not even God, can help her. He promises to heal her, and so at last she tells her story.

She has been loyal to love for seven or eight years, devoted to her friend with all her heart, so that nothing else in all life intefered: he was her hope, her joy, her every thought and desire, all her solace, treasure, and comfort. Their hearts were a pair in perfect accord, and there was no trace of villainous thought in their love; but now her joy has turned to sorrow and her once-bright days are filled with darkness and unhappiness: nothing can help her but death, death who has done her a terrible wrong, having taken her beloved. The poet, hidden in the bushes, sees her faint at the end of her lament.

When the lady revives, the knight assures her that her suffering is nothing compared to his own: her beloved is dead, his has proved unfaithful. The lady asks how it's possible for her pain to be less severe than his, and he promises to prove his contention providing that she will listen intently and put aside her unhappiness so her attention is wholly his.

He begins his tale with an account of his service to the god of love. Then he tells how once, in a company of ladies, he saw his beloved, sent by Fortune—a lady who outshone all others as the sun outshines the moon. He tells at great length how he saw her dancing, singing, and laughing so beautifully that there was no greater treasure on earth. Her hair was like spun gold, neither too blond nor too brown; her eyes opened by degrees, never too widely, seeming to offer mercy—eyes not set too far apart; her color was lively, fresh and rosy, and her white neck had neither wrinkle nor bony lump. She had long arms, white hands, long fingers, white small breasts, and a beautiful straight young body with well-formed legs. As for the rest which he could not see, that too seemed well fashioned. She was so beautiful, in fact, that if nature wished to make another such beauty, this lady alone could be the pattern or example.

The knight was afraid to express his love, he says, until he came to be assured that such beauty cannot exist without mercy. Yet when it came to telling her of his painful desire, he trembled and stood transfixed and couldn't say a word. In this misery he endured for many days until at last he gathered courage to tell her he loved her and to beg for her mercy. Even as he spoke he was afraid she would scorn him, but her look seemed to encourage him to say more until, to his horror, she interrupted, refusing him and telling him he should address himself not to her but to love, apparently because it seemed to her that he was in love not with her but with love itself.

Despite the refusal, it seemed to the knight that the lady's eyes really did say yes, and he rehearsed to himself her qualities, such as her soft, humble face, example for all beauty.

And so he served her devotedly, and finally she accepted him as her friend. He felt resurrected as if from death to life, so happy that his happiness cannot be described even now. He thanked his lady for the noble gift of her mercy and for having filled him with bliss and health, promising to serve loyally, guarding her honor, and he tells his present listener that that is indeed how he thanked his lady for the gift of her mercy. Thus he lived in happiness for a long time.

Then comes his lament, including a tirade against Fortune, who caused his fall: his lady took another friend! His listener interrupts, objecting that his loss is less than hers since he can always see his beloved again, as she can not. The knight answers that his ability to see his lady means, alas, that he can never forget, then complains of her changeableness, now here, now there, now by the fire, now at the table, uncertain as a game of chance. He sees her often and cannot forget her and at the same time, to his even greater pain, does not in fact wish to forget her, since that would make him an unfaithful lover.

The argument has by now reached an impasse, and the lady suggests that they find an arbitrator, to which suggestion the knight courteously agrees. The poet hidden in the bushes decides he can help and comes out to approach them. As he does so the lady's little dog begins to bark, then seizes the poet's robe in his teeth. The poet smooths down the fur of the dog and hands him back to his lady, then salutes the two of them (both pale with grief), explains that he has heard all, and offers to tell them the name of a judge competent to decide which of them has most suffered. They agree and the poet names the king of Bohemia (the patron for whom Machault is writing), who is fortunately in residence at a nearby castle. The castle is on a mountaintop surrounded by water and a beautiful valley ringing with the songs of birds. When they arrive at the castle they are met by allegorical figures and the noble king. The king consults with Reason, Loyalty, and Youth, then finds for the knight. After the judgment, dinner is served, the party remains for eight days and then comes away with precious gifts. The poem ends with an anagram containing the poet's name and praise of his lady.

Obviously a good deal of the *Book of the Duchess* is drawn directly or indirectly from Machault's compliment to the king of Bohemia; large, general ideas like the comparison of lovers in different situations, the promise to play physician by listening attentively, and so forth, and also particular ideas and images like the "eight years," the puppy, the conflict with Fortune, the game of chance, the lady's hair (in Chaucer) which was neither too red, too brown, nor too yellow, but like spun gold — and many, many more. Moreover, as Robinson's notes show (or, better, those of Albert I. Dickerson, Jr.).[30] Chaucer takes over numerous lines in straight translation. For instance, Chaucer writes:

> And eek the wlken was so faire,
> Blew, bright, clere was the air,
> And ful atempre, for soth, it was,   [temperate]
> For nother cold nor hoot it nas.

> [BD, 339–42

reflecting Machault's

> Et li jours fu attemprez par mesure,
> Beaus, clers, luisans, nés et purs,
> Sans froidure.

("And the days were tempered by measure, blue, clear, shiny clean, and pure without coldness") — all stock details in descriptions of the earthly paradise, details which Machault, too, borrowed. We find an abundance of such echoes; in fact, the whole of the Black Knight's eulogy to his lady might be described as scrambled Machault, or, rather, Machault recategorized under the headings Truth, Goodness, Beauty, and so forth. Yet Chaucer is equally indebted to several other French poems, for instance Machault's *Remedy of Fortune* (*Remede de Fortune*) — which I must summarize more briefly.

The *Remedy* is a sort of didactic treatise on love and fortune, in which a mature lover tells of his love-education. He begins with the twelve rules necessary for learning any art (compare Chaucer's fusing of the art of love and the art of poetry in *Parliament of Birds* and, less obviously, here in the

Book of the Duchess), then speaks of how, when he was young, his works were fleeting. He placed himself, he says, in his lady's tutelage, since she was endowed with all that is beautiful and good. He loved merely according to his youthful understanding, but love intervened in his behalf. He dared not refuse his emotion, but he had, he says, doubts that even with all the qualities of such renowned personages as Solomon, Alexander, Job, and so forth, he could be worthy. Love took care of him nevertheless, and his lady's character, mirror and example of all good, encouraged him toward virtue.

For a long time he served his lady devotedly, though he dared not reveal his love to her and could only confess his passion in secret poetry, one specimen of which he reproduces. Then, to his profound embarrassment, one of his poems came to the lady's attention. She asked him who wrote it, and he fled in confusion to a garden where he complained against love and Fortune, comparing the latter to the victor in a chess game. In all this misery, his lady is, he thinks, the only possible physician. He meets another lady, whom we later find to be Hope, and she reminds him that his beloved has all the qualities of goodness, including pity. Hope gives him a ring which restores him to health, and describes herself as the castle, fortress, and physician of desirous lovers. She tells the young poet how to deal with Fortune, explaining that happiness is the result of patient suffering, then disappears. The poet doubts again, is again cheered up by Hope, whom he now himself describes as his tower. Then he goes to where he can see his lady dancing in a garden near a tower, in company with ladies and gentlemen. He works up his courage to ask her forgiveness for his discourtesy, describes her as his paradise, and at last wins her mercy. That evening he attends chapel and a feast at the castle, and later he and his lady exchange rings. Unhappily, the lady's kindness does not last, or so it seems to the poet. He accuses her and when she defends her loyalty, the poet can only half believe her. He closes with a signature-anagram and an homage to love.

Again one can see at a glance that Chaucer borrowed numerous details — the idea of the futility of private poetry, of youthful love that "koude no good," of catalogues of famous

men and women, of love as fortress (the love of Blanche of
Lancaster, "the long castel with walles white," the New
Jerusalem), the idea of the chess game with Fortune, and so
on. And again, as the annotated editions of the poem show,
Chaucer quotes some of the *Remedy*'s lines word for word,
especially in the Knight's description of his lady. But everywhere — and this is the point — Chaucer's organizing imagination reshapes, enriches, magically transforms. In Machault the
parallels between the love religion and Christian religion have
become frozen metaphor, mere elegant convention. Chaucer
thaws them, reawakening the ideas at the heart of the
conventions. From the *Canticles* he borrows the image of the
beloved's throat as an ivory tower:

> Hyr throte, as I have now memoyre,
> Semed a round tour of yvoyre,
> Of good gretnesse, and noght to gret
>
> [BD, 945-47

And thus he reinforces at once the chess-game imagery which
runs throughout the poem (the lady is a chesspiece, hence a
victim of Fortune), the traditional idea of Christ as a fortress,
and the Platonic idea of the beloved as a vector toward
absolute good (the lady as temporary savior), so that, like the
crucified lover, the lady is both vanquished (as flesh) and
victorious (as spirit), capable of saving the lover from loss and
failure, victimization by Fortune, if the lover can properly
understand her merely physical death.

So it goes with the rest of Chaucer's borrowings and
allusions. The lion in Machault's *Dit dou Lyon* provides
Chaucer with some details for his treatment of the whelp
"Chaucer" meets in the animal-filled forest of the *Book of the
Duchess*, but the lion brings more than sharp visual detail.
Machault's lion is dangerous except to true lovers, the orchard
he protects is called "The Trial of True Love," and the lion's
allegorical character as patient sufferer of "attacks of envy" is a
proof that "he who suffers, overcomes." All this, for Machault,
has to do with honorable versus dishonorable courtly love; for
Chaucer and for those in his audience who remember the

context from which he borrows, it has to do with all life and death. The same is true, as I've suggested already, in his borrowing of Machault's retelling of Ovid's tale of Seys and Alcyone, in the *Fountain of Love*. Chaucer, emphasizing Christian possibilities in the story, accepts those details that work for him (Morpheus opening just one eye) and changes those that don't (whereas in Machault the messenger wakes Morpheus with gentle speech, Chaucer gives her a trumpet).

In short, a key element in Chaucer's style is poetic allusion, and one of the things one needs to watch in reading his poetry is his manipulation of sources, not just French poetry — though this would be important to him all his life, so that even a relatively late poem like the *Legend of Good Women* can take its scheme from a poem by Machault (in this case, the *Judgment of the King of Navarre*) — but also patristic writings, Italian poetry, the Bible, occasionally even the half-wit pop tunes of fourteenth-century England. This is not to say that one cannot read Chaucer without knowledge of everything he ever read. In Chaucer's poetry, as in the Bible as patristic exegetes understood it, "Nothing is in one place revealed obscurely that is not elsewhere set down plainly." But it is to say that wherever Chaucer's texture seems lifeless, like a faded place in an ancient fresco, the likelihood is that the culprit is Time, not Chaucer.

ii

The *Parliament of Birds* ~~~~~~
Order and the Appearance of Chaos in Art and Life; or, Chaucer as Dim-witted Puppet and Wise Puppeteer

HAUCER MAY OR MAY NOT HAVE written the *Parliament of Birds* for a specific occasion, the proposed marriage treaty between Richard of England and Marie of France; but whatever may have prompted the poet to write it, the poem is as brilliantly worked out as the *Book of the Duchess* and has many things in common with that poem — among others, virtual inaccessibility to readers attuned to a modern aesthetic, and the use of a comic narrator, in this case (as in that) one who has only the dimmest understanding of the poem he's inside.

The poem's inaccessibility to modern readers has two main causes, its dependence on a body of knowledge now forgotten and its seeming coldness, or detachment. The narrator is a delightful man, but as Kemp Malone once put it, he "serves as reporter of what he sees and hears, not as a participant in the action," [1] and that tends to put us off. On the surface, he simply looks at things and records his none-too-bright responses. Insofar as he understands the allegory of the poem at all, it is revealed for him as on a movie screen. In fairly typical medieval fashion, the allegory takes the place of drama (in the modern sense of drama), and symbolic juxtapositions and ornamental devices — catalogues, ironic contrasts, amusing asides, and poetic allusions — substitute for profluence. The real drama is of a kind immediately obvious to a medieval audience, for whom the disparity between what the narrator understands and what the audience understands is tension enough.

For the modern reader, the poem also presents — like most of Chaucer's work — a further difficulty. By our aesthetic, which is to say, really, our metaphysical assumptions, a work tends to be unconvincing and vaguely annoying when — as in some of the stories of Ring Lardner, for instance — a narrator reveals more than he himself understands, presenting a neat symbolic system he lacks the intelligence or background to construct. We feel the ego of the writer smirking down at the character telling the story. Perhaps medieval poets felt that too, to some extent, and for that reason made their half-wit narrators caricatures of themselves. But also, they worked with a different metaphysic. For a medieval poet who assumes a neat and orderly universe no one but God and his angels understand, a befuddled narrator in an orderly work is not only excusable but quite normal, poetically reflecting the usual condition of mankind. This is especially true, of course, for the poet influenced by nominalism, which denies that knowledge can be achieved. Thus in most of Chaucer's poetry we must deal with two "Chaucers" — the master artist in the corner of the universe slyly supervising and paring his nails, and the clown narrator who is at least to some extent unaware that his world is taken care of.

Though all Chaucerians are now conscious of the two Chaucers, few have quite managed to deal with them, it seems to me, which is the reason a number of critics at the moment mistakenly think Chaucer's poems solemn meditations of one sort or another. Focusing on the larger structural patterns, the work of the master craftsman in the background — finding a systematic consolation pattern in the *Book of the Duchess*, or in the *Parliament of Birds* an ingenious, numerologically ordered universe built on principles out of Boethius' *De Musica*[2] — they celebrate Chaucer's nobility and sobriety and seem inclined to dismiss the clown in the foreground as a curious distraction. The trouble, of course, is that the clown in the foreground is exceedingly visible. He is not merely one of those miniature figures we find at the bottom of a medieval painting, and not a mere ornament or ruse for the wrongheaded (carnal) reader: he is emphatically human, with particular worries and physical problems (nearsightedness, love-problems, a tendency toward fat). Or to put it another way, in the noble and orderly architecture of Chaucer's poems (an image of God's order), he is a worried nominalist wringing his fingers and squinting in confusion. The "truth" in Chaucer's poetry is not that the world is orderly and good yet man is man — restless and unhappy, hungry, a comi-tragic misfit, which is to say, fallen. The poems are not lessons, in other words, but works of art. They are not dead, like old cathedrals, but charged, like cathedrals with people inside. If they seem to us lessons, the reason is that what Chaucer and his audience took as their premise by revelation — the well-made cosmos — sounds to us like news, something Chaucer is "suggesting" or "leading up to." For Chaucer, the orderly Creation is simply the stage or backdrop; the comedy played before it is the life of man — and the life of the poem.

§ 1

ONE OF THE MOST IMPRESSIVE demonstrations of the *Parliament*'s orderliness of structure is David S. Chamberlain's "The Music of the Spheres and *The Parlement of Foules.*"[3] The whole poem, Chamberlain shows, is built on Neoplatonic and Neo-Aristotelian musical principles which Chaucer may have found in any number of writers — Augustine, Cassiodorus, Isadore, or Boethius, among others. "Music" as one of the branches of the quadrivium implied more in the Middle Ages than it does today. It was a philosophical study which dealt with all aspects of proportioning — by one standard formulation, *the music of the world* (the rhythm of the seasons, and so

forth), *human music* (the rhythm and harmonious proportioning of parts of the body and soul), and *the music of instruments*.
World music derives, according to writers like Boethius, from
exemplars in God and the "hymning" of the spheres, and is
revealed in everything there is.

The whole subject, though fascinating, is much too large
for treatment here; it will be enough to give merely some
indication of Chaucer's use of musical philosophy in the
poem's structure. As Chamberlain says, Chaucer "weaves
through the structure and themes of the poem all four medieval
species of music, and numerous subspecies," and controls by
musical principles "the very form of the poem, its meter,
stanza, and length." [4] Begin with this last, the form.

In all standard editions, the *Parliament of Birds* is 699
lines long, but this, Chamberlain argues, is a mistake; in the
roundel which ends the poem a refrain line has been dropped
(after line 686). The poem is really 700 lines long, ending
with a roundel of 14 lines (or 7×2), composed of seven-line
stanzas with 10 syllables to a line (average), or stanzas of 70
syllables. All these sevens and perfect multiples of seven reflect
the "seven tones" of the spheres in Platonic and medieval
music philosophy, and also the harmonious make-up of man
(the four elements — earth, air, fire, water — plus three faculties of soul). There are various other appearances of the
number *seven* in the *Parliament*: the poem has seven main
sections,[5] matching the seven chapters of the "dream of
Scipion," summarized by Chaucer in seven stanzas, and the
poem treats seven kinds of music, as music was categorized in
Chaucer's day — trinitarian, angelic, Edenic, mondial, human,
social, and instrumental.

Chamberlain's argument on the length of the roundel and
thus of the poem is not entirely satisfactory: Chaucer's other
roundels are all exactly like this one, and other numerological
considerations make a thirteen-line poem ideal at this point.
The number 699, besides its own numerological significance,
is obviously pushing hard on 700, and I think we need not alter
the text to agree, in principle, with Chamberlain. Seven
symbolism appears in other seven-line poems by Chaucer,
most strikingly in the *Troilus* and the unfinished *Anelida and*

Arcite, which is definitely composed (as another brilliant line-counter has noticed) of seventy-line sections mostly in seven-line stanzas.

We find also numerous patterns of *four* and *three*, the numbers respectively of matter (the four elements) and spirit (the Trinity and the three faculties of soul). Together, of course, four and three, matter and spirit, make up the whole universe this side of heaven (home of the angelic, strictly spiritual nine legions — intermediaries between the perfect music of the Trinity and the music of the world). The angels' perfect, intellectual singing is, by one extremely common account, the real music of the spheres ("thrys thre"); and it is the fact that man is both four and three, in other words that he has two inclinations, one toward earth, one toward heaven, that causes him his trouble. What joins matter and spirit, or body and soul, according to Boethius, is "love" — the musical term *concordia*, reflected in Chaucer's verbal repetitions, in the *Parliament*, on *acord, acordaunt*, and so forth (e.g., lines 197 and 203). The importance of fours and threes in the poem, like the importance of the number seven, is also built into the stanza, in the relation of quatrain and tercet.

But Chaucer's use of musical principles for form does not end here. The stanza's rhyme-scheme, Chamberlain writes,

> embodies the three principal consonances of instrumental music, the perfect fourth or *diatessaron* (4:3), the perfect fifth or *diapente* (3:2), and the octave or *diapason* (2:1), which were also the principal consonances among the spheres. In Chaucer's stanza, the relation of quatrain to tercet is *diatessaron* (4:3); the relation of rimes within the tercet (bcc) is *diapason* (2:1); and the relation of b's to a's and of b's to c's in the whole stanza (ababbcc) is *diapente* (3:2). The only other relationship that can be found in the stanza is equality or *unisonus* (1:1) appearing in the a:b relation in the quatrain (2:2) and the a:c relation in the whole stanza (2:2), and it was considered the best of all consonances by Augustine.[6]

If one believes all this — and analyses of this kind are always more incredible than unconvincing — one may ask why

Chaucer should go to all this trouble. The easy answer is that he was a medieval poet and thought it was his duty (Dante and hundreds more had done it). But needless to say, there's more to it than that. Chamberlain has set down part of the answer:

> The idea of imitating the sound of the spheres appears in most of Chaucer's . . . sources. Boethius explains that seven strings of the gamut imitate the music from Saturn to Moon; and Dante declares that angels "ever accord their notes after the notes of the eternal wheels." But the idea is most vivid in the *Dream of Scipio* itself. "Those eight motions," Africanus says, "produce seven different tones, which number is the key of nearly all things. Learned men, imitating this music on stringed instruments and in songs, have gained for themselves a return to the sky, just as others have who, with outstanding talents in human life, have pursued divine studies." *Learned men, that is, win heaven by imitating the music of the spheres!* [7]

To get the rest of the answer we must turn from the noble and orderly superstructure to the narrator's terrible problem and the events of the poem.

§ 2

AS JOHN P. MC CALL POINTED OUT not long ago, critical accounts of the *Parliament of Birds* tend to be inconsistent and frustrating because critics have been looking for the wrong thing, a hidden answer or resolution of the poor questing narrator's trouble.[8] What the poem in fact offers is a great mix of conflicting elements held together by "concord" and balance — the music of heaven, the cackling of birds; true love, false love; selfishness and lust, the "common profit"; in a word, "heaven and hell, and earth." If there is any resolution to the narrator's trouble, it is the poem itself, in which the superstructure, as Chamberlain demonstrates, is ideal Neo-platonic art, an imitation of the singing universe in Plato's *Timaeus*, while the inner structure — the narrator's quest — is disorderly and baffling, as tortured as the narrator's heart.

The narrator's trouble is simply this: he's a poet who wants to understand and write about love. He knows perfectly well, after he has read the *Dream of Scipio*, what he ought to write about and concern himself with: eternal things, love in its highest manifestation. He should write like, say, Dante. But while this may be all right for the master poet Chaucer who manipulates the stanzas as God looks after the seven fixed stars — the nine spheres, counting the sun and moon — it leaves the comic-narrator Chaucer unsatisfied. He's a man incapable of such noble calm: though not a lover, he's hungry, eager, too deeply involved in the beauty and ugliness of the world to be ruled by good sense.

Like the *Book of the Duchess*, the *Parliament* opens with the narrator's reflections on his condition.[9] He's a poet hungry for knowledge of the world's basic principle (according to Boethius), "love," — so hungry and confused that he's miserable, like some poor half-crazy lover. He wrings his hands and moans:

> The lyf so short, the craft so long to lerne,
> Th'assay so hard, so sharp the conquerynge,
> The dredful joye, alwey that slit so yerne:
> [slides away so quickly]
> Al this mene I by love, that my felynge
> Astonyeth with his wonderful werkynge
> So sore, iwis, that whan I on hym thynke,
> Nat wot I wel wher that I flete or synke.   [float]
> For al be that I knowe nat Love in dede,
> Ne wot how that he quiteth folk here hyre,
> [pays people their hire]
> Yit happeth me ful ofte in bokes redde   [it happens to me]
> Of his myrakles and his crewel yre.
> There rede I wel he wol be lord and syre;
> I dar nat seyn, his strokes been so sore,
> But "God save swich a lord!" — I can na moore.   [know]
> [PB, 1–14

The first line of course calls up the aphorism, "Ars longa, vita brevis," and sets up the poem's major motif, one of the traditional subclasses under *musica humana, poetry,* which Chaucer will treat here as in the *Book of the Duchess* as an exercise of love. The second line, read literally, calls up the image of a siege, a stock courtly love metaphor. The oxymoron "dredful joye" is a commonplace of love-poetry (drawn, of course, from religious emotion) and prepares for the explanatory "Al this mene I by Love." We assume momentarily that the poet means broad Boethian love, the "fair chain" in Chaucer's translation of Boethius' *Consolation*; but the remaining lines of the stanza and all of the second stanza seem to confuse harmonious Boethian love and the kind of love that leads to discord and sorrow, love as represented by Cupid. This apparent confusion — actually what McCall describes as the harmonious duality of life — extends to the whole poem.

The second section of the poem (parallel to the Seys and Alcyone section of the *Book of the Duchess*) presents the narrator reading a book, *Tullyus of the Drem of Scipioun.* It is Macrobius' account of and commentary on Cicero's dream of Scipio, in which Scipio, in company with "his auncestre, Affrycan," soars above earth and sees that it is a trifle. This mortal life, Scipio learns, is nothing but a kind of death, no matter where one travels or what one achieves, but if one is righteous one goes from this world to a sort of heaven. The whole book treats the subject of love in the Boethian sense and ought to tell the narrator all he wants to know.

It's in seven chapters, symbolically binding *four* and *three,* as do the spheres' seven tones (as Macrobius comments), and it treats the whole universe, "heavene and helle / And erthe" — that is, the cosmic extremes and the earth that lies between them. It tells of the "nyne speres" (Cicero spoke of eight; Chaucer, to get his symbolic "thrys thre," shifted to another cosmology), the cosmic "welle . . . of musik and melodye [and] armonye," that is, divine (trinitarian and angelic) source of all music's proportions, namely *measure* ("musik"), *melodic line,* and *harmony.* It tells of cycles of time, another musical consideration (a part of *musica mundana* or world music), a binding force or love-force. As the audience familiar with Macrobius would recall, reminded by Chaucer's short précis, the book speaks of forms of human love — the "acord" of *friends* (Scipio and Massinissa, whom wise Scipio persuaded away from the seductress Sophonisba), the accord of *relatives* (Scipio and "Affrycan so deere"), and the accord of *men in the just society,* which results in "commune profyt." It speaks, finally, of love gone wrong, that of "likerous [lecherous] folk," the concupiscent who, as a result of their sins, "whirle aboute th'erthe alwey in peyne." This book, in short, tells Chaucer both about love and about music, mother of his "craft," poetry. It tells him, in effect, to look heavenward and write according to those large and noble principles which order the stars and, in the form of common profit, maintain states.

The book leaves the narrator excited but unsatisfied. For all its richness, the book leaves out the lush details elaborated in Petrarch's extravaganza, the *Africa* — a poem Chaucer must surely have known or heard about, since it was considered in Italy to be Petrarch's masterpiece. As Petrarch tells us at delightful length, Scipio met his beloved general Massinissa to win him back to duty from the seduction of black-eyed Sophonisba. It was after this success that Scipio dreamed of his ancestor. The whole Macrobius story, Scipio's dream, has plenty to do with love's "wonderful werkynge"; but the juicy parts are gone, everything rushing to Affrycan's advice on the base kind of love which nearly destroyed Massinissa, the love of the "likerous," and spiritual love, the love of noble souls.

> "Know theyself first immortal,
> And loke ay besyly thow werche and wysse
> To commune profit, and thow shalt not mysse
> To comen swiftly to that place deere
> That ful of blysse is and of soules cleere."
>
> [PB, 73–77

Tired out by his long day of reading, still restless of soul — "For bothe I hadde thyng which that I nolde [did not want] / And ek [also] I nadde [had not] that thyng that I wolde" — half beast, half angel (as his imagery reminds us — the animals who must lie down, the book he must put aside) — the narrator falls asleep and begins to dream. Affry-can comes and, to requite the narrator for working so diligently at Macrobius' long book, takes him to a walled park with a gate of ambiguous significance — one gatepost sign promises joy, the other sorrow — and impatiently shoves him in. After admiring the park, the narrator enters an artificial garden within the park and, little by little, makes his way past personified abstractions, graceful dances, and elegant devices to the sultry temple of Venus — from which he flees. Thanks to the shifting and unpredictable landscape of dreams, he happens to come upon a "launde" where all the birds in the world are gathered around Dame Nature for the purpose of choosing their mates in an orderly parliament, and watches as Dame Nature tries to get through the whole business quickly. Her attempt fails since three courtly eagles spend the whole day debating which of them most loves the beautiful formel whom one of them must choose. The formel asks for time to consider; Nature grants it; and the birds all join in singing a pretty roundel. The poem ends:

> And with the shoutyng, whan the song was do
> That foules maden at here flyght awey,
> I wok, and othere bokes tok me to,
> To reede upon, and yit I rede alwey.
> I hope, ywis, to rede so som day
> That I shal mete som thyng for to fare
> The bet, and thus to rede I nyl nat spare.
>
> [PB, 693–99

At first glance, as this summary should indicate, the poem seems the disjointed and confused sort of thing a poet might write if he set out in high spirits to rhyme a while with no general plan worked out beforehand. And the tone of the poem may seem at first to support such a notion. The introductory stanzas on the poet's state have obvious touches of comic irony,[10] but the Dream of Scipio, which follows, is presented with perfect seriousness. After a serious transition on the nature of dreams comes the broadly comic episode in which, parodying Dante among others, Chaucer presents his narrator's uneasiness before the ambiguous gate and Affrycan's forceful resolution of the narrator's dilemma. Next, presenting the lovely, conventional park and the garden of love within, Chaucer seems one moment to be writing with perfect seriousness, the next to be faintly mocking;[11] and the description of Venus, Professor Muscatine rightly observes, has a "hothouse closeness . . . which, missing the full sensuality of the Italian [i.e., Boccaccio's version], hits on a voyeurism that is unique in Chaucer." [12] Then, bursting in like something out of a different poem entirely, comes the comic realism of the Valentine's Day parliament of birds.[13]

Seeming confusion and a disparity of poetic styles is not unusual in medieval poetry and need not drive us — as it did a number of early critics of the *Parliament* — to a conclusion that Chaucer did not know what he was about;[14] neither are we forced to account for the changes in tone, together with the narrator's statement that he is seeking "a certeyn thing to lerne" (20), by interpreting the poem as sober Christian philosophy, arguing — with Huppé and Robertson, for instance — that the seriously rendered asceticism of Cicero's book, judged against the comic material found elsewhere, and also against the noise, ineffectiveness, and mundane interests of the birds, establishes an essentially grim contrast between heavenly love, or true felicity, and "false felicity." [15]

Chamberlain's demonstration of the poem's tight form wipes out the notion that the poem is merely careless. What is wrong with the Christian ascetic reading is that it ignores the poet's clear and unashamed delight in this world. (It also ignores textural and structural detail.) If Chaucer disapproves of his chattering birds, he also enjoys them, and so do we. Insofar as the birds represent human failings — the persistent desire of some people to murder others, for example — they represent fairly serious failings; but Chaucer has written them down as birds, not people. No one, I think, would seriously argue that the creators of Donald Duck and Bullwinkle Moose are, respectively, sober moral and political reformers. More important, one can hardly miss the narrator's sometimes simple, sometimes mingled feelings of dread, joy, and wonder within the dream — all quite proper Christian responses to nature. It is true and exceedingly important that the narrator is, as Professor Muscatine remarks, a bookworm[16] and, like most of Chaucer's narrators, something of a learned dolt; but he is not a bookworm who relishes the *contemptus mundi* of Cicero's book.[17] Having read excitedly all day, believing he was at last on the track, he has in the end a *contemptus mundi* he understands but would prefer to do without.

What needs to be noticed, if the poem's controlling comic method is to work, is that the narrator's condition, involving confusion and loss of sensation, is directly comparable to the melancholy condition of the conventional sorrowing lover, like the narrator in the *Book of the Duchess*, but the cause of the present narrator's state is not that he is in love. What numbs him is love's "wonderful werkynge" — the *process*. As poet and as quester for truth, the narrator is fascinated by — and sick with desire to understand — an incredible power in the world, love. Whereas Affrycan gives the tormented Scipio the vision he needs (a vision of the cosmic plan), Affrycan gives to the narrator what *he* desires: brief insight into the order and significance of "inclinations" *below* the Galaxy. The two views are of course not mutually exclusive, although, as Affrycan's rough handling of the narrator suggests (153–54), one is considerably lower than the other. Both views come from Affrycan, the truth-teller. Beginning with a view of Affrycan as one of those gifted pagans who "touched the truth" and, in this case, firmly grasped it, Chaucer draws Affrycan back to what he ought to know best, as a pagan, the "law of kind."

If the point of the poem were merely the point made in Scipio's dream (as Huppé and Robertson believe) or merely the comic irony in a bookworm's being tricked into writing on earthly love (as Professor Muscatine thinks), there would be no need for all three of the dream's symbolic locales, "hevene and helle / And erthe" (Chaucer has altered Cicero here) — that is to say, 1) the fused earthly paradise and heaven where trees have leaves "that ay shal laste" (173; cf. the trees the narrator finds in *Pearl*), where "swetnesse everemore inow [enough] is" (185), where birds sing "With voys of aungel in his armonye (191), and where "ne nevere wolde it nyghte"

(209), that is, where daylight is everlasting; 2) the artificial love-garden and temple, at the center of which lovers suffer as in hell; and 3) the "laund," where Dame Nature presides and birds, like men, can make their choices of better or worse. If the joke were a philosopher's having to deal with sex, then the final episode, Dame Nature's parliament, would be sufficient alone.

It is equally inadequate to try to account for the presence of all three locales in Charles O. Macdonald's way, by claiming that Chaucer intended a simple contrast of bad and good.[18] Both the paradise and the temple garden have some bad and some good in them. Consider, for example, the trees, which Macdonald finds attractive because of the qualifying adjectives:

> The byldere ok, and ek the hardy asshe;
> The piler elm, the cofre unto carayne;
> The boxtre pipere, holm to whippes lashe;
> The saylynge fyr, the cipresse, deth to playne;
> The shetere ew; the asp for shaftes pleyne;
> The olyve of pes, and eke the dronke vyne;
> The victor palm, the laurer to devyne.
>
> [176–82

Along with things pleasant, Chaucer summons up coffins, whips, graveyards, arrows, drunkenness. As trees in paradise, these species can suffer no decline (their leaves never die); but to the human narrator's mind they suggest the baffling complexity of the human condition, man caught between elements and spirit, sorrow and joy; and what makes the whole problem of man so difficult is that not all joys are spiritual or all sorrows caused by physicality: building (with oaks), ornamenting one's mansion with pillars (of elm), or sailing (with masts of fir) are joyous activities of physical existence.

The idea that the formel eagle is a spoiled young lady of noble birth must also be rejected. As J. A. W. Bennett has pointed out, "The main emphasis here . . . is on the ennobling, the maturing effect of service by which the brashness, the callousness of youthful love, is rubbed away; and by which the sincerity of the rivals' claims can be tested." [19] Compare with this the Black Knight's year of humble service in the *Book of the Duchess*. In fact the formel is not spoiled but, as we'll see, timid and fearful, recognizing love's dangers.

In the *Parliament of Birds*, then, the central contrast is not between the bliss of love and heaven's bliss but between, on one hand, the unreasonable desire to possess (not merely "use with delight," in Augustine's words) the object of one's desire, and, on the other hand, a selfless delight in that which seems good, in other words, a desire which takes some account of the total order of the universe or, here below heaven, the total order of nature — the "commune profit." The focus is not primarily on "carnality" in its simplest (that is, sexual) form — the point that might have most interested a patristic writer at such a parliament. The focus is on the "carnality" we would describe as general self-interest, or self-love, the human being's almost unavoidable concern about his private welfare at whatever cost[20] — a point naturally interesting to a philosophical poet (and member of the English parliament). The view Affrycan offers in the Proem is not unlike Chaucer's scheme in the *Book of the Duchess*, a sharp contrast between lasting heavenly bliss and earthly bliss which is of short duration, if possible at all; and Chaucer makes the contrast as Christian as he can, insisting upon Cicero's virtually Christian treatment of "likerous folk" who

> after that they ben dede,
> Shul whirle aboute th'erthe alwey in peyne,
> Tyl many a world be passed, out of drede,
> And than, foryeven al hir wikked dede,
> Than shul they come into this blysful place,
> To which to comen God the sende his grace.
>
> [79–84

But it is not this austere view that controls the poem. (The point is Bennett's.) Even granting that Affrycan is right when he tells us that nature, this world, is a trifle beside "the Galaxye," still, however "lyte" our world, it is not quite Plotinus' worthless passing shadow; it is a priceless though minute part of the whole, a place that imitates the cosmic rhythm (consider the poem's verbal repetitions on "day by day" and "year by year"), a place of selflessness and joy as well as selfishness and sorrow.[21] Though this world is certainly not the "welle of musik and melodye," it echoes that music, abounding with birds which have, like men, a double nature; they can sing like angels or squabble like devils.

One may be tempted at first to say that since the time of the *Book of the Duchess* Chaucer has broadened his concept of "this world's bliss" to include not only the love of a dear physician but love of all nature. But even in his first dream vision, Chaucer presented nature as beautiful and good, and the self-concerned, sorrowing lover as something nature, with her cycles and seasons, cannot tolerate. Chaucer has simply shifted his focus and, with it, his narrative technique. Concentrating now not on the plight of a particular lover but on the total order in which particular lovers (both human lovers and birds) play their tragic or comic parts, the master poet behind the poem chooses as his puppet narrator not a man comically pitiful because hopelessly in love but a man who has lost his taste for all that — a philosopher-poet comically pitiful because, though he is interested in the total order, not in exclusive possession of some lady, and is thus a man in an excellent position to make reasonable choices (as the narrator of the *Book of the Duchess* was not), he fails to make those reasonable choices. Like any ordinary lover, the narrator unreasonably yearns to possess; and the object of *his* desire is knowledge.

§ 3

THE IRONICALLY ANALOGOUS POSITION of the philosopher and the lover, together with the general focus in the poem on the total order as against the desires of the particular creature, enforce a revaluation of those artifices constructed by the highly civilized as opposed to the brute: a revaluation not only of law and the common profit in the political sense but also of that elaborate codification, courtly love. To focus on a given

courtly lover (a creature by nature and situation likely to be
incapable of Boethean reasonableness) is to see courtly love as
the way of sorrow. Consider the Knight in the *Book of the
Duchess*; consider poor Dido in the *House of Fame*; or consider
what the narrator of the *Parliament* sees in the temple of
Venus:

> And, as I seyde, amyddes lay Cypride,   [Venus]
> To whom on knees two yonge folk ther cryde,
> To ben here helpe. But thus I let hire lye,
> And ferther in the temple I gan espie
>
> That, in despit of Dyane the chaste,
> Ful many a bowe ibroke heng on the wal
> Of maydenes swiche as gonne here tymes waste
> In hyre servyse; and peynted overal
> Of many a story, of which I touche shal
> A fewe, as of Calyxte and Athalante,
> And many a mayde of which the name I wante.
>
> Semyramis, Candace, and Hercules,
> Biblis, Dido, Thisbe, and Piramus,
> Tristram, Isaude, Paris, and Achilles,
> Eleyne, Cleopatre, and Troylus,
> Silla, and ek the moder of Romulus:
> Alle these were peynted on that other syde,
> And al here love, and in what plyt they dyde.
>
> [277–94

But to focus on the total order of Providence is to see the
courtly-love scheme as necessary for the preservation of one of
nature's kinds, the spiritual aristocrat. For in the *Parliament* as
elsewhere in medieval verse, that side of love which represents
dark, sensual passion is dangerous: one must approach Venus
slowly and cautiously, making certain that more is involved in
one's love than mere sexual hunger. It is this danger that
Chaucer suggests in ordering his garden and temple of love as
he does.

Professor Bennett has called attention to the progression.
(I modify Bennett slightly, introducing the Neoplatonic

faculties of soul.) One sees, at the outset, only the noble, innocent, and good — the mighty, angel-like "Cupide, oure lord" (cf. the Cupid of the *Legend of Good Women*, Prologue G), who can be, at best, a figure of man's highest, rational part, which inclines love to what is noble; then one sees "Wille, his doughter," the Platonic irascible part (*animositas, magnanimitas*), the faculty by which men feel righteous indignation, loyalty, and pity; and after that one sees allegorical figures which begin well but decline toward perverted will (fierce loyalty to what is bad) and desire, that is, from Plesaunce, Aray, Lust (not in the modern sense but in the sense of "joy" or "assiduity"), Curteysie, Craft (art), Delyt, Gentilesse, Beute, and Youthe, down, gradually, to Foolhardynesse, Flaterye, Desyr, Messogerye (covert message sending), Meede (bribery) and three more too horrible to name, the three qualities (whatever they may be) which are closest to the temple of Venus, here a figure of Plato's third faculty, the "concupiscent part," desire.

When we reach the door of the temple we find the same, for desire, like will, can be good or bad: outside, Dame Pees, Dame Pacience, Byheste, and Art (all noble desires); inside, rank fecundity, phallicism, drunkenness, gluttony, death. If there is an ugly voyeurism in Chaucer's treatment of what he finds in the temple of Venus, nothing could be more appropriate: it's an ugly, perversely exciting place, a hell on earth. The spatial separation of Cupid and Venus is thus an allegorical indication of their difference in quality: Cupid represents the noble, potentially uplifting side of love — reasonable love — and Venus, at the heart of her temple, the extreme of the destructive, carnal side. Chaucer's description of the two reinforces the contrast. Thus the formel eagle, saying she will serve neither Cupid nor Venus (652) is holding back, presumably out of fear (like Emelye in the *Knight's Tale*) from her natural duty, that is, she insists she will not mate at all, neither well nor badly.

If this account is right, then Chamberlain's identification of the garden and temple as "helle" is oversimple. It has hell at its center, heaven at its rim; in other words, like nature itself it is ambiguous, containing both good and evil (as the two gateposts warned). The place is, as all its artifice suggests, the garden and temple of this world conceived as Art, which can be mistaken for hell but is finally a very different place. Compare the idea in the *Book of the Duchess* that poetry can be harmful or helpful, and compare the traditional, half-right view of Art as the devil's work.

One implication of the progression from beauty to ugliness in the narrator's movement from rim to center is that if the formalism and high-flown, verbose debate of courtly lovers (presented in the poetry of courtly love) seem ridiculous, they are nevertheless useful, metaphorically suggesting the same right state of affairs encountered in the "launde" full of birds. "Nature, the vicaire of the almyghty Lord," does not stop the eagles although they declaim from dawn to sunset. Chaucer has now reached a balanced view of the poetry of courtly love. He laughs at the interminable talk of the eagles but he approves, for the premise of courtly-love ritual is common rather than personal profit.

The speeches of the three eagles carry implicit theories of love but carry also theories on that political common profit central to the dream of Scipio and suggested by the very idea of a parliament.[22] The first and most noble of the three suitor eagles is harmonious of soul — he speaks with "wil, and herte, and thought," a balance of the three faculties, and bases his claim on his unselfish wish to serve the formel rather than himself. His only appeal (like the Christian's appeal to God) is for mercy, which is to say, the complement to his selflessness, her willingness to place another's happiness ahead of her own. And his final statement is that, whatever the judgment, he will abide by nature's law. (I don't accept Chamberlain's idea that the eagle should have said "thought" first, then "will," then "heart." His judgment of the emphasis suggested by placement is arbitrary, and both the traditions of love-poetry and Christian doctrine support the eagle's selfless appeal as proper.) The politically analogous position is that view of *quod principi plaquit* stressed by, for instance, Bracton (echoed in Wyclif), the idea that the king's pleasure, subservient to law, is not his selfish pleasure but the pleasure or welfare of the state. King and state are to be mutually dependent upon one another, each serving the other according to the (ultimately religious) doctrine of patience.[23]

The two eagles who speak next are far less courtly, and the politically analogous positions are less admirable. Their language of course shows it as clearly as their thought. The first cries, forgetting that his station is beneath that of the first eagle, "That shal nat be! / I love hire bet than ye don, be seint John — " And then, remembering his manners: "or at the leste I love hire as wel as ye." He bases his claim on an inferior theory of social order, not feudal interdependence based on love but feudal dependence based on obligation. The formel must marry him because she *owes* it to him, in payment for his long service. The analogous political doctrine — of which both monarchists and publicists made use during the Middle Ages — is that the state owes service to the king (or vice versa). This thesis troubled the whole history of feudalism, as Professor Ganshof has shown;[24] and it was a thesis frequently attacked by English poets of the period, especially as Richard's absolutist theory began to take shape.[25]

The third of Chaucer's eagles offers the only argument left to him, an argument as base as one can offer without going to the lengths of the vulgarly selfish lower hookbills. After quickly dismissing the argument about length of service, he says:

> "I saye not this by me, for I ne can
> Don no servyse that may me lady plese;
> But I dar seyn, I am hire treweste man
> As to my dom, and faynest wolde hire ese.
> At shorte wordes, til that deth me sese,
> I wol ben heres, whether I wake or wynke,
> And trewe in al that herte may bethynke."

[477–83

The eagle pays lip service to the code's prescription of humility, and lip service to the idea of common profit; but mainly what he says is that the formel ought to choose him because he is the one most eager to prove satisfying to her (to give someone "ease" was often used in a sexual sense, as when the Wife of Bath says it) — an appeal neither to mutual selflessness nor to obligation but to the selfishness of the formel. The difference between this eagle and the lower aristocratic birds is merely that the latter are frankly and contentiously concerned about their own welfare.

The rest of the birds comment on the ideal in other ways, and the chief point, as McCall notes, is that none of the lesser birds' alternatives is even remotely relevant. Each speaks according to his kind, proving merely that he has no conception of what it is to be an eagle. Ironically, they all represent private as opposed to common profit (Chaucer is almost certainly satirizing the so-called Good Parliament of 1376), and yet all, it seems, must have their say on the same grounds that the formel must have *her* say: for Dame Nature to arbitrate without consulting "the many wills" (as Dante says) which the one monarchial will is to resolve would be tyranny.[26]

At first glance (momentarily dismissing the confusion introduced by the lesser birds), it seems obvious that the formel should choose the first eagle and be done with it (as the son of the falcon understands); and certainly the long debate is ludicrously inefficient. But if the first eagle speaks well, there is no proof "by experience" that he's telling the truth. The second and third eagles, less skillful with language, may in the end be more worthy lovers; and so the conventional debate, and the equally conventional year's delay, are right. Though Chaucer laughs at the interminable courtly talk, he ends his poem with a roundel written in the manner of Machault or Deschamps, the tune of which "imaked was in France," land of elegant artifice.

We can now see more clearly the significance of the contrasts between the paradise, the garden and temple of love, and the "launde" where Dame Nature holds her parliament. The paradise, where there is no mutability, establishes the ideal, but one not directly available in a mutable world; the second, thoroughly artificial, seems at first to have no connection with that common profit of which Scipio learned or the harmony and accord of paradise. It is the conventional love-paradise found in hundreds of love poems and seems meant, indeed, to be tediously conventional, since Chaucer has elaborated and expanded his source, introducing stock images and devices everywhere possible.[27] It seems, moreover, a place Chaucer intends us to scorn, since he himself treats it, at numerous points, comically or ironically, remembering the lesson of Scipio's dream about lecherous folk. The "launde" of Dame Nature, on the other hand, seems designed to represent, despite its comic inefficiency, a more natural and right state of affairs, where law governs lovers much as the clumsy English parliament governed England. This more natural kind of love does have some relationship to Scipio's discovery, and love in nature therefore at first seems preferable to the artifice of *amor cortois*. But the debate of the eagles, which Dame Nature allows to pursue its whole course, suggests that there are natural reasons for the courtly paraphernalia in the love garden and temple — which is to say, there are good reasons for artifice.

In fact — as the poem's superstructure shows — nature is ordered, as are love poetry and the ceremonies of courtly love. Whereas Chaucer found in the artificial garden an ordered series of personified abstractions, he finds in the surrounding park that neatly organized medieval world picture schematically laid out in Martianus Capella's *De Nuptiis Philologiae et Mercurii* and, more important for this poem, the *Anticlaudianus* of Alanus de Insulis, mentioned at line 316, significantly both a philosophical treatise on order and a poem. The great trouble with nature, the whole *Parliament* insists, is that it's changeable, various. This is one of Macrobius' main points in his *Commentary*, the book which triggered the dream, and it's the point enforced by the darker adjectives applied to the trees, 176 et seq. Like the paradise Dante finds on the Mount of Purgatory, the Chaucer paradise seems everlasting and immutable and is heavily furnished with traditional eschatological trappings — spices, light, and so forth. But insofar as this paradise recalls the world as it is, it warns us to guard against changes of heart, changes of loyalty, and of thought. The poet who, bored with the artifice of poetry, would like to turn to nature for his inspiration finds himself forced back, inevitably, to art.

So the *Parliament of Birds*, like the *Book of the Duchess*, is partly a poem about poetry, and the central character is that "noble philosophical poet" Chaucer, disguised and caricatured; and the dream he dreams is on art — man's various arts. Having sought diligently for order in the chaos of love as it's known on earth, he deserves some reward, and in a *somnium* both *animale* and *coeleste,* the shade of Affrycan brings it to him. He takes the narrator to what is, in effect, three approaches to the whole question of love: the ideal, that is, the Platonic "Form"; the Platonically ordered garden and temple of artifice;[28] and then to nature. The narrator rejects the garden and temple, since at the heart of courtly-love artifice lies the foul pit of Venus; but in the park of Nature he comes to see the value of the place he earlier rejected.

Recognizing the focus and progression of the poem, we see that Chaucer's cackling birds are not simply debaters, like the Owl and the Nightingale, for instance, but the poet's allegorical summary of the singing of the universe, from the "Kek kek! kokkow! quek quek!" of geese and cuckoos and ducks to the "voys of aungel" or, to stop this side of the Galaxye, the singing of long-winded knights to their ladies. Indeed, the universe *is* music, in the sense of rhythm and proportion, essence of all existence:

> so huge a noyse gan they make
> That erthe, and eyr, and tre, and every lake
> So ful was, that unethe was there space   [not easily]
> For me to stonde, so ful was al the place.
>
> [312–15

And so despite the difficulties — *Ars longa, vita brevis* — and despite the fact that this world we sing in is "lyte" in comparison to the whole, the poet Chaucer returns to his books in hopes of finding some theme or dream-trigger by means of which he can join, by writing another poem, the universal hymn. So bookish a response to a love-vision is manifestly comic, and to praise it as virtue is to distort the poem: bookishness and rhyming are all the poor, sadly limited narrator is good at. But however comic, the response is right, for every creature serves the total order in his own way, and they also serve who only read and write.

As always in Chaucer, the counterpoise of ideas is complex. Judged against the sublime vision of Scipio, the anguish of sexual lovers is ludicrous, and reason seems an excellent thing; indeed, one is almost prepared to say, as one critic does, "Reading is the symbol of the good life. It delivers the mind from the spears of desire and lifts it to the truth of heaven." [29] But if the "spears of desire" happen to be, as they are for the narrator, the spears of desire for knowledge, then reading is as ludicrous as sexual love. At the same time, if sexual love and the love of knowledge both serve, at their best, the common profit which carries us to Scipio's heaven, both, however ludicrous, are good.

In the *Parliament* writing poetry *is* in fact love. In the paradise section, Chamberlain points out, the three traditional kinds of sonorous music are all present, each created by a different form of life — the vegetable leaves, the animal (bird) voices, and unseen "instruments" (manual art). The air that moves the leaves "belongs to Aristotle's lowest order of nature, sheer existence," but also "the gentle wind suggests, as in *Genesis* and Dante, the love of God who 'breathes' the soul into man and generally animates creation," [30] that is, joins disparate physical and spiritual things by "euene noumberis of acord," as Boethius says. It is true (the point is again Chamberlain's) that the true artist is for Chaucer, as for Boethius, the one who fully understands what he's doing, not the artist who merely plays his instrument or sings. The master poet behind the poem is the one who understands; but the metrical singing of any poet — even the narrator, who only dimly understands — does the kind of thing God does with his breath of love: joins disparates together by even numbers of accord.

iii

The Unfinished *Anelida and Arcite*
and a Few of Chaucer's Short Poems,
a Chapter Brief and Disorganized,
but Rich in Curiosities ✧✧✧✧✧✧✧✧
*A Trinket Shop at the Foot
of the Mountainous Chapter 4,
on TROILUS AND CRISEYDE*

HAUCER WROTE HIS SHORT POEMS
at various times and for various reasons. They
range from early invitations to love to late
begging poems addressed to kings or friends at
court. They have never received much critical attention and
will not get much here, since they are fairly accessible works,
so that nothing much need be said except on two or three of
the more complex. But though few of the poems require
comment, the fact remains that if nothing else of Chaucer's
had survived, the short poems alone would be enough to tell us
he was an extraordinary poet. As F. N. Robinson and others
have pointed out, the short poems show, more than anything
else in the poet's work, Chaucer's interest in prosodic
experimentation. If he did indeed write the *ABC* for Blanche
of Lancaster, as tradition holds, the poem is one of the first to

use in English what was later to become the mainstay of serious English poets, iambic pentameter. (Chaucer's French original was in tetrameter.) And for some readers, at least, the poem has other, more curious metrical oddities. Frank T. Zbozny points out that in all but two stanzas heavy stress falls on the first syllable of the stanza's first line; that is, a trochee replaces the expected iamb, emphasizing the poem's alphabet pattern in much the way an illuminated capitol might do in a fancy manuscript.[1] In the *Complaint unto Piety* and the *Complaint to his Lady* he used rhyme royal, probably for the first time in English, and the latter contains also the first attempt in English at Dante's *terza rima*. Elsewhere among the short poems he tries the French roundel (in *Merciles Beaute*), the French balade form (*To Rosemounde, Womanly Noblesse, Fortune, Truth, Gentilesse, Lak of Stedfastnesse,* and *Against Women Unconstant*), and stanzas apparently constructed for numerological appropriateness, notably the seven and nine line stanzas in the *Complaint of Mars*.

The short poems of course have more than clever prosody to recommend them, though the subtler virtues of a first-rate lyric are always hard to talk about. In some, what stands out as especially fine is the voice, the gusto, partly an effect of the choice of words, partly an effect of the rhythmic rush — as in these lines from *Lak of Stedfastnesse*, Chaucer's angry poem to his lord and friend, Richard:

> Trouthe is put doun, resoun is holden fable;
> Vertu hath now no dominacioun;
> Pitee exyled, no man is merciable;
> Through covetyse is blent discrecioun.
> [Through covetousness, discretion is blinded]
>
> [15–18

Needless to say, every reader will scan the lines somewhat differently, one reader denying the hovering stresses I suggest, another emphasizing *man* rather than *no,* and so on; but the rush of unstressed syllables will remain by any account, as will the language that, pretending to speak of general evils, subtly strikes out at the king himself — truth "put down" like a rebellion, "domination" stolen from the rightful ruler, Virtue, and the quality of mercy "exiled."

In other lyrics what stands out most is the wit, the Donne-like punning in *Truth*, for instance:

Flee fro the prees, and dwelle with sothfastnesse,
[crowd, rabble]
Suffyce unto thy good, though it be smal;
For hord hath hate, and climbing tikelnesse,   [instability]
Prees hath envye, and wele blent overal;   [weal blinded]
Savour no more than the bihove shal;
Reule wel thyself, that other folk canst rede;   [counsel]
And trouthe thee shal delivere, it is no drede.

Tempest thee noght al croked to redresse,
In trust of hir that turnet as a bal:
Gret reste stant in litel besinesse;
Be war also to sporne ayeyns an al;   [press against an awl]
Stryve not, as doth the crokke with the wal.
Daunte thyself, that dauntest otheres dede;
And trouthe thee shal delivere, it is no drede.

That thee is sent, receyve in buxumnesse;
[submissiveness, or bigness]
The wrastling for this world axeth a fal.   [asketh]
Her is non hoom, her nis but wildernesse:
Forth, pilgrim, forth! Forth, beste, out of thy stal!   [beast]
Know thy contree, look up, thank God of al;
Hold the heye wey, and lat thy gost thee lede;
And trouthe thee shal delivere, it is no drede.

Envoy

Therfore, thou vache, leve thyn old wrecchednesse;   [cow or ox]
Unto the world leve now to be thral;
Crye him mercy, that of his hy goodnesse
Made thee of noght, and in especial
Draw unto him, and pray in general

For thee, and eek for other, hevenlich mede;   [reward]
And trouthe thee shal delivere, it is no drede.

The neatest pun in the poem is "vache," which Edith Rickert long ago identified as the name of the man for whom the poem was written, Sir Philip la Vache, husband of the daughter of Chaucer's friend Sir Lewis Clifford. (During the period of Gloucester's dominance in government affairs, before 1390, Vache was in disfavor, and it was no doubt this that prompted Chaucer's poem.) But punning and rapid association are the poem's chief devices. The phrase "hord hath hate" means "the crowd is full of hate" but also "treasure (a hord) gets hatred." "Temptest thee noght" means "don't distress yourself," but the word *tempest* brings on by rapid association (through weather) the turning world image, that is, Fortune. (Chaucer frequently identifies Fortune's wheel and the world. As an astronomer he of course knew that the world is round; he tells us he once wrote a book on the subject, a companion piece to the *Astrolabe* and he perhaps also wrote the *Equitory of the Planets*.) But the cosmos also turns like a ball. Beyond the cosmos (the spheres) stands the unmoved prime mover, the realm of Dante's heaven, the place of "great rest" — an idea Chaucer uses in the *House of Fame*, *Troilus*, and elsewhere. Thus by puns, heaven is contrasted with the realm of flux, the mercantile world or, at any rate, "besinesse." The sphere image turns into a pottery image, calling up Biblical associations, God as potter, man as clay. In the next stanza *buxumnesse*, "submissiveness" suggests, in its secondary sense, "bigness," the image of a wrestler, which in turn suggests a "fall" in wrestling, which in turn suggests the effect of Adam's attempt to be master of the world, "the Fall." The loss of Eden introduces the idea of the world as a wilderness (as in Augustine), life as a pilgrimage (a stock image to be used again in the *Knight's Tale* and the *Parson's Tale*), man as part animal, part spirit, that is, man as part cow or ox (an image with rich exegetical associations), and the cow or ox image sets up the poem's final pun, *mede*, which means "reward" but also "mead" or "meadow," the comically suitable reward for a *vache*.[2]

In still other poems, what is most striking is the humor — in the middle-aged poet's love poem *To Rosemounde*, for instance, where conventional love-longing and Chaucer's love of food get comically mixed up, or in *Lenvoy de Chaucer a Scogan*, where Scogan's sensible dropping of his mistress (since she refused to notice him) causes Chaucer to shudder and cry out in fear that Scogan's sin may bring revenge from Cupid, who may refuse forever after to shoot his darts of love at all who, like Chaucer, "ben hoor [silver haired] and rounde of shap." The funniest, perhaps, is *The Complaint of Chaucer to his Purse*, the poet's appeal for patronage when Henry IV became king, a poem in which Chaucer merrily turns the high-minded conventions of courtly love to the purpose of comically outrageous begging. His purse is his "lady dere," and as a lady may become "lyght" (faithless) so his purse, to the poet's unspeakable sorrow, is light (empty). As the Petrarchan lady is "lyk the sonne bryght," so his purse, at one time, "of yelownesse hadde never pere [peer]." Chaucer goes wildly all the way. As the worthy courtly lady leads the soul heavenward, though she is not really, herself, keeper of that treasure, so the purse is to do, a thing only proper since, though he may not be especially holy, in his baldness at least he's like a friar:

> Now purse, that ben to me my lyves lyght
> And saveour, as doun in this world here,
> Out of this toune helpe me thurgh your myght
> Syn that ye wole nat ben my tresorere;   [treasurer]
> For I am shave as nye as any frere.
> But yet I pray unto your curtesye:
> Beth hevy agen, or elles moot I dye!
>
> [15–21

Critics have debated what Chaucer means by "this toune." One suggestion is that "toune" should be taken in the older sense of "walled enclosure," hence that it refers to the enclosed house by Westminster Abbey where Chaucer moved for sanctuary against his creditors. Chaucer did have, we know, considerable trouble collecting what was owed him by the crown and was frequently sued for private or government debts. But the word "toune" here has also a burlesque religious sense. After such language as "my lyves lyght," "saveour," and "doun in this world here," the religious meaning of "this toune" is certainly "this world, the Old Jerusalem," as the word is used in the pun-riddled *Prima Pastorum* of the Wakefield Cycle, where we read:

> *2 Pastor.*   Hay, ha!
> Ar ye in this toune?
> *1 Pastor.*   Yey, by my crowne!
> *2 Pastor.*   I thoght by youre gowne
> This was youre aray.

Here as throughout the play, the grubby world of the shepherds parodies heaven, the perfect "towne" where all God's children get a "crowne," a "gowne," and splendid "array." [3] Chaucer pays his purse the ultimate courtly lover's compliment. It will save his soul. King Henry was apparently amused. Anyway, he paid.

§ 2

THE SHORT PIECES sort into three main groups: religious or philosophical meditations (*ABC, Truth,* and so forth), poems of courtly love (*The Complaint of Mars,* and so forth), and comic pieces (*Rosemounde, Scogan, Chaucers Wordes unto Adam,* and so forth). To sort the poems in such a way is to lay out in handy categories the three main components of Chaucer's way of looking at the world. As background and foundation he has his premises as a citizen of the Age of Faith, a set of emotions and ideas that here in the short poems he often presents straight. Alongside this he has his interest in ennobling human love. And to soften any potential conflict between the two, he has his comic sense.

The straight religious or philosophical poems are of course the most obviously medieval. They take orthodox positions — *contemptus mundi,* for instance, the position toward which Chaucer urges Vache. Usually — and this is equally medieval — the poems richly ornament the old positions by puns and other subtleties but do not test or doubt. The courtly-love poems are slightly more modern but not much. However the code's ideals are treated, but especially when they're presented straight (with a minimum of biblical and exegetical allusion and thus a minimum of irony) they advance the courtly-love tradition toward — as Frank J. Chiarenza puts it — "a concept of love *sui generis*: more credible than the distantly medieval because more modern, and less alien than the Renaissance distemper because less discouraging." [4]

It is frequently suggested and has lately come to be, in some quarters, an article of faith that we should take such love poetry as nothing but a game, since courtly love, we are told, never had any existence outside poetry. Insofar as that notion pretends to be scholarly, it can be — and has been — demolished on scholarly grounds; but it is objectionable on other grounds as well. We should be slow to admit that great writers like Chaucer merely fool around with form, writing roundels, say, because roundels are all the rage this season, not because they express real feeling. (This is not to deny that all art is partly play.) And then there's common sense. If there was only literary courtly love in the courts of Edward III and Richard II, there was nevertheless also (well-documented) lovemaking, and why should lovers like Gaunt or Edward III ignore literary models? Why should a lady who's read Chretien de Troyes settle for less than Lunette got from Gawain? The heart of the argument against courtly love is that courtly love poetry is always ironic: it condemns what it pretends to praise. That argument is demonstrably false, but more important, it's pernicious.

Love has been a powerful force in Western civilization for centuries, and long before Byron, Shelley, and Keats, poets made up the rules for how men and women should practice it. "Courtly love" was the best set of rules in its day, elevating the lady — a thing much needed in that misogynist age — and scorning the man who treated his lady as a sex object or dared to force her to his will. If people didn't try to live by the poets' code of courtly love, they should have. John of Gaunt, we know, did live by it. So did Edward III. If Geoffrey Chaucer was serious about love — not just Boethean love, but the love exchange between men and women — his short poems on love are significant works.

Chaucer found he had two choices for dealing with courtly love in verse. One was to present it straight, as in other short poems he presented his religion and philosophy; the other was to set it in counterpoise with another system of values, the religious system courtly love imitated. He writes straight poetry in, for instance, *A Complaint to his Lady* and *Womanly Noblesse*. More often, throughout all his poetry, he uses counterpoise like that in the *Book of the Duchess* or *Parliament of Birds*, setting love and religion (or art and life, or some other opposition) in ironic balance and thus writing in a more modern way, not simply ornamenting old ideas but testing them, forcing some compromise, reaching toward insight.

§ 3

THOUGH *ANELIDA AND ARCITE* is not really a short poem but an unfinished long poem, it was for Chaucer a crucial experiment in this technique of counterpoise and can help us appreciate the more ambitious of Chaucer's short poems. The date is conjectural. F. N. Robinson places the poem before the *Parliament of Birds* on the grounds that "*Anelida* bears every indication of having been Chaucer's first attempt to utilize the *Teseida*" (source of the later *Knight's Tale*). And he adds that the *Parliament* "is at all events a more finished work." [5] Certainly *Anelida* looks like a failure, and conceivably it was Chaucer's recognition of what went wrong here that led him, in the *Parliament*, to his view of the courtly-love conventions as at once sublime and ridiculous. On the other hand, artists don't always get better poem by poem, and in many respects *Anelida* looks like a transition between the *Parliament* and *Troilus*.

James I. Wimsatt points out that *Anelida and Arcite* is

composed of seventy-line sections:[6] the epic introduction offers seventy lines of rhyme royal; Anelida is introduced at line 71 and the story of her love runs for 70 lines, after which the story of Arcite's treason runs for 70 lines. In Anelida's Complaint, the introduction and strophe run for 70 lines, and the antistrophe and conclusion run for 70 more. Wimsatt projects a poem 700 lines long (the length of the *Parliament*, if Chamberlain's account is accepted — and the two articles, I might mention, appeared simultaneously, so the discoveries were probably independent). Wimsatt thinks the poem would be in ten sections of 70 lines each, and he convincingly argues, on the basis of symmetries already introduced, that the last 350 lines were to correspond in form and content to the first 350.

According to Wimsatt's theory — far superior to any other yet advanced,[7] or so it seems to me — "It is possible that the first additional 70 lines, like the introduction of the poem, were to be occupied with epic material, specifically the description of Mars' temple which Chaucer promises [at the end of the Anelida Complaint]. The next 140 lines might have been devoted to continuing the story, with Anelida praying to Mars, and Mars acting on her behalf. This could have led to the appearance of Arcite who could end the poem with a 140-line 'Comfort' that would exactly balance Anelida's Complaint." [8]

The use of sevens as a formal device in both the *Anelida* and the *Parliament* strongly suggests that the poems were written at about the same time, just before the *Troilus* where sevens are again important. Unlike the *Parliament*, the *Anelida* is an attempt at straight narrative poetry, epic poetry at that (heading toward *Troilus*), or epic balanced with amorous complaint, and not a first-person narrative or dream vision. The absence of a narrator — the whole cause of the poem's failure, in my opinion — suggests a technical stage transitional between Chaucer's use of omnipresent narrators in the early poems and his skillful handling of an unobtrusive but sharply characterized narrator who can fade his voice in and out as Chaucer does in the *Troilus* and *Canterbury Tales*.

Also — though now we're on soggier ground — the *Anelida* seems psychologically right as a next step after Chaucer's conclusion in the *Parliament* that, silly as it may seem, the poetry of love is a stretta in the elaborate counterpoint of the cosmic hymn. With lofty purpose and a touch of overconfidence, Chaucer may have turned from the *Parliament* to his first attempt at writing a long poem in the "heigh stile."

The central contrasts in the *Anelida* are among those Chaucer explores in the *Troilus*. Most of them have little to do with anything we've seen up to now in Chaucer's work. The contrast between the immutable and the mutable, heaven and earth, to be found in the first dream visions, is present in *Troilus*, but along with that contrast there appears in the *Troilus* and in *Anelida*, and nowhere before, a contrast between the intense present moment and the vast sweep of time (a favorite theme in Virgil and Dante), a contrast between confined and panoramic vision, and a contrast — only faintly implied before — between the world of action and the world of passion. In the *Anelida* the contrast seems clumsy: the character of Theseus makes the character of Anelida seem trivial and silly (a narrator-voice could have saved this); but in Troilus — a hero who is both soldier and lover — and also in the contrast of Troilus and Pandarus, one an idealist, the other (for the most part) a realist — the balance of epic action and romantic passion works beautifully. The same balance, and also a related Theban story, appears in the *Knight's Tale*, another middle-period work probably begun while *Troilus* was in progress. One suspects that Chaucer learned from his failure in *Anelida*.

The poem opens with an invocation like nothing thus far seen in Chaucer. In place of the tongue-in-cheek invocation in the *Parliament*, Chaucer opens *Anelida* with an invocation that might have suited the trumpet of John Milton. Most of the invocation is as memorable and as perfect, in its own way, in anything in the classical epics.

> Thou ferse god of armes, Mars the rede,   [fierce; red]
> That in the frosty contre called Trace,
> Within thy grisly temple ful of drede
> Honoured art, as patroun of that place,
> With thy Bellona, Pallas, ful of grace,

Be present, and my song contynue and guye;   [guide]
At my begynnyng thus to the I crye.

For hit ful depe is sonken in my mynde,
With pitous hert in Englyssh to endyte   [compose]
This olde storie, in Latyn which I fynde,
Of quene Anelida and fals Arcite,
That elde, which that al can frete and bite,   [age]
As hit hath freten mony a noble storie,
Hath nygh devoured out of oure memorie.

Be favorable eke, thou Polymya,
On Parnaso that with thy sustres glade,
By Elycon, not fer from Cirrea,
Singest with vois memorial in the shade,
Under the laurer which that may not fade,   [laurel]
And do that I my ship to haven wynne.   [bring]
First folowe I Stace, and after him Corynne.

[1–21

Chaucer begins the poem proper with a sure hand — a solemn epigraph, some noble classical authorities, and a sweeping panorama that calls to mind the huge worlds of Virgil or Dante. In the opening stanzas, the dignity of Chaucer's verse is unbroken: highly poetic diction, measured cadence. The emphasis throughout is on bigness: mighty reaches of time and space, mighty gentlemen and ladies who shine in the streets like gods. Instead of colloquial understatement of the kind which opens the *Knight's Tale*, where Theseus brings Ypolita "hoom with hym in his contree / With muchel glorie and greet solempnytee" (*CT*, I, 869–70) and where the pomp and circumstance of the homecoming would be "to long to heere" (I, 875), Chaucer opens *Anelida* with epic pomp:

When Theseus, with werres longe and grete,
The aspre folk of Cithe had overcome,   [bitter]
With laurer corouned, in his char gold-bete,
Hom to his contre-houses is he come;
For which the peple, blisful al and somme,
So cryeden that to the sterres hit wente,
And him to honouren dide al her entente.

Beforn this duk, in signe of victorie,
The trompes come, and in his baner large   [trumpeters]
The ymage of Mars; and, in token of glorie,
Man myghte sen of tresour many a charge,
Many a bright helm, and many a spere and targe,
Many a fresh knyght, and many a blysful route,   [battalion]
On hors, on fote, in al the feld aboute.

Ipolita his wif, the hardy quene
Of Cithia, that he conquered hadde,
With Emelye, her yonge suster shene,
Faire in a char of gold he with him ladde,
That al the ground about her char she spradde
With brightnesse of the beaute in her face,
Fulfilled of largesse and of alle grace.

[22-42

The same epic note sounds in Chaucer's catalogue of over-thrown kings (57–63; a catalogue he will echo in *Troilus*) and in his first presentation of Anelida:

Among al these Anelida, the quene
Of Ermony, was in that toun dwellynge,
That fairer was then is the sonne shene.
Thurghout the world so gan her name springe,
That her to seen had every wyght likynge;
For, as of trouthe, is ther noon her lyche,   [like]
Of al the women in this worlde riche.

[71-77

Then the poet shifts his ground. The story of Anelida and Arcite, as Chaucer tells it, is a melodrama. Set against the world of action — the world summed up in the name "Theseus" — the world of Anelida and Arcite lacks magnitude. Anelida and Arcite are neither demigods nor people, merely conventions, graceful artifices of the sort made in France. The usual comment, that the poem begins and ends well but sinks to bathos in the middle, misses the point: the middle might not trouble us if it were not for the figure of Theseus in the background. We might not shudder in finding in a frankly artificial poem such lines as these:

She wepith, waileth, swowneth pitiously;   [swooneth]
To grounde ded she falleth as a stone;
Craumpyssheth her lymes crokedly;
She speketh as her wit were al agon;
Other colour then asshen hath she noon;
Non other word speketh she, moche or lyte,
But "merci, cruel herte myn, Arcite!"

[169–75]

In fact the image here of convulsively cramped limbs, like the vividly realized madness that follows, is quite fine. And Anelida's Complaint, everyone agrees, is as good as anything of its type. What Chaucer seems to have recognized, judging from his later practice, is that the conventions of love and the vision implicit in the epic opening, if not somehow brought into accord, must conflict.

In short, Chaucer had miscalculated — and this is not, I think, mere modern prejudice. Having concluded in the *Parliament* that in certain ways the poetry of courtly love could be philosophically serious, and having known all his life that dualism was a false dichotomy, he had resolved to write a poem partly in the high or epic style, partly in the artificial style of amorous complaint, and to take as part of his subject courtly love, the self-regarding, love-sick individual's place in the state or common profit that surrounds him. Exactly how the poem was to develop is anyone's guess, but, thematically at least, the outlines are clear. Cherniss has summarized the main details:

> Anelida has become the central figure about whom a philosophical dilemma unfolds itself, and this dilemma seems to me to embody the theme of the poem. Clemen, taking special note of the repetitiousness with which Chaucer reminds the reader of Anelida's fairness and her lover's falseness, suggests that "trouthe" is the dominant theme, while Madeline Fabin long ago noted the lack of optimism and the emphasis upon destiny in the "complaint." Close examination reveals what appears to be several views of Anelida's plight, and these views do not seem to be entirely compatible with one another. Both

the narrator (148–54, 197–203) and Anelida herself
(211–19, 311–16) claim that her suffering is the result of
Man's natural inclination toward falseness and that,
because of this inclination, "trouthe" like hers is never
justly rewarded. At the same time, however, Anelida
blames "destinee" (243, 339, 348), "aventure" (324) and
"chaunce" (348) for her plight. Some sort of resolution
of these views seems desirable.[9]

The poem's two invocations — to Mars, god of arms (also
lover of Venus), and to Polymya, muse of sacred hymns — undoubtedly suggest the general principle whereby the thematic
question would be resolved. The poem was to explore some
such set of contrasts or polar oppositions as the secular versus
the ecclesiastical (the latter in terms of pagan love-religion, as
in *Troilus*); action versus passion; the marital binding or
knitting of things versus the poetic or musical (as in the
Parliament); public versus private good, and so forth. All these
contrasts Chaucer used in poem after poem, so nothing more
need be said of them here. But in conceiving the poem,
Chaucer had perhaps neglected an important fact: he had an
instinct for decorum and aesthetic efficiency, which is not to
say that he objected to mixing styles or that he objected to the
highly artificial, but that he objected to giving equal weight —
equally serious consideration — to things great and small. He
could believe in the mythic grandeur of Theseus and could
believe in the validity of courtly love in its relation to the total
order; but when he turned from stylized treatment of
important matters (the justice of Theseus and tyranny of
Creon) to an equally stylized treatment of the sorrows of an
abstract, conventional lady, he couldn't help but notice that his
poem had gone thin, as when a trombone springs a leak. His
vision was large and calm. He loved the common profit,
disliked bigotry and injustice, understood human unhappiness;
but the conventional courtly lover's habit of seeing the
moment as all important, and the present emotion as more
significant than the slow maturation of a lifetime, was, he
knew, a kind of foolishness. The shortsightedness of the
conventional courtly lover is at the heart of the comic scene in

the *Reeve's Tale* wherein fat, flat-nosed Molly parts with the clerk who, a perfect stranger, has been kind enough to swyve her. The clerk leaves Molly with the pretty cliches of courtly love: "But everemo, wher so I go or ryde, / I is thyn awen clerk, swa have I seel [soul]!" (I, 4238–39). Molly is touched, as what miller's daughter wouldn't be, talked to like a lady in literature! — and her equally literary response is comically pathetic:

> "Now, deere lemman," quod she, "go, far weel!
> But er thow go, o thyng I wol thee telle:
> Whan that thou wendest homward by the melle,
> Right at the entree of the dore bihynde
> Thou shalt a cake of half a busshel fynde
> That was ymaked of thyn owene mele,
> Which that I heelp my sire for to stele.
> And goode lemman, God thee save and kepe!"
> And with that word almoost she gan to wepe.
>
> [I, 4240–48

The same shortsightedness wrecks Troilus. What saves him as the hero of a poem, making him tragic as well as sometimes comic, is that Troilus is not a papier-mâché dolt who toys with empty love-conventions but a convincing character, an ambitious and noble idealist who defies destiny for love, at least partly knows what he's doing, and has a dramatically valid reason for turning to the conventions — his passionate love for the real and beautiful Criseyde.

In studying the failure he had on his hands and in thinking back to the technique of counterpoise more successfully worked out in his dream visions, Chaucer realized that henceforth he must choose between, on one hand, the use of a narrative voice implying a real man speaking and, on the other hand, a use of artifice that keeps all concrete reality at arm's length. Either he must keep the two separate or he must combine them in such a way as to make one a comment on the other or, better yet, each a comment on the other. From this point on, Chaucer was a poet sure of his grounds.

Part of the time he chose artifice. He may have written

the *Complaint of Mars* before *Anelida* or he may have written it immediately after; either way, it's a splendid example of what pure artifice can do.[10] The poem opens as prettily as anything ever sung by an English bird, and it holds up beautifully to the end. More often, Chaucer chose to undercut artifice by playing its devices against narrative-voice realism. The device shows up again and again in the *Canterbury Tales* — in the Clerk's realistic comments on his quasi fairy tale of Walter and Griselda; in the Nun's Priest's juxtaposition of language suitable to that lovable fop of a chicken, Chaunticleer, and plain talk suitable to the dull "povre wydwe"; in the Knight's juxtaposition of ordinary speech about story-telling or Boethian order and mock-elegant speech on the chaos of passion. In his best works, Chaucer makes the play of artifice against natural voice not simply a poetic technique but a dialectic method, a means of perceiving.

§4

LIKE MUCH POETRY AND PROSE in Middle English, as I've said, the religious and philosophical short poems have as their chief purpose not abstract philosophical discovery by way of the concrete situation or image (a usual purpose in later English verse) but revitalization of received and established truth of one kind or another.[11] Such rediscovery was of course at the heart of medieval Christian experience. We see it in the earlier medieval Christian writer's fondness for imagining in grisly detail the sufferings of Christ: in Richard Rolle, for instance, who imagines Christ's Passion in every particular, then implores the Virgin to help him keep it vivid in his mind, lest he grow ungrateful. The same general purpose of giving emotional vitality to old truth informs the many dialogues of Christ and man, Christ and the Virgin, or body and soul, and we see the same in the mystery plays, the beast allegories, the secular lyrics or in symbolic or allegorical longer poems — "Summer Sunday," the poems of the *Gawain*-poet, and so forth.

But another group of Chaucer's short poems depends for effect on plays of wit in a more elevated sense, looking forward even more than a poem like *Truth* to the poetry of Donne or George Herbert. With these trickier poems, or with four examples of these, we'll be concerned for the rest of this chapter. The kind of wit to be found in these (and also, in less compressed form, in Chaucer's long poems) is not something completely unprecedented in medieval poetry, but for control like Chaucer's I think one has to travel clear to Italy, to Dante and Petrarch.

Take first a simple example, the *Complaint unto Pity*. The controlling device here is Chaucer's old gimmick, the myopic, dim-witted narrator, caricature of himself, whose literal-mindedness makes the complaint a comically "realistic" treatment of allegorical devices and conventions — roughly the medieval equivalent of the man who shoots back at the movie screen. In the opening stanzas a realistic sounding and therefore comic version of the conventional grieving lover seeks the conventional personified abstraction "Pity," finds her dead and buried "in an herte," and responds as one would if Pity and her death and burial were all real. All that is left for the narrator, Love being governed entirely now by cold Beauty, Lust, and the rest, is "kepynge the corps" of Pity. And then the narrator says that since Pity is dead there is now no one to whom he can present his love complaint, which was going to read as follows — and he presents the complaint. The comic revelation of what cannot be revealed is like Donne's revelation of what cannot be revealed in "The Undertaking." Just as Donne has it either way — he reveals his secret to those worthy to understand it and not to those who are not — so Chaucer has it both ways: if Pity is indeed dead, Chaucer has recognized the fact and, unlike conventional lovers who do complain, preserves his dignity; but if the lady *should* happen to be capable of mercy — if she *should* accept the noble promise which the poet now does and does not make, his promise to be hers forever — then without even risking his dignity, the poet has won his lady. From the conventional viewpoint a lover's unwillingness to take a chance for the sake of love would be ludicrous (even today, cartoon books tell us, the lover is supposed to go down on his knees to propose marriage); from a realistic viewpoint, the folderol of love is ridiculous. In the *Complaint unto Pity*, each viewpoint throws the other into comic perspective, lighting up the age-old paradox: what the lover does to show his love is ridiculous, no man of sense would do it; but lovers are nobler (more daring, more selfless) than people with dignity and good sense.

The *Complaint of Mars* is a far more complex juxtaposition of conventions and a much more serious analysis of love. As Skeat, Manly, and others have shown in detail, Chaucer's story of the love of Mars and Venus, Venus' dread of jealous Phoebus, and Venus' removal to the protection of Cilenius (Mercury), is built of astrological materials: the events of the plot are an ingenious interpretation, in terms of the conventions of courtly love, of the movement of the stars. This use of astrological phenomena for the plot of a love poem inevitably urged for the poet's immediate audience an ironic view of love: if the stars in their courses (closely associated in medieval thought with the idea of destiny) can suffer the conventional tribulations of lovers, then the joys and sorrows of lovers may be interpreted as fixed and involuntary, and thus, in rational creatures, more or less comic. But Chaucer goes beyond this easy joke on lovers: unable as he is to deviate from his fixed course, Mars nonetheless sees his way, at last — as any lover can — to rise, through love, into freedom; that is, he sees that he has allowed himself to be caught up in mere Fate. One passage from Boethius is especially helpful. (I give Chaucer's translation.)

> But I ne ordeyne nat (as who seith, I ne graunte nat) that this liberte [i.e., the freedom of rational creatures to seek or avoid] be evenelyk in alle thinges. Forwhy in the sovereynes devynes substaunces (that is to seyn, in spiritz) jugement is more cleer, and wil nat incorrumped [will is uncorrupted], and myght redy to speden [power ready to push along] thinges that ben desired. But the soules of men moten nedes be more fre whan thei loken hem in the speculacioun or lokynge of the devyne thought; and lasse fre whan thei slyden into the bodyes;

and yit lasse fre whan thei ben gadrid togidre and
comprehended in erthli membres. But the laste servage is
whan that thei ben yeven to vices and han ifalle fro the
possessioun of hir propre resoun. For aftir that thei han
cast awey hir eyghen fro the lyght of the sovereyn
sothfastnesse to lowe thingis and derke, anon thei derken
by the cloude of ignoraunce and ben troubled by felonous
talentz; to the whiche talentz whan thei approchen and
assenten, thei hepen and encrecen the servage which thei
han joyned to hemself; and in this manere thei ben caytifs
fro hir propre liberte.

[5, PROSE 2, 20 ff.

As examples of this turning away from light, the church writer
might cite Adam, who turned from God to Eve, or any man
who turns from God to earthly treasure. The Christian Fall, in
terms of Boethius' view of freedom and slavery ("servage"), is
a fall into Fate.

The *Complaint of Mars* is, from first to last, pagan, not
Christian, but pagan exactly the way Greek poetry was to
Boccaccio: a Christian view of life is adumbrated throughout,
both in imagery and diction and in the organization of the
argument; and the poem ends in two ways at once — with a
pagan question, and with an implied Christian answer.

The bird sings to lovers in the Proem:

Wyth teres blewe, and with a wounded herte,
Taketh your leve; and with seint John to borowe,
Apeseth sumwhat of your sorowes smerte.
Tyme cometh eft that cese shal your sorowe:
The glade nyght ys worth an hevy morowe!

[8–12

But the idea that a joyful night is worth sorrow in the morning
is not in accord with the view of Mars in his Complaint:

Thus, whether love breke or elles dure,
Algates he that hath with love to done
Hath ofter wo then changed ys the mone.

[233–35

A short paraphrase of the complaint, with comment on what is implied if we interpret situations falling under the law of kind in the light of the law of revelation, will be sufficient to show the centrality, in Mars' complaint, of the religious question, "Where is God's justice?"

Mars laments (164–72), "Ever since I was first created by Him that governs each intelligence [i.e., both each astrological influence and each rational nature; but see also Robinson's note], I have truly served the finest thing I found in the universe, Venus." What Mars does not know, but what the Christian audience does, is that the loveliest thing in nature is not identical with the Supreme Good. For if Venus stands here as an emblem of celestial love, as she does in *Troilus* and the *Knight's Tale* (as in Dante), she is merely the emblem, not celestial love itself. In the same way, Eve and her antitype, the Virgin, are the effects of heavenly love, not, in themselves, proper objects of worship. As Boethius has it, " 'Thise thynges thanne,' quod sche [Philosophie] (that is to seyn, erthly suffysaunce, and power and swiche thynges), 'outher thei semen lyknesses of verray good, or elles it semeth that thei yeve to mortel folk a maner of goodes that ne be nat parfyt. But thilke good that is verray and parfyt that mai thei nat yeven.' " (3, prose 9, 171 ff.)

Mars continues (173–90), "Venus my lady is the source and well of beauty, lust, freedom. What wonder, then, that I place myself in her service, since she is all-powerful?" But again Mars is perceiving imperfectly: God, not Venus, is the source and well of good. Indeed, the "well" or "well-spring" is so common an image of Christ — appearing in Boethius, in the work of all the Church writers, and in much of the poetry of Chaucer's time — that the irony would be impossible for Chaucer's audience to miss. Moreover, as Mars himself notices in a moment, Venus is *not* all-powerful. She cannot even help herself. (Cf. Boethius' ironic remark, "O, a noble thyng and a cleer thyng is power that is nat fownden myghty to kepe itself!" [3, prose 5, 7 ff.].)

" — And so to whom shall I complain?" Mars continues (191–217). "Venus is helpless, and even if she is preserved from death it can be none of my doing. Ah, poor lovers!

Whichever way they turn they find sorrow! And my sorrow is intensified by the sorrow of my lady." In Part III of his complaint, Mars grows philosophical. He says first — and here it is necessary to quote:

> To what fyn made the God that sit so hye,   [end]
> Benethen him, love other companye,
> And stryneth folk to love, malgre her hed?
> And then her joy, for oght I can espye,
> Ne lasteth not the twynkelyng of an ye,
> And somme han never joy til they be ded.
> What meneth this? What is this mystihed?   [mystery]
> Wherto constreyneth he his folk so faste
> Thing to desyre, but hit shulde laste?
>
> [218–26

Chaucer's audience knows well enough the answer to Mars' first question. Man is to "love other companye" but is to refer his pleasure to its source, that which is immutable. Mars' next question, "And somme han never joy til they be ded. / What meneth this?" means to Mars, "Some never achieve joy at all; what can it mean?" But to the Christian, Mars' words have another meaning, namely that one can find joy *after* death, for true joy comes from union with God. Now Mars speaks of mutability:

> And thogh he made a lover love a thing,
> And maketh hit seme stedfast and during,
> Yet putteth he in hyt such mysaventure
> That reste nys ther non in his yeving.
> And that is wonder, that so juste a kyng
> Doth such hardnesse to his creature.
> Thus, whether love breke or elles dure,
> Algates he that hath with love to done
> Hath ofter wo then changed ys the mone.
>
> [227–35

But it is not a wonder that so just a king should behave so unkindly toward his creature if we understand, with Boethius, that

yif blisfulnesse be the soverayn good of nature that lyveth
by resoun, ne thilke thyng nys nat soverayn good that
may ben taken awey in any wise (for more worthy
thyng and more dygne [noble] is thilke thyng that mai
nat ben take awey); than scheweth it wel that the
unstablenesse of fortune may nat atayne to resceyven
verray blisfulnesse. And yit more over, what man that
this towmblynge welefulnesse ledeth, eyther he woot that
it is chaungeable, or elles he woot it nat. And yif he woot
it nat, what blisful fortune may ther ben in the
blyndnesse of ignoraunce? And yif he woot that it is
chaungeable, he mot alwey ben adrad that he ne lese that
thyng that he ne douteth nat but that he may leesen it (as
who seith he mot bien alwey agast lest he lese that he
woot wel he may lese it); for which the contynuel drede
that he hath, ne suffreth hym nat to ben weleful, or elles
yif he lese it, he weneth to ben despised and forleten.

[3, PROSE 4, 142 ff.

In the next stanza the irony becomes still more apparent:
the pagan Mars happens on the metaphor of his god as a
fisherman, man as wounded fish, and so unwittingly antici-
pates the idea of Christ as fisher of men, identified with the
sign of the fish. Unaided by revelation, Mars sees the Maker as
cruel, not loving, and so inverts the scriptural signs, confound-
ing the wages of joy and the wages of sorrow:

> Hit semeth he hat[h] to lovers enmyte,
> And lyk a fissher, as men alday may se,
> Baiteth hys angle-hok with som plesaunce,
> Til many a fissh ys wod til that he be
> Sesed therwith; and then at erst hath he
> Al his desir, and therwith al myschaunce;
> And thogh the lyne breke, he hath penaunce;
> For with the hok he wounded is so sore
> That he his wages hath for evermore.

[236–44

In Part IV Mars begins to see more clearly, as a rational
creature can do even without divine revelation, according to
Boethius (and all the later Church writers would agree). It

occurs to Mars that the things we desire — for example, "the broche of Thebes" — are not harmful in themselves but 1) in the curse placed on them and 2) in the covetousness of the would-be possessor. It is impossible to miss the parallel between the brooch and the forbidden fruit. The identification of woman (the basis of Adam's fall) and riches (gold, gems, and so forth) is ancient and finds support in patristic descriptions of the Fall. With regard to the basis of Adam's fall, Hugh of Saint Victor writes:

> Yet Adam was not seduced [by the devil's promise], because he knew that what the devil promised was false. And he did not eat the forbidden apple on this account, as if through that eating he believed that he could be made equal to God or even wished to be made equal, but only lest by resisting her will and petition he might offend the heart of the woman who had been associated with him through the affection of love, especially since he thought that he could both yield to the woman and afterwards through repentance and supplication for pardon please the Creator.[12]

As for the traditional identification of woman and riches, consider Scotus' remarks on the subject. After identifying Adam's misinterpretations of Eve's beauty with any misinterpretation of beauty, Scotus writes:

> Let us suppose two men, one a wise man in no way tickled or pricked by the goad of avarice, but the other stupid, avaricious, everywhere transfixed and lacerated by the thorns of perverse cupidity. When these two have been placed in one location, let there be brought a vase made of refined gold, decorated with precious stones, fashioned in a beautiful shape, fit for royal use. Both look at it, the wise man and the miser [watch, reader, here comes the old tripartite soul again] both receive the image of the vase in the corporal sense, both place it in the memory and consider it in thought. And the man who is wise refers the beauty of this vase whose image he considers within himself completely and immediately to the praise of the Creator of natural things. No allurement

of cupidity subverts him, no poison of cupidity infects his
pure mind, no libido contaminates him. But the other, as
soon as he takes the image of the vase, burns with the fire
of cupidity.[13]

(Mars' comments on the ancient brooch even more closely
parallel Boethius' comments on worldly riches, 2, prose 5.)

Perceiving at last that the fault is not in the brooch,
parallel to transient love, but in the curse placed on it and in
the covetousness and ignorance of him who would possess it,
Mars draws the rational — and incipiently Christian — conclusion:

> She was not cause of myn adversite,
> But he that wroghte her, also mot I the,
> That putte such a beaute in her face,
> That made me coveyten and purchace
> Myn oune deth; him wite I that I dye,
> And myn unwit, that ever I clamb so hye.

[266–71]

Mars perceives his fall. His only recourse is to ask that knights
better than himself (as he says), ladies who are true and stable,
and other lovers like himself complain and thus not only share
his suffering and that of Venus but also, hopefully, obtain
mercy from . . . somewhere.

On the pagan level, the ending offers very little hope:
unable to say what intercessor the knights, ladies, and lovers
might invoke, Mars can only ask a general complaint. But
Chaucer's audience could give Mars the name of the intercessor and comforter. All that Mars conventionally ascribes to
Venus, comforter of lovers, more truly applies to the Virgin.
(Or, to put this another way, here as everywhere in Chaucer,
the love-scheme and the Christian are parallel.) It is the Virgin
"that with unfeyned humble chere / Was evere redy to do
yow socour"; it is the Virgin "that evere hath had yow dere";
the Virgin is truly mistress of "beaute, fredom, and manere,"
the Virgin who "endeth your labour," and the Virgin who is
"ensample of al honour" and who "never dide but al
gentilesse" (290–98).

All this is not to ignore the fact that the adaptation of church language to the religion of love was conventional. Yet what is involved in the *Complaint of Mars* is something new, the convention viewed from its last logical extremity. Only on the grounds I've indicated, I think, is it possible to account in other than arbitrary fashion for the sequence of argument in Parts III, IV, and V of Mars' complaint. Now let us turn to the *Complaint of Venus*.

An old tradition, broken by Furnivall and all editors since, makes the *Complaint of Venus* a pendant to the *Complaint of Mars*. There is certainly nothing to Shirley's theory that the *Mars* was written with reference to an intrigue of Isabel, Duchess of York, and the Duke of Exeter, and that the *Venus* was composed (that is, translated and adapted) for Isabel; and it is probably true that the *Venus* is somewhat later than the *Mars*. Nevertheless, the poems may be related. It seems possible that the topical interpretation was brought forward to explain a nearer connection which Shirley or someone before him failed to see.

The argument that the title of the *Complaint of Venus* is wholly inappropriate is nonsense. The title is traditional (like the poem's original position following the *Complaint of Mars*), and while it's true that two of the original French ballades are, in the French, explicitly written about a lady, Chaucer's version keeps nothing to suggest the original context. And the word *Princesse*, or the variant reading *Princes*, which appears in the Envoy, has no bearing on the case. The Envoy is a separate piece of work, a tag probably added later when the poet decided to send in the poem as a plea for favor. It has nothing in common with the subject matter of the complaint. The supposed chief absurdity in the assignment of the poem to Venus, that the goddess should look above to "Love" is not an absurdity in the light of the last stanza of Mars' complaint or in the light of Chaucer's characterization of Cupid elsewhere as servant of a higher power (e.g., *LGW*, Prologue G). Venus' power is manifestly intermediate: as lovers complain for themselves to Venus, so now they are to complain *for* Venus. If Chaucer had in mind here the scheme he sometimes used elsewhere, Venus could look above because, as one of the celestial spheres Venus is intermediary in the harmony ("acord," or "love") of the universe — between mondial music and trinitarian. Finally — and the chief reason we should hesitate to disturb the poem's traditional placement — the poem is appropriate to the plot of the Mars-Venus story told in the *Complaint of Mars*. Separated from her lover, Venus consoles herself with the thought of his excellence (Ballade I), fights her tendency toward jealousy (II), then reaffirms her love (III). Three possible objections to this view are that Venus describes her lover as "the best that ever on erthe went" (60), that the Envoy speaks of one complaint, not two, as it might if the complaints belonged together, and that in terms of the astrological scheme in the *Complaint of Mars*, Venus does not remain faithful but sleeps with Mercury. The first objection seems to me not very bothersome: Greek and Roman gods, though astrological, do walk around on earth in classical poetry. As for the second, the Envoy tells us only that the *Complaint of Venus* was at some time used as an appeal for favor; it does not tell us that Chaucer himself never thought of the two complaints as companion pieces. And as for the third, the astrological scheme is not all that clear, and even if it could be shown (as it cannot) that the Venus-Mercury conjunction invariably implies lechery, the reasonableness attributed to both Mars and Venus — their ability to rise above Fortune through thought — frees them from Fortune's mechanics: Venus has a choice. At all events, the poems are built on the same principles and work well side by side.

We have seen that Mars' complaint, though pagan on the surface, consistently implies a Christian interpretation of the story, though one Mars cannot quite grasp. In the *Complaint of Venus* the same adaptation of church language to a love situation is evident, but with a contrasting effect: Venus' complaint sets up a pagan reading of experience, again parallel point for point to the Christian reading, but this time philosophically adequate. If we read the poem with Mars' complaint in mind, or with the language of either prologue to the *Legend of Good Women* in mind — since there too "jealousy" and the like have Edenic associations — the pagan vision in Venus' complaint becomes more impressive in that, like the tales in the *Legend*, it parallels the Christian vision without ever becoming subject to it.

All that Venus says of Mars might equally well be said of Christ, with the possible exception of line 14, "Therto so wel hath formed him Nature," which clearly defines Mars as (in effect) mortal (but Christ was part man in the orthodox view); and Boethius or any other medieval Christian might easily say of Christ, as Venus says of Mars,

> Ther nys no high comfort to my pleasaunce,
> When that I am in any hevynesse,
> As for to have leyser of remembraunce
> Upon the manhod and the worthynesse,
> Upon the trouthe and on the stidfastnesse
> Of him whos I am al, while I may dure.
> Ther oghte blame me no creature,
> For every wight preiseth his gentilesse.
>
> [1–8

But clearly the lines do *not* refer to Christ, in Venus' mind, nor do they suggest that Venus *ought* to look to Christ rather than Mars: as the pious look to Christ in "any hevynesse," Venus looks to Mars, for which no creature ought to blame her. Religious overtones become more insistent in the second stanza, yet nothing but a legitimate parallel is implied. If "bounte, wisdom, governaunce, / Wel more than any mannes wit can gesse" call to mind the infinite bounty, wisdom, and governance of God (or, to be precise, the Trinity), which are beyond the grasp of human reason, they equally suggest conventional hyperbole; and if the perfect glory of knighthood suggests the commonplace view of Christ as chivalric lord or knight (*miles*), it suggests just as strongly the ideal chivalric lover. The statement "Honour honoureth him for his no-blesse" submits to the same type of interpretation, but nothing in Chaucer's lines requires us to contrast the "noblesse" of the beloved and the Supreme Good. And all of the third stanza — including the phrase "verrey sikernesse" — may also be read either as Christian or simply as the language of the love religion.

The second ballade has the same sort of overtone: love's

"noble thing" might be read as parallel to Christian salvation, but to read in this way is not to see the value of human love diminished. "Jelosie" which, like Eve, "wolde al know thurgh her espying" carries overtone suggestions of concupiscence, but Venus *rejects* jealousy. In the final stanza of this ballade, language again recalls the Eden story:

> A lytel tyme his yift ys agreable,
> But ful encomberous is the usyng;
> For subtil Jelosie, the deceyvable,
> Ful often tyme causeth desturbyng.
> Thus be we ever in drede and sufferyng,
> In nouncerteyn we languisshe in penaunce,
> And han ful often many an hard mischaunce,
> Al the revers of any glad felyng.

[41–48

If we identify Love's gift to man with God's original gift, paradise, then certainly it is a gift which is agreeable only for a while. Soon the use of paradise becomes a vexation, for Jealousy, Eve's jealousy of God's station — all too easily "deceyvable" — causes disturbance. As a result, mutability sets in — fear of death, suffering of pain, uncertainty — and "we languisshe in penaunce." But the literal pagan level and the adumbrated Christian level come in the end to the same thing: the speaker in the poem rejects the temptation — jealousy of the beloved or jealousy in general.

In the third ballade, Venus reaffirms her love for the absent Mars, choosing the way of patience: "Sufficeth me to sen hym when I may"; and she vows that she will love him as long as she lives. She recognizes that for her beloved she is indebted to that undefined Love which stands above her, and having referred "grace" to its proper place, she may without fault resolve to seek no further. She makes no unreasonable demands: she will be satisfied with what she has, which is not happiness but "suffisaunce unto my pay [delight]." The resolution does not come easily:

> Herte, to the hit oughte ynogh suffise
> That Love so high a grace to the sente,

To chese the worthieste in alle wise
And most agrable unto myn entente.
Seche no ferther, neythir wey ne wente,
Sith I have suffisaunce unto my pay.
Thus wol I ende this compleynt or this lay;
To love hym best ne shal I never repente.

[65–72

Taken by itself, the *Complaint of Venus* has perhaps nothing in it that urgently signals us beyond the most literal reading. (I don't really believe that. The more one reads of medieval literature, the more blatant these seemingly faint hints become, whether the purpose, in a given case, be religious, blasphemous, or something else.) But read in the light of techniques and ideas set up in the *Complaint of Mars*, techniques and ideas seen again and again in the poetry of Chaucer and in the courtly-love tradition in general, the *Complaint of Venus* becomes a richer poem. Chiefly, it gains dramatic force as a result of our sense, partly developed in the earlier complaint, of Venus as, in psychology at least, a lifelike woman.

One last Boethean wit poem:

J. S. P. Tatlock, commenting on *The Former Age*, describes the poem as

based on the fifth poem in Boethius' second book, and describing one of the classical ideas of the simple life projected back into the beginnings of the human race: subsistence on the natural fruits of the earth, without agriculture or milling or cookery or wine; no dyeing, no building, no commerce, no mining, no luxury, conquest, or warfare. The picture is more attractive, especially to the imaginatively indolent, than the Garden of Eden, where man must till the soil. Hebrew literature throughout had the ethical spirit of the prophets. The classical ancients, while they also had a more strenuous picture of the golden age, could surrender their ethics and their good sense for a while to an existence of lolling; even so strenuous an idealist as Boethius could surrender to its combination with peaceableness; it would appeal as much

at moments to Christians who accepted the orthodox
unstrenuous idea of heaven.[14]

This will do well enough as a description of what Boethius'
poem and Chaucer's have in common, but something remains
to be said about differences, for Chaucer's poem is no mere
translation.

Unlike Boethius' poem, Chaucer's is rich in concrete
imagery: the contrast between the Golden Age and the
troubled modern world is sharp. But Chaucer's imagery is not
designed merely to lend vividness. It's also symbolic. Whatever may be said about the ethical spirit of Hebrew literature,
Chaucer's poem identifies the classical idea of the Golden Age
and the Christian idea of the Garden: by introducing the
words *blisful* and *fruits*, which have no parallels in Boethius,
by transforming Boethius' "streams" into "the colde welle,"
which suggests the spring in Eden and its symbolic equivalent,
the well-spring, Christ,[15] by focusing on — to mention only
the most obvious details — grain, the vine, fleece, sweaty
business (cf. Genesis 3:19), and the conventional paradise
image of gemmed streams (cf. *Pearl*, 61 et seq.), by introducing the familiar Christian idea of "our sorwe broghte" by
"coveytyse," by describing the people as "lambish" (cf. the
Twenty-Third Psalm), and by introducing the Old Testament figure Nimrod (builder of the Tower of Babel, according to Augustine in the *City of God*, XVI, iv), Chaucer fuses
the pagan First Age and the Christian. The poem ends:

> Yit was not Jupiter the likerous,
> That first was fader of delicacye,
> Come in this world; ne Nembrot, desirous
> To regne, had nat maad his toures hye.
> Allas, allas! now may men wepe and crye!
> For in oure dayes nis but covetyse,
> Doublenesse, and tresoun, and envye,
> Poyson, manslauhtre, and mordre in sondry wyse.

> [56–63]

Here suddenly, in dense, swift verse (there is nothing of the
kind in Boethius) unity gives way to chaos, universal harmony

and love to war. Against the unified human tradition artisti-cally established in the poetic fusion of the Golden Age of Greek tradition and the Garden of Christian tradition, stands Nimrod's Tower, cause of the diversion of tongues. And against the tranquil hierarchy, God and man in an interrela-tionship informed by love, there is the god who lusts after mortal girls and the king who with overweening pride, that is, love of self, hungers to be God. With the breaking of divine unity, the corruption of the relationship between god and man, the rise of tyranny, and the dispersion of mankind, all order collapses and all mankind are at one another's throats. As in Boethius or Plotinus, or as in musical theory on mis-matched proportions, with the collapse of love Oneness explodes into Manyness. There is "doublenesse and treason, and envye, / Poyson, manslauhtre and" — the perfect final touch — "mordre *in sondry wyse.*" This same idea of the tragic conflict within the realm of the many will be a focal idea in Chaucer's greatest work so far, *Troilus and Criseyde.*

ib

The Double Sorrow (and Joy) of Love in *Troilus and Criseyde*; or, Chaucer's Double Vision ~~~~~~~~~~~~~~

Love in the Realms of "the Many" and "the One"

T WAS NOT BEFORE THE EARLY OR mid 1380s, judging by the poetry and by the apparent date of the *Treatise on the Astrolabe* (1390 or so, since the Chaucerian compilations are for 1391), that Chaucer became seriously interested in the workings of the heavens. Poems commonly believed to have been written before this time have only general and abstract allusions to the character and movements of the stars and planets, often mistaken or merely poetic allusions, references which would be, to an astronomer, trivial, meaningless, or incorrect. He treats the nine spheres symbolically in his early poetry, much as Boethius does in *De Musica*; but he never at this stage goes beyond the knowledge or practice of his poetic contemporaries — John Gower, for instance, whose pseudo-explanations of cosmic functions reveal that he knew nothing whatever of the heavenly clockwork.[1] In his poetry of the mid-eighties, however — that is to say, in the *Complaint of Mars*, in *Troilus and Criseyde*, and in various sections of the *Canterbury Tales* — Chaucer shows a knowledge of astronomy, and a fascination with astrological forces, that can be matched in the writing of no other medieval poet except Dante.

In the book or books he wrote for little Lewis, Chaucer shows his grasp of the technical, or strictly astronomical, side of medieval astrology. In the *Astrolabe* he explains computation of the movement of the stars. He seems to mention there an earlier account of *The Solid Sphere* (the earth),[2] and it is at least possible that he also wrote a later account (as tradition holds) dealing with the third element of the cosmos, the planets — a manuscript which perhaps survives, *The Equitorie of the Planetis*, since this manuscript has much in common with the *Astrolabe* and contains what may be a Chaucer signature (also, on the last page, an amateur's mistake in computation!).[3] Elsewhere, especially in *Troilus and Criseyde* and the *Canterbury Tales*, he shows his grasp of astrological theory, the influence of the stars on the fortunes of men.[4]

As Professor Smyser has suggested, this interest in astronomy and astrology probably comes mainly from the poet's profound and lasting interest in the philosophy of Boethius, for whom the stars and planets and "this little earth" circling at the center of their circling (by the Ptolmaic system Chaucer knew) make up the realm of Fortune. In *Troilus and Criseyde* the whirling cosmos *is*, in fact, Fortune, or rather, Chaucer's own brilliant version of "Fortune's wheel." Beyond the wheel lies Aristotle's unmoved Prime Mover, the God of Macrobius, Aquinas, and Dante: the benevolent controlling intelligence. As Macrobius, Boethius, Aquinas, and Dante understood the cosmos, the stars and planets are intermediary between God and man: below the moon, seeming uncertainty and chaos, perpetual change; above the moon, increasingly clear indications of God's fixed nature, serenity, and majesty. (Cf. the "under the moon" repetitions in *Pearl*.) Both the Christian who's been granted divine revelation and the intuitive pagan like Cicero (according to Macrobius' account) could understand the universe as Fortune in the hands of Providence — could understand, that is, that what happens in the world is blind, heartless Fate if we look no farther than the

immediate cause, Fortune, but God's benevolent, universal
plan if we look beyond Fortune to the final cause. It was to
explore this view and to dramatize its meaning in human
lives — its effect on human freedom, its implications with
regard to human love — that Chaucer turned to scientific study
of the heavens. Part of what he learned, if he followed Aquinas
and Dante — and in *Troilus and Criseyde*, as we'll see, he
did — is that what lies beyond Fortune is one and immutable,
whereas all that lies below, in the realm of the many, has
inherent contradictions and thus mutability, whatever its
momentary value.[5] One may love things mutable and profit by
that love (as Chaucer had been arguing since the *Book of the
Duchess*), but sooner or later one must watch them fall apart.
Astrology gave Chaucer new depth and scope. His poetry
becomes, in the classical sense, metaphysical.

At the same time, of course, he keeps older metaphoric
systems spinning. As Professor Peck has shown in a superb
essay, here as in the *Complaint of Mars* and *Parliament of Birds*
(in some ways rough drafts for the background scheme in
Troilus), Chaucer makes use of numerology and the philosophy of music — elements I must slight for lack of space.[6] And
he keeps the old system of pagan religion as adumbratively
Christian, his much-used device of the double narrator (but
with curious new twists),[7] and much, much more.

Needless to say, this chapter cannot possibly treat fully
the whole vast subtlety of *Troilus and Criseyde*, or even
properly acknowledge the work of the Chaucerians who, in
recent years, have cracked this once-largely-mysterious poem.
Yet rather than throw up my hands in dismay or deal with the
Troilus with gross superficiality, I should like to speak as fully
as human patience allows about how the poem works,
presenting others' discoveries and certain of my own, always
on the assumption that the reader has read through the poem
already and has sensed its worth; for the *Troilus* is a
masterpiece, an almost perfect work of art, and when we've
said all there is to say in the dull, humble style that suits mere
explanation, it still looms above us like the cathedral at
Cologne.

§ 1

THE MAIN THING to be said about *Troilus and Criseyde* is that it
is first and last a great love story. If I seem to forget that in the
progress of this chapter, the reason is that I am trying to make
obscure things clearer, so that the love story can stand out
plain. The story's depth and power comes partly from
Chaucer's use of antique ideas which once contributed to his
central purpose but may now obfuscate it. In fact they have
made some critics doubt that the poem *is*, in fact, a love story.
It is, emphatically: the love story of a man and a woman and in
a larger sense — in the supporting story of the narrator and his
materials — a Christian story and metaphysical defense of
man's love for his fellow man. The humane and forgiving
position Chaucer takes and justifies was not an easy one to
take in the mid-1380s, when Gloucester's star was rising
and Chaucer and many of his friends were in trouble. Old-
fashioned Christian notions of good and evil (bad Gloucester,
good King Richard) were more comforting, less troublesome.
But Chaucer's essential "tenderness," as Professor Michio
Masui somewhere calls it, ruled out such gross simplifications
of complex events. For a court full of anger and suspicion,
Chaucer celebrated gentleness and patience, and proved
betrayal, whether sexual or political (the *Troilus* deals with
both) a part of the universal order of things, not shameful or
monstrous but tragic. That, when the poem was first read, was
the highest of its virtues.

THE *TROILUS* HAS BEEN READ in a variety of ways, some better,
some worse — as a poem largely influenced by Boethian
thought,[8] as an argument for or against courtly love,[9] as an
orthodox Christian "tragedy" of man's fall to the seduction of
"false felicity." [10] Recently the opposing camps have begun to
come to harmony, working toward a balance between the two
traditional pitfalls of *Troilus* criticism: the mistaken view that

Troilus' love is good *although* un-Christian, a view which makes the epilogue irrelevant to the poem, and the mistaken view that Troilus' love is a *foil to* or *fall from* Christian virtue, so that the poem is, so to speak, irrelevant to the epilogue.[11]

Several recent studies have demonstrated that the love of Troilus and Criseyde is not in fact something the Christian audience must automatically condemn — no surprising conclusion when we remember that Chaucer's original audience included such people as Katheryne Swynford, John of Gaunt, and King Richard, son of that noble old one-time-mistress, later-wife of the Prince d'Angleterre, Joan. So far as the machinery of Fate and human limitation allow — our lack of omniscience and omnipotence — Troilus and Criseyde are true and faithful lovers;[12] their sexual attachment has the uniqueness and intimacy that belongs to love, not mere lust,[13] and their love — unlike that in Chaucer's source — resolves misunderstandings, makes each lover more humane, and makes the listening audience more aware of its concomitantly sexual and spiritual humanness.[14] If such a love fails, it can only be because all love on earth runs at least the strong risk of failure.

In a neglected doctoral dissertation, "The Goddes and God in the *Troilus*," Sister Mary Angelica Costello[15] has provided a clue to the specific reason for the failure. Pointing to the medieval commonplace that the pagan religious scheme adumbrates the Christian, Sister Costello opens the way to the view that Troilus' destruction derives not so much from the *character* as from the *multiplicity* of the gods he must serve. But the contrast of manyness and oneness is a more pervasive idea in the poem than a strictly religious interpretation can suggest.

Structurally and thematically, *Troilus and Criseyde* is a dramatic exploration of the inherently tragic contrast between the many and the one (unity and diversity) of Neoplatonic thought as it comes down through, among others, Macrobius, Boethius, Aquinas, and Dante. For all the complexity of Chaucer's development of his theme — for all the richness of characterization, social commentary, lyrical and imagistic play, poetic and scriptural allusion, and philosophical speculation — the theme itself can be expressed simply: *In this world of manyness, higher, lower, and equal but mutually exclusive goods produce conflicts which cannot be resolved in this world but which are resolved in the realm of the Absolute.* The first three books dramatically establish the potentially conflicting goods and foreshadow their conflict; the concluding books (in the usual fashion of five-movement tragedy) dramatize the conflicts and the resulting disintegration.[16]

What's involved in the reading I've just sketched out is not really something new but a shift in critical emphasis, a shift which enables us to describe more precisely the unity of the poem. We need to notice here, as in Chaucer's earlier work, that earthly love is a positive good (cf. Macrobius on virtue in his *Commentary on the Dream of Scipio*); that love is of many kinds, each earthly kind more or less noble but potentially threatening to other kinds; that our world of manyness is not actively evil but doomed to corruption by its substantial nature; and that freedom and love — closely related ideas, for Chaucer — lead to affirmation and charitable forgiveness, while necessity and the failure of love lead to wrath and self-annihilation. All that is not to suggest that Chaucer's philosophy is, like Dante's, thoroughly schematic. But neither is it thoroughly impressionistic.

§ 2

IN THE *BOOK OF THE DUCHESS* Chaucer had developed a comparison of heaven's bliss and this world's bliss; had made human love the figure of this world's bliss and had, through Lady White, symbolically linked human love and nature itself, both of which we are forced to view as positive goods. The same comparison and the same devices and attitudes appear in *Troilus and Criseyde*. Various critics have pointed out in a general way Chaucer's treatment of Criseyde as a lower good on the Platonic scale. One such statement is Professor Muscatine's:

> The meaning of the poem does not hinge on so fortuitous
> a fact as Troilus' placing his faith in the wrong woman or

in a bad woman, but in the fact that he places his faith in
a thing which can reflect back to him the image of that
faith and yet be incapable of sustaining it. The rendering
of Criseyde's betrayal is rather symbolic than psychological. The whole denouement is a symbolic repetition, seen
now in a wider and more impersonal context, of what has
been and what, indeed, may be again. . . . Chaucer has
succeeded, drawing equally on [realism] and on the
idealizing imagination of the courtly tradition, in creating
in Criseyde one of the most compelling symbols of
secular life:

> thynketh al nys but a faire
> This world, that passeth soone as floures faire.
>
> [1840–41

Were the world not fair, it would not have its deep and
tragic attractiveness; were it not mutable and passing, it
would not be the world. Criseyde's ambiguity is as the
world's.[17]

Criseyde, like Lady White, is repeatedly identified by
imagistic means with nature at its best, substance informed
with spirit. She is described as a paradise; her hair is like
sunlight; she is like April and like May, very commonly
associated with spiritual awakening (cf. the opening of the
General Prologue to the Canterbury Tales). When Troilus is
hopeless, Pandarus tells him, "And thynk wel, she of whom
rist al thi wo / Hereafter may thy comfort be also" (I,
944–45). For Chaucer's audience, the lines recalled the
traditional Christian idea of woman in her double character,
natural and spiritual, the natural pole represented by Eve, "of
whom rist al thi wo," the spiritual embodied by the second
Eve, Mary, man's comfort later.[18] For illustrations, Pandarus
turns, in conventional fashion, to images drawn from ambiguous nature itself, each image a common emblem in medieval
poetry and painting.

> For thilke grownd that bereth the wedes wikke
>
> [wicked weeds]
> Bereth ek thise holsom herbes, as ful ofte;

Next the foule netle, rough and thikke,
The rose waxeth swoote and smothe and softe; [sweet]
And next the valeye is the hil o-lofte; [aloft]
And next the derke nyght the glade morwe;
And also joie is next the fyn of sorwe. [end]

[I, 947–52

He falls later into using other analogies of Criseyde and the world. For example:

Peraunter thynkestow: though it be so [peradventure]
That Kynde wolde don hire to bygynne
To have a manere routhe upon my woo, [pity]
Seyth Daunger, "Nay, thow shalt me nevere wynne!"
So reulith hire hir hertes gost withinne, [spirit]
That though she bende, yeet she stant on roote;
What in effect is this unto my boote?

Thenk here-ayeins: whan that the stordy ook
                                    [on the contrary]
On which men hakketh ofte, for the nones, [nonce]
Receyved hath the happy fallyng strook,
The greete sweigh doth it come al at ones, [fall]
As don thise rokkes or thise milnestones; [millstones]
For swifter cours comth thyng that is of wighte, [weight]
Whan it descendeth, than don thynges lighte.

[II, 1373–86

The opposition of *Kynde* and *Daunger* (the ruling "gost" which resists the lower inclinations of nature) seems a species of the nature-spirit opposition familiar in both pagan and Christian Neoplatonism; and the contrast of weight and lightness can of course be read in the same terms: things lower on the Platonic scale are heavier, so when "gost" is overcome, the rest will come down crashing.[19] The narrator, too, uses natural metaphors when speaking of Criseyde:

But right as when the sonne shyneth brighte
In March, that chaungeth ofte tyme his face,
And that a cloude is put with wynd to flighte,

Which oversprat the sonne as for a space,
A cloudy thought gan thorugh hire soule pace,
That overspradde hire brighte thoughtes alle,
So that for feere almost she gan to falle.

[II, 764–70

Reading with Neoplatonic spectacles, one finds the form-substance antithesis in the contrast of sun and cloud, for the Macrobian Neoplatonist not only a contrast between light and dark but also one between lightness and heaviness. (For a brief review of Neoplatonic tradition and imagery, see note 20.)

All of these images have in common an identification of Criseyde and nature — nature in its double (lower and higher) character, as both substance and spirit. She is a woman of flesh and blood, Chaucer insists throughout; but also she is "aungelik," "lik a thing inmortal," seemingly "an hevenyssh perfit creature, / That down were sent in scornynge of nature" (I, 102–5). In the crowded temple where Troilus meets her she stands foremost in beauty, "makeles" [matchless, also, mateless], in her widow's habit, "under cloude blak so bright a sterre" (I, 172 et seq.).

THE IDENTIFICATION of Criseyde and nature does more than simply establish symbolic relationship between loving a woman and loving the world. Criseyde, unlike earlier medieval heroines, is a "real" woman, a human being with needs and aspirations, and thus not just a "beloved" but a "lover" — the role usually reserved for the medieval (or modern) male. Because she's presented as a lifelike person, not just a stock counter in a mechanical love-poem, her metaphoric identification with nature makes her (as Shakespeare's imagery makes Cleopatra) larger than life: with thoughts like the whole March sky, with a hauteur which, once broken, lets her crash down like an oak or an avalanche, Criseyde becomes heroic, justifying a hero's love for her and commanding the reader's sympathy and respect. Nothing could be farther from the truth, in other words, than that view of the *Troilus* which

makes Chaucer an antifeminist or a man oblivious to women as
people; and to argue Criseyde's humanity is not to "modern-
ize" the poem but to recognize the effect of the poem's
startling new uses of traditional poetic devices, especially
Chaucer's presentation of Criseyde as herself torn (as normally the male courtly lover is torn) between higher and
lower desires. That is: whereas usually the lady is simply the
object to which the knight either wisely or with cupidity
responds (as to Scotus' jewelled vase), here Troilus is as much
a temptation to Criseyde as is Criseyde to Troilus. Notice, for
instance, how the choice usually held out to the male, between
higher or lower love, is held out to Criseyde in Antigone's
song (II, 827–75). The poem's main focus, even so, is on
Troilus — that is, the poem's main principle of suspense —
which is why Criseyde, more often than Troilus, is identified
with ambiguous Nature, the mutability inherent in substance,
in other words, with doom — both her own and that of
Troilus — the "destinal forces" evident in the world of the
poem from the beginning.[20] It is when Phoebus, enemy of
Troy, comes into the ascendent that we first begin to hear
about Criseyde's "sunnish" hair. (She will later be metaphorically identified with the changeable moon.) *Yet Criseyde loves
the idealistic Troilus and is ennobled by that love, so that with a
part of her mind and heart she stands opposed to those forces of
natural change — the degenerative effects of the substantial part —
with which her lower elements have come to be identified. This is
why her fall is tragic.*

Troilus' situation is more usual of course. Males are quite
normally considered human in the Middle Ages. Insofar as
Troilus loves Criseyde for what is best in her (and there is no
indication that Troilus' love is essentially base),[21] his love is
virtuous. As in the *Book of the Duchess*, so in the *Troilus*,
Chaucer not only uses but insists on the conventional idea that
the devotion of the lover (male or female) is analogous to
Christian devotion.[22] Troilus wins his bliss partly because of
his great worthiness and his unstinting service, partly through
the complement to his devotion, his lady's *grace*, her extension
of mercy. This is standard in the lover-beloved model of the
courtly-love relationship. What follows changes the model,

each in the pair functioning as both lover and beloved. In the bedroom scene, on that rainy night in Pandarus' house, we encounter repeatedly the idea of the loved one's forgiveness (parallel to God's forgiveness) of a lover who by nature cannot be worthy of the "mercy" he — or she, in turn — asks. (The "smoky rain" from Fortune, ultimately from God, perhaps undercuts, perhaps gives urgency to the love-religion by reminding us of more awesome powers; but it doesn't for a moment deny the love-religion's validity within its sphere.) Each lover, by virtue of his (her) nobler part, plays god to the other's role as worshipper. Instances:

When Troilus is half dead with shame at having used a trick to reach his lady, Pandarus cries, "Say 'al foryeve,' and stynt [ended] is al this fare!" [business] (III, 1106) and Criseyde says she will do so. Immediately afterward, Troilus comes to and discovers with horror that he's in bed with Criseyde, and Criseyde, after coyly teasing him a moment, "hire arm over hym she leyde, / And al foryaf" (III, 1128–29). Again, when Troilus has elaborately lied about the supposed rumor of Criseyde's unfaithfulness to him, Criseyde, seeing through him, dismisses the fault with cheerful forgiveness: "And she answerede, 'Of gilt misericorde! / That is to seyn, that I foryeve al this' " (III, 1177–78). But if the bliss of Troilus is an effect of mercy, so is the bliss of Criseyde: " 'And now,' quod she, 'that I have don yow smerte, / Foryeve it me, myn owene swete herte' " (III, 1182–83).

The lover is saved not only by the grace of his beloved but also by that of the god of love. Troilus tells Criseyde:

> "Here may men seen that mercy passeth right;
> Th'experience of that is felt in me,
> That am unworthi to so swete a wight.
> But herte myn, of youre benignite,
> So thynketh, though that I unworthi be,
> Yet mot I nede amenden in some wyse,   [must]
> Right thorugh the vertu of youre heigh servyse."
> [III, 1282–88

To the god of love Troilus says in language quite as Christian:

"Benigne Love, thow holy bond of thynges,
Whoso wol grace, and list the nought honouren,
                              [wishes not to honor thee]
Lo, his desir wol fle withouten wynges.
For noldestow of bownte hem socouren   [succor]
That serven best and most alwey labouren,
Yet were al lost, that dar I wel seyn certes,   [certainly]
But if thi grace passed oure desertes."

                                             [III, 1261–67

That the whole course of human love parallels the course of religious devotion — and that manyness (the plurality of gods) can lead the soul toward the One — is also evident from diction like this:

> But Troilus, al hool of cares colde,
> Gan thanken tho the blisful goddes sevene.
> Thus sondry peynes bryngen folk to hevene.
>   [III, 1202–4

In the *Troilus*, then, as in various of Chaucer's other poems (e.g., the *Complaint of Mars*), the setting and characters are pagan while the poem is Neoplatonic-Christian. Natural love, a religion looking to Cupid and others, need not be bad but may lead to most if not all of the Christian virtues; and a pagan god or pagan intuition of a god may not be altogether false but may point toward the true God.[23] As everyone knows, the end of Book III shows clearly that Troilus' love for Criseyde is ennobling. Directly after Troilus' song paraphrasing Boethius (III, 1744–71), the narrator tells us, in some of the handsomest verse in the poem:

> In alle nedes, for the townes werre,
> He was, and ay, the first in armes dyght,
> And certeynly, but if that bokes erre,
> Save Ector most ydred of any wight;
> And this encrees of hardynesse and myght
> Com hym of love, his ladies thank to wynne,
> That altered his spirit so withinne.

In tyme of trewe, on haukyng wolde he ride,   [truce]
Or elles honte boor, beer, or lyoun;
The smale bestes leet he gon biside.
And whan that he com ridyng into town,
Ful ofte his lady from hire wyndow down,
As fressh as faukoun comen out of muwe,
Ful redy was hym goodly to saluwe.

And moost of love and vertu was his speche,
And in despit hadde alle wrecchednesse;
And douteles, no nede was hym biseche
To honouren hem that hadde worthynesse,
And esen hem that weren in destresse.
And glad was he if any wyght wel ferde,
That lovere was, whan he it wiste or herde.

For, soth to seyn, he lost held every wyght,
But if he were in Loves heigh servise,
I mene folk that oughte it ben of right.
And over al this, so wel koude he devyse
Of sentement, and in so unkouth wise,
Al his array, that every lovere thoughte
That al was wel, what so he seyde or wroughte.

And though that he be come of blood roial,
Hym liste of pride at no wight for to chace;
Benigne he was to ech in general,
For which he gat hym thank in every place.
Thus wolde Love, yheried be his grace,
That Pride, Envye, and Ire, and Avarice
He gan to fle, and everich other vice.

[III, 1772–1806

It is true that again and again throughout history human love
has proved false, and that fact might seem to urge a rejection of
human love altogether for celestial love. But to read such an
argument into the poem — even into the narrator's conclusion
— would be oversimplification. What Troilus' ascending soul
discovers is no more than Scipio discovered in the *Parliament
of Birds*, that this world may be "held al vanite" in *comparison
to* "the pleyn felicite / That is in hevene above." Whatever

the general tendency — as Troilus angrily points out to Cassandra — human love is not always false. Man's proper course is to love, recognizing that his beloved may prove false and forgiving faults "in charite," as the narrator does.

Boethian and scriptural echoes are found throughout *Troilus and Criseyde* not because Chaucer is imposing Christian values upon a pagan story but because, in the view of the best minds of Chaucer's age, those values are inherent in the pagan story. The identification of Cupid and the Supreme Good, the "binding force," Boethian love, is usually so close that no real distinction between pagan and Christian is possible. Here, for example:

Forthy ensample taketh of this man,
Ye wise, proude, and worthi folkes alle,
To scornen Love, which that so soone kan
The fredom of youre hertes to hym thralle;
For evere it was, and evere it shal byfalle,
That Love is he that alle thing may bynde,
For may no man fordon the lawe of kynde.

That this be soth, hath preved and doth yit.
For this trowe I ye knowen alle or some,
Men reden nat that folk han gretter wit
Than they that han be most with love ynome;   [taken]
And strengest fok ben therwith overcome,   [strongest]
And worthiest and grettest of degree:
This was, and is, and yet men shal it see

And trewelich it sit wel to be so.   [suits]
For alderwisest han therwith ben plesed   [the wisest of all]
And they that han ben aldermost in wo,   [most of all]
With love han ben comforted moost and esed;
And ofte it hath the cruel herte apesed,
And worthi folk maad worthier of name,
And causeth moost to dreden vice and shame.

[I, 232–52

Troilus has just scorned Cupid, but the language of Chaucer's comment, in his long departure from *Il Filostrato*, clearly points to Boethius' view of love as one of the two great forces, the second being nature in Boethius' special sense, derivative from Neoplatonism. As one commentator on Boethius explains it:

> Nature is the god-given principle which enters into every object, celestial or terrestrial, and which causes it to possess a certain definite motive power, propelling it in a certain definite direction. But left to itself, each object would pursue its course independently of all other objects. The universe would be a flux. The light things would rise forever up; the heavy things would sink forever down. The moist things would become irrevocably separated from the dry things. All the diverse elements of the universe would rush together or fly apart in continual warfare. Heavenly bodies would collide in riotous chaos; and all things would follow without control or direction the principle of self implanted within them. But to rescue the universe from this confusion, exists the bond of Love, emanating from Providence. It restrains unalterably and binds together the diverse elements so that serenity is brought out of chaos.[24]

The "fredom of youre hertes" of which Chaucer speaks (I, 235) is, in Christian language, the "freedom" of pride, self-will; and "the lawe of kynde," as the phrase is used here (I, 238), is not simply the casual effect of substance but the law of nature Neoplatonically conceived, as substance and form in interpenetration: Troilus' "light" soul inclines to fly up, his substantial body inclines to sink, but governing love enforces balance, making the willful heart "thrall" not to body but to providential order. No aspect of man's tripartite soul, Chaucer says in the next two stanzas, can escape this law: wisdom, power, and goodness (men of great "wit," "strengest folk," and the "worthiest and grettest of degree") are equally subject.

The ethical standard outlined here, the necessary renunciation of natural will, is accepted not only by the Christian and humane narrator but by the characters as well. Pandarus assures Troilus that Criseyde will love him because everyone must submit to either terrestrial or celestial love, and Criseyde is too young to be naturally inclined toward celestial love. Criseyde, echoing Boethius (and echoing, also, Mars' complaint), recognizes in Christian language the contrast between willful desire, leading to false felicity, and love of the total order:

> "O God!" quod she, "so worldly selynesse,   [foolishness]
> Which clerkes callen fals felicitee,
> Imedled is with many a bitternesse!"
>
> [III, 813–15

(The whole of Criseyde's meditation, III, 813–40, is relevant.) Troilus' acceptance of the same standard is evident from, for instance, his Boethian song, III, 1744–71. It is incorrect, then, to say that there are "two layers of meaning in the poem symmetrically adjusted to each other: Troilus was guilty of sinning against the Court of Love, and was punished by Criseyde's infidelity; from the Christian point of view, he was guilty of yielding to blind pleasure, and he suffered." [25] Both systems find Troilus guilty on the same counts. His sin against the pagan god was the error of Mars, as Mars discovers in his complaint — pride. The narrator insists on the point. Whereas Boccaccio shows us Troilo's pride as he twits his companions about love (*Il Filostrato*, I, 22; cf. *Troilus*, I, 194–203), leading Boccaccio to an exclamation against Troilo's pride, not against the pride of man, Chaucer shifts the position of the moralizing outcry, generalizes it, and greatly expands it, beginning:

> O blynde world, O blynde entencioun!
> How often falleth al the effect contraire
> Of surquidrie and foul presumpcioun;   [pride]
> For caught is proud, and caught is debonaire.
> This Troilus is clomben on the staire,
> And litel weneth that he moot descenden;
> But alday faileth thing that fooles wenden.   [expect]
>
> [I, 211–17[26]

§ 3

BUT TO SAY that in one standard medieval view pagans and
Christians may fall in the same terms is not quite to explain the
terms. Neither is it finally sufficient merely to note that
earthly love is lower than love of God because it is transitory.

It is of course true that here as in the *Book of the Duchess*
Chaucer suggests that earthly bliss is perhaps only a splendid
dream — a traditional Neoplatonic and patristic image of the
transitory, our world as phantom.[27] The idea is implicit from
the start of the poem, but it becomes explicit and dramatically
forceful in Book II and, as a result, it tints with dramatic irony
the sincere but foredoomed protestations of Criseyde in Book
IV and the still more desperate self-delusion of both Criseyde
and Troilus in Book V. In Book III, when Troilus and
Criseyde are in bed, the narrator says,

> . . . lo, this was hir mooste feere,
> That al this thyng but nyce dremes were;
> For which ful ofte ech of hem seyde, "O swete,
> Clippe ich yow thus, or elles I it meete?"
>
> [Hold; dream]
> And Lord! so he gan goodly on hire se,
> That nevere his look ne bleynte from hire face,
> And seyde, "O deere herte, may it be
> That it be soth, that ye ben in this place?"
>
> [III, 1340–48

Though the embrace is real, the sense of security is false, as
Troilus will discover — in a dream.

Nevertheless, Chaucer's account of why this world fails
depends directly neither on Boethius nor on Augustine, whose
fundamental *contemptus mundi* would at once "pass through"
the real Criseyde for the ideal she embodies. Boethius'
explanation of trouble in our world, the province of God's
agent Fortune, is simply that this world is distant from the
source of things.[28] Boethius leaves unexplained what it is,
exactly, that Fortune does to bring about chaos and misery

(though he does imply the answer in his remarks on even and uneven numbers, accord and discord); and his discussion of the relationship or bond of things does not treat in detail the kinds of things bound together. In particular, Boethius' philosophical focus precludes his treating civilized man's conflicting commitments.

For Chaucer, as for Aquinas and Macrobius, manyness itself is the root of the trouble. This is the significance of Sister Costello's demonstration that Chaucer is careful to maintain the special powers and provinces of the pagan gods; but more than gods are finally involved. As Bonaventura tells us, this world of substance succinct with spirit contains traces, *vestigia*, of the divine hand. According to Bonaventura's view (in *The Mind's Road to God*, chapter 1), reminiscent of Plato's argument in the *Symposium* and distant, in attitude, from the views of Boethius or Augustine, objects in this world are the splendid first rung of the ladder by which the soul ascends to God. The soul's great difficulty, as another Neoplatonic account makes clear, is that spirit, as it sinks into substance, becomes forgetfully "drunk" (cf. Criseyde's cry upon first seeing Troilus, "Who yaf me drynk?"); in other words, forgetful of its origin, the soul tends to mistake the *vestigia* — each of the *vestigia* — for the hand itself. Macrobius says in his *Commentary on the Dream of Scipio*,

> When the soul is being drawn towards a body in this first protraction of itself [from the indivisible to the divisible — cf. *Timaeus*, 35A] it begins to experience a tumultuous influx of matter rushing upon it. This is what Plato alludes to when he speaks in the *Phaedo* [a work available to Chaucer] of a soul suddenly staggering as if drunk as it is being drawn into the body; he wishes to imply the draught of onrushing matter by which the soul, defiled and weighted down, is pressed earthwards. . . . Now if souls were to bring with them to their bodies a memory of the divine order of which they were conscious in the sky, there would be no disagreement among men in regard to divinity; but, indeed, all of them in their descent drink of forgetfulness, some more, some less. Consequently, although the truth is not evident to all on

earth, all nevertheless have an opinion, since opinion is born of failure of the memory.[29]

To love the whole order of this world insofar as it reflects love of the One which, here in this world, Macrobius says, is "like a countenance reflected in many mirrors arranged in a row," [30] is to love what Chaucer called the "commune profit" (*Parliament*, I, 75), or to possess, as Macrobius says earlier, the *political virtues.*

> Man has political virtues because he is a social animal. By these virtues upright men devote themselves to their commonwealths, protect cities, revere parents, love their children, and cherish relatives; by these they direct the welfare of the citizens, and by these they safeguard their allies with anxious forethought and bind them with the liberality of their justice; by these "They have won remembrance among men." [31]

When Boethius' "fair chain of love" (Homer's "golden chain," Macrobius says)[32] is taken together with the chain or net of social relationships maintained by the political virtues, the sum is what Chaucer and the *Gawain*-poet sometimes call "courtesy," the proper (not merely necessary) relationship of men to their superiors, their equals, and their inferiors on the social and metaphysical scales. The premise of cosmic courtesy is love, evident in every area of human experience. The relationship between God and the Church (i.e., all Christians) is one of husband and wife; the king is married to the state; the priest is husband to the congregation, and so forth.

In other words, for the fourteenth century generally — as in Boethius' thought — all relationships are love-commitments. The trouble with this world, where no man can see the total plan, is that love-commitments can conflict, with the result that love of one good thing can lead to betrayal of — and finally hatred of — another.

CONFLICTS OF *courtesy* — conflicts within the scheme of interdependence based on love — account for every relationship and breakdown of relationships in *Troilus and Criseyde*: the relationship of god and god, god and man, king and state, citizen and king (or state), friend and friend, lover and beloved. Chaucer insists stylistically upon the similarity of each kind of "love" *by treating each in the language and forms of another.*[33] Consider a few examples.

The pact of Calkas and the Greeks is in effect a feudal commendation. When Calkas asks for his boon, he says:

> "Lo, lordes myn, ich was
> Troian, as it is knowen out of drede; [doubt]
> And, if that yow remembre, I am Calkas,
> That alderfirst yaf comfort to youre nede, [first of all]
> And tolde wel how that ye shulden spede.
> For dredeles, thorugh yow shal in a stownde [time]
> Ben Troie ybrend, and beten down to grownde. [burned]
>
> "And in what forme, or in what manere wise,
> This town to shende, and al youre lust t'acheve, [wreck]
> Ye han er this wel herd me yow devyse:
> This knowe ye, my lordes, as I leve. [believe]
> And, for the Grekis weren me so leeve, [beloved]
> I com myself, in my propre persone,
> To teche in this how yow was best to doone,
>
> "Havyng unto my tresor ne my rente
> Right no resport, to respect of youre ese.
> Thus al my good I lefte and to yow wente,
> Wenygn in this yow, lordes, for to please. [expecting]
> But al that los ne doth me no disese. [distress]
> I vouchesauf, as wisly have I joie,
> For yow to lese al that I have in Troie,
>
> "Save of a doughter that I lefte, allas!
> Slepyng at hom, whanne out of Troie I sterte. [fled]
> O sterne, O cruel fader that I was!
> How myghte I have in that so hard an herte?
> Allas, I ne hadde ibrought hire in hire sherte!
> For sorwe of which I wol nought lyve tomorwe,
> But if ye lordes rewe upon my sorwe.

"For, by that cause I say no tyme er now
Hire to delivere, ich holden have my pees;
But now or nevere, if that it like yow,
I may here have right soone, douteles.
O help and grace! amonges al this prees,
Rewe on this olde caytyf in destresse,
Syn I thorugh yow have al this hevynesse."

[IV, 71–98

Notice that the feudal plea of Calkas sounds oddly like the plea of a lover to his mistress — his emphasis on his entirely selfless devotion, his assertion that he is about to die of sorrow, his appeal for "grace," and so on. It is no accident that Pandarus and Troilus speak of faithlessness in love in the language of a different (political) commitment, describing love-betrayal as "treason," or that every event in the poem turns on the agency of some friend — Hector, Deiphebus, Eleyne, Criseyde's ladies, Pandarus — who may or may not be tricked or betrayed in the transaction. Again and again throughout the *Troilus*, characters swear eternal service to one another and promise to "deserve well" of each other, and again and again characters are called upon to remember old love-commitments.

Beside Calkas' assertion that his service has been selfless, consider Pandarus' assertion (one of many) to Troilus:

But God, that al woot, take I to witnesse,
That nevere I this for coveitise wroughte,
But oonly for t'abregge that distresse
For which wel neigh thow deidest, as me thoughte.

[III, 260–63

As Calkas says he will die if not granted his wish, Pandarus tells Criseyde that if she refuses to grant him his wish — the happiness of Troilus — both he and Troilus will die:

But sith it liketh yow that I be ded,   [pleases]
By Neptunus, that god is of the see,
From this forth shal I nevere eten bred
Till I myn owen herte blood may see;
For certeyn I wol deye as soone as he.

[II, 442–46

(The appeal to changeable Neptune, sometimes a medieval emblem of the devil, does not say much, perhaps, for Pandarus' deep sincerity at this moment.) Troilus hardly dares write a letter to Criseyde for fear she will not receive it, and says, "Than were I ded, ther myght it nothyng weyve" [waive] (II, 1050). On the other hand, as Calkas' service to the Greeks merits service in return, so Pandarus' service to Troilus merits a return, for Troilus says:

> And that thow hast so muche ido for me
> That I ne may it nevere more diserve,
> This know I wel, al myghte I now for the
> A thousand tymes on a morwe sterve. [die]
> I kan namore, but that I wol the serve
> Right as thi sclave, whider so thow wende,
> For evere more, unto my lyves ende.
>
> [III, 386–92

Troilus' remark that Pandarus has served him more than he can deserve suggests a view of Pandarus' "grace" parallel to Troilus' view of Criseyde's grace in a passage quoted above (III, 1282–88) — that is, friendship is like love;[34] and parallel, too, to the grace of the god of love, which "passed oure desertes" — that is, friendship is like religion. At the same time, however, one seeks to deserve well of one's lord in this metaphorical love, religion, or feudalism:

> This Pandarus, tho desirous to serve
> His fulle frend, than seyde in this manere:
> "Farwell, and thenk I wol thi thank deserve!"
>
> [I, 1058–60

And when Troilus is looking forward to seeing Criseyde, in Book III, the narrator says:

> And for the more part, the longe nyght
> He lay and thoughte how that he myghte serve
> His lady best, hire thonk for to deserve.
>
> [III, 439–41

By means of verbal echoes and parallels of this sort, Chaucer treats the relationship of Troilus and Criseyde, Troilus and Pandarus, Troilus and the state, Criseyde and the state, Pandarus and the state, and so forth, as being all of the same kind, even though some may be higher and nobler "loves" and others lower. Courtly love, rooted in selflessness, feudal courtesy rooted in a selfless concern for the common profit, and Christian devotion, rooted in otherworldliness, are analogous, as the innumerable verbal repetitions insist; hence betrayal of a woman, betrayal of a king, and betrayal of a god are all one: each can serve as a metaphor for the other.

§ 4

THE DOOM OF TROY, which comes to be at least metaphorically one with the doom of this world, is presented from the outset as inevitable and just from a pagan, from a Christian, and from a metaphorically feudal point of view. Within the realm of the mutable, love on all levels is replaced by betrayal. Abnegating the law of love, men betray their gods (or their God), and men betray nature, which in turn betrays; kings betray kings; citizens betray king and state, and kings and states betray their citizens; sons betray fathers and fathers their sons; brother betrays brother, friend betrays friend, lover betrays lover, and man betrays himself. Only the love of God is sure, for in Him unity and diversity come together. Oddly enough, to say that the world is treacherous is not to say that it is evil. Love of every kind, from the love of the citizen for his state to Criseyde's love for her good name, partakes of the virtue of heavenly love. *And no one betrays love except from one cause: love.* Thus the harmony of nations is broken by Paris' love for Helen, and from this betrayal — if not from Adam's — all others follow; for as Professor ap Roberts has pointed out by different means, this is the root of every conflict of loyalties in the poem. To recognize this is to recognize that no character in the poem — certainly not Criseyde — must necessarily be thought wicked. Our proper attitude is that which the narrator himself assumes at once (as Professor Cook has shown). As lovers plead mercy of their ladies, so the narrator begs the compassion of lovers — which is to say, given the extension of love just now described — the compassion of all human beings, for whom, in turn, the narrator feels compassion. (See I, 47–51.)

The story opens, as it will close, with betrayals. Calkas, "a lord of gret auctorite," learns by astrological and oracular means that his native Troy will fall, and he flees to the Greek camp and there turns traitor, assisting the enemy with its plans. As though he were a king, or a god, or a mistress, the Greeks "in curteys wise" do him "worship and servyse." Calkas' betrayal is actually triple: he abandons not only his country but also his honor (I, 107) and his daughter, a woman unprotected either by a lord (husband) or by friends (I, 97–98). The daughter, Criseyde, throws herself on the "mercy" of Hector, son of the king, just as her father will later throw himself on the mercy of the Greeks in asking a boon from them, and Hector promises Criseyde state protection and "al th'onour that men may don yow have" (I, 120). Though we will never be allowed to forget the march of the destinal forces, from here until the turning point in the action (near the end of Book III),[35] the emphasis will be on love, not the betrayal of love.

Criseyde's dependence on the "mercy" of the state is reflected in her concern with public opinion — granting that Chaucer may also be interested in psychological realism and granting, too, that for medieval poets the line between realism and symbolism may be faint. Having no immediate lord (since Pandarus' position with respect to Criseyde is as vague for her as it is for us), she looks for her welfare to the people around her, concrete representatives of her protector, the state. Her attitude toward Troy is just what we might expect, whether we choose to see it in psychological or in metaphorically feudal terms: a combination of dread and the desire to please. (A lord is always "beloved and drad," both loving and powerful, "mellowing the ground," as George Herbert says, "With showres and frosts, with love & aw.") It is both from fear of the people and from shame (91 et seq.) that she turns to the

prince, Hector, for "excusynge," [36] and when she has been
dissociated from her father's crime, the narrator tells us that,

> in hire hous she abood with swich mayne   [retinue]
> As til hire honour nede was to holde;
> And whil she was dwellynge in that cite,
> Kepte hir estat, and both of yonge and olde
> Ful wel biloved, and wel men of hir tolde.

[I, 127–31]

Her concern with public opinion is strongly emphasized
throughout. It is involved in her response to Pandarus when he
invites her to dance:

> "I? God forbede!" quod she, "be ye mad?
> Is that a widowes lif, so God yow save?
> By God, ye maken me ryght soore adrad!   [adread]
> Ye ben so wylde, it semeth as ye rave.
> It sate me wel bet ay in a cave   [suits me; better]
> To bidde and rede on holy seyntes lyves;
> Lat maydens gon to daunce, and yonge wyves."

[II, 113–19]

When Pandarus teases her curiosity with the news that he has
news he cannot tell her because "proudder woman is ther
noon on lyve" (II, 138), Criseyde's first question is of the
welfare of Hector, whom she describes as "the townes wal and
Grekes yerde" [rod] (154). Pandarus knows his niece's
concern with those around her, and he plays to it: he prepares
the way for Troilus' love-suit by describing Troilus as the best
known, most honored, and best loved of all the Trojan heroes
(II, 190–210); and having told her of Troilus' love he urges his
friend's good faith by declaring,

> "And also think wel that this is no gaude;   [trick]
> For me were levere thow and I and he
> Were hanged, than I sholde ben his baude,
> As heigh as men myghte on us alle ysee!"

[II, 113–16]

—less an appeal to her fear of death than to her fear of public shame. He does not forget to assure Criseyde that if she permits Troilus to come to her house no one will talk (II, 365–70). And when he swears that if she will not have mercy on Troilus, he, Pandarus, will kill himself (presumably an appeal to her familial love for himself), Criseyde's horrified response is not to the thought of Pandarus' death but to the thought of what people might think "if this man sle here hymself, allas! / In my presence" (459–60). Criseyde decides she had better string along. She compromises, they talk of other things, and then, when she thinks her uncle's guard is down, she casually asks,

> "O good em . . . [uncle]
> For his love, which that us bothe made,
> Tel me how first ye wisten of his wo.
> Woot noon of it but ye?" [knows]
>
> [II, 499–502

What she really wants to know is whether Troilus has been talking publicly of his love. Pandarus praises Troilus' secrecy, and Criseyde, craftily enough, still worrying about her reputation, tries another gambit: "Kan he wel speke of love?" she asks coyly; "I preye, / Tel me, for I the bet me shal purveye" [advise myself]. Pandarus sees through the trick, as these two almost always see through one another:

> Tho Pandarus a litel gan to smyle, [then]
> And seyde, "By my trouthe, I shal yow telle."
>
> [II, 505–6

And he represents Troilus (truthfully, despite poetic license) as such a figure of secrecy that at last Criseyde's fears are allayed. When Pandarus lets it slip out that what Troilus really wants is her favor in bed — *that* was not in Criseyde's compromise — Criseyde laughs merrily at her uncle's false move and instantly forgives him. Real honor is not the point.

When Pandarus leaves, Criseyde sits at her window worrying, and just then Troilus happens by on his way home

from battle. She falls in love with the glorious man, and part of
the reason, though only a part, is that

> Ascry aros at scarmuch al withoute,   [outcry; skirmish]
> And men cride in the strete, "Se, Troilus
> Hath right now put to flighte the Grekes route!"
> With that gan al hire meyne for to shoute,
> "A, go we se! cast up the yates wyde!   [gates]
> For thorugh this strete he moot to paleys ride."
>
> [II, 611–16

His glory alone might make a woman giddy; but the shouting
of the people helps.

> And ay the peple cryde, "Here cometh oure joye,
> And, next his brother, holder up of Troye!"
>
> Fro which he wex a litel reed for shame,
>   [embarrassment]
> When he the peple upon hym herde cryen,
> That to byholde it was a noble game,
> How sobrelich he caste down his yen.   [shyly]
> Criseyda gan al his chere aspien,
> And leet it so softe in here herte synke,
> That to hirself she seyde, "Who yaf me drynke?"
>
> [II, 643–51

Finally, however, it is the knight himself that Criseyde loves.
If his renown is part of his attractiveness, it is overshadowed
by "his excellent prowesse, / And his estat . . . His wit, his
shap, and ek his gentilesse" and, above all, the fact that "his
distresse / Was al for hire" (II, 660 et seq.). The point is not
that she is flattered, though she is. The point is that given
power over Troilus, Criseyde responds, as is proper, with
mercy.

　　And now suddenly — and it is one of the beautiful effects
in the poem — those values previously central to Criseyde's
character become her rationalizations for a love she cannot yet
confess to herself. She argues that she ought to accept Troilus'
love because if she does not he might, as a king's son, be

dangerous; and then, after toying with the idea that if Troilus were to ruin her, public opinion would blame Troilus, not herself, she reflects that in accepting Troilus she would become the envy of the town. The last step in her shift of allegiance from Troy to Troilus comes when she declares:

"I am myn owene womman, wel at ese,
I thank it God, as after myn estat,
Right yong, and stonde unteyd in lusty lesse,
Withouten jalousie or swich debat:
Shal noon housbonde seyn to me 'chek mat!'   [checkmate]
For either they ben ful of jalousie,
Or maisterfull, or loven novelrie."

[II, 750–56

But the shift of allegiance is of course not complete. Criseyde's ladies are always about her, guarding her honor. We are constantly aware of their presence in the next room — and so is Criseyde — when Troilus and Criseyde meet at Pandarus' house.

The ironic end is that the people of Troy, her preservation, decide that their only hope lies in trading Criseyde for the hero Antenor — who will in fact betray them to the Greeks. "Altheigh that Ector 'nay' ful ofte preyde," the parliament will not listen: they betray at once their lords, one of Troy's citizens, and — unwittingly — themselves.[37] However, the town's immoral betrayal of Criseyde (she is a citizen, not a prisoner of war, so she's not in fact tradable) is to some degree balanced by Criseyde's psychological betrayal (not, of course, immoral) of the town for Troilus. Brokenhearted at the thought that she must leave her beloved, Criseyde weeps; her ladies-in-waiting grieve for her, and the narrator says, slipping into the tone of Criseyde's thought (through his sympathy):

And thilke fooles sittynge hire aboute
Wenden that she wepte and siked sore
                                    [imagined; sighed]
Bycause that she sholde out of that route   [company]
Departe, and nevere pleye with hem more.

And they that hadde yknowen hire of yore
Seigh hire so wepe, and thoughte it kyndenesse,
And ech of hem wepte eke for hire destresse.

And bisyly they gonnen hire conforten
Of thyng, God woot, on which she litel thoughte.

[IV, 715–23

Nevertheless, it is partly her social sense (and her sense of honor) that takes Criseyde to the Greek camp. She realizes she can stay with Troilus only if he renounces Troy and, indeed, all civilization, to become an exile.

Secondary to Criseyde's love-commitment to society is her love-commitment to family. With respect to Calkas she feels at the outset nothing but shame; but she does feel affection for Pandarus, little though she trusts him. Her banter with him, her anticipations of his thought, her grief when he suggests that she is not getting any younger, all show fondness between them. When she catches him in his one real slip, both her delighted mockery and her quick forgiveness show affection. And her affection for him — and his for her — show clearly in the scene in which Pandarus comes to Criseyde's bedside to ask how she enjoyed her night with Troilus (III, 1555 et seq.). However, Criseyde's feelings change. Though she knows it's important to Pandarus — for the sake of his love for Troilus — that she return to Troy, she stays in the Greek camp, betraying both lover and uncle. As for her father, she tells Diomede:

"I woot my fader wys and redy is;
And that he me hath bought, as ye me tolde,
So deere, I am the more unto hym holde.

[V, 964–66

As always, Criseyde has more or less convinced herself of what Fortune makes it comforting, if not downright necessary, to believe; but for Chaucer's audience, the statement rang with sad irony. Calkas contrasts with the truly "wys and redy" father recalled in the common Middle English phrase "him that us dere bought." Whereas God died on a cross for his beloved, Calkas, a mere mortal and not a very good one, runs out on his daughter in the middle of the night to save his skin.

Pandarus in turn betrays Criseyde — and himself as well. At the beginning of the affair, Pandarus says,

> But wo is me, that I, that cause al this,
> May thynken that she is my nece deere,   [niece]
> And I here em, and traitour eke yfeere!
> [uncle; both together]
> [III, 271–73

Elsewhere he says, with apparent sincerity, that he has interceded for Troilus only out of love for him and a conviction that Troilus is a man of honor (III, 239–343); what he has done for Troilus he would do for no one else. But he says in Book IV, when Criseyde seems bound to leave,

> This town is ful of ladys al aboute;
> And, to my doom, fairer than swiche twelve
> As evere she was, shal I fynde in som route,
> Yee, on or two, withouten any doute.
> Forthi be glad, myn owene deere brother!
> If she be lost, we shal recovere an other.
> [IV, 401–6

He goes on to allude to Zanzis (that is, the Greek painter Zeuxis, of Cicero's *De Inventione*) and how Zanzis found that different women have different beauties — one more twist of the manyness theme.[38] For one love, here in this world of refractions, far from heaven where there *is* just one love (to borrow Macrobius' image of the mirrors), Pandarus is desperately rationalizing betrayal of another.

Besides her commitments to Troilus, her father, and so forth, Criseyde has also a commitment to nature. Like Troilus and Pandarus, she serves "the lawe of kynde," that is, here, the pre-Christian law of natural love. Having taken Troilus as her lover, she repeatedly swears that she will not "repent." [39] By her very nature (higher nature) she loves Troilus, she says, and she cannot do otherwise. Learning that she must go to the Greek camp, she exclaims, alone in her room,

"To what fyn sholde I lyve and sorwen thus? [end]
How sholde a fissh withouten water dure? [endure]
What is Criseyde worth, from Troilus?
How sholde a plaunte or lyves creature
Lyve withouten his kynde noriture?
For which ful ofte a by-word here I seye,
That 'rooteles moot grene soone deye.' "

[IV, 764–70

But if the real nature of Criseyde is spiritual idealism, nourished by Troilus' idealism, she does in the end betray her higher nature; and Dame Nature, in any case, inevitably betrays Criseyde. Although Criseyde is associated throughout most of the poem with spring — March, April, and May — Criseyde is no young Juliet. The first hint of her age, discounting the fact that she is a widow who may or may not have children (Chaucer departs from Boccaccio to say he doesn't know), is Pandarus' *carpe diem* speech:

"Thank ek how elde wasteth every houre [age wastes (things)]
In ech of yow a partie of beautee;
And therefore, er that age the devoure,
Go love; for old, ther wol no wight of the.
Lat this proverbe a loore unto yow be: [lesson]
'To late ywar, quod beaute, when it paste';
And elde daunteth daunger at the laste.

"The kynges fool is wont to crien loude,
Whan that hym thinketh a womman berth hire hye,

[bears herself]

'So longe mote ye lyve, and alle proude,
Til crowes feet by growen under youre ye,
And sende yow than a myrour in to prye,
In which that ye may se youre face a morwe!'
Nece, I bidde wisshe yow namore sorwe."

[II, 393–406

When Pandarus finishes, he looks at the floor, and Criseyde cries. Then when the narrator describes Diomede, Criseyde, and Troilus in Book V, he speaks of both Diomede and Troilus as young but in his description of Criseyde confines himself to her physical and spiritual qualities and, as for her age, says only, pointedly, "But trewely, I kan nat telle hire age" (V, 826).

Troilus, like Criseyde, is doomed by the conflict implicit in manyness. He is the very figure of Macrobius' "political virtues," and this, ironically, is his ruin. His devotion to his father, his brothers, the people of Troy, and the gods is emphasized throughout, and in every form Troilus' devotion parallels the devotion of courtly love. When the people shout his praises he blushes like a maid and "soberly" looks at the ground; on the other hand, betrayal of Criseyde would be, he says, "treason." Immediately after the parliament has voted to send Criseyde away, Pandarus' suggestion to Troilus that he forget Criseyde meets with a response which establishes the direct parallel in Troilus' mind between the parliament's betrayal and the proposed betrayal by Troilus:

> "Frend,
> This lechecraft, or heeled thus to be, [medical craft]
> Were wel sittyng, if that I were a fend,
>   [suitable; fiend]
> To *traysen* hire that trewe is unto me!
>   [commit treason on]
> I pray God lat this conseil nevere ythe; [give ease]
> But do me rather sterve anon-right here,
> Er I thus do as thow me woldest leere! [teach]
>
> "She that I serve, iwis, what so thow seye,
> To whom myn herte enhabit is by right,
> Shal han me holly hires till that I deye.
> For, Pandarus, syn I have trouthe hire hight,
> I wol nat been untrewe for no wight;
> But as hire man I wol ay lyve and sterve,
> And nevere other creature serve."
>   [IV, 435–48]

Troilus inhabits Criseyde's heart as he inhabits Troy; and just as state and citizen are interdependent, so Troilus and Criseyde are bound by a form of feudal interdependence, must shun "traysen." Calling himself her *man*, Troilus again speaks the language of feudalism, not specifically the language of love.[40] At the same time that Troilus' diction identifies him as Criseyde's temporal lord and, also, servant, it hints at a parallel between temporal and celestial lordship. Pandarus' advice would be suitable if Troilus were a fiend. The suggestion is faint if we take the passage out of context but much less faint if we recall earlier passages (e.g., IV, 260–87) where Troilus complains to Fortune in language as appropriate to courtly love as to religious service, appealing for "grace," recalling his humble and loyal service, asserting that he must "evere dye and nevere fulli sterve," and asking "how maistow in thyn herte fynde / To ben to me thus cruwel and unkynde?" And as devotion to the goddess Fortune is analogous to devotion to a lady, so in IV, 289–94, devotion to the god of love is analogous to a vassal's devotion to his lord. Troilus addresses the god as "verrey lord" and speaks of the love between him and Criseyde as a law which has been "repeled." Soon after this, Troilus addresses Criseyde as "lady sovereigne" and asks her to receive his soul "in gree," that is, in court favor.

With the parliament's decision to trade Criseyde for Antenor, Troilus' loyalties come into conflict. His only hope, as Pandarus sees, is to ravish Criseyde, but Troilus says he cannot do it. The gods would blame him, men would blame him, his father would blame him, and Criseyde's good name would be ruined — in short, he would have to abnegate all his love-commitments. (See IV, 547 et seq.) Pandarus mocks him for thinking so "corteisly" (590) and leads him to a change of mind.[41] Troilus' one modification of Pandarus' scheme is that Criseyde must agree to the plan — a modification based, again, on the concept of courtesy. Soon Troilus learns to speak as glibly of social and familial defiance as Criseyde herself. If in the end Troilus remains true to his father, his brothers, and the people of Troy, his good faith is accidental and without much spiritual meaning: by betraying him first (unable to do otherwise), Criseyde robs Troilus of any chance to betray.

Pandarus, too, is a more or less worthy lover caught in a conflict of love-commitments. He is emphatically not, as some have thought him, an entirely amoral figure, a symbol of obsequious, grasping middle-class England, much less a devil, but indeed, for what it's worth, the true lover of Troilus.[42] Philosophy tells Boethius in the *Consolation* that in sending him troubles Fortune has been good to him at least in that it has shown him who his true friends are. The idea was important enough to Chaucer to provide the dramatic climax of a short poem, "Fortune." In the *Troilus*, Pandarus is the friend whose loyalty adverse Fortune cannot shake.

To take so serious a view of Pandarus is not to deny that he is comic and, in his handling of some of his commitments, a trifle unscrupulous, but to recognize that, where love is concerned, he is comic partly because, to preserve his dignity, he chooses to be so. In love, he tells Criseyde, "I hoppe alwey byhynde," and with Troilus he dismisses his own hopeless suit with similar levity; nevertheless, he loves his unnamed lady in earnest. Chaucer is far more insistent on this than was Boccaccio. He develops from the merest suggestions in Boccaccio (*Il Filostrato* II, 9, II, 11, and IV, 47) his elaborate treatment of Pandarus' sentimental misery — his anguish at the song of the nightingale, his banter with Criseyde about his own actually painful emotion, his attempt to evade his grief by telling himself "japes" (II, 1096–99), and so forth. If his attitude toward Troilus' love is practical, realistic, even cynical at times, Pandarus is with respect to his own affair as idealistic as Troilus himself [43] – and Troilus knows it. When Pandarus suggests that Troilus abandon Criseyde for someone new, Troilus lashes out:

> "But telle me now, syn that the thynketh so light
> To changen so in love ay to and fro,
> Whi hastow nat don bisily thi myght
> To chaungen hire that doth the al thi wo?
> Why nyltow lete hire fro thyn herte go?
> Whi nyltow love an other lady swete,
> That may thyn herte setten in quiete?"
>
> [IV, 484–90

As we've seen already, Pandarus' service of Troilus parallels the courtly lover's service of his mistress. As the lover swears that he will die for want of his lady's grace, so Pandarus swears repeatedly that he will die if Troilus' suit is not granted. As the lover's joy is wholly unselfish, so Pandarus never "for covetise wroughte"; his joy is all in the joy of Troilus — and in the joy of Pandarus' second beloved, Criseyde. When Troilus swears to Criseyde, in the first of the bedroom scenes in Book III, that he will kill himself if she will not have him, Pandarus' sympathy is ludicrously earnest:

> And Pandare wep as he to water wolde,
> And poked evere his nece new and newe,
> And seyde, "Wo bygon ben hertes trewe!
> For love of God, make of this thing an ende,
> Or sle us both at ones, er ye wende."
>
> [III, 115–19

And when Criseyde accepts her lover — as decorously as is possible, considering the time and place — Pandarus' joy is as great as anyone's:

> Fil Pandarus on knees, and up his eyen
> To heven threw, and held his hondes highe,
> "Immortal god," quod he, "that mayst nought deyen,
> Cupid I mene, of this mayst glorifie;
> And Venus, thow mayst maken melodie!
> Withouten hond, me semeth that in towne,
> For this merveille, ich here ech belle sowne."
>
> [III, 183–89

The matchmaker's joy — as his prayer, his choice of the word "merveille," and the image of invisibly rung bells all suggest — is positively religious, and rightly so, both in psychological terms and in terms of the symbolic structure of the poem: Pandarus' wish for the happiness of Troilus and Criseyde is, like all selfless love, holy.

Structurally parallel to the exchange of vows between Troilus and Criseyde (III, 1107) is the exchange of vows between Troilus and Pandarus (III, 239 et seq.). The poet makes the parallel as explicit as possible. After Eleyne and Deiphebus leave,

> Pandarus, as faste as he may dryve,
> To Troilus tho com, as lyne right,

And on a paillet al that glade nyght
By Troilus he lay, with mery chere,
To tale; and wel was hem they were yfeere.

[III, 227–31

And the exchange between Troilus and Criseyde, as well as
the exchange between Troilus and Pandarus, has yet another
parallel — an odd one. After Criseyde's first night with
Troilus, Pandarus comes to her bedside and this is what
happens:

And ner he com, and seyde, "How stant it now
This mury morwe? Nece, how kan ye fare?"
Criseyde answerede, "Nevere the bet for yow,
Fox that ye ben! God yeve youre herte kare!
God help me so, ye caused al this fare,
Trowe I," quod she, "for al youre words white.
O, whoso seeth yow, knoweth yow ful lite."

With that she gan hire face for to wrye
With the shete, and wax for shame al reed;
And Pandarus gan under for to prie,
And seyde, "Nece, if that I shal be ded,
Have here a swerd and smytheth of myn hed!"
With that his arm al sodeynly he thriste
Under hire nekke, and at the laste hire kyste.

I passe al that which chargeth nought to seye.
What! God foraf his deth, and she al so
Foraf, and with here uncle gan to pleye,
For other cause was ther noon than so.

[III, 1562–79

Needless to say, Boccaccio has nothing remotely resembling
this. Chaucer has introduced the scene in order to skirt as close
as possible to a direct parallel with the two earlier scenes (one
between Troilus and Pandarus, one between Troilus and
Criseyde) in which mercy is exchanged and a bed shared.

As Criseyde places her honor in Troilus' hands and as
Troilus in turn promises to love and serve her faithfully as long

as he lives, so Pandarus places his honor in the hands of Troilus, his "alderlevest [most beloved] lord, and brother deere" and Troilus, in turn, swears everlasting gratitude and service to Pandarus (III, 360 et seq.).

Pandarus is faithful to his commitment to Troilus, but he can manage the feat only by violating other love commitments. Only by desperate rationalization can he acquit himself of his own charge that he is both uncle and traitor to Criseyde, and just as he subjugates familial love to his love for Troilus, he subjugates social commitments. He makes Deiphebus, "which hadde his lord and grete frend ben ay," an unwitting tool for the satisfaction of Troilus' desire, and he draws in, as well, most of the nobility of Troy before he is through. (For this effect, too, Chaucer departs from Boccaccio. The whole Deiphebus affair — II, 1394–1757 — is Chaucer's own.) But Pandarus' love, like Troilus's love, is at last betrayed; and just as Criseyde's betrayal of Troilus is beyond her own control, so Troilus' betrayal of Pandarus is beyond Troilus' control: Pandarus' chief desire is the joy of Troilus, but in this world joy is fleeting.

Besides those love-conflicts dramatized within the lives of the three central characters, Chaucer introduces further love-conflicts in his handling of the minor characters. The most interesting case is Calkas. In Boccaccio there is only a brief suggestion of Calkas' avarice. He is "old and avaricious," Griseida tells Troilo; she will ask her father for permission to return to Troy for the safety of his property there, and she is sure that "for avarice he will allow [her] return" (IV, 136). Out of this Chaucer makes a passage six stanzas long (IV, 1373–1414). Criseyde says she will ask her father's permission to return for the "moeble" she has been forced to leave behind, and she is sure he will allow it, for he is "old, and elde is ful of coveytise" (IV, 1371). In effect, Calkas is to *spend* Criseyde for the other (IV, 1373–79). She will so seduce him with her "sawes" that

> ". . . right in hevene his sowle is, shal he meete   [dream]
> For al Appollo, or his clarkes lawes,
> Or calkulyng, avayleth nought thre hawes;   [forecasting]

Desir of gold shal so his soule blende, [blind]
That, as me lyst, I shal wel make an ende."

[IV, 1396–1400

In short, Criseyde introduces (or hopes to introduce) in Chaucer's version of the story, conflicts within Calkas between love of his daughter, love of his possessions, and love of his god and sciences.

§ 5

ALL OF THE PERSONAL BETRAYALS in the poem, as well as betrayals of self, king, and society, take place in the shadow of Troy's cosmic betrayal — indeed, this world's cosmic betrayal — for, as ap Roberts has shown, it is Fortune, not poor, shortsighted man, that plays the villain in Chaucer's piece. If man could know what Providence knows, his crimes would be monstrous; but he knows very little and for the most part freely chooses as best he can. The reader, who sees both why the characters act and what Providence has designed, can only grieve the failures, learn charity, and try for submission to God's larger purposes.

The doom shaped for Troy is the doom shaped long before for Thebes when the ancient king Meleagre killed the boar of the goddess Diane to please the most beautiful of all the women alive in that dimly remembered time. The curse incurred by Paris devolves upon Troy and Troilus; Diane's curse, like Cassandra's narrative, "so descendeth down from gestes olde / To Diomede." Finally, as Christian overtones suggest throughout, the curse goes back to Adam, from whose mistake comes man's dimness of vision, that is, his inability to see God directly.[44] Thus the Muse invoked for Book I is Dante's sorrowing Fury, Tesiphone, who torments and weeps. The narrator of the poem is Tesiphone's instrument, and he shares her paradoxical nature (I, 6–11). Knowing all that went before and all that will follow, the narrator sees as if with the eyes of divine Providence; and because he cannot change the historical outcome — bound by old "sources," most of them fictitious — he weeps. In *Troilus and Criseyde* then, as in the closing lecture on Providence in the *Knight's Tale*, Time and Space work as a further elaboration of the contrast between manyness and oneness.

Morton W. Bloomfield has pointed out Chaucer's emphasis on the vastness of Time, past, present, and future:

> Throughout, Chaucer tries to give us a sense of the great sweep of time which moves down to the present and into the future and back beyond Troy, deepening our sense of the temporal dimension. He tells us that speech and customs change within a thousand years (II, 22 ff.) and that this work he is writing is also subject to linguistic variability (V, 1793 ff.). Kingdoms and power pass away too; the *translatio regni* (or *imperii*) is inexorable — "regnes shal be flitted / Fro folk to folk" (V, 1544-45). The characters themselves reach even farther backward in time. Criseyde and her ladies read of another siege, the fall of Thebes, which took place long before the siege of Troy (II, 81 ff.). Cassandra, in her interpretation of Troilus' dream (V, 1450-1519), goes into ancient history to explain Diomede's lineage.[45]

Against this sweep of time, Bloomfield says, Chaucer plays limited time. Henry W. Sams adds the observation that though the action takes three years, Chaucer symbolically relates the action to the progress of a single year, the four seasons.[46] And the peak of intensity in the poem is the passing of the ten terrible days — then eleven, then twelve, then more and more — of Troilus' wait for Criseyde's return. It is worth adding that the bulk of the references to Time in the *Troilus* are original with Chaucer. In some cases major changes of Boccaccio's organization are involved. For instance, Boccaccio presents Troilo's dream of the *cinghiar* under whose feet Griseida lies (Fil. VII, 23 et seq.) and immediately thereafter the interpretation, not merely that Grieseida is unfaithful (as Troilus guesses from his dream), but that she has given her love to Diomede. Chaucer postpones the interpretation of Troilus' dream, both to build tension and to provide Cassandra with an opportunity to recount the story of the Calydonian hunt.

Space is an equally important motif. Professor Bloomfield
writes:

> The events of the poem take place in faraway Asia
> Minor. . . . At times we seem to be seeing the Trojan
> events as from a great distance and at others we seem to
> be set down among the characters. This sense of varying
> distances is most subtly illustrated in the fifth book when
> Chaucer, after creating a most vivid sense of intimacy
> and closeness in describing the wooing of Criseyde by
> Diomede, suddenly moves to objectivity and distance in
> introducing the portraits of the two lovers and his heroine
> (799 ff.) — a device taken from Dares.[47]

We must add that more than aesthetic distance is involved
here. Panoramic views alternate with close-ups throughout the
poem, and the emphasis becomes increasingly, toward the end,
on the panoramic. We see at the very beginning the vast
spectacle of ships at sea:

> the Grekes, stronge
> In armes, with a thousand shippes, wente
> To Troiewardes, and the cite longe
> Assegeden.
>
> [1, 57–60

Soon after, we see the crowded temple, and Troilus leading his
young knights "up and down / In thilke large temple on every
side." Throughout the first three books we shift again and
again from the immediate story, bound in by rooms, to
panoramic views of the war, the long crowded street where
Troilus rides, the forest where he hunts, the Boethian chain of
trees, rivers, hills, winds, stars. Book IV opens with an epic
view of spears, arrows, darts, swords, maces flashing in the
sun, and through much of Book V we stand with Troilus on
the Trojan wall looking out toward the enemy camp far in the
distance. The contrast between limited space and infinite space
is at its sharpest in this book, for against the view from the wall
there is Troilus' fascination with particular locations which his
love has given significance: Criseyde's house, with "hire dores
spered [barred] alle," nearly breaks his heart in two. And:

Fro thennesforth he rideth up and down,
And every thyng com hym to remembraunce
As he rood forby places of the town
In which he whilom hadde al his plesaunce.   [formerly]
"Lo, yonder saugh ich last my lady daunce;
And in that temple, with hire eyen cleere,
My kaughte first my righte lady dere.

"And yonder have I herd ful lustyly   [merrily]
My dere herte laugh; and yonder pleye
Saugh ich hire ones ek ful blisfully.
And yonder ones to me gan she seye
'Now goode swete, love me wel, I preye;'
And yond so goodly gan she me biholde
That to the deth myn herte is to hire holde.

"And in that corner, in the yonder hous,
Herde I myn alderlevest lady deere
So wommanly, with vois melodious,
Syngen so wel, so goodly, and so clere,
That in my soule yet me thynketh ich here
The blisful sown; and in that yonder place
My lady first me took unto hire grace."

[v, 561–81

In this world one hour betrays the next, one place betrays another.

This Time-Space motif Chaucer vastly extends by astrological imagery: throughout the poem, characters and events turn, twist, circle, and so forth, like Fortune's wheel. Astral influences conflict with astral influences, houses (planetary swings through time) conflict with houses. Finally the changeable characters themselves are identified with the turning celestial bodies which make up the cosmic wheel. In Book V, when Diomede leaves Criseyde, the behavior of the stars and planets parallels that of the characters. Criseyde's lower inclination — "hot passion," if you will — relates her to Phoebus, while her wish to remain pure relates her to Cynthea (Diana). Thus, as Diomede walks smiling and scheming back to his tent,

The brighte Venus folwede and ay taughte
The wey ther brode Phebus down alighte;
And Cynthea hire char-hors overraughte
To whirle out of the Leoun, if she myghte;
And Signifer his candels sheweth brighte,
When that Criseyde unto hire bedde wente
Inwith hire fadres faire brighte tente,

[v, 1016–22

The conflicts between times and within Space — the fundamental principles of the world of substance and, of course, the essential difference between this world and the Absolute, where Time gives way to Eternity (in which all is known) and Space is reduced to what Dante called divine *mente* — point to the thoroughgoing (and thoroughly Boethian) Christianity of the poem's Neoplatonism. Troy is doomed not simply because it is distant from the Supreme Good but because it is "fallen." Troilus is doomed because, like the Theban king, Meleagre, he recapitulates the sin of Adam, the sin of overconfidence, or "pride."

At a religious festival, Troilus mocks the god of love and denies that anyone or anything can make him love against his will. It goes without saying that he is denying the lordship of the god; but it needs pointing out that implicit in his denial is a view that lordship is based upon *power*, not love: I am stronger than the god, Troilus says, and so I will not serve him. When order grounded on love is denied, power takes over: "He kidde anon his bowe was naught broken" (I, 208). (Criseyde makes the same mistake, it should be noted. Just before she sees Troilus in the street she assures herself that she cannot be made love to against her will. And Pandarus well-meaningly encourages this mistake throughout — e.g., IV 617–20). Struck down by love, Troilus grows religious, carefully observing the rituals of the gods whose power he now perceives.[48] Yet at every setback Troilus turns on the gods with curses and vows that he will no longer serve them, once again assuming that the relationship between the human and the divine is one of negative obligation: having gotten nothing, one owes nothing.

Opposing medieval man's knowledge of the cosmic order established by love (that is, the order of "courtesy") was his tendency to slide into the false persuasion that order on every level had power as its premise. The error was one that bothered theorists like Bracton,[49] and it was an error often treated by poets. In the *Pearl*, for example, the jeweller demands his rights, not mercy, mistakenly believing courtesy to be grounded on station and obligation, in other words, power, not mutual love. He is astounded to find that, as he supposes, his three-year-old child has overcome all rival lovers of Christ to become queen of heaven. The same opposition of power and love informs the alliterative *Patience*, where Jonah learns at last that power not governed by love would mean total destruction. Cain's mistake in the *Mactacio Abel* of the Wakefield Master is that he fails to see that God rules by love, not obligation. Having borrowed "neuer a farthyng" from God, he will pay God nothing; but when he murders Abel, incurring a debt he cannot repay, he assumes his situation to be hopeless and, self-damned by despair, runs to hide. His response to cosmic power is exactly that of Criseyde (who makes the same mistake about power) — he fearfully caves in — and exactly opposite to that of Criseyde's psychological complement or "double," Troilus, who shakes his fists and, impotently, goes down raging.[50]

As both lover and soldier, Troilus looks both to Venus and to Mars.[51] (The Wife of Bath has, of course, the same problem.) For a time the two elements of Troilus' character are able to exist in harmony; but at last love and war conflict. Here as in *The Complaint of Mars* it is the sun that drives out Venus and isolates Mars.

The movement begins gently enough. Hearing the cock crow, Criseyde, lying in Troilus' arms, cries out against daylight:

> "O blake nyght, as folk in bokes rede,
> That shapen art by God this world to hide
> At certeyn tymes wyth thi derke wede,
> That under that men myghte in reste abide,
> Well oughten bestes pleyne, and folk the chide,

[complain]
That othere as day wyth labour wolde us breste,
That thou thus fleest, and deynest us nought reste."

[III, 1429–35

For Criseyde, the complaint is merely against sunrise; but for
the reader it is more. Having been given hints that the bliss of
lovers is all too brief, we see in sunrise the doom of love. This
implication Troilus picks up from Criseyde's complaint. He
says:

"O cruel day, accusour of the joie
That nyght and love han stole and faste iwryen,
Acorsed be thi comyng into Troye,
For every bore hath oon of thi bryghte yen!
Envyous day, what list the so to spien?
What hastow lost, why sekestow this place,
Ther God thi light so quenche, for his grace?

Alas! what have these loveris the agylt,
Dispitious day? Thyn be the peyne of helle!
For many a lovere hastow slayn, and wilt;
Thy pourynge in wol nowher lat hem dwelle.
What profrestow thi light here for to selle?
Go selle it hem that smale selys grave; [seals]
We wol the nought, us nedeth no day have."

[III, 1450–63

In Troilus' phrase "Acorsed be thi comyng into Troye" and in
the images which follow — light bursting through every chink
and crack, hundreds of blazing eyes — we catch still grimmer
overtones, of which Troilus himself is unaware. It is with day
that lower love is revealed for what it is (hence the
introduction of mercantile imagery), and it is with day that
the fighting resumes, eventually to bring in treason and the
destruction of Troy. Grim overtones continue to be heard,
rising to the narrator's observation:

But cruel day, so wailaway the stounde! [alas the time]
Gan for t'aproche, as they be sygnes knewe;
For which hem thoughte feelen dethis wownde.

So wo was him that changen gan hire hewe,
And day they gonnen to despise all newe
Callyng it traitour, envyous, and worse,
And bitterly the dayes light they curse.

[III, 1695–1701

Then, robbed of his love, Troilus turns on Phoebus just as earlier he turned on Cupid, this time saying that "for the sonne hym hasteth thus to rise, / Ne shal I nevere done him sacrifise" (III, 1707). Phoebus, enemy of Troy, is the wrong god to defy.

In the opening of Book IV, the book of betrayals, the grimly ironic equation of sunlight and death enters as a major theme. The word *day* sounds again and again in the first twenty-eight lines, and for description the principle of selection is anything that shines. There is fine irony, after all this, in the narrator's description of the sincerely heartbroken Criseyde upon her discovery that she must leave for the Greek camp:

Criseyde, ful of sorweful pite,
Into hire chambre up went out of the halle,
And on hire bed she gan for ded to falle,
In purpos nevere thennes for to rise;   [thence]
And thus she wroughte, as I shal yow devyse.

Hire ownded heer, that sonnyssh was of hewe,   [hair]
She rente.

[IV, 731–37

As I mentioned earlier, this is Chaucer's first allusion to Criseyde's yellow hair, but from now on the poet will call attention to it often. If it is terrible to Troilus that his beloved should be faithless, and if it is terrible to Criseyde herself, it is nevertheless as inevitable as the rising and setting of the sun. Criseyde's mistake is not her faithlessness in love but her idealistic underestimation of the strength of body, and her overestimation of her ability to maintain by will her spiritual inclination. Troilus falls by the same error. Like Hector, who

promises to defend Criseyde from her enemies in Troy,
Troilus promises more than man, mere animal that he is (cf. I,
218), can deliver. It is not that such idealistic promises are bad;
they are the basis of order in the state, order in the family, and
order in the heart; they are the things of art and philosophy,
and they make man almost a god, which is a good thing to be;
but at last they can crush him. The sorrow of Criseyde is what
seems to be her tragic loss of stature: ennobled by love
revealed to herself as no natural creature subject to the
all-inclusive chain of love but, instead, a pure and shining
spirit, she is forced to say of her fall from her own impossible
ideal:

> "Allas! of me, unto the worldes ende,
> Shal neyther ben ywriten nor ysonge
> No good word, for thise bokes wol me shende.   [wreck]
> O, rolled shal I ben on many a tongue!
> And wommen moost wol haten me of alle.
> Allas, that swich a cas me sholde falle."
>
> [v, 1058–65

The tragedy of Troilus, on the other hand, is that his pride
reduces him, not to humility and the universal human bond of
charity, but to rage and self-destruction of the kind that so
fascinated Christopher Marlowe. Whether he rightly affirms
love or wrongly affirms power as the basis of order in the
universe, he cannot avert Troy's doom or his own loss of
Criseyde; but he need not sink, either by the pagan or
by the Christian system, to impotent wrath. The conflict
in Troilus, between belief in love and belief in power, results in a breakdown of order in the microcosm, Troilus,
which is analogous to the breakdown of order in the macro-
cosm.

When things go well for Troilus, the Venus in him
supports the Mars: for love of honor, family, and country —
later for love of Criseyde as well — he is "the first in armes
dyght" and "save Ector most ydrad of any wight"; but when
his luck is bad, the two parts of his nature (elements of his
multiplicity) war with one another, his faith in love being

undermined by his sense that here his power is futile. (The foundation of the idea that "Mercy passes Right" is that man cannot be saved by his works. If no man is righteous in God's sight, if salvation must come from childlike acceptance of grace beyond merit, the man notable for his works — Simon the Pharisee [Luke 7:36–47] or Troilus — is in an unhappy position.) Throughout the first two books we see Troilus, alternately, in two situations: scouring the plain like a very lion, or lying, helpless and hopeless, in his bed. The conflict reaches fulfillment in Troilus' predestination speech (IV, 958 et seq.).[52] Until now his aid when will left him was the human love of his friend and, in a sense, vassal, Pandarus; now when Troilus seems beyond the help of human love he goes to a temple, where one might seek the aid of divine love, and there, ironically, he turns not to faith but to reason. Rehashing the old debate of clerks, he concludes the "al that comth, comth by necessitee." If effect, he denies cosmic love and asserts that man is robbed of power by the omnipotence of the gods. As Patch and others have pointed out, Troilus misses the conclusion of the Boethian argument implicit in the Neoplatonic-Christian imagery throughout the poem — lucidity versus darkness, lightness versus heaviness, temple versus marketplace, height versus depth, and so forth.[53] As Scipio learned, man has the freedom to serve the common profit — in Boethian language, the freedom to accept the bond of love which relates him with the whole order, not merely some particular object of desire. And man has also the freedom to reject the balance of nature, higher and lower; pitch his tent on the cosmic railroad tracks and be annihilated. Once again Pandarus' love comes to the rescue, revitalizing Troilus' enfeebled will; but the check on Troilus' self-destructive tendency, rooted in his increasingly inclusive rejection of love as ordering principle, can only be momentary. When Hector is dead and Criseyde lost, human resources are exhausted. Pandarus "kan namore seye."

The last order to crumble is the order of Troilus' tripartite soul — that is, in the common medieval view which goes back to Plato, the interdependent hierarchy of the rational, irascible, and concupiscent souls. In the healthy tripartite soul, reason (the rational part) gives man knowledge of the total order and ultimate good; "mettle" or "will" (the irascible part) gives man the power to pursue the good of which reason informs him; and desire (the concupiscent part) leads man to wish for the highest good. The perverted soul, "blind" with its fall into substance — "the darkness of the blood," Macrobius says — replaces reason with selfish unreason, replaces pursuit of the good with defiance, and replaces desire for the highest good with desire for that which is below or counter to the highest good. So Troilus. He turns from life to pursuit of death at the hand of whatever man or god has the power to dispense it. He hates Criseyde: she gave his brooch to Diomede not out of weakness or "slyding corage," Troilus thinks, but out of imperatorial scorn, or at any rate, "despit" (i.e., power not love); and if he does not hate Pandarus as well, Pandarus nevertheless feels he must disclaim any part in Criseyde's "treason." The end of Troilus' life is given over to a madness of destruction, to "ire, day and nyght," and to hunger for vengeance on Diomede. But though he slays thousands, Troilus' wrath, lashing out against Fate, is impotent: he cannot kill the man he's after. And at last his "visible and invisible foon," brought together in the demigod Achille, destroy him—"dispitiously."

Though multiplicity can ennoble as well as debase, the partisan narrator's final angry comment, though fierce, is partly just:

> Swich fyn hath, lo, this Troilus for love!
> Swich fyn hath al his grete worthynesse!
> Swich fyn hath his estat real above,
> Swich fyn his lust, swich fyn hath his noblesse!
> Swych fyn hath false worldes brotelnesse!
> And thus bigan his lovying of Criseyde,
> As I have told, and in this wise he deyde.
> [v, 1828–34

The love of the One, God, is the logical resolution of the human dilemma, the ambiguity inherent in the realm of the

many. Though love of particular goods in the realm of
manyness can be ennobling, love of God runs no risk of
exclusiveness, the betrayal of one value for another. God is the
ultimate resting place for the human love-impulse (though
only the man first hurt by Fortune can readily understand it)
because in God unity and diversity come together, and here
the limits of time and space no longer have force. Hence the
narrator's prayer:

> Thow oon, and two, and thre, eterne on lyve,
> That regnest ay in thre, and two, and oon,
> Uncircumscript, and al maist circumscrive,
> Us from visible and invisible foon
> Defende, and to thy mercy, everichon,
> So make us, Jesus, for thi mercy digne,
> For love of mayde and moder thyn benigne;
>   Amen.
>   [v, 1863–69

The "payens . . . olde rites" are "corsed" only insofar as they
are incomplete and misleading. They fail to warn explicitly of
the destructive potential of manyness, by which both men and
women may be wrecked (V, 1779–85). Indeed, pagan religion
itself can be a mistaken affirmation of the many, ascribing to
each god his separate and exclusive virtue.

> Lo here, what alle hire goddes may availle;
> Lo here, thise wrecched worldes appetites;
> Lo here, the fyn and guerdoun for travaille
> Of Jove, Appollo, of Mars, of swich rascaille!
>   [v, 1850–53

The multiplicity of gods, reflecting the multiplicity of desires
lower on the Platonic ladder, leads — or can lead — to disrup-
tive self-will, reduction of the "fair chain" to chaos. Troilus
laughs, in the end, because like Scipio (whose journey through
the heavens is directly behind Troilus' journey), he has at last
seen "armonye" (V, 1812). He turns his back on nature, that
jangling, often discordant world Chaucer pictured earlier in

the *Parliament of Birds*, but in turning away, Troilus is no more a model for man that was Criseyde when, affirming her higher nature and denying her lower, she went to bed and swore she would never get up. Troilus is not a man but a ghost, which makes all the difference; if he loves heaven's order, he has forgotten the similarly beautiful order he experienced for a little while on earth. For a natural creature, acceptance of the bond of love means acceptance of the world, love of the world but love not based on the "vanyte," or error, of belief that to please one's own wish the world's goods will last, much less that by one's own might one can make what one loves endure.

The argument is not at all that man should not struggle to achieve great things — a beautiful woman, or victory in war, or a poem. The poet-narrator himself, as always in the *Troilus*, establishes the moral norm:

> Go, litel bok, go, litel myn tragedye,
> Ther God thi makere yet, er that he dye,
> So sende myght to make in som comedye!
> *But litel book, no makyng thow n'envie,*　　[vie with]
> *But subgit be to alle poesye;*
> *And kis the steppes, where as thow seest pace*
> *Virgile, Ovide, Omer, Lucan, and Stace.*
>
> 　　　　　　　　　　　　　　[v, 1786–92; my italics

He does not ask to be absolute master among poets but only that he be among Poetry's most diligent and ennobled servants, one who kisses the steps (lover-like) of still greater poets. Chaucer's request that he be granted the might to write some comedy "er that he dye" is entered in the proper spirit, ambitious but selfless. And knowing the mutability of things, Chaucer asks not for a suspension of the laws of nature but only for preservation, by some means, of the poetic quality and meaning of his work (V, 1793 et seq.). The narrator submits, as all men must strive to submit, to total order — to all "lovers," all "poesye," the Good.

§ 6

ONE LAST BRIEF WORD — about the narrator.

Like the *Parliament*, the *Troilus* has, in a sense, a puppet narrator who is manipulated by an all-wise puppeteer artist; but puppet and puppeteer are much closer in the epic than in the earlier poem. The puppet here is not half-informed, as in the *Parliament*; he's an involved narrator who knows exactly what the artist knows — that the pagan, Christian, and courtly-love religions are harmonious, each at least potentially guiding men and women heavenward, though admittedly the pagan and the neo-pagan courtly-love religions see dimly what Christian revelation shows clearly. The puppeteer-artist lays out the structure of the poem — the destinal forces that undermine character-intentions and pounce on errors (effects of non-omniscience) and on the wrong responses of people who think themselves weaker than they are (overreactions to non-omnipotence: Troilus' defiance, Criseyde's tendency toward cowardice). The puppet-narrator, though a character in the poem, understands the whole system in the *Troilus*. But unlike the master artist behind him, the puppet is intensely involved, in the strict sense passionate;[54] for all his knowledge, he gets carried away, as all decent human beings do. He loves his characters, hates their enemies, and desperately rationalizes or excuses their mistakes, though he knows them mistakes. When at the end, in the so-called Retraction, he turns against the multiple pagan gods, he does so in anger and disappointment, accusing them unfairly just as Troilus accused Criseyde of acting "for despit." The puppet-narrator, in other words, is the poem's humanizing influence. Just as, despite his historical omniscience, he excuses his beloved young lovers' errors, thus "erring" himself — but erring for love — so, despite his omnipotence as poetic creator, he reacts with uncalled-for rage — rage because of love. Then gradually, in the poem's long windup, the puppet-narrator grows wiser, more calm, and submits, becoming virtually one with the stately puppeteer.[55]

His final dramatic justification of his characters' faults is that he shares them — as we all do, and as his poetry has made sure the audience must do. What makes frosty condemnation of sin impossible in *Troilus and Criseyde* — as in the story of Christ and the woman taken in adultery — is that here on earth there is no one fit to cast the first stone. Forgiveness is the only available option — the theme of the scene between the lovers in bed, the theme of all Chaucer's art.

b

The *House of Fame*, or "Dante in English"

Experience, Authority, and the Comedy of Self-love, or Pride

CRITICS HAVE HAD A FAIRLY DIF-
ficult time with Chaucer's unfinished *House of Fame*, partly because they've usually misdated it, most of them placing it before the *Parliament of Birds*, only a few, like ten Brink and Skeat, correctly treating it as composed at around the time of the *Troilus*, perhaps even *after* an early draft of that poem.[1] In terms of theme and, to a lesser extent, imagery and allusion, it clearly belongs with *Troilus* and the *Legend of Good Women*, not with the *Book of the Duchess* or *Parliament of Birds*; and since Chaucer mentions in the *House of Fame* his work at the customhouse, which ended in 1385 — a year in which he was writing the *Troilus* (as we know by one clear astronomical reference) — a fair guess is that he wrote what we have of the *House of Fame* shortly before he began the *Troilus* or as spin-off from a *Troilus* early draft, perhaps in 1383 or '84, while he was still living at Aldgate, devoting a good deal of his time to his poetry and to study of, besides poetry, philosophy and science. It may have been simply his move from Aldgate, and from the customs job to less slavish occupation (minor

clerk of king's works and entertainer to Queen Anne) that inclined Chaucer to abandon his poem. The move from Aldgate, after all, wrecked part of the poem's premise, the narrator moving doltishly from customhouse to Aldgate, poring over books, so imprisoned by vocation, inclination, and his wife that no one could help him but Saint Leonard, patron saint of prisoners and henpecked husbands (among other things). As a prominent member of the queen's retinue, dividing his time between Eltham, Sheene, and Greenwich, he could no longer caricature himself as myopic scholarly drudge; and to delete from the poem that comic device is to blast away the foundation of its splendid architecture.

One might offer numerous proofs of the *House of Fame*'s place in the chronology of Chaucer's work. Like the *Legend of Good Women*, the *House of Fame* is directly influenced by Ovid's *Heroides*;[2] like the *Troilus* it shows the strong influence of Dante and a fully digested Boethius;[3] compared to the *Book of the Duchess* and the *Parliament* it has relatively few imitations of French poetry, and the few found are free and distant.[4] The *House of Fame* shares ideas and particular lines with Troilus (e.g., *HF*, 639–40; *T*, I, 517–18) and shares images and ideas with the *Legend* (e.g., the image of stellification, not found elsewhere except in the *Knight's Tale* — another work regularly assigned to this middle period and one which shares verbal-repetition patterns with the *House of Fame*, for instance the pattern "up and down").[5]

But the most important evidence of the relationship between the *House of Fame* and the larger epic which followed it is thematic. Both poems deal centrally with "experience" and "authority," [6] with earthly as opposed to heavenly "fame," and with the fallibility of human perception — moral, poetic, and scientific. And both — in ways I will discuss in detail later — draw more heavily than anything Chaucer had written before on the poetry of Dante, partly, of course, because Dante gave Chaucer his greatest medieval epic model, and partly because Dante too, especially in the *Inferno*, had made "fame" one of his important themes. The main concern of most of Dante's damned is their reputation among the living.

Dante's influence shows up again and again in both the *House of Fame* and the *Troilus*. In the *Troilus* Chaucer writes:

> Go, litel bok, go litel myn tragedye,
> Ther God thi makere yet, er that he dye,
> So sende myght to make in some comedye!
> But litel book, no makyng thow n'envie,
> But subgit be to alle poesye;
> And kis the steppes, where as thow seest pace
> Virgile, Ovide, Omer, Lucan, and Stace.   [Statius]
>   [v, 1786–92

The poets named here, borrowed from Dante, are the same poets who hold up the pillars in the temple of Fame, except that there two more are added, Josephus and Claudianus, and Homer is provided with subalterns (*HF*, 1429–1512). The idea in *Troilus* (V, 1789, above) that a poem might "envie" — contend against or vie with — some other for laurels recalls a major theme in Chaucer's comic epic, poetic fame; and the *Troilus* narrator's Dantesque humble stance (kiss the steps of Virgil, and so forth) reverses the stance of the jubilant *House of Fame* narrator, who insists that no man who ever lived has dreamed such a dream as *he* just had.

Both the comic or mock epic *House of Fame* and the epic *Troilus* are adorned with Dantesque invocations, extended similes, and other epic devices relatively uncommon in the poetry of Chaucer; both use Dante's device of the slightly unreliable narrator, the *House of Fame* in slapstick terms, the *Troilus* in direct imitation of Dante, where Dante as puppeteer creates the majestic architecture of the *Comedy* and Dante the puppet-narrator moves through the poem responding with his judgments and emotions. Except with regard to the narrator, the *House of Fame* is more directly and openly Dantesque, so that it seems an excellent candidate for that position left vacant by Lydgate's reference to the otherwise lost Chaucerian work, "Dante in English." From Dante comes Chaucer's comic eagle, the dreamer's visit to three symbolic places ironically related to Dante's Inferno, Purgatorio, and Paradiso, and much, much more.

To point to specific lines and images Chaucer borrowed from Dante is to suggest only feebly the English poet's indebtedness to the Italian. Chaucer's high-spirited "survey of the whole world of mortal endeavor," as Kittredge called it,[7] is a comic variation on the whole Dantesque theme. Like the *Divine Comedy*, Chaucer's poem is a spiritual journey in quest of wisdom (but Chaucer goes largely against his will, from Book II forward, and gets second-rate wisdom for which he has little desire and less use). Whereas Dante's experience is initiated and guided by a beautiful and highly spiritual woman, Chaucer's is triggered and at one point helped along, we are led to believe, partly by a nagging wife. As Dante travels from hell to purgatory to paradise, so Chaucer travels, but every scene he visits turns out to be a comic false paradise. What the message of the "man of great authority" was to be (supposing he was meant to offer any) will never be known, thanks to the truncated state of the poem, but the poem's whole tendency is toward an affirmation Christian by default, which ironically confirms and comments on Dante's affirmation.

The problem now is to make all this as plain as the poem is, which is to say, to bring into synthesis the sometimes violently opposed readings Chaucerians have advanced, this past few years, showing how well they in fact fit together and how the poem that emerges from their various interpretations is a typically Chaucerian — and splendid — work. Begin with the poem Chaucer carefully did *not* write but intended us to notice as a shadow on the wall behind the poem — like the background "music" in the *Parliament of Birds* — B. G. Koonce's "Advent poem," or, so to speak, hymn on Christian honor.

§ 1

IN *CHAUCER AND THE TRADITION OF FAME*, Koonce argued — to the surprise of many and the disgust of not a few — that what we'd all been reading as the hilariously funny *House of Fame* is in fact a serious Christian meditation on celestial as opposed to earthly fame. His principle, drawn from D. W. Robertson, Jr., and the ill-named school of "historical" criticism, is that the surface of the poem is a sort of ruse, a distraction for the sinful or uninitiated, that is, a trick like the surface illusion in the *Canticle of Canticles* which, by traditional exegetical theory, makes the songs seem sensual love songs to the ignorant, whereas in fact, on the deeper, allegorical level, they're chaste and holy love-songs of Christ to his Church.

Any reader can perceive at a glance that Koonce is wrong, and his book has been largely ignored except by a few for the most part unimpressed reviewers. But in fact, though Koonce is indeed wrong finally, his book is a valuable introduction to the poem. All satire depends on some standard set of values the satirist shares with his audience. Because we all know how decent Greeks ought to behave, we laugh at the antics of Aristophanes' fools; because we all know how politics ought to be run (and how, alas, politicians really work) we laugh at the political animals of the late Walt Kelly. In the *House of Fame* Chaucer provides reminders of how things ought to be, according to orthodox Christian theory. By subtle hints which his original audience could easily catch, he sketches, himself, the value base. What Koonce misses, as we will find, is that the surface of the *House of Fame* is no mere satire: it threatens, even eats away at, traditional belief.

Koonce points out, with heavy documentation, that for the orthodox Middle Ages

> true fame is heavenly fame, which has its beginning and end in God. God's own fame, or glory, expresses his perfect goodness and is manifested in the praise given him by his creatures. The fame of the Father is shared by the Son, who as deliverer of mankind was "crowned with glory and honor" and gained "a more excellent name" than that of the angels. . . . As long as Adam lived in harmony with God, his own fame was fame in heaven, his actions and speech a glorification not of himself but of God and the divine image within. But with the Fall human fame acquires new meaning; for Adam's sin, symbolizing the mind's turning away from God to the world, involved an irrational confusion between temporal

and eternal glory. Unlike heavenly fame, which lies in
the opinion of God, earthly fame comes to mean the
opinion of man's fellow creatures, whose judgments may
be equally impaired as a result of Adam's sin. As
elaborated in Scriptural commentary, Adam's transgres-
sion reflects the vainglory of Satan, the prototype of those
who seek fame for its own sake. Satan's purpose in
tempting Adam was to ruin man's fame in the eyes of
God, thereby preventing his participation in the eternal
fame forfeited by himself and the other fallen angels. The
Christian doctrine of redemption is an answer to Satan's
design and an affirmation of God's charity in allowing
man through Christ to regain the eternal fame lost by
Adam.[8]

Koonce quotes the standard church fathers — chiefly Augustine, of course — whose work Chaucer knew and repeatedly
echoed throughout his poetry, and thus illuminates image after
image in the *House of Fame*: pleasant scent as an emblem of
good works, foul odor as emblematic of evil deeds, excessively
sweet odor as emblematic of hypocrisy; the trumpet not only
as an image of Gabriel's horn but also as emblem of "those
who 'sound a trumpet' before them as they perform their good
works" in hopes of worldly praise; earthly fame as a swelling
of wind, also smoke, which "the higher it ascends, the more
quickly it dissipates, and the lower it descends, the denser it
becomes — an apt comparison, [John of Salisbury] concludes,
since the desire for praise has its origin in Satan, the prince of
all vanity." [9]
   Koonce traces, partly following earlier critics, the tradition of fame as brought down by Chaucer's dearest mentor,
Boethius, again illuminating Chaucer's imagery: slavery, like
that of the narrator when the poem begins; Fortune's false gift
of reputation, whereby man "areysen hem as heyghe as the
hevene"; the world as nothing but "a prykke at regard of the
gretnesse of hevene"; the image of thought as "fetheris" which
can bring man "hool and sownd" to his proper "house" or
"contree"; and so forth. He traces the literary tradition of
fame, mainly Chaucer's most obvious sources, Virgil, Ovid,
Dante, Petrarch, and Boccaccio, again illuminating Chaucer's

imagery: Fortune's temple on a mountain of ice, the traditional relationship between Fame and Venus, and so on. He turns next to prophetic tradition, which gives him, among many other things, a clue to the symbolic date of Chaucer's dream, Ezechiel's prophetic flight "to the mountain and house of God on 'the tenth day of the month' — an event paralleled in Scriptural commentary with John's similar flight to the holy mountain and city," [10] supported, in Chaucer's poem, by astrological machinery:

> Of basic astrological importance to Chaucer's dream from Jupiter is [the fact] that the sun on December 10 is in the sign of Sagittarius, the mansion of Jupiter, and the ninth of the twelve houses of the zodiac. Like the other houses, the ninth is assigned special attributes or "influences" that have acquired value as Christian symbols. As distinguished from the others, the ninth house is the house of faith and religion, and its powers, we are told, are exerted especially in such spiritual matters as prophetic dreams, pilgrimages, and heavenly tidings,[11]

an idea Koonce supports with a quotation from Roger Bacon's *Opus Majus*.

What Koonce demonstrates beyond a shadow of a doubt (despite some mistakes and forced arguments) is that much of Chaucer's imagery in the *House of Fame* called up in the minds of his original audience religious, literary, and philosophical associations which contrasted the whole crazy action of the poem with what ought to be. Where Koonce goes wrong is in supposing that the narrator of the poem is a serious quester for religious truth, that the loquacious eagle is Chaucer's "spiritual physician," and that Chaucer, in his strange celestial travels, is really getting somewhere, namely to the "man of gret auctorite" who is about to lay on Chaucer "Christ's New Law." The poem Koonce finds in the *House of Fame* is really there, but there as a flickering background vision, an aurora borealis of orthodoxy against which the characters play their comic roles and which, however they may try, they cannot see. Their blindness may be a sign of Adam's fall, but it's real blindness, and it's total; and *that*, not the truth of revelation, is the subject of the poem.

§ 2

IN THE INTRODUCTION to his *Opus Majus*, which was a Bible up at Oxford, where Chaucer was soon to send his little son Lewis, Roger Bacon speaks with considerable fervor of 1) true and false "authority," by which he means, on the one hand, revealed doctrine and whatever accords with it, and, on the other, mere received opinion, or tradition, or, to use his own word, *fame,* and 2) "experience," by which he means scientific experiment, or "observation." His purpose, he tells his patron (Pope Clement IV), is to promote true knowledge: "For by the light of knowledge the Church of God is governed, the commonwealth of the faithful is regulated, the conversion of unbelievers is secured, and those who persist in their malice can be held in check." [12] He rails at length against "fame" — that authority, he writes,

> which without divine consent many in this world have unlawfully seized, not from the merit of their wisdom but from their presumption and desire of fame — an authority which the ignorant throng concedes to many to its own destruction by the just judgement of God. For according to Scripture "owing to the sins of the people frequently the hypocrite rules"; for I am speaking of the sophistical authorities of the irrational multitude, men who are authorities in an equivocal sense, even as the eye carved in stone or painted on canvas has the name but not the quality of an eye. [13]

He lists the causes of error (submission to faulty and unworthy authority, the influence of custom, popular prejudice, the concealment of our own ignorance), then describes the true road to non-revealed wisdom: *true authority* (i.e., sound philosophy or rigorous logic) *supported by experience.* After this introduction, Bacon, in the first five sections of his book, summarizes the wisdom of the greatest of the ancients, shows its correspondence with Christian revelation, and shows how this wisdom can show up the tricks of conjurers and magicians. He closes with a section on the principles of experimental science and a section on moral philosophy.

Much of what Bacon has to say has relevance for the poetry of Chaucer, but rather than spell out particulars let me plunge straight to the heart of the matter. Bacon in his great book admits the existence of one grave problem — a problem already just visible in Ockham and one which grew clearer and clearer with time until it precipitated Descartes: except for the authority of divine revelation, at which, Bacon says, we can only wonder, if proofs are unattainable, *authority* (that of Plato and Aristotle, for instance) can only be trusted when confirmed by experience; but *experience lies,* as when myopics see rainbows when there's no rainbow there,[14] so that experience must be confirmed by authority (reason or sound tradition). In other words, for imperfect, fallen man, *nothing outside revelation can be certain.* "For sins weaken the powers of the soul," [15] causing shortness of life and stupidity.

The problem was one that had troubled Bacon's teacher, Robert Grosseteste, or "Great Head," whose study of optics first sharply raised the question; it was the one great epistemological problem philosophers confronted in the fourteenth century, as Laurence Eldridge points out. Eldridge makes it the basis of his own interpretation of the *House of Fame.*[16] Thinkers who followed the so-called *Via Antiqua,* or ancient way, concerned themselves, generally, with the relationship of God and man. Thinkers who, under the influence of Ockham's nominalism, believed God's nature and ways unknowable, developed the so-called *Via Moderna* and emphasized logic and epistemology, the study of how we find out what we find out. Such thinkers — Grosseteste and Bacon, for instance — understood that if their fundamental principle was right, that is, if God's absolute power could alter all the laws of the universe in a flash, then their whole study was, at least potentially, an exercize in futility. Nevertheless they labored on — as twentieth-century scientists labor on, confronted by similar imponderables. In so doing they made a major logical advance, "the introduction," as Eldridge puts it, "of three-valued logic." Eldridge explains:

> Up to the fourteenth century a proposition was either true or false. But in dealing with the problem of future contingents, some philosophers found that a third category was needed, a proposition that is neither true nor false but simply neutral. The reasoning went something like this: if God knows with perfect certainty what events are to come in the future, then neither those events nor His knowledge are contingent; rather they are certain, and thus divine foreknowledge necessarily means a deterministic universe in which there is no place for human freedom. In order to preserve contingency and freedom of the will, these philosophers concluded that propositions concerning the future, whether uttered by God or man, were neutral — their truth or falsity could not be determined until the event had actually taken place. . . . And as far as fourteenth-century thought is concerned, the use of this third value in logic justifies the application of the term "skeptic" to followers of the *Via Moderna*.[17]

Denying the certainty of statements by God can lead, of course, to theological embarrassments. One response — as Eldridge does not go on to say — was "skeptical fideism," the springboard to Sheila Delany's somewhat blurry book *Chaucer's "House of Fame": The Poetics of Skeptical Fideism*.[18] For the skeptical man of faith, Delany says, there are two truths, the truth of logical necessity and the truth of revelation: when logical necessity conflicts with revelation, the skeptical fideist simply believes both, snatching his hat off and devoutly granting that the revealed truth is, naturally, "higher." To such paradox, there could be no reasonable response, as Chaucer understood, but slapstick comedy. (That or the heresy of Siger of Brabant or Boetius of Dacia, who set reason above faith.) And so Chaucer sketched in his background vision, the poem B. G. Koonce has explicated, and trotted out before it his poor, proud, stupid, child-of-Adam philosopher "Geffrey."

Geffrey's whole problem from beginning to end, Eldridge points out, is that like any decent skeptic he can't make up his mind. His Proem opens with a rapid-fire summary of nearly all the dream lore the Middle Ages knew; but

> his attitude toward dream lore is that all of the propositions he mentions are neutral — that is, they may or may not be true, but he is in no position to assert the validity of any one of them. In fact, all he can do is throw up his hands (". . . the holy roode / Turne us every drem to goode!") and move on to tell of one particular dream. And in this movement away from theory toward evidence, away from the general toward the particular, we can see additional signs of a follower of the *Via Moderna*[19]

— a movement toward "experience." In his dream Geffrey finds himself in the temple of Venus, where the whole story of the *Aeneid* is written out, a story handed down by ancient authority — or rather by at least *two* ancient authorities (as Delany points out), Virgil, who views Aeneas as a hero in the control of his destiny, and Ovid, who views Dido as a cruelly betrayed lady.[20] Nothing in experience can arbitrate the conflict of the two traditions unless, following Bacon's advice, Chaucer can find out "whoo did hem wirche [them work] " (*HF*, 474) and choose the more stable authority. He leaves the temple, exploring like a proper scientist (Eldridge says), and finds outside it a barren desert, which proves the whole thing is illusion. Like a sensible fideist, he calls out to the only authority left: "O Crist! . . . / Fro fantome and illusion / Me save!" Down plummets the eagle, who may be a messenger from Christ, or even a comic Christ-Logos himself. The eagle comes, he claims, from "Jupiter," who by one tradition represents Jaweh and by another tradition stands for pagan stupidity. And so it goes throughout the poem. Geffrey seeks truth by "authority" and "experience," and learns more and more particulars (which is why the poem's books grow longer and longer) but in terms of real truth learns — as a nominalist could have predicted — less and less.

"What Geffrey seems to want," Eldridge points out, "is

the right theory, but what he [shows us] is a mind poorly disposed to accept any theory at all." *21* When the Dantesque golden eagle snatches him up, our expectation is that all Geffrey's problems will be solved in the traditional way, by transcendence. So Dante had gotten truth from a celestial journey, and Scipio the Younger, and many another in poems no longer read. But that's not what happens. Eldridge writes:

Consider . . . what happens when Geffrey looks down at the little earth:

>   And y adoun gan loken thoo,
> And beheld feldes and playnes,
> And now hilles, and now mountaynes,
> Now valeyes, now forestes,
> And now unnethes grete bestes;   [with difficulty]
> Now ryveres, now citees,
> Now tounes, and now grete trees.
> Now shippes seyllynge in the see.
>   But thus sone in a while he
> Was flowen fro the ground so hye
> That al the world, as to myn ye,
> No more semed than a prikke;
> Or ellles was the air so thikke
> That y ne myghte not discerne.
>
> [HF, 896–909

This glance corresponds to the moment when other celestial travelers look back at the earth, as Troilus will do later, and smile at the pettiness of it all. But here something goes awry. In the first place the details of the earth do not become so small as to be insignificant, but on the contrary the larger features of things are still clearly visible [and, one might add, fascinating] to Geffrey. When the eagle flies higher and the earth becomes as small as a pinpoint, it seems that the desired perspective is finally coming to pass. But then an alternative explanation is offered and the traditional meaning of transcendence vanishes. What has happened here, I think, is that a skeptical habit of mind intrudes upon the narrator, with the result that while he is sure of what he is seeing he is not sure of the reasons why he sees just that.[22]

Thus the celestial journey in the *House of Fame* is a parody of the celestial journey which brings transcendent wisdom. Starting out as a poor drudge of a poet, a married man who writes love poems but knows nothing about love except what he reads in books, he seeks true love-tidings on a transcendental journey, but "instead of discovering that multiplicity resolves itself into one, he has found the complications of one love story have become so multitudinous and so varied in their relevance that it is impossible to know the significance of anything." [23] Or rather, to put the matter more precisely, it is impossible to know anything either by experience or by reason and tradition (authority). Theoretically, of course, one still might know how things stand by plain faith. But in the *House of Fame* that too is ruled out, at least for poor Geffrey, for Geffrey is a born victim, a butt of the cosmic joke, a klutz. Except for one fact, which we'll get to in due time, his tale would be the black comedy of a soul cut off utterly, abandoned in a senseless universe.

§ 3

THE *HOUSE OF FAME* is from beginning to end one great, wild rush. Professor Bennett says, commenting on how the opening lines leave the narrator breathless, "Even while we hurry after those quick octosyllabics we are being attuned to the dominant *allegro* of the poem proper. Speed — sometimes bewildering speed — crowded scenes, swift action, and swift change — these belong equally to each part of the poem as they belong to the lofty lady who sits at the center of it." [24] The poem's rush and clutter are partly reflections of the narrator's character. Though he has, as Eldridge says, a mind poorly disposed to accept any theory, he's an eager and lively quester and a jubilant storyteller, fascinated by the surfaces of things and, if not indifferent to deeper meanings, incompetent at working them out. Professor Clemen says:

> The poet spies eagerly about to see whatever is to be seen in and from the heavens. But what he sees is not linked

up with any philosophical or didactic material [at least within the narrator's mind]; Chaucer was now concerned simply with observation as such, not with knowledge deduced from what might be perceived. When for instance the poet, looking down from the vault of heaven, says that the earth is no larger than "a prikke" (907), this might have been an echo of the *Somnium Scipionis.* In that work, however, the earth's minuteness is stressed solely to show how futile it is to strive for earthly fame. Chaucer makes his observation for its own sake.[25]

(Eldridge's reading of course complements Clemen's.) The same comic myopia accounts for the narrator's earlier roaming up and down through the curious "temple ymad of glas," examining, as in a museum or a lady's boudoir, the portraits and figures, and for his later inspections of the houses of Fame and Rumor. The sober deductions he does make and the connections he sees between what he is experiencing and what he has read or heard "men say" are in general comically simpleminded (though not always wrong) and often comically moral or else pious. Think, for example, of his reaction to his discovery that the mountain on which the castle of Fame stands is ice, not steel. As if rolling his eyes up and ducking to his knees, he thinks:

> "By seynt Thomas of Kent!
> This were a feble fundament   [foundation]
> To bilden on a place hye.
> He ought him lytel glorifye
> That hereon bilt, God so me save!"
>
> [HF, 1131-35

His inspection of books, like his inspection of life, shows the liveliest possible curiosity but no depth. He is willing to take on faith what his authors tell him, so long as it appears to make a kind of sense, and though it at times pleases him to discover that what he has read is true, he is not so thirsty for knowledge that he cares to learn, at his age, the names of the stars. In fact, the narrator's greatest pleasure is not in knowledge but in citing it — to himself, to the reader, or to the eagle:

Tho gan y loken under me
And beheld the ayerissh bestes,
Cloudes, mystes, and tempestes,
Snowes, hayles, reynes, wyndes,
And th' engendrynge in hir kyndes,
All the wey thrugh which I cam.
"O God!" quod y, "that made Adam,
Moche ys thy myght and thy noblesse!"
And thoo thoughte y upon Boece,
That writ, "A thought may flee so hye,
Wyth fetheres of Philosophye,
To passen everych element;
And whan he hath so fer ywent,
Than may be seen, behynde hys bak,
Cloude," — and al that y of spak.

[HF, 964–78

The upshot of the narrator's sally into the *Consolation* is comically significant: Boethius' statement that a *thought* may rise up through every element stirs in Geffrey the anxious question, or philosophical dilemma, whether he is rising "in body or in *gost*" (981). In the poem, in short, the chief concern of the childlike Geffrey is Geffrey, as surely as the eagle's chief concern is (after his duty to Jupiter) the eagle. Though the eagle has a great advantage, the two are very similar, each lecturing the other at length, with frequent appeals to authorities and empirical proofs, and neither caring to hear too much of any lecture by the other. It is while Geffrey is discoursing on the veracity of Marcian and Anteclaudian that the eagle interrupts to offer his lecture on the stars (985–90).

Though the eagle *ought* to be (as Koonce feels) Geffrey's "spiritual comforter," he's in fact not much better than Geffrey. Of all those critics who've studied the eagle, John Leyerle is the man who best understands his nature and function. The eagle, he says, "is the first major comic character in English poetry," a bird who talks well, "but perhaps the tone is a shade too condescending and not a little self-satisfied." [26] Yet the humor goes deeper than that, Leyerle shows. The eagle was the standard symbol of the apostle John (whose revelations were a good deal more spiritual than those of Geffrey's eagle), and as John's symbol, the eagle was commonly carved into lecterns (Latin *aquila*, "eagle," was in fact a medieval Latin word for "lectern"). Strange to say,

> such lecterns seem likely to have been a source of the tradition of the speaking eagle, because the Gospels when heard from below an eagle lectern would seem to come from the bird. . . . That the eagle lecterns were intended to be thought of as animated is indicated by a drawing in the sketchbook of Villard de Honnecourt which shows a pulley mechanism inside the eagle so designed that the reader can turn the eagle's head left or right, or even all the way around to face him. . . . There is a weight that returns the head to a forward position so that a skilful reader could seem to be having a dialogue with the bird.[27]

Obviously the powerful church associations called up by Geffrey's eagle (compare Chaucer's emphatic treatment of Venus' temple as a "church") give comic irony to the eagle's insistent role as modern scientist — an experimenter with the force of gravity, for instance:

> "loo, thou maist alday se
> That any thing that hevy be,
> As stoon, or led, or thyng of wighte,   [weight]
> And bere hyt never so hye on highte,
> Lat goo thyn hand, hit falleth doun."
> [HF, 737–81

The eagle's allusion to gravity of course has dire implications for poor Geffrey, hanging in those talons. The eagle has repeatedly made mention of Geffrey's annoying heaviness, has spoken of him as "dumb as stone," and has mentioned in passing that he eats too much (660). Though the remarks seem light enough, Geffrey trembles in fear, and for good reason. Medieval eagles were famous for dropping even their own children, especially those who (like Geffrey) have mediocre eyes. In a twelfth-century Latin bestiary translated by T. H. White, we read:

It is claimed that an eagle presents his young to the sunbeams, and holds the children up to them in middle air with his talon. And if one of them when stricken with the sun's light, uses a fearless gaze of his eyes, with an uninjured power of staring at it, that one is made much of, because it has proved the truth of its nature. But the one which turns away its eyes from the sunbeam is thrown out as being degenerate and not deserving of such reward. Nor is it considered worth educating such a mollycoddle, as if it were not worth bothering about it.[28]

Telling the eagle he would rather not learn about the stars for fear his staring at them might cause blindness, Geffrey takes his life in his hands. The prolix eagle answers, for once, in just four grim words: "That may wel be" (1017). But falling is not the poet's only worry. Leyerle writes:

There is, as might be expected with Chaucer, a humorous side to the discourse on "eyr [air] ybroken"; when one recalls the position of the nether-riding passenger, the remarks inevitably have a scatological sense.

"Soun ys noght but eyr ybroken,
And every speche that ys spoken,
Lowd or pryvee, foul or fair,
In his substance ys but air;
For as flaumbe ys but lyghted smoke,
Ryght soo soun ys air ybroke."

[HF, 765–70

The lecture on sound is, apparently, an elaborate joke on flatulence.[29]

The rule of Geffrey's existence, in short, is that anything that can turn up to make him miserable will turn up. Nevertheless, he courageously hears the eagle out, or anyway pretends to, and shows his interest with lectures of his own.

The engaging spiritual myopia which Geffrey and the eagle share is an important part of Chaucer's burlesque of poetry in general and epic form in particular — points I will elaborate later — but it is also the chief cause of the poem's disjunctive character, the seeming disunity which for a time so puzzled critics and led W. P. Ker, for one, to call the poem "not honest." The myopic narrator is Chaucer's means of focusing attention moment by moment on particulars of the dream journey, not on connections between the journey's parts. We are expected to enjoy the trip for itself, like Geffrey — but not to the extent that "the baffling result in this poem is that as structural materials [the parts] seem to have almost no connection with each other." [30]

The connections, as most critics now agree, are solidly there — though no two critics, so far as I can tell, see quite the same connections. [31] (This, perhaps, is exactly as it should be in a farcical dream vision on the stupidity of man.) The main principle of unity, pointed out by Paul G. Ruggiers, is the Boethian premise of the poem. Though the *House of Fame* narrator is comically stupid, he is that same theoretician of love who was astonished, in the *Parliament*, by love's "wonderful workings" and who would write in the *Troilus*,

> For I, that God of Loves servantz serve,
> Ne dar to love, for myn unliklynesse,
> Preyen for speed, al sholde I therfore sterve,
> So fer am I from his help in derknesse.
> But natheles, if this may don gladnesse
> To any lovere, and his cause availle,
> Have he my thonk, and myn be this travaille!
>
> [TROILUS, I, 15–21

As Troilus' Boethian hymns and Chaucer's scriptural echoes show, the god of love in the *Troilus* is to be understood as a pagan adumbration, however imprecise, of the true god of love, Christ. The explicitly Christian invocations to Book I of the *House of Fame*, the narrator's assertions that, though a servant of love, he knows nothing about love between men and women, the eagle's long lecture on the order of the universe, and the narrator's insistent piety throughout the poem all suggest that we must understand love here as we do in the *Troilus*, that is, as the fair chain, God's providence, which binds the universe together. And just as the force opposing love in the *Troilus* is pride (Criseyde's concern about her reputation, Troilus' concern about his dignity), the force opposing love in the *House of Fame* is that pride inherent in concern with *fame* in any of its overlapping medieval senses: "report, rumour, tidings; reputation (good or bad); widespread reputation, renown; ill repute, infamy." [32] Leyerle reminds us, tightening the argument, that the "Old English word *lof,* meaning 'praise' or 'glory,' survived into late Middle English and occasionally appears spelled 'love' (see the *OED,* s.v. *lof*)." [33] This is in a way merely to restate Koonce's point, that the opposite of love (outgoing charity) is self-love (pride), or Barry Sanders' point, that in his search for love Chaucer gets nothing because the order of the universe has broken down, all love collapsing into self-love. It is from shame over her bad reputation that Dido kills herself; it is about the mechanics of fame that the eagle talks (with such obvious delight in the impression he's making); it was for tidings that Chaucer visited the houses of Fame and Rumor, which he now with such boundless pride tells us about.

If the main principle of unity in the poem is the Boethian fair chain of love, or rather its breakdown through self-love, or love of fame, the main supporting connection between the three books is the vehicle of fame, *sound* — noises, voices, instruments. The poem is the talkiest, noisiest Chaucer ever wrote: in the Proem the narrator bombards us in one vast, rambling sentence with a host of theories on dream interpretation, all of which come down to — nothing. In the first book he "sings" us, as well he can, the story of Aeneas, introducing, wherever possible, shouts of "Allas! and welaway!" or moralizing asides or high-style laments the length, inappropriateness, and implausibility of which the narrator has no time to notice:

> But what! when this was seyd and doo,
> She rof herselve to the herte,
> And deyde thorgh the wounde smerte.
> And al the maner how she deyde,
> And alle the wordes that she seyde,
> Whoso to knowe hit hath purpos,
> Rede Virgile in Eneydos
> Or the Epistle of Ovyde,
> What that she wrot or that she dyede;

And nere hyt to long to endyte,
Be God, I wolde hyt here write!

[HF, 372–82

The second book introduces the pedagogical eagle and the almost equally pedagogical Geffrey prattling upward (along with other noises, from the whispers of secret lovers to the squeak of a mouse) toward the house of Fame. And in the third book, once Geffrey has scrambled mumbling up the mountain, we find a host of musicians, a crowd "crying many oon, / 'A larges, larges, hold up wel!' " the pillars of poets, Fame's supplicants, the two mighty trumpets, and, in the house of Rumor, the chattering bearers of tidings.

This focus on sound, together with our consciousness of Geffrey as a poet in the service of love, calls attention to a further unifying element in the poem, poetry, fame's essential tool. Though we need not follow J. L. Simmons in his view that the *House of Fame* is a bid for patronage, he is certainly right about the role of the poet as the Middle Ages frequently understood it: "only the poet can give an enduring fame to mortals." [34] Early mistranslations of Aristotle's *Poetics* gave prestige to that opinion. Aristotle's distinctions between tragedy and comedy were blurred, in Arabic versions, to poems of praise and poems of blame (satires). One of the universe's tricks on poor Geffrey is that it shows him that his whole heavy labor as a poet is ridiculous.

§4

THE IMPORTANCE OF POETRY in the *House of Fame* is obvious on the surface, in Geffrey's quest for poetic subject matter, [35] but it also helps organize the poem's structure, each book dealing with a branch of the trivium, the whole field of the linguistic arts. The point is Professor William S. Wilson's:

The synopsis of the *Aeneid* in Book I illustrates the techniques of medieval exegetical grammar on the ideal

illustration of grammar, the *Aeneid*; the scene in the court
of Fame in Book III illustrates the techniques of medieval
dialectic on a medieval dialectician, the goddess Fame.
Book II . . . illustrates the techniques of Ciceronian
persuasive rhetoric on a relevant science, the physics of
sound.[36]

Wilson's discovery represents, I think, a major advance in our
understanding of the *House of Fame*, but his arrangement
reverses the order of the second and third branches of the
trivium and doesn't fit the poem. (I also disagree on another
point which I'll mention in a moment.) The right order is:
Book I, grammar; Book II, dialectic (or rather, sophistry); and
Book III, rhetoric, or eloquence. Since I accept Professor
Wilson's reading of Book I, I'll simply refer the reader, if he's
curious, to Wilson's article for detailed discussion.[37]

My opinion that Book II deals with dialectic rests partly
on John of Salisbury's distinction, in the *Metalogicon*, between
dialectic and rhetoric:

Speech is an instrument used in common by both
dialectic and rhetoric. Rhetoric, which aims to sway the
judgment of persons other than the contestants, usually
employs prolonged oration and induction, owing to the
fact that it is addressed to a larger number of people and
generally solicits the assent of the crowd.[38]

Certainly Chaucer's eagle uses some "figures" and "colors,"
despite his boast, but this is allowable within dialectic, and his
object is to persuade Geffrey alone. Along with the comically
inappropriate appeals to Venus and the Muses (this second
book will contain neither love nor "art," unless very, very
metaphorically), the invocation in Book II includes an appeal
to "thought" — which means not memory, as some critics
suppose, but "thought," equivalent to the broad *mente* in the
source. "Thought" is not to be taken too seriously, however, as
is evident from Chaucer's diction:

O Thought, that wrot al that I mette,   [wrought; dreamed]
And in the tresorye hyt shette   [closed]

Of my brayn, now shal men se
Yf any vertu in the be,
 To tellen al my drem aryght.
Now kythe thyn engyn and myght!

[HF, 523–28

The invocation to Book III — the book which mocks eloquence, as John calls it — includes Chaucer's famous disavowal
of interest in "art poetical."

If Book II concerns logic, then the eagle certainly
represents not *demonstration,* which is "independent of the
assent of its listeners," nor yet *probable logic* (dialectic),
"concerned with propositions which, to all or to many men, or
at least to the wise, seem to be valid," but rather *sophistry,*
"which is 'seeming, rather than real' wisdom. . . . It has no
care at all for facts. Its only objective is to lose its adversary in
a fog of delusions." [39] However valid the eagle's lecture on the
movement of sound in medieval terms, the eagle's science
comes to lend plausibility to what is blatantly a fiction.[40] The
whole of the eagle's lecture handily illustrates John's characterization of sophistry:

> It often brings about acceptance of an opinion, which is
> not actually true or probable, but only seems to be so.
> Sometimes it even uses true and probable arguments. It is
> a shrewd deceiver, and often sweeps one along, by means
> of detailed interrogations and other tricks, from the
> evident and true to the doubtful and false. It transforms
> itself into a minister of light, and like Neptune, exposes
> anyone it can lead astray to shoals and shame.[41]

All this is of course not to say that the eagle is wicked. He says
himself, "Take yt in ernest or in game" (822).

For the *House of Fame* is not, as Professor Wilson
imagines, a serious "exploration" of the relevance of grammar,
logic, and eloquence to poetry. (It would be remarkable if
Chaucer were seriously to question their relevance, accepted
even by Dante.) The truth is that whereas heroic poetry
makes a noble use of the best available grammatical, logical,
and rhetorical instruction and devices, Chaucer's mock-heroic

poem, or mock-skeptical attack on poetry itself, makes a cunning use of *bad* grammar, logic, and rhetoric, arts here perverted by the self-importance of the speakers.

Let me briefly trace Chaucer's burlesque of the trivium book by book. In the first book, the commentary tradition founded on Fulgentius' "grammatical" analysis, which for the Middle Ages revealed in the *Aeneid* a clear adumbration of the whole scheme of Christian wisdom, Aeneas representing Christ, and Rome representing the New Jerusalem — a scheme accepted by Dante, who found in it evidence that the one true Holy Ghost guides all high-minded poets — gives way to the ludicrously sentimental "grammatical" analysis of Geffrey's translation, wherein Virgilian and Ovidian traditions are crossed and the poet's abbreviations and amplifications make the confusion total. Dutifully but dimwittedly obeying the precepts of medieval *grammatica*, which taught students how to interpret and imitate poems, Geffrey reduces what most educated medieval people thought to be the greatest of pagan "theological" stories to a rubble heap, parody both of epic tradition and of the courtly lay.[42]

And as the first book burlesques grammar the second burlesques logic. On the lecture on sound Professor Clemen writes:

> In the final words of [the eagle's] exposition of the laws of sound the eagle refers with satisfaction to the "empirical proof" (preve by experience, 878; cf. 787) which is to follow and provide the needed support for what has been postulated. He had already mentioned many observations and experiments which anyone can make for himself in the world of nature (737, 774, 777, 788, 814). On the other hand the eagle makes use of the medieval method of logic, priding himself on his "conclusions" "skilles" and "sentences," and basing his assertions on the authority of classical writers (Aristotle and daun Platon / And other clerkys many oon; 759). The exposition he gives is constructed like one of those "problemata dialogues" which open with the question to be discussed (here, typically, it is the eagle himself who poses the question) and proceed with a sequence of logical "conclusions"

leading on to the final clarification. In his speech the eagle thus unites what are in fact two contrary methods of proof; and we find Chaucer being slightly ironical about each of them.[43]

Clemen adds a moment later that the eagle involuntarily makes fun of his own proof, which he calls "lewed," for "skilles" so palpable that one "can shake them by the bill" amount to "a comic contradiction in the sphere of abstract logic." [44]

With the conclusion of the eagle's demonstration on sound, the direct burlesque of logic ends; but the subject matter of the rest of Book II is not altogether irrelevant to the burlesque. Nearly all the remainder of this book plays "proof by experience" against proof by ancient authority, the province of the medieval grammarian, called up in Book I; and the argument runs: given proof by experience, on one hand, and proof by authority (old authors), on the other, who needs the authority of logic? Geffrey needs no demonstrations when he looks down and sees fields, plains, and so forth (896–903). On the other hand, when they fly higher and can no longer see such details, poetic authority suffices for explanation:

> for half so high as this
> Nas Alixandre Macedo;
> Ne the kyng, Daun Scipio
> That saw in drem, at poynt devys,
> Helle and erthe and paradys;
> Ne eke the wrechche Dedalus,
> Ne his child, nyce Ykarus,
> That fleigh so highe that the hete
> Hys wynges malt, and he fel wete
> In myd the see, and ther he dreynte,
> For whom was maked moch compleynte.
>
> [HF, 914–24

The last line here directly recalls the subject of Book I (cf. Dido's complaints) and recalls, indirectly, the fideist comment on this mode of proof, Geffrey's cry to Christ, "Fro fantome and illusion / Me save!" (493–94).

Next the eagle directs Geffrey's attention upward to the "eyryssh bestes," mentioned by "Daun Plato," and to the "Galaxie," treated in the myth of Phaeton; and once again authority is supported by observation. Geffrey himself provides the comment:

> And than thoughte y on Marcian,
> And eke on Anteclaudian,
> That sooth was her descripsion
> Of alle the hevenes region,
> As fer as that y sey the preve;
> Therfore y kan hem now beleve.
>
> [HF, 985–90

The inevitable next step in the comic argument is that one does not even need proof by experience (much less logic); once he has found that the poets and clerks, like the eagle earlier, "feythfully to me spak" (963), Geffrey concludes he has no need whatever for proof by experience (which troubles the wits of a middle-aged man [995] and might even end up blinding him). In other words, Geffrey has no need for the very thing kind old Jupiter has sent him, firsthand knowledge. And so we come to Book III and the subject of eloquence, the "betynge of the see."

Classical and modern views of poetry as an approach to knowledge stand in flat opposition to the prevailing medieval view.[45] Professor Robert O. Payne puts it this way:

> But beginning perhaps even before Augustine's *De doctrina*, and certainly clearly systematized in that document, Christianity had bound knowledge and moral value inseparably together and subjected both to a priori determination, doubly based on direct revelation (the Passion) and indirect revelation (the pattern of history and the created universe). Augustine thus stands very near the head of a new traditionalist and institutionalist theory of knowledge, which leads at once (already in Augustine's writing, as well as in Jerome's) to the separation of the useful from useless knowledge; with salvation at stake, the distinction of useless from useful

knowledge in turn demands authoritarian and systematic enforcement. So, the rhetoric which Augustine defines in Book IV of *De doctrina* is a system of persuasion which specifically does *not* involve its user in any choices about the content or direction of argument.[46]

Thus, Payne adds later,

> Poetry as an art must remain, as long as the framework of medieval belief stood, a process of arousing favorable response to a fittingly dignified statement of pre-existing truths. At least those were the only terms in which its theoricians could discuss it. Thus *inventio,* if it remains in the discussion at all, becomes a process of verbal ingenuity or a search for a theme.[47]

Chaucer's burlesque of eloquence in Book III takes "invention" in this special medieval sense. Eloquence seeks to sway the crowd to acceptance of what is so. What makes eloquence absurd, here, is that everyone has his special version of what is so, and the arbiter of what shall be heard is whimsical Lady Fame.

It is here in Book III that we encounter, for the first time in the poem, mock-heroic images and similes:

> And on hir fet woxen saugh y
> Partriches wynges redely.
>
> [1391–92

> The halle was al ful, ywys,
> Of hem that writen olde gestes
> As ben on trees rokes nestes;
>
> [1514–16

> I herde a noyse aprochen blyve,
> That ferde as been don in an hive
> Ayen her tyme of out-fleynge:
>
> [1521–23

> This Eolus, with harde grace,
> Held the wyndes in distresse,

And gan hem under him to presse,
That they gonne as beres rore,

[1586–89

Wente this foule trumpes soun,
As swifte as pelet out of gonne,
Whan fyr is in the poudre ronne;

[1642–44

Out of his trumpes mouth it smelde
As man a pot of bawme helde
Among a basket ful of roses;

[1685–87

And whan they were alle on an hepe,
Tho behynde begunne up lepe,
And clamben up on other faste,
And up the nose and yen kaste,
And troden fast on others heles
And stampen, as men doon aftir eles.

[2149–54

The mock-heroic technique is familiar and scarcely needs comment. Whether Chaucer introduced "partriches wynges" by accident (mistranslating Virgil's *pernicibus, Aeneid*, IV, 180) or on purpose, the grand is here yoked with the mundane. (At 1383, to increase the disparity, Chaucer took an image from the Apocalypse.) The Virgilian and Dantesque bee image (at 1522) is comic by its colloquial treatment ("That ferde as been don . . .") and by misapplication: what is focal is not the grim and dangerous rage of the bees but the noise they make (cf. *Inferno*, XVI, 1). So it is with the remaining examples. The points to be noted are two: Book III is the first of the books to make repeated and ostentatious use of the devices of eloquence, and the devices are all used (from an epic poet's point of view) absurdly.

In contrast to the first book, Book III makes comically elaborate use of allegory — the very soul of medieval eloquence.[48] Both the temple in Book I and the houses in Book III contain "queynte maner of figures," but whereas Book I dismisses all these in a few lines (120–27 and 470–73), Book III develops the allegory in great detail, always playing it against the commonsensical, middle-class, wrongheaded realism — the unimaginative myopia — of the narrator.

The narrator climbs the mountain of ice slowly, laboriously not wondering at its majesty but puzzling over what it is made of.

> But up I clomb with alle payne,
> And though to clymbe it greved me,
> Yit I ententyf was to see,
> And for to powren wonder lowe,
> Yf I koude any weyes knowe
> What maner stoon this roche was.
>
> [HF, 1118–23

Here in the realm of allegory, familiar country to medieval readers, Geffrey confuses the *letter* and the *sentence,* or the surface appearance for the true meaning.[49] Forgetting his earlier, somewhat confused opinion that firsthand knowledge is of slight importance, and mistaking "the fair show of things" for the underlying meaning (i.e., eloquence for sentence), he studies the mountain grammatically and logically. When he discovers that the carved names are nearly obliterated on one side he makes the sober observation, "But men seyn, 'What may ever laste?' " This is nothing other than "moral interpretation," like Geffrey's earlier generalization on the falsity of men as seen in Dido's case (383–426), that is, the sort of interpretation exegetical *grammatica* taught the student or "translater" to impose on a classical poem. Then when Geffrey discovers that the names are still visible on the other side, he draws upon logic for a choice between alternative explanations of the phenomenon (storm versus heat):

> Thoo gan I in myn herte caste
> That they were molte awey with hete,
> And not awey with stormes bete.
> For on that other syde I say
> Of this hil, that northward lay,
> How hit was writen ful of names

Of folkes that hadden grete fames
Of olde tyme, and yet they were
As fressh as men had writen hem here
The selve day ryght, or that houre
That I upon hem gan to poure.
But wel I wiste what yt made:
Hit was conserved with the shade
Of a castel that stood on high —
Al this writynge that I sigh —
And stood eke on so cold a place
That hete myghte hit not deface.

[1148–64

(The logic is just a little weird; notice the shadow and *also* the coldness of the hill.)

The absurdity of Geffrey's way of dealing with the mountain depends, of course, on the conventionality of the mountain as elegant device or allegorical "veil." One need not search far for occurrences of mountains like this one. Whatever the significance of the fact that "Hier stant ther non in Spayne," [50] various details here recall Saint John's mountain in the *Apocalypse*, "that hilltop" of which the *Pearl*-poet speaks, "the New City of Jersualem" (*Pearl*, 791–92). The *Pearl*-poet's mountain, like Chaucer's "was lyk alum de glas, / But that hyt soon ful more clere" (cf. *Pearl*, 990 and 1025); both have "a castel that stood on high" and (in different connections) a list of names. Chaucer's allegorical mountain has a generalized list of famous people, while the *Pearl*-poet's castle gates have scriptural names (*Pearl*, 1039–40). Both poets make a point repeatedly of their inability to put their dream-experience into words. The *Pearl*-poet speaks repeatedly and at length of mortal man's inability to describe heaven's sights and sounds (e.g., 223–28), and Geffrey has the same experience:

Thoo gan I up the hil to goon,
And fond upon the cop a woon,   [top; dwelling]
That al the men that ben on lyve
Ne han the kunnynge to descrive
The beaute of that ylke place,
Ne coude casten no compace   [cast, or conceive; means]

Swich another for to make,
That myght of beaute ben hys make,   [mate]
Ne so wonderlych ywrought,
That hit astonyeth yit my thought,
And maketh al my wyt to swynke,   [toil]
On this castel to bethynke,
So that the grete craft, beaute,
The cast, the curiosite
Ne kan I not to yow devyse,
My wit ne may me not suffise.

[HF, 1165–80

And whereas the *Pearl*-poet's New Jerusalem contains the traditional 144,000 inhabitants, Geffrey's has, he tells us more than once, "Many thousand tymes twelve." In short, Geffrey's dream has brought him to a factitious New Jerusalem: the rhetorical device — the *permutatio,* if you like — identifies Fame as a false paradise.

Like Dante in *De Vulgari Eloquentia* and Deschamps in *L'Art de Dictier et de Fere Chançons,*[51] Chaucer seems to think of poetic eloquence under two headings, music and meaning. This, at all events, would account for the appearance, around the house of Fame, of various musicians and other entertainers and, within the house, poets. Neither fares well in Chaucer's poem. The musicians make up a vast host, all tooting their various instruments at the same time. At the feet of the chief harpers sit "smale harpers" who, in obedience to the rhetoric books, "countrefete hem as an ape, / Or as craft countrefeteth kynde." [52] Behind these stand others playing "al be hemselve" — a conglomeration of shepherds, Greek heroes, "Pipers of the Duche tonge," trumpeters, and so forth. Like a good rhetorician (as he thinks) Geffrey cuts his list short and introduces a moral observation: "For tyme ylost, this knowen ye, / Be no way may recovered be" (1256–57).[53] Then Geffrey gives, in the form of an elaborate *expolitio,* a list of other entertainers.

Lists of this kind are not something new in this poem; we have seen already, for example, the lists of false men in Book I, the lists of authorities in Book II. But Book III is made up *chiefly* of these comically long-winded lists. In other words, here one of Chaucer's central purposes seems to be burlesque of that rhetorical dilation so dear to men like Geoffrey of Vinsauf.

Eloquence is the very gate to fame, Chaucer ironically suggests, for as eloquence is made up partly of nature, partly of art,[54] so the castle gate

> so wel corven was
> That never such another nas;
> And yit it was be aventure
> Iwrought, as often as be cure.
>
> [HF, 1295–98

Chaucer turns next to a generalized description of Fame's complainants, that is, another of the prescribed ornamental lists; to a highly allusive *descriptio* of Fame herself; then to his elaborate allegory of the poets. Like the musicians earlier, the poets work at cross purposes, each seeking to maintain the fame of his own kingdom and various poets of a single kingdom sometimes working against one another, as in the case of those who bear up Troy (1465–79).

The central event in Book III, Fame's audience with the nine groups of soliciters, comments on eloquence in two ways, figuratively through the two trumpets Laud and Slander, literally through the appeals of the solicitors and the whimsy of Fame's judgments. Of the figurative trumpets nothing need be said except, perhaps, that the ugliness of rhetorical and persuasive slander has never been better described:

> What dide this Eolus, but he
> Tok out hys blake trumpe of bras,
> That fouler than the devel was,
> And gan this trumpe for to blowe,
> As al the world shulde overthrowe,
> That thrughout every regioun
> Wente this foule trumpes soun,
> As swifte as pelet out of gonne,
> Whan fyr is in the poudre ronne.
> And such a smoke gan out wende
> Out of his foule trumpes ende,

> Blak, bloo, grenyssh, swartish red,
> As doth where that men melte led,
> Loo, al an high fro the tuel.   [chimney]
> And therto oo thing saugh I wel,
> That the ferther that hit ran,
> The gretter wexen hit began,
> As dooth the ryver from a welle,
> And hyt stank as the pit of helle.
> Allas, thus was her shame yronge,
> And gilteles, on every tonge!
>
> [HF, 1636–56

And the cloying sentimentality of hollowly eloquent praise is summed up as forcefully in Chaucer's image of "a pot of bawme held / Among a basket ful or roses" (1686–87).

As for the comment on eloquence in the literal-level appeals of Fame's solicitors and the whimsy of her judgments, the point to be noted is that neither the requests (some presented in indirect discourse) nor the responses contain a shred of eloquence: all nine appeals are bluntly factual, and all nine responses (like some of the appeals) are distinctly low-style. Only the narrator's comments — for instance his comparison of the roar of the winds to the roar of bears (1587–89) — introduce high-style devices; for the rest, we have commonplaces such as "No wyght shal speke of yow, ywis, / Good ne harm, ne that ne this" (1565–66), or " [they] seyden they yeven noght a lek [leek] / For fame ne for such renoun" (1708–9). The basis of fame, just or unjust, is unpoetic fact and Fame's own unpoetic whim. And what makes the unpoetic (or ineloquent) quality of Fame's audience noticeable is its setting, for it follows the highly rhetorical catalogues and precedes the rhetorical *descriptio* of the house of Rumor, which reaches its climax in the bombastic flight:

> And over alle the houses angles
> Ys ful of rounynges and of jangles
> Of werres, or pes, of mariages,
> Of reste, of labour, of viages,
> Of abood, of deeth, of lyf,
> Of love, of hate, acord, of stryf,

Of loos, of lore, and of wynnynges   [fame; experiences]
Of hele, of seknesse, of bildynges,   [health]
Of faire eyndes, and of tempestes,
Of qwalm of folk, and eke of bestes;
Of dyvers transmutacions
Of estats, and eke of regions;
Of trust, of drede, of jelousye,
Of wit, of wynnynge, of folye;
Of plente, and of gret famyne,
Of chepe, of derthe, and of ruyne;
Of good or mys governement,
Of fyr, and of dyvers accident.

[HF, 1959–76

What Geffrey finds within the house of Rumor is as ineloquent as what he hears in Fame's audience, though his description of what he hears employs all the figures and colors. Ironically enough, his description of the babble of truths, half-truths, and lies closely echoes his description of the effect of Eolus' trumpet (1641–44 and 1650–53):

Thus north and south
Wente every tydyng fro mouth to mouth,
And that encresing ever moo,
As fyr ys wont to quyke and goo
From a sparke spronge amys,
Til al a citee brent up ys.

[HF, 2075–80

When the doctrine which eloquence is designed to adorn depends on the babble of the crowd followed by the arbitrary judgment of Fame, eloquence is absurd. But Chaucer's comically outrageous attack on poetry goes still further. Another of the *House of Fame*'s unifying elements, and one at which it is now time to look more carefully, is the poem's burlesque of Dante, a poet not of earthly but of heavenly fame.

§ 5

DANTE TRAVELS in his spiritual journey from hell to purgatory to heaven. Geffrey moves from the "illusion" of Venus' temple to a purgatorial ascent with the eagle (but no evils are purged), to a false paradise — or rather two of them (a paradise where manyness is unresolved).

In Book I Geffrey finds himself in the "church" of Venus. Since elsewhere in Chaucer we are given reasons for men's dreams — in the *Book of the Duchess* the anxiety of a melancholy man, in the *Parliament* the restless anxiety of a man "too curious in study" — it is natural, despite Geffrey's own disclaimers, to look for a reason here. The only clue is Geffrey's character, his drudgery at the customhouse and the fact that he has made a pilgrimage "myles two / To the corseynt Leonard, / To make lythe [easy] of that was hard" (116–18). Presumably if sleep came from physical exhaustion, the dream came through the intercession of Saint Leonard. What Geffrey finds in Venus' church at first seems to support this presumption: like the temple in the *Book of the Duchess*, Venus' church abounds with stock exegetical emblems: glass, gold, "ryche tabernacles," jeweled "pynacles," a "rose garlond whit and red" (one of the images Chaucer introduces into the *Legend of Good Women*, Prologue G, when he transforms Cupid into a Dantesque angel); and here Geffrey finds the *Aeneid*, which has strong Christian associations as an allegory. In terms of the conventions with which Chaucer is working, the assumption that Venus' temple is a "chirche" is natural: found within a fecund love-garden (as it is in the *Book of the Duchess*), the temple would be read by any medieval interpreter as an adumbrative paradise,[55] the rich green countryside surrounding it representing resurrection. But this temple, surprisingly, is surrounded by sand and contains nothing alive, only artifices, traditionally the Devil's work. And so the narrator, always optimistic, calls to Christ. Not even Virgil and his *Aeneid*, Dante's help, have proved helpful.

An eagle very much like Dante's great symbol of

Justice — but also much like Christ,[56] since he is a "phoenix" and is repeatedly identified with the Christ of the Apocalypse — picks Geffrey up and, after much talk, brings him in Book III to another false paradise, or rather two-in-one. The mountain of course recalls, among other things, Dante's mountain of purgatory at the top of which stands the entrance to heaven. For Geffrey, no such luck. The keeper of the castle on the mountaintop, Fame, sits in a throne of ruby, a gem exegetically identified with martyrdom or the passion of Christ (1360–63);[57] she changes shape like Boethius' Lady Philosophy, who guides one to true religion (1369–76); she has as many eyes as "weren on the bestes foure / That Goddis trone gunne honoure, / As John write in Th'Apocalips" (1383–85); she is surrounded, like the heavenly throne of Dante's paradise (and the *Pearl*-poet's) by "the hevenyssh melodye / Of songes, ful of armonye" (1395–96), a music which continues "ever mo, eternally" (1403). She pronounces judgments, as does God, by means of trumpets, instruments which call to mind the trumpets of the Last Judgment — a comparison enforced by diction. One trumpet "fouler than the devel was" (1638); it blows "As al the world shulde overthrowe" (1640); it is associated with "fyr" and "smoke" (1644–45); and so on. The other trumpet blows, like Gabriel's "est, and west, and south, / And north" (1680–81), "as lowde as any thunder" (1681), another apocalyptic image; and this trumpet is sweet, like "a pot of bawme" — exegetical emblem of grace, and so forth[58] — and roses (1686–87); too sweet, in fact, suggesting hypocrisy rather than goodness. Whereas the Judgment of God "may do nothing but right" (*Pearl*, 496), the judgments of Fame are pure madness.

The house of Rumor is yet another false heaven, a small, rickety version of Dante's paradise. The narrator says:

> And ever mo, as swyft as thought,
> This queynte hous aboute wente,
> That never mo hyt stille stente.   [stopped]
> And therout com so gret a noyse
> That, had hyt stonden upon Oyse,   [the river Oise]
> Men myghte hyt han herd esely

To Rome, y trowe sikerly.
And the noyse which that I herde,
For al the world, ryght so hyt ferde,   [traveled]
As dooth the rowtynge of the ston
That from th'engyn ys leten gon.

                        [HF, 1924–34

The house parodies heaven philosophically conceived, the "rest" of Dante's (and Chaucer's) unmoved Prime Mover, whose idea of absolute motion is the inclination of the spheres. He is pure Mind (*mente*), hence the joke "so swyft as thought," and eternal, hence "ever mo"; and he is the source of Christendom's information which goes chiefly "To Rome." The simile of "the rowtynge of the ston" is an outlandish allusion to the music of the spheres (or the trinitarian music behind theirs), the noise supposedly made by the planets in motion. The eagle's exclamation, "Petre!" (2000) is thus comically appropriate: in such a paradise, the function of Peter, keeper of the keys to heaven, is to fly like hell and get the soul aboard.[59]

This house is constructed

      of twigges, falwe, rede,
And grene eke, and somme weren white,
Swiche as men to these cages thwite,   [weave]
Or maken of these panyers,   [breadbaskets]
Or elles hottes or dossers;   [two kinds of back-basket]

                        [HF, 1936–40

The colors yellow, red, and white are stock colors of the earthly paradise (in the *Roman*, the *Book of the Duchess*, the *Pearl*, and so forth — cf. *Pearl*, 27), and green either points (ironically here) to the vital and everlasting quality of this paradise (the colors of Beatrice and of the Trinity were, in Dante, green, red, and white) or, more directly, to the falseness and changeableness of the place (cf. the short poem "Against Women Unconstant").[60] The image of birdcages points to the stock identification of souls as birds; "panyers" parodies the idea of the Body of Christ as wheat or bread. (As for "hottes" and "dossers" I can't explain them except by a farfetched association, Persius' image of faults or sins carried on one's back where one cannot see them.)[61] Whereas in the New Jerusalem, as represented in the Apocalypse and in *Pearl*, the gates are always open (*Pearl*, 1065), in the house of Rumor, Geffrey says,

> And be day, in every tyde,
> Been al the dores opened wide,
> And by nyght, echon, unshette;
>
> [HF, 1951–53

But there is never rest in the house of Rumor (1956); in fact the place of Rumor's "congregacioun" is more like Dante's hell, where Dante can hardly believe Death had undone so many (*Inferno*, III, 55–57). Chaucer's echo goes:

> in the world nys left
> So many formed by Nature,
> Ne ded so many a creature.
>
> [HF, 2038–40

Here Christian revelation, the "new tidings" of the gospel, is burlesqued:

> And every wight that I saugh there
> Rouned everych in others ere   [mouthed]
> A newe tydynge prively,
> Or elles tolde al openly
> Ryght thus, and seyde: "Nost not thou
> That ys betyd, lo, late or now?"
> "No," quod he, "telle me what."
> And than he tolde hym this and that,
> And swor therto that hit was soth —
> "Thus hath he sayd," and "Thus he doth,"
> "Thus shal hit be."
>
> [HF, 2043–53

The undependability of the new tidings of what "was" and "is" and "ever shall be" is patent. It seems unlikely — indeed, as Paull F. Baum says, "monstrous" — that any true "man of gret auctorite" should be discovered in such a place.[62]

Chaucer's poem comically reflects Dante's not only in that it is an allegorical search for paradise and in that, like the *Troilus*, it borrows some of Dante's invocations, but in another way as well. For Chaucer as for Dante, Venus adumbrates the more elevated Christian idea of love, and earthly love is the grammar school of celestial love. The great difference is that, whereas Dante's Beatrice was a sublime Platonic idea, Geffrey's wife — if the usual interpretation of the "mannes vois" is at least on one level correct — was a common, human frau.[63] We will never know how fully Chaucer developed (in a lost, complete version of the poem) or meant to develop (in the version we have) the idea set up at the start of the *House of Fame*, and it may seem foolhardy to look closely (for perhaps the thousandth time) at the function of the briefly mentioned "oon I koude nevene." However, we have seen already that there is a good deal of order in this poem, as in all of Chaucer's writings, so the investigation is not altogether immaterial. We have two passages to go on, lines 111–18, which tell of Geffrey's visit to the shrine of Saint Leonard and the lines which tell how the eagle spoke

> In mannes vois, and seyde, "Awak!
> And be nat agast so, for shame!"
> And called me tho by my name,
> And, for I shulde the bet abreyde,   [wake up]
> Me mette, "Awak," to me he seyde,
> Ryght in the same vois and stevene   [tone or pitch]
> That useth oon I koude nevene;   [name]
> And with that vois, soth for to seyn,
> My mynde cam to me ageyn,
> For hyt was goodly seyd to me,
> So nas hyt never wont to be.
>
> [HF, 554–65

The first lines mentioned seem to identify Geffrey as a henpecked husband who might naturally seek (futilely, alas) tales of successful and happy love and might naturally moralize on the Dido story,

> Hyt is not al gold that glareth.
> For also browke I wel myn hed,   [bet, or pawn]

Ther may be under godlyhed
Kevered many a shrewed vice.   [HF, 272–75

Seemingly he, too, has been disappointed. But the eagle's cry
"in mannes vois" throws strange light on this. Whereas in the
Book of the Duchess and somewhat more etherially in Dante
(and throughout medieval poetry) a beautiful lady can raise a
man from death to life, in the *House of Fame* a nagging wife's
voice raises the dead — for such is the narrator's situation: "al
my felynge gan to dede" (552). The result of the eagle's cry
in the voice of Geffrey's wife is that,

> here-withal I gan to stere,
> And he me in his fet to bere,
> Til that he felte that I had hete,
> And felte eke tho myn herte bete.
> And thoo gan he me to disporte,
> And with wordes to comforte,
> And seyde twyes, "Seynte Marye!"
>
> [HF, 567–73

Incredibly, even the unromantic but substantial love of
married people can elevate and comfort just as Jove's messenger (or Christ, who also spoke "in mannes vois") comforts and
as, traditionally, "Seynte Marye" provides comfort. It should
be noted that Geffrey's two apparent references to his wife are
separated by nearly 450 lines and that no other joke of this
kind appears in all of Chaucer's poetry, though other men's
troubles with their wives come up often enough. The wife is, I
think, no accidental intrusion into the poem but a realistic and
comic affirmation of Dante's more elevated Neoplatonic view
of love. If all this is true, the wife may have been meant to
appear at least once more, at the end of the poem, if only to
cry "Awak!"

§6

THE HEART of Geffrey's problem is that, like Dante before his
ordeal, he is not loving but proud. He's proud of what he

knows, proud of what he doesn't know, proud of his art and of his artlessness. With the eagle, he delights in lecturing on all he's discovered in books; in the Proem, on the other hand, he takes pride in the fact that he does *not* know — and doesn't pretend to know — what causes dreams. You will not get from *him* (as from those highfalutin French poets) arrogant pretensions to knowledge of dream lore! However, his cheerfully hectic list of what he doesn't pretend to make sense of handily shows off his in fact encyclopedic knowledge of the subject.[64] The real reason he will not pronounce upon dream theory, one cannot help suspecting, is his nominalist pretense to piety (cf. the comic piety of the narrator in the *Book of the Duchess* or the "Chaucer" of the *Canterbury Tales*). In a burlesque of right reason, he leaves the whole business of dreams to God in his opening line — "God turne us every drem to goode!" So William of Ockham or Roger Bacon would do. And at the end of his digression he returns to the same stance. As if with great humility, he says

> Wel worthe, of this thyng, grete clerkys,
> That trete of this and other werkes;
> For I of noon opinion
> Nyl as now make mensyon,
> But oonly that the holy roode
> Turne us every drem to goode!
>
> [HF, 53–58

But his next lines give him away:

> For never, sith that I was born,
> Ne no man elles me beforn,
> Mette, I trowe stedfastly,
> So wonderful a drem as I.
>
> [HF, 59–62

He is the best dreamer ever, the luckiest of men.

Also, he would have us understand, he knows about poetry. He points out, at the start of his invocation to Book I, that he knows the forms:

> But at my gynnynge, trusteth wel
> I wol make invocacion,
> With special devocion,
> Unto the god of slep anoon.
>
> [HF, 66–69

But if he knows the forms, he seems not to understand poetic substance as medieval critics understood it. His invocation to the god of sleep, to a medieval critic used to interpreting pagan deities as adumbrations of Christian figures, would be an invocation to the Devil, ruler of sleep and death; but Geffrey apparently doesn't see this, even though his own diction (reworking a passage from the *Book of the Duchess*) insists on it:

> the god of slep anoon,
> That duelleth in a cave of stoon
> Upon a strem that cometh fro Lete,
> That is a flood of helle unswete,
> Besyde a folk men clepeth Cymerie, —
> There slepeth ay this god unmerie
> With his slepy thousand sones,
> That alwey for to slepe hir wone is.
>
> [HF, 69–76

His second invocation, to the Prime Mover, and his third, to Christ, make comically obvious his concern about what people think of his poem — his concern, in other words, with fame. Nothing could be farther from the stance of the *Troilus* narrator, who bids his poem, "But subgit be to alle poesye" and "be understonde, God I beseche!"

In the invocations which introduce his second book, the narrator shows the same comic pride in his extraordinary dream, calling it

> So sely an avisyon,
> That Isaye, ne Scipion,
> Ne kyng Nabugodonosor,
> Pharoo, Turnus, ne Elcanor,
> Ne mette such a drem as this!
>
> [HF, 513–17

And for the invocation to his third book, Geffrey turns again to the false humility of his Proem, explaining to Apollo, for instance:

> Nat that I wilne, for maistrye,
> Here art poetical be shewed;
> But for the rym ys lyght and lewed,
> Yet make hyt sumwhat agreable,
> Though som vers fayle in a sillable;
> And that I do no diligence
> To shewe craft, but o sentence.
>
> [HF, 1094–1100

This book, of course, contains *all* of the poem's imitations of epic simile, a majority of the ornamental lists, and the poem's most fully elaborated allegory.

All this is not to say that Geffrey is speaking ironically when he says to the man at his back in Book III (1868–82) that he did not come to the house of Fame for personal fame. He knows his Boethius (972 et seq.) and undoubtedly knew before his trip all about Fame except the mechanics of her house and rule. The joke is that, knowing the worthlessness of human fame (even without the help of the dream vision which he lacks the wit to understand), Geffrey rejects fame as an ideal, feels pleased with himself at having done so, and makes every effort to convince his audience of his extraordinary virtue. Once again, possibly, the greatest and proudest of Italian poets is the butt of the joke. Not exclusively, however. The caricature is of Chaucer himself, whose wife, whose customhouse reckonings, and whose poetic efforts are all conspicuously introduced. As always in Chaucer, the moral statement has humorous detachment, the basis of that charity the narrator (at line 108) insists that he lacks.

But there's at least one further irony in the *House of Fame*, the irony at the heart of the poem's effect, its crazy, splendid quality of celebration. Though God is in his heaven (as Koonce's shadow poem makes clear), and though Geffrey is too myopic, physically and spiritually, to glimpse the higher meaning of his remarkable adventures, the dream which makes a fool of him nevertheless fills him with joy and, indeed, a frantic eagerness to tell us all about it. Since conflicts of authority (the conflict of Virgilian and Ovidian poetic traditions, for instance) and Geffrey's pride-dimmed reason give him, together, no way of grasping what the vision really says, the whole dream is for him pure experience — life lived — something he can never hope to understand, can only thank God for — however ludicrous, even prideful, his piety. In other words, neither by the prattling revelations of an eagle, by lower authority (tradition and logic), nor by experience can poor foolish man *know*; but God's old authority has the universe in hand, and God's gift, man's experience, is a splendid thing in its own right. The poem forecasts (and goes somewhat beyond) the wisdom of the sly old Wife of Bath: "I thank it God / That I have had my world as in my time."

The *Legend of Good Women*

*How and Why Chaucer Revised his First
Prologue to Make his Second, and How and
Why he Made the Stories*

HAUCER'S DISCIPLE GAVIN DOUGLAS
once said, "Chaucer was always a friend to
women." The truth of that statement shows
everywhere in Chaucer's poetry — in his sympathy for Criseyde, in his delight in the wit and
vitality of the Wife of Bath, in his sharp perception of how
women feel, from the caged wife to the jubilant wench (as in
the *Miller's Tale*) to the yielding and devoted ideal of the
Middle Ages, Griselda on one hand, on the other childlike
Thisbe; but nowhere does his friendship toward women show
more clearly than in the much neglected, delightful *Legend of
Good Women.*

He tells us in his prologue that he is writing the poem by
order of someone he calls "Alceste," as a punishment for
writing earlier stories of faithless women, and that he's to take
it, when he's finished, to the queen at one of the two favorite
royal manors, Eltham or Sheene. All this is mostly artifice, of
course. Chaucer had never slandered women in his poetry and
had nothing to repent; and though John Gower sometimes
wrote poems because a royal patron asked him to, poetry like

Chaucer's rarely comes from commands, though it does sometimes come — like *Alice in Wonderland* — in response to some dear friend's request. The prologue, in other words, does *not* tell us, as many critics have believed, that the plan of the *Legend of Good Women* came from someone other than Chaucer and was one he recognized from the start as burdensome. It probably does tell us that someone close to Queen Anne — the most likely guess is King Richard's mother, Princess Joan — asked Chaucer if he wouldn't please write something for her, or for Queen Anne, or for both of them (Princess Joan and Queen Anne were frequently together), or perhaps that something "Alceste" said gave Chaucer the idea, some remark like, for instance, "Geoffrey, why do poets never write about *nice* women?" But however it all happened, Chaucer did write the poem for the court of Queen Anne, and wrote it with great pleasure, as the zest and lightness — the beautifully balanced earnestness and teasing — of the whole poem show.

Among scholars of the present century, the *Legend* has only very recently begun to be popular.[1] The prologue to the *Legend*, or rather the two prologues, the so-called F text and G text, have always been a delight, but the collection of short tales which makes up the *Legend* proper has had, in recent times, not many adherents. It has been assumed pretty generally that Chaucer wrote half-heartedly and in haste, as he tells us himself (but the claim is part of an elaborate joke), and so the poem has largely gone unread. That's a shame, as I mean to show by palpable proofs. But first let us look at the prologues. I think the best way to see how they work — and at the same time to glimpse Chaucer's way of revising — is to compare the two versions and see how and why he revised.

§ 1

VARIOUS EXPLANATIONS HAVE BEEN PROPOSED to account for Chaucer's revision of Prologue F into Prologue G,[2] some of which have been generally dismissed, some of which have been generally accepted as correct as far as they go. None, so far, has managed to close the case. One can't help feeling that when the right answer comes it will be plain as day. But unfortunately, complex literary questions seldom admit of brilliantly simple solutions. The true solution, which I offer in this chapter, is complex, but no more so than the problem: what general principles explain *every single change* from Prologue F to Prologue G? What I think I show is that Chaucer revised for two main reasons, one practical (and already generally recognized), the other artistic. Though I privately believe some changes to be merely scribal errors, my theory doesn't require an appeal to scribal error but merely admits the possibility. If my argument seems involved, the reason is that neither of Chaucer's purposes in revising admitted of simple and direct solutions. He was dealing with a poem, an organic whole, and his object was a new, in certain respects more satisfying organic whole, so that changing one detail meant changing another — and so on through a complex process of evolution. Since my explanation depends partly on a sorting of older opinions, partly on close analysis of the two prologues as separate and distinct poems, it will be useful to begin with a quick review of earlier theories.

Four theories have been advanced. One, Tatlock's theory, begins with the suggestion that to please Queen Anne and the "mentally feminized society" her reign encouraged, Chaucer "affected transports over a sweet little flower, which afterwards in a belated maturing he was to acknowledge tacitly as a trifle silly." When Anne died, Tatlock writes, Chaucer revised the prologue, both to get rid of the silliness and to please Richard II by removing all reference to the queen; for Richard was "a highly neurotic man, emotionally very dependent on her, who after her death among other signs of feeling ordered the house at Sheene where she died torn down, though a favorite residence." [3] The second theory, which F. N. Robinson accepted, is that Chaucer wanted to improve the general organization and clarity of the prologue. A third theory, which Professor Malone tentatively held, is that the revision reflects Chaucer's altered sense of what constitutes good poetic style. The fourth theory, first advanced by D. D.

Griffith, argues that Chaucer's object was to revise out "the obvious use of the Christian service," for which Chaucer in his mature years felt increasing respect.[4]

None of the theories is fully acceptable. It is true that Queen Anne is missing from Text G, and Chaucer's wish to spare Richard's feelings may indeed be behind the change. But the notion that the author of the *Parliament of Birds, House of Fame,* and *Troilus* suffered a belated maturing is ridiculous. As for the second of the two main theories, it is true that Prologue G is notable for its logical structure and, in some respects, clarity, but it is not true that the comic confusion in Prologue F is a defect. Moreover, the clarity of Text G is by no means always greater than that of Text F. Throughout Text G — unless one attributes every one of the many minor changes to careless Adam, scrivener — Chaucer seems to have demonically thrown particular idea and image relationships out of focus. For example, in Text F (3–4) we read: "And I acorde wel that it ys so; / But, natheles, yet wot I wel also." The corresponding lines in G (3–4) substitute an imprecise "this" for "yet." Again, where the progressive relationship of *feyth, ful credence,* and *reverence* is clear in F, where Chaucer's use of the words in a new context maintains the normal progression of religious emotions, Chaucer breaks up the relationship and dilutes the church language in G. Here are the passages:

> And to hem yive I *feyth* and *ful credence,*
> And in myn herte have hem in *reverence.*
>
> [F, 31–32

> And to the doctryne of these olde wyse
> Yeven *credence,* in every skylful wyse,
> And trowen on these olde aproved storyes
> Of holynesse, of regnes, of victoryes,
> Of love, of hate, of othere sondry thynges,
> Of which I may nat make rehersynges.
> And if that olde bokes weren aweye,
> Yloren were of remembraunce the keye.
> Wel oughte us thanne on olde bokes leve,   [believe]
> There as there is non other assay by preve.   [proof]

And as for me, though that my wit be lite,
On bokes for to rede I me delyte,
And in myn herte have hem in *reverence*,
And to hem yeve swich lust and swich *credence*
That there is wel unethe game non
That fro my bokes make me to gon.

[G, 19–34

The word *feyth* drops entirely in the revision, replaced by *lust;*[5] *credence* is introduced earlier, in proximity to *doctryne,* on one hand, *trowen* (cf. *leven*) on the other;[6] the progression from faith to belief to reverence is suppressed. All this is not to deny that idea and image relationships are sometimes improved in G; it is merely to say that the theory that Chaucer was out to improve the clarity of his earlier prologue is inadequate.

The third theory, which I'm unfairly imputing to Professor Malone (see note 4), is also unsatisfactory. Dissatisfied with the clean, musical sound of his opening line, "A thousand tymes have I herd men telle," Chaucer substituted, according to this line of argument, a rougher, for him more pleasing line, "A thousand sythes have I herd men telle."[7] Here *sythes* picks up the *s* and *i* in modified form, the *th* of *thousand,* killing the alliteration of *tymes* and *telle,* to produce cacophony. Again in line 5 Chaucer suppresses the musical quality of "That ther nis noon dwellyng in this contree" for the dryer sound and less regular meter of Text G's "That there ne is non that dwelleth in this contre." The same principle explains the change from F, 10 to G, 11, in which "But God forbede but men shulde leve" gives way to "But Goddes forbode, but men shulde leve." According to this stylistic theory, Chaucer must also have come to dislike tight writing and so expanded well-made lines with flab. And occasionally, we must say, he changed lines out of sheer whimsy, throwing away F, 39, "Farewel my bok, and my devocioun!" and introducing G, 39, "Farewel my stodye, as lastynge that sesoun!" The doubtful assumption behind this theory is that a poet's style in textural matters reflects his stage of development, simply, and has nothing to do with his larger artistic purpose. If this were true, the speeches of Hotspur and Owen Glendower would be indistinguishable.

    If one closely examines the texture of the two prologues, making the tentative assumption that the two fundamentally different styles reflect differences not in Chaucer's taste but in his artistic purpose, one notices at once that one striking feature of Chaucer's revision is the one Professor Griffith first noted: again and again possible religious overtones present in Text F disappear or weaken into pure convention in Text G. For example, the phrase which occurs in F, 39, "and my devocioun," is replaced by a phrase without religious possibilities, G, 39, "as lastynge that sesoun." Again, in Text F we read:

> To hem [daisies] have I so gret affeccioun,
> As I seyde erst, whanne comen is the May,
> That in my bed ther daweth me no day   [dawneth]
> That I nam up and walkyng in the mede   ] meadow]
> To seen this flour ayein the sonne sprede,
> Whan it upryseth erly by the morwe.
> That blisful sighte softneth al my sorwe,
> So glad am I, whan that I have presence
> Of it, to doon it alle reverence,
> As she that is of alle floures flour,
> Fulfilled of al vertu and honour,
> And evere ilyke faire, and fressh of hewe;
> And I love it, and ever ylike newe,
> And ever shal, til that myn herte dye.
>
>   [F, 44–57

The revision reads simply:

> To hem have I so gret affeccioun,
> As I seyde erst, whan comen is the May,
> That in my bed there daweth me no day
> That I n'am up and walkynge in the mede
> To sen these floures agen the sonne sprede,
> Whan it up ryseth by the morwe shene,   [beautiful]
> The longe day thus walkynge in the grene.
>
>   [G, 44–50

The phrase "blisful sighte" can have religious nuances, like the phrase which follows in F, "softneth al my sorwe." (The

revision of "erly by the morwe" reflects merely the need for a
new rhyme when "sorwe" is removed.) The word *presence*,
too, has a spiritual range of nuances, still borne in such modern
locutions as "the divine presence," and the word *reverence*,
broader in the Middle Ages than today, has similar religious
range, though the word as often appears in medieval discussions of politics or love. The phrases "evere ilyke faire" and
"ever ylike newe" are extremely common in medieval
references to heaven's bliss. (Cf. *BD*, 1288.) Whatever the
purpose of the faintly religious language in Text F of the
prologue, Chaucer has clearly gotten rid of it in the passage
under discussion from Text G.

The trouble with Griffith's theory is, first, that there is
not a scintilla of evidence that Chaucer grew increasingly
religious as he got older; indeed, a growing number of critics,
sensible and otherwise, interpret all of Chaucer's poetry
allegorically and find it essentially religious. Second, the very
analogy Griffith thinks Chaucer out to suppress is at the heart
of the expanded speech by Cupid in Prologue G. And third,
Griffith's theory does not work equally well at all points in the
two prologues. The passage on the service of the birds (F, 125
et seq.), full of religious nuances, is maintained in G (113 et
seq.). And the description of Cupid (F, 226 et seq.; G, 158 et
seq.) has clearer religious nuances in the revision than in the
original. Thus Griffith points us in the right direction but fails
to explain why some religious passages are suppressed, others
kept or intensified.

To get at Chaucer's actual principles of revision, we need
a reasonably complete catalogue of the revisions. Most of the
changes do indeed involve religious nuances. One such passage
appears at F, 84–96, for which no corresponding passage
occurs in G:

> She is the clernesse and the verray lyght
> That in this derke world me wynt and ledeth.
> The hert in-with my sorwfull brest yow dredeth
> And loveth so sore that ye ben verrayly
> The maistresse of my wit, and nothing I.
> My word, my work ys knyt so in youre bond

That, as an harpe obeieth to the hond
And maketh it soune after his fyngerynge
Ryght so mowe ye oute of myn herte bringe
Swich vois, ryght as yow lyst, to laughe and pleyne.
Be ye my gide and lady sovereyne!
As to myn erthly god to yow I calle,
Bothe in this werk and in my sorwes alle.

[F, 84–96

Here again the vocabularies of love and religion interpenetrate. As churchmen identify God with light, "the verray sonne" of Chaucer's Boece, so the love poet associates the sun and his lady. As man is God's harp, according to Augustine,[8] so the lady plays her lover's heart. And as God, man's sovereign, leads man through the world's darkness, so the "lady sovereyne," an "erthly god" leads and, again like God, comforts. (Chaucer's humor requires us to understand that he is *not* talking, at least at this point, about either God or a lady but about an as yet unallegorical daisy.)

The next change, not especially noteworthy at first but interesting in the light of Chaucer's thus far consistent deletion of possible religious overtones in Text F, occurs at F, 99–100, which corresponds approximately to G, 83–84. In F we read that "men mosten more thyng beleve / Then men may seen at eye, or elles preve." The vague and therefore possibly suggestive "more thyng" of the earlier version is nailed down in the revision: we are not to believe mysteries but "autoritees."

Then at F, 103, Chaucer speaks of "My besy gost, that thursteth alwey newe." The possibility of an Augustinian reading, in which the human soul is seen as ever restless, ever thirsting, vanishes in the revision. Other religious possibilities also drop out when Chaucer revises the passage:

My besy gost, that thursteth alwey newe
To seen this flour so yong, so fressh of hewe,
Constreyned me with so gledly desir
That in myn herte I feele yet the fir
That made me to ryse, er yet were day —
And this was now the firste morwe of May —
With dredful hert and glad devocioun,

> For to ben at the resureccioun
> Of this flour, whan that yt shulde unclose
> Agayn the sonne, that roos as red as rose
> That in the brest was of the beste, that day,
> That Agenores doghtre ladde away.
>
> [F, 103–14

The revision reads:

> When passed was almost the month of May,
> And I hadde romed, al the someres day,
> The grene medewe, of which that I yow tolde,
> Upon the freshe dayseie to beholde,
> And that the sonne out of the south gan weste,
> And closed was the flour, and gon to reste,
> For derknesse of the nyght, of which she dredde,
> Hom to myn hous ful swiftly I me spedde.
>
> [G, 89–96

The image of the burning heart is dropped; the time is changed from the first of May, which patristic writers associate with resurrection,[9] to near the end of the month, where no such association is likely; and the word *resurrection* vanishes.

In F, 115 et seq., Chaucer gets down on his knees to the daisy. In G the image of kneeling is dropped for one equally effeminate and silly (a point which militates against the theory of Chaucer's belated maturing) but clearly more burlesque-pagan than burlesque-Christian:

> And in a lytel herber that I have,
> Ybenched newe with turves, fresshe ygrave,   [turfs]
> I bad men shulde me my couche make;
> For deynte of the newe someres sake,   [pleasure]
> I bad hem strowe floures on my bed.
>
> [G, 97–101

Up to this point, revisions of Text F remove possible religious implications, however faint these implications may seem. But in the passage which follows next in both versions, the principle of revision changes. The conventional earthly paradise image is maintained intact (F, 119 et seq., G, 107 et seq.), and possible religious overtones in the discussion of birds and the "foweler," whom a patristic exegete would associate with the Devil, are also preserved. Text F speaks of birds

> That from the panter and the net ben scaped,   [fowling trap]
> Upon the foweler, that hem made awhaped   [confounded]
> In wynter, and distroyed hadde hire brood,
> In his dispit hem thoghte yt did hem good
> To synge of hym, and in hir song despise
> The foule cherl that, for his coveytise,
> Had hem betrayed with his sophistrye.
> This was hire song, "The foweler we deffye,
> And al his craft." And somme songen clere
> Layes of love, that joye it was to here,
> In worship and in preysinge of hir make;   [mate]
> And for the newe blisful somers sake,
> Upon the braunches ful of blosmes softe,
> In hire delyt they turned hem ful ofte,
> And songen, "Blessed by Seynt Valentyn."

[F, 131–45

The whole passage is of course conventional. The fowler is the Devil; his snares are the traps he sets for unwary Christians;[10] his "coveytise" refers to his envy of man's right to paradise[11] and his "sophistrye" refers to the false arguments with which he tricked Eve and still seeks to trick mankind. The birds' "worship and . . . preysinge of hir make" would, from a narrow exegetical point of view, be a case of sinful concupiscence.[12]

Not only does Chaucer refrain from cutting out these possibilities, he cuts a joke in Text F which might work against a serious reading of the passage. At F, 148 et seq., he tells how the birds kiss and do other "observaunces / That longeth onto love and to nature," then says impishly: "Construeth that as yow lyst, I do no cure." The suggestive line is missing in Text G, 134 et seq.

Another change has to do with the characterization of Cupid. Alceste says in Prologue F:

> A god ne sholde nat thus be agreved,   [annoyed]
> But of hys deitee he shal be stable,

And therto gracious and merciable.
And yf ye nere a god, that knowen al,
Thanne myght yit be as I yow tellen shal:
This man to yow may falsly ben accused,
Ther as by right him oughte ben excused.
For in youre court ys many a losengeour,   [flatterer]
And many a queynte totelere accusour,   [sly, tattling accuser]
That tabouren in youre eres many a sown,   [drums]
Ryght after hire ymagynacioun,
To have youre daliance, and for envie.
These ben the causes, and I shal not lye.
Envie ys lavendere of the court alway,   [laundress]
For she ne parteth, neither nyght ne day,
Out of the hous of Cesar.

[F, 345–60

Compare Text G:

. . . A god ne sholde not thus been agreved,
But of his deite he shal be stable,
And therto ryghtful, and ek mercyable.
He shal nat ryghtfully his yre wreke,   [ire avenge]
Or he have herd the tother partye speke.
Al ne is nat gospel that is to yow pleyned;
The god of Love hereth many a tale yfeyned.
For in youre court is many a losengeour
And many a queynte totelere accusour,
That tabouren in youre eres many a thyng
For hate, or for jelous ymagynyng,
And for to han with you som dalyaunce.
Envye — I prey to God yeve hire myschaunce! —
Is lavender in the grete court alway,
For she ne parteth, neyther nyght ne day,
Out of the hous of Cesar.

[G, 321–36

The fourth and fifth lines from the Text F passage above
contain an ironic suggestion, dropped from Text G, that the
god of love is not as almighty as he pretends to be. For the
word *gracious* (F, 347) Chaucer substitutes the less courtly,
more Christian word *ryghtful.* Text G adds the phrase

"ryghtfully his yre wreke." The rhyming line (G, 325) might be included only for the rhyme, but it does suggest that in some situations wrath is legitimate. The word *gospel,* introduced in the next line, has no parallel in F and of course has a strong Christian association. Other new details, notably "For hate" and the exclamation "I preye to God" contribute to Chaucer's shift in tone toward the more serious.

As we might now expect, the description of the god is also changed, and the force of the change is evident at a glance. In F:

Yclothed was this myghty god of Love
In silk, enbrouded ful of grene greves   [embroidered; branches]
In-with a fret of rede rose-leves   [ornament]
The fresshest syn the world was first bygonne.   [since]
His gilte heer was corowned with a sonne,
Instede of gold, for hevynesse and wyghte.
Therwith me thoghte his face shoon so bryghte
That wel unnethes myghte I him beholde;   [uneasily]
And in his hand me thoghte I saugh him holde
Two firy dartes.

[F, 226–35

In the revision the god has lilies as well as roses, and he blazes still more blindingly, like a Dantesque angel (apparent source of Chaucer's image):

Yclothed was this myghty god of Love
Of silk, ybrouded ful of grene greves,
A garlond on his hed of rose-leves,
Stiked al with lylye floures newe.
But of his face I can not seyn the hewe;
For sikerly his face shon so bryghte
That with the glem astoned was the syghte;
A furlong-wey I myhte hym not beholde.
But at the laste in hande I saw hym holde
Two firy dartes.

[G, 158–67

The god in Text G also talks like a Christian. He refers to Saint Jerome (284), then points out that those women true to the service of Love have done as much as Christian women have done in steadfast pursuit of the best they know, for, like the Christian martyrs,

> some were brend, and some were cut the hals   [neck]
> And some dreynt, for they wolden not be fals.   [drowned]
> For alle keped they here maydenhede,
> Or elles wedlok, or here widewehede.
> And this thing was nat kept for holynesse,
> But al for verray vertu and clennesse,
> And for men schulde sette on hem no lak;
> And yit the were hethene, al the pak.
>
> [G, 292–99

No one need be shown that both Text F and Text G are comic. In both, the narrator is a comic figure so stupid he scarcely notices what sinful trash he translates (F, 364–65; G, 341–43), a burlesque nature lover who in F kneels to a daisy and in G sleeps in a bed of flowers. But it is apparent that verbal detail pushes the comedy in one direction in the first version and in another in the second.

Chaucer revised his first text, excellent though it was, for two reasons. First, as Tatlock and others have argued, he meant to revise out references to Queen Anne and her poetastering court (note the deletion of F, 69–72 and change from *ye*, F, 73, to *folk*, G, 61, and similar changes in the lines which immediately follow in each text). Second, he revised Prologue F because it was not consistent with the *Legend* it was designed to introduce — probably because Chaucer changed his mind about how the stories should be told. (The first legend, "Cleopatra," is pure satire; if they were all pure satire — as one might expect them to be in the Middle Ages — the earlier prologue would work.) Prologue F gently satirizes what I have been calling the love religion by presenting a foolish god of love and, in the narrator, a comically simpleminded worshipper. The revision honors love devotees through slightly more elevated characterization of the god of love and through comic presentation of a narrator who, stupidly, is *not* a worshipper.

Chaucer's use of Neoplatonic love doctrine in the *Legend of Good Women* is at once serious and tongue in cheek. His explicit statements present orthodox tenets of the love religion, but irony hints that the orthodox views, though right in principle, need qualifying. For instance, the courtly love doctrine that the lady is superior to her lover and thus can lead him upward becomes, in the *Legend*, comic melodrama: the narrator insists (as his assignment requires) that women are excellent, men foul and wretched, and that exceptions like Piramus prove the rule. The truth is slightly more compli-cated. Love *ought* to be ennobling, and the virtuous constancy of the love martyrs in the stories (some of them men) points toward the ideal; but, by undercutting, Chaucer grants that the ideal is easily misunderstood and hard to reach. The first of the two prologues makes fun of love by openly burlesquing its silliness. The second, like the stories themselves, asserts the ideal but qualifies the assertion by comically exaggerating, among other things, the true lover's virtue and the non-lover's stupidity.

Chaucer's narrator in the original prologue is a caricature of the devotee, a creature too dainty, too gentle, too childlike for this world. Our pleasure in him is double: we recognize both that his world is lovely, far lovelier than ours, and that his delight in the world is ludicrous, grounded, in fact, on sentimental and distinctly effeminate misapprehension of the world we too live in. His mental limitation is patent. The sweetness of his verse is excessive, and he is incapable of recounting his experience without getting mixed up or losing himself in digression.

This sweet dim-wittedness is at the heart of the logical structure of the early prologue. In precise, musical verse the narrator tells us that he most certainly believes, as do all decent people, "That ther ys joy in hevene and peyne in helle," even though he has never seen either place. Then he argues, with charming simplemindedness (especially for a man who'd read Roger Bacon), that since a thing may be true even though we have no empirical evidence, we ought to believe every word we read in old books, as long as no empirical evidence shows what we read to be false. (A confusion of divine authority and authority by tradition.) The argument is of course closely related to the comic argument developed in the *House of Fame*, wherein Geffrey gives up "preve" for old books (991–1017).[13] But in Prologue F to the *Legend* the comic argument is more explicitly "religious": since Christian notions of heaven and hell are not grounded in empirical knowledge but are nonetheless true, it follows that old stories also found in books but not empirically known must also be true — *and therefore holy*. This implication is carried by diction:

> On bokes for to rede I me delyte,
> And to hem yive I feyth and ful credence,
> And in myn herte have hem in reverence
> So hertely, that ther is game noon
> That fro my bokes maketh me to goon.
>
> [F, 30–34

As we have seen already, both diction and the psychological progression here establish the religious character of the narrator's study. But the narrator does leave his book religion occasionally ("But yt by seldom") on holy days. And invariably ("certeynly")

> whan that the month of May
> Is comen, and that I here the foules synge,
> And that the floures gynnen for to sprynge,
> Farewel my bok, and my devocioun!
>
> [F, 36–39

If it is true, as the narrator imagines, that reading old books is a form of religious devotion, then the narrator's tripping off to look at daisies is something of a fall from virtue, though the gleeful narrator fails to notice his slip. And if it is also true that Chaucer's reference to the "leef" and the "flour" (F, 72) has to do with the fact that (as Robinson says in his note to line 72) "Court society . . . was apparently divided into two parties or amorous orders devoted respectively to the Flower and to the Leaf," and if the whole prologue looks to the convention of the marguerite poem, then for Chaucer's courtly audience the joke must have been obvious: instead of satirizing

daisy-poets from a somber Christian point of view, Chaucer
sets up daisy worship (a pagan sort of business) as a departure
from virtue in non-Christian terms — that is, as a departure
from the virtuous service of books. Since we do not take the
book religion seriously, the ironic comment on service to
the Flower and Leaf has humor without bite, especially since
the narrator himself is a daisy worshipper par excellence and
completely misses the impiety in it. In the lines which follow
this pseudo-logical introduction (F, 44–59) we have as
pretty — and as ludicrous — a piece of daisy worship as
literature affords. The narrator loves his daisy as a courtly
lover loves his lady, "no wight hotter in his lyve." And when
evening comes the narrator runs — as a *not* so courtly lover
might run to peek at his girl undressing — to watch the lovely
daisy go to bed. Oh that he had English, "ryme or prose," he
cries, "Suffisant this flour to preyse aryght!" (F, 66–67).
Perhaps lovers will help him; since he comes late, all the
prettiest phrases have been used up — indeed, he is embar-
rassed to confess, he may at times have to steal others' phrases,
for which he hopes he will be excused. The humor of course
lies both in the narrator's incompetence and in Chaucer's sly
dig at the marguerite-poets' fondness for cliches.

At this point the narrator breaks into his account to say,
"As for what I started out to tell you — about old stories and
how we ought to reverence them and about how people ought
to believe in things they haven't seen — I'll get back to all that
when I can; a person can't say everything at once and keep
track of his rhymes too." Whereupon he returns merrily to his
digression. This interruption is often described as a structural
flaw, but in fact it reinforces the reader's sense of the childlike
simplemindedness of the narrator and, more important, recalls
the narrator's book religion, his earlier subject, that form of
devotion which throws ironic light on daisy worship. It is
appropriate that the reader be reminded just here of the book
religion, for the lines on the daisy which immediately follow
will go so far beyond conventional application of church
language to the ritual of love that they tend to identify the
daisy not with a courtly lady but with Christ himself. We are
within the bounds of conventional hyperbole in such expres-

sions as "the clernesse and the verray lyght / That in this
derke world me wynt and ledeth" (84–85). But the introduction of spiritual thirst is a trifle extreme, and when we
encounter the "resureccioun" of the daisy we are well outside
the usual limits. Now consider the rest of the passage. The
narrator rises

> With dredful hert and glad devocioun,
> For to ben at the resureccioun
> Of this flour, whan that yt shulde unclose
> Agayn the sonne, that roos, as red as rose
> That in the brest was of the beste, that day,
> That Agenores doghtre ladde away.
>
> [F, 109–14

After "resureccioun" and the surrounding words with a
religious range of nuance it is not unnatural to read "sonne" as
a pun and "rose" as a Christian emblem of heavenly love. At
this point and also in the next line (reading "beste" as a pun)
there comes a comic reversal: the ironic juxtaposition of the
daisy cult and one of the narrator's "olde appreved stories."

The earthly paradise images and the fowler passage
(discussed above) continue the good-humored satire of the
amorous cults. The birds' hymns to their mates remind us,
though not too seriously, that a mate is not really the source of
all bliss, and oaths taken "on blossoms" perhaps pass as "soone
as floures faire." But the narrator remains enraptured: he sinks
"ful softely" to the ground and there, lying on his side and
leaning on his elbow (like Dante Gabriel Rossetti, who meant
it) watches one little daisy from dawn until sunset.

The narrator's dream, like his waking experience, gently
satirizes the amorous cults. The rather confused narration,
interrupted for instance by a song of praise to the beautiful
lady, burlesques the ecstasies of Leaf and Flower poets, and the
god of love is characterized, ironically enough, as mean and
vengeful, also pretentious in that he does not really have the
omniscience he claims to have. Alceste is almost as fierce as the
god. When the poet tries to tell her that he has always been on
the side of love, she hushes him: she is not interested in

arguments but only in reading him the cruel sentence. He is to spend the rest of his natural days writing legends of good women, with some mention of the wickedness of men, and when the book is finished he's to take it to Queen Anne.

Now the god of love asks the poet if he knows who has befriended him, and when the poet says he does not, the god tells him that the lady is Alceste, whose story is found in old books and who was transformed into a daisy. The moment is significant. Until now, daisy worship and devotion to books have stood in ironic counterpoise, as in turn, Christianity and devotion to books stood in counterpoise at the outset. But in the figure of Alceste the two paganish schemes are brought together: leaving one's books to look at a daisy is not, after all, a failure of piety. (The comic discovery, notice, exactly parallels the poet's discovery, in the *Parliament*, that love of nature need not necessarily be a fall from love of God.)[14] If book worship and daisy worship are finally analogous, possibly Christian devotion, book worship, and daisy worship are also capable of being brought into harmony.

As everywhere in Chaucer, pagan religion adumbrates Christian. Just as certain pagan thinkers, particularly poets and philosophers, touched and almost grasped the truth, so love martyrs who died true to the best they knew may be seriously considered "types" of Christian constancy. Such will be the explicit comment of the god of love in Chaucer's revision of the prologue.

Prologue G differs from Prologue F, then, chiefly in that it presents a new, more serious view of love, with the result that the narrator must be made, throughout, more realistic without ceasing to be comic, and with the further result that the logical (or pseudo-logical) structure of the original prologue must be abandoned in favor of one much simpler and, unfortunately, less delightful.

What Chaucer may have felt, looking back over the *Legend* sometime after the writing of Prologue F, was that the relationship between the prologue and the *Legend* was one of flat contradiction. If *amor cortois* is conceived as a religion analogous to true religion, then the saints of love must be treated with some respect. If the god of love is a complete fake, then those who die for this god, however admirably they may die, die deluded. Perhaps the first change Chaucer made, then, was his characterization of the god of love. He described the god in more distinct Christian terms and gave the god a long speech on the relationship between love martyrs and Christian martyrs.

But to view the god of love as a servant or vicegerent of God is necessarily to reconsider the poets of love. If human love typifies divine love, then the poets who sing of human love are not to be scorned. The fool, indeed, is the poet who does *not* praise human love but deprecates it. The F-narrator's comic rhapsodies on the daisy must go, for they satirize the wrong thing, and the ironic analogy of daisy worship and Christian worship must also go, for the parallel between the two is ultimately valid. If ironic religious overtones must be dropped from passages involving the daisy, so, in turn, must the ironically religious treatment of the narrator's love of books, that form of worship which casts ironic light on daisy worship. The result is a more realistic, less "poetic" narrator, one who does not speak as precisely or as musically as the F-narrator but speaks like a real man, using loose transitions, hitting upon rougher, more colloquial language, and so forth. Realistically characterized, the narrator does not go into transports over daisies or anything else; he does not whimsically break into his narrative with a song but gives it to the god's attendants (hence the "improved" structure); he does not actually hear birds talking but only dreams he does. He remains a credulous reader of books and a flower-enthusiast, but since he can no longer be a creature of misdirected piety, he must be made interesting in some other way. Chaucer's solution was to make him a man who, reading old stories constantly, missed the obvious best and picked the worst, or, as the god of love has it, picked up "The draf of storyes and forgete the corn." The god's line neatly echoes the narrator's poetry metaphor earlier (G, 61 et seq.), suggesting here that the narrator has picked bad poetry instead of good — indeed, the chaff, which the wind driveth away. The point looks back to the Augustinian notion that in reading scripture, especially books like the Song of Songs, one must look for the *fruyt*, as

Chaucer says elsewhere, and throw away the *chaf*. Thus Chaucer caricatures himself in the second prologue approximately as he will caricature himself in the *Canterbury Tales*, where he tells, as the only poem he knows, the "drasty" rhyme of *Sir Thopas*.

§ 2

HATING THE INDIVIDUAL LEGENDS in the *Legend of Good Women* is like hating dogs and children: it's a mark of vulgar overseriousness, pedantic stupidity, stillborn imagination. On the other hand, to defend them on the grounds of their subtlety, or their escape from the hobble of medieval tradition, is like defending dogs and children on the grounds that when they grow up they may be Rin Tin Tin or Socrates. What Chaucer does in the legends is in a way intensely serious: he writes a group of poems of a kind unknown before in England, poems seriously concerned with women — with a few exceptions, like "Cleopatra" — that is, not poems in which women are simply the pasteboard objects of the devotion of courtly lovers, not poems in which women are mere symbols of false felicity, not poems in which women are inscrutable creatures to be laughed at, but poems about lifelike wives and maidens who worry, make mistakes, prove themselves worthy of the same honor men get. That serious purpose is a striking thing to find in fourteenth-century England and Chaucer of course knew it, but the knowledge did not drive him to self-righteous solemnity. With his usual light touch he lays out in his prologue (either prologue) what he means to do but also in his prologue (either prologue) sets up his principle of undercutting. He's doing all this against his will. A whole poem about good women? Ridiculous!

The result is a brilliant collection of lighthearted serious tales, tales of the kind one writes for one's family at Christmas, or for an old friend on the occasion of his marriage. The prologue is thus not a mere ornament, a picture frame, but Chaucer's means of establishing his relation with his audience, his tone. The subject matter is important (Alceste has told him it's important, and whatever he may think he must treat it as important), but its importance will not prevent him from venturing an occasional joke, an occasional trick on the ladies in his audience (if he thinks he can get away with it) or an occasional complaint that the punishment is really *too* severe. To put this another way, the prologue establishes the character of the narrator, the whole work's "voice," that magic, binding force in any first-rate poem or novel that makes a banquet of materials the expression of a single personality, so that even when, to the casual eye, nothing of much interest appears to be happening, the reader goes on reading as a child goes on listening to his grandfather's voice after "Once upon a time. . . ."

When one's said this much, there's in fact not much more to say about the legends.[15] They offer no complex symbolic structure which the critic can cunningly explicate; they do show, as Eleanor Jane Winsor proves, ingenious manipulation of source materials, but since nobody reads the sources anymore, talking about the ingenious manipulation is like discoursing at length on how Carrol's "You Are Old, Father William" makes fun of "The Battle of Blenheim."

What Chaucer brings off in the individual legends is deft storytelling of the kind he will use in the *Canterbury Tales* (except that there he gives himself more voices to play with) — storytelling in which swift, sure strokes lay out the necessary exposition, and all the rest is done by sharply imagined closeup scenes with transitions enriched by the narrator's chat. So in "Cleopatra," for instance, he manages to make Cleopatra the rich queen of Egypt and to sail Antonius over to her in just eight lines; in eighteen more he turns Antonius against Rome, gets him his divorce, and rehabilitates him as a chivalrous lover; and in nine more throws Cleopatra violently in love with him and gets the pair married. At the same time, of course, he's set up the legend's basic ironies, partly because of the narrative speed: "faithful" Cleopatra remarries after the death of her husband (though the legend will praise her for dying out of faithfulness), "faithless" Antonius who, married to Caesar's sister, "lafte hire falsly, or

that she was war [before she knew what was happening] / And wolde algates han another wyf" (593–94), becomes immediately "Worthi to any wyght that liven may."
The narrator of course pretends to notice none of this. He's
rushed the plot to the point of the first closeup, innocently, as
if mindlessly suggesting by that very rush the insanity of the
passion — he's even mentioned, hardly noticing it himself, that
"love hadde brought this man in swich a rage" (599) — so now
he pauses for chat, breaking the pace, shifting our attention
from the story to the storyteller and his wearysome burden,
the punishment imposed by Alceste:

> The weddynge and the feste to devyse,
> To me, that have ytake swich empryse   [enterprise]
> Of so many a story for to make,
> It were to longe, lest that I shulde slake
> For men may overlade a ship or barge.
> And forthy to th'effect thanne wol I skyppe,
> And al the remenaunt, I wol lete it slippe.
>
> [LGW, 616–23

Then — back to the old grind — he rushes in Octovyan and
gives the poem's first actual scene, a violent sea battle:

> Up goth the trompe, and for to shoute and shete,   [shoot]
> And paynen hem to sette on with the sunne.
> With grysely soun out goth the grete gonne,   [gun]
> And heterly they hurtelen al atones,
> And from the top doun come the grete stones.
> In goth the grapenel, so ful of crokes;
> Among the ropes renne the sherynge-hokes.
> In with the polax presseth he and he;
> Byhynde the mast begynnyth he to fle,
> And out ageyn, and dryveth hym overboard;
> And styngeth hym upon his speres ord;   [point]
> He rent the seyl with hokes lyke a sithe;   [scythe]
> He bryngeth the cuppe, and biddeth hem be blythe;
> He poureth pesen upon the haches lidere;
> With pottes ful of lyme they gon togidere;
> And thus the longe day in fyght they spende,
> Tyl at the laste, as every thyng hath ende,

Antony is schent, and put hym to the flyghte,   [ruined]
And al his folk to-go, that best go myghte.

[LGW, 635-53

Cleopatra flees "with al hire purpre sayl," Antony kills himself
in a fit of madness, and the narrator pulls back once more for
talk:

But herkeneth, ye that speken of kyndenesse,
Ye men that falsly sweren many an oth
That ye wol deye, if that youre love be wroth,
Here may ye sen of wemen whiche a trouthe!
This woful Cleopatre hath mad swich routhe
That ther is tonge non that may it telle.

[LGW, 665-70

Now comes the poem's second fully elaborated scene. Cleopatra makes a splendid shrine, makes the snake pit beside it,
delivers a solemn parting speech explaining that she'll die
because she promised to share Antony's joys and sorrows, and
kills herself. The narrator closes with four lines:

And this is storyal soth, it is no fable.
Now, or I fynde a man thus trewe and stable,
And wol for love his deth so frely take,
I preye God let oure hedes nevere ake!   Amen.

[LGW, 702-5

The effect is very fine, though to explain it is probably to
weaken it. Both closeup, fully elaborated scenes summon up
violence — the frantic, fighting ships (on which we see no sign
of Antony and Cleopatra, only "he and he," nameless, panting
commoners), and then the splendidly bejeweled shrine, the
corpse, the naked queen, the writhing snakes. The two scenes
of course stand out starkly from the rest — the narrator's
leisurely talk about writing, his leisurely allusion to the trivial
world of courtly love where men swear they will die if their
ladies "be wroth," his lighthearted mock pious, mock despond-
ent conclusion, "until I find such a true and stable man may
we never have headaches!" In short, in his first legend in

obedience to Alceste, Chaucer does what he's supposed to do, praises a faithful woman; but what his story implies is that love is violence and madness, one big headache. For his original audience, which had never heard — at least never in English — Cleopatra's story, the effect was no doubt even more striking. So now we're ready to expect a collection of legends which slyly scoff at love — legends in the predictable antifeminist tradition so common in the Middle Ages. Instead, we get the legend of Thisbe, the straightest love story Chaucer ever wrote.

In this legend, for all his love of tricks, Chaucer plays no tricks except of course the great one of making careful art seem artless. As Professor Frank has pointed out, Chaucer increases the childlike innocence of the lovers, supports it with colloquial and relaxed narrative diction, cuts anything that detracts from the story's purity and simplicity, gives the characters thoughts and emotions not present in his source. When Thisbe is sitting absolutely still in the dark cave, hiding from the lion, it occurs to her that Piramus may be out there, and Chaucer gives her the frightened thought: "If it so falle that my Piramus / Be comen hider, and may me not yfynde, / He may me holde fals and ek unkynde" (855–57). When she decides to kill herself with Piramus' sword because Piramus is dead, Chaucer gives her, instead of some high-style complaint, a gentle and colloquial understatement:

> "My woful hand," quod she,
> "Is strong ynogh in swich a werk to me;
> For love shal yeve me strengthe and hardynesse
> To make my wounde large ynogh, I gesse."
> [LGW, 890–93

Throughout the poem he avoids ironic comment, in fact virtually effaces himself as narrator until the end, when he lets out just a touch of low-key irony and then immediately retreats from it to a serious statement about women:

> Of trewe men I fynde but fewe mo
> In alle my bokes, save this Piramus,

And therefore have I spoken of hym thus.
For it is deynte to us men to fynde
A man that can in love been trewe and kynde.
Here may ye se, what lovere so he be,
A woman dar and can as wel as he.

[LGW, 917–23

I think I need not go through more legends; the main point is surely clear enough. Chaucer's ideas about love have not really changed since the *Book of the Duchess*. It can ennoble, as love ennobles Piramus and Thisbe; it can confound, as it does Antony and Cleopatra; or it can do anything in between. But in *Troilus* and the *Legend*, as in the *Canterbury Tales*, Chaucer has moved well beyond the usual position of the courtly-love poet to a serious and sympathetic interest in women as human beings whose virtues and defects are similar to men's. He has turned that fascination with the particular which we saw comically presented in the *House of Fame* to precise observation of particular kinds of women, applying here something of the same skeptical fideism (not really faith in ancient books but faith that God has things in hand and the world still has some good in it). It may be — in fact it's very likely — that in *Troilus* and the *Legend* he was consciously writing for women, in particular Queen Anne, and that the nature of his audience subtly led him to his discoveries. If so we have reason to be exceedingly grateful to that gentle, faithful wife King Richard brought to England from Bohemia.

vii

To Canterbury, and Beyond ✂✂✂✂

*Introductory Remarks on the Medieval
and the Modern in Chaucer's
CANTERBURY TALES*

ITH THE *CANTERBURY TALES* WE
come to Chaucer's most realistic and modern
work, though a work containing more medi-
eval elements than may at first meet the eye — curious old
philosophical categories, old fashioned attitudes, and the
elegant, ungainly allegorical machinery that gives the Middle
Ages their unique dignity and charm. In the *Legend of Good
Women*, Chaucer had virtually abandoned allegorical machinery for straight retelling of old stories coupled with direct
observation, "experience." Thisbe is a lifelike girl; she is not
on any level of the poem an emblem of, say, the contemplative
life, or one of the three faculties of the soul. In the *Canterbury
Tales* the machinery is back in all its creaking, gewgawed
splendor, bright-framed jewel-studded mirrors flashing, elves
and painted ladies peeking out from significant painted forests,
even the lifelike prattling Pilgrims arranged for their portrait
in symbolic groups; but the machinery by no means pulls the
poem back home to the sober Christianity of the early Middle
Ages. Chaucer had now such perspective on the machinery
that he could use it unsuperstitiously. The English critic
Trevor Whittock hits the point exactly:

> Chaucer, living towards the end of the medieval period,
> was actually conscious of the assumptions and implica-

tions inherent in modes of sensibility which were beginning to retreat before the new ways that finally made the Renaissance. That moment of time he inherited enabled him to set out and criticize these very assumptions and implications.[1]

The *Canterbury Tales* (a "Canterbury tale" is, in Middle English slang, a "lie") is the culmination of a lifetime of reflection, doubt, faith, and brilliant, meticulous writing. It holds all the poet's usual opinions and attitudes, along with some new ones, and all his favorite techniques. In a book meant for nonspecialists, it would be impossible to present a full line-by-line analysis of the whole work, much less a full appreciation of its magnificence as poetry, and for the reader who's labored through this book this far, no such analysis or detailed appreciation should be necessary; generalities and brief analysis should suffice. (If any reader desires more, he can easily get it from others by tunneling through my notes.) Let me begin with some remarks about what makes this poem, perhaps more than anything else in Chaucer, modern.

COMPLEXITY WAS PRIZED in medieval art. We find it in music, in architecture, in schematic painting, and in interlace work, as well as in poetry and prose; and we find it not only in aristocratic art but also in the art of the middle class — in popular lyrics and the mystery play, for instance. But medieval art — especially early medieval art — is not intricate in the same ways as the art of later periods: it is at once more baffling and more simple. As long as art remains truly medieval, its complexity is a matter of ornamentation: it embellishes and points out connections, it does not qualify or define reality in a new way. The reasons why ornamentation became a highly valued quality in this art need not concern us at the moment. One might point to medieval pride in workmanship, undermined later by the introduction of machines and, within Chaucer's lifetime, something like mass production; one might point to the influence of the Near East, where poetic ornamentation seemingly for its own sake went back to the age of the *Gilgamesh* and where the Islamic injunction against representing figures had helped to produce a wholly ornamental art; or to the Christian ideal of glorifying God with every stitch one sewed. Above all, of course, there was the brute fact that fixed and largely unalterable Christian doctrine precluded any form of artistic exploration except the reshuffling and embellishing of established truths. This restriction, together with the Augustinian notion — reiterated by Boccaccio and other late medieval critics — that what is gained by diligence is of greater value than what comes easily, would be sufficient to account for the high place given to ornamental elaboration in the Middle Ages. And in an age in which all knowledge seems to cohere, incontrovertibly expressing the underlying simplicity of an outwardly complex universe, the embellishment of any given idea seems virtually inevitable.

Whatever the causes, it was to ornamentation that medieval rhetoricians gave the greater part of their attention. In fact, the whole process of poetic creation as medieval rhetoricians understood it is reducible to a system of ornamentating doctrine. The poet began not by making something up but by choosing, from the storehouse of "olde appreved stories" and conventional devices, those materials he would bring together in his poem. At the second stage, he planned the arrangement or disposition, his aim being to crystalize and release the presumably inherent meaning in each part of his matter by setting it in significant relationship to all other parts. The third step in the poetic process was nothing more than touching up the ornaments, adding, cutting, focusing, shifting, renovating, polishing. Nothing could be farther from the classical view expressed by Aristotle, that poetry is at the core nothing less than original philosophical investigation — not, as Plato thought, a distant imitation of ideas but the only direct imitation in the world of the *process* of unfolding reality.

What marks a poem as medieval is not the extent to which it uses traditional materials. Dante uses materials from real life; Chaucer, though in some ways more modern, generally works with traditional materials, even in his last, most realistic poem. The medievalness of a poem lies mainly in its concern with *demonstrating* rather than *exploring*. From the medieval point of view, the more elaborate, encyclopedic, and complex the demonstration — the richer the ornamentation of the central idea — the greater the work.

From the modern point of view, the *reductio ad absurdum* of this tendency toward elaboration is seen in the medieval prose romances, preeminent among them the so-called Vulgate Cycle of Arthurian romances from the thirteenth century. We are dumbfounded by the proliferation here of plots and characters, and with our Aristotelian prejudice in favor of art which is perspicuous, we blanch, throw away our pencils, and retire in confusion. Perhaps medieval readers were actually able to keep all the innumerable strands in mind, as Professor Vinaver has tentatively suggested,[2] but considering the non-Aristotelian premise of medieval art, that seems unlikely. It seems more plausible that to writers of the Vulgate Cycle — as perhaps to the creators of the more intricate forms of interlace work — the appeal of this complex art lay precisely in its imitation of the infinite complexity, and only secret orderliness, of life itself. In any case, though the Vulgate Cycle cannot be grasped in its un-Aristotelian entirety, at least by modern minds, it allows us comforting stays. For all its elaboration, its widely separated and yet apparently significant repetitions of language, imagery, and situation, its tortuous, seemingly pathless wanderings of plot — the form itself a reflection of what Vinaver has seen as the writers' central symbol, the seemingly boundless medieval forest — the cycle never loses sight of its plan, or at any rate its principle of growth. The moral norms of the Cycle are orthodox, they are not defined but merely elaborated within the work; and so, though we are lost, we are not lost hopelessly. Moreover, in the Vulgate Cycle just as in Dickens (and for a similar reason) the plots are all indispensable in the end. In Dickens all mysteries are finally resolved in the reunion of families, and the hidden relationships of characters seemingly far apart in society are at last brought to light, showing that men are not, after all, isolated and free of responsibility. In the Vulgate Cycle the knights of Arthur's court go out, each on his separate quest, and suffer more delays, distractions, and reversals than the mind can comfortably retain; and yet, incredibly, out of all this seeming chaos, order emerges. As in life, where the secrets of God's plan are unknown, adventures develop, however inscrutibly, by plan, every detail or adventure ingeniously preparing for another detail much later. The baffling echoes and repetitions within the Cycle (for instance two widely separated scenes, in the first of which Gawain borrows Arthur's sword to help Sir Lancelot, and in the second of which he borrows it to fight him, both times speaking the same words to Arthur) are at least to some extent *intended* to be baffling. They hint, as if in subliminal suggestion, that the underlying order is still there. A century of critical interpretation might locate nearly all of the Cycle's subtle, and probably orderly, relationships; but to understand the Cycle in this fashion might well be to miss its real meaning. Like Gothic cathedrals, medieval works are not intended to be taken in at a glance or at any time recognized as wholes.

Other literary works from the Middle Ages have other kinds of ornamentation. *Sir Gawain and the Green Knight* is relatively straightforward in plot but thick with allegorical emblems, subtleties of diction, numerological tricks, and ingenious juxtapositions. The alliterative *Patience* embellishes the Jonah story by the introduction of puns, images, and situations which underscore the typic relationship, traditionally mentioned by scriptural exegetes, between Jonah and Christ (false patience and true). And so on.

But as I've said, whether the embellishment of accepted doctrine is presented on the surface, as it is for the most part in the Vulgate Cycle, or presented both literally and allegorically, it remains medieval as long as the doctrine itself remains stable. When intricacy begins in any significant way to qualify meaning, in other words, when the artist begins to derive both thought and feeling from within, we are on our way out of the Middle Ages and into the Renaissance. Spenser's *Faerie Queene* superficially resembles other Arthurian romances; but the doctrine of the poem, however derivative, is the gospel according to Spenser. Like earlier romances, the *Faerie Queene* moves clumsily, as if aimlessly, like a bear with amnesia, through every cave and glade its innumerable characters happen to stumble on. But though the author and his characters wander, Spenser is never lost. Every knight is emblematic, and whatever the adventure a knight comes upon, Spenser knows what question to ask: "What bearing has this on the abstract quality this particular knight represents?" If the answer is "None," the adventure must be evaded, hurried over as transitional, or revised out of the poem. Discounting the flowers and cockleburs of Spenser's verse, there is no reason the *Faerie Queene* could not have been composed by several hands, like the Vulgate Cycle — except for one. Its principle of organization is Protestant: Spenser's tendency is to look not to authority but to his own mind and heart, and his object is to see what can be said by Edmund Spenser, in sometimes allegorical, sometimes symbolic, and sometimes strictly literal fashion, about "the twelve private morall virtues, as Aristotle hath devised." (Even the appeal to the authority of Aristotle seems partly modesty. Spenser no more intends to follow the Philosopher than he will entirely rely on his nearer sources, Lodowick Bryskett or Piccolomini.) Not that Spenser was a modern individualist who, like James Joyce, proposed to deduce the universe from the structure of his own personality. Spenser undoubtedly assumes that all men of judgment will agree with his findings about the moral virtues. Nevertheless, the findings are his own.

This shift from ornamentation to original statement is evident in Arthurian romance at least as early as Malory, whose complex and slightly confused cycle[3] presents an attitude in many respects original with Malory. It is true, as critics have repeatedly observed, that Malory greatly simplifies the traditional romance, and if we ask only what he did to untangle the interwoven plots in his sources, we may conclude that Malory's central purpose was to get rid of ornamentation and complexity altogether. But recent critics have shown that if we look more closely at what Malory kept and what he changed we discover that Malory does not merely simplify the traditional stories, reducing them to pure adventure; he seems to be adapting them to a new concern — perhaps not a clearly articulated thesis in Malory's mind but a settled emotional conviction about the world. All of the adventures in the *Morte Darthur* in one way or another elaborate a single idea which may well have entered more heads than just Malory's in the treacherous days of Edward IV: civilization rises more or less pointlessly and inevitably falls by its own nature, mysteriously borne down by both its virtues and its defects. Malory untangles traditional plots and cuts traditional details in such a way that what remains forces the reader into an uneasy — and finally unmedieval — ambivalence. Launcelot's love is both more beautiful and more terrible than Tristram's selfish love; Launcelot's noble behavior and Gawain's base behavior contribute about equally to the Round Table's fall. In short, what we get in *Le Morte Darthur* is the sort of ironic counterpoise we have seen at work in Chaucer, the same sort of counterpoise that will inform the plays of Shakespeare (the balance of Othello and Iago, Hamlet and Laertes). Both the ideas and the feelings of Malory's "doctrine" evolve at least partly from within.

In short, the post-medieval or proto-renaissance poet does not manipulate traditional materials to crystallize and release the meaning which the Middle Ages conceives as inherent in all elements, real or fictional, of the vast array of emblems; his manipulation *explores and finally denies* at least certain elements of the orthodox view. What makes this exploration possible is that, however traditional his materials, the proto-renaissance writer's art is in one important sense realistic.[4]

When the interrelationship of statements grounded on realism and arranged in ironic counterpoise grows very complex, the intellectual and emotional synthesis which the counterpoise was first introduced to serve may be refined out of existence. That is not to say that a work of art which is in this respect tortuously constructed must necessarily be bad or meaningless; it is rather to say that its complexity approaches that of life itself, and an adequate critical description of the work must amount to a full-fledged metaphysic.

The world of the *Canterbury Tales*, like the world of the *Troilus*, is the Neoplatonic realm of the many, where mutual goods, not all of equal value but all having some ennobling potential, struggle with one another as the Pilgrims, with all their virtues and defects, struggle within themselves and among themselves on the road to Canterbury. Like the whole process of Troilus' story, the pilgrimage may lead in the end to God and to the renunciation of the world which the Parson recommends; but Chaucer's reasons for renouncing the world, insofar as we can infer them from the form of the poem, are not identical with the Parson's. Chaucer's method, like Malory's, is to look closely at what is immediately before him — people, ideas, old stories and ways of telling stories, the ground at his feet where, with any luck, he must sooner or later "fynde an hare." It is in part the method of the secure Neoplatonist — a method Chaucer will simultaneously defend and mock in the chatter of the Wife of Bath. Whatever abstract truth there may be in the world (Chaucer surely has no doubt that there is abstract truth, whether or not human beings can ever reach it), the approach to it is through the palpable, through careful comparisons of this gnarled tree and that one; and since the approach depends on the fallible human mind, it may be simply that, as the nominalist would insist, we can't get there from here.

The *Canterbury Tales* is built from end to end out of contrasts similar in principle to the contrast between the idealistic Troilus and the realistic Pandarus. Critics have long recognized this as the central dramatic principle of the tales and have pointed out the various ways in which rivalries between pilgrims generate attacks and counterattacks and thus provide Chaucer's collection with a kind of profluence not to be found in, say, the *Decameron*. But I am speaking here of more than dramatic profluence. I mean that in each of the structural blocks or groups of tales in the total collection, Chaucer's pilgrims offer rival points of view on a series of traditional topics — the nature of justice (the theme Professor Olson has pointed out in Fragment I); the idea of authority; the basis of power in the world; and so forth. In other words, I mean that not just in the so-called marriage group, where Kittredge saw the principle at work in a limited way, but throughout the collection, and consistently, profluence is dialectical — or rather "flawed-dialectical," since every one of the Pilgrims is subtly wrong.[5] To put this still another way, the aesthetic model of the *Canterbury Tales* is not simply the "collection" — the form represented by the *Decameron*, Ovid's *Metamorphoses*, Gower's *Confessio Amantis*, and so on — but the "collection" form combined with the medieval "debate," represented by *The Owl and the Nightingale*, for instance. It is a characteristic of the latter form that the author or narrator takes no stand in the argument, that he simply observes or (as in *The Owl and the Nightingale* and in Sir John Clanvowe's *Cuckoo and the Nightingale*) comments doltishly, comically missing the point. Some medieval debates do come to a conclusion — for example "The Thrush and the Nightingale" — but these are exceptional. Normally the decision is deferred or left to an absent judge, which is to say, in effect, left to the reader.[6] The original assumption behind the form, presumably, was that the reader will come to the right decision and that it will be orthodox; but the form allows the widest possible latitude to conflicting ideas and emotions and had from the beginning the potential of becoming truly dialectical.

Chaucer, like other debate narrators, takes no stand except in comic or ironic terms — unless we count the Retraction at the end of the tales. But though Chaucer's debates in the *Canterbury Tales* are grounded in medieval debate tradition, the very complexity of the characters and the tales through which they develop their positions, together with the closeness of Chaucer's scrutiny of the reality his tales and narrators fictionally embody, precludes any obvious or thoroughly orthodox Christian abstraction, though the *Canterbury Tales* is, of course, Christian. When we ask, "In *what* sense is the collection Christian?" we are driven to recognition that the tales have in fact *no* final doctrine: they are mere art; they are, that is, what the philosopher-novelist William Gass calls "metafictions." The tales have direction (from Southwerk to Canterbury, Nature to Spirit, pagan order to Christian, Fortune to Grace), but no conclusion and no possibility of coming to conclusion: even the *Parson's Tale* is a mere point of view. Part of the reason for this is that much of the *Canterbury Tales* was, for its original audience, political — far more so than anything else Chaucer had written. But we soon recognize a deeper philosophical reason for the work's inconclusiveness.

In Chaucer's groups of tales on a single theme, conflicting attitudes undermine or cancel one another and thus justify at least a measure of Christian withdrawal. In the tales, all human points of view have something to be said for them and something to be said against them (which is not to say either that Chaucer is a Laodicean or that he is a modern moral relativist but only that he can find in nearly everything some moral use), so that, finally, the only right point of view, Chaucer might say, is a point of view beyond the reach of art (since all views in art come from fallible human beings, that is, characters): total abnegation of any personal and self-regarding point of view for selfless and prayerful love of God and one's fellow human being. This is not to deny that in the *Canterbury Tales* some positions are better than others, as we guess from the fact that some of the characters are nicer people than others. Chaucer's way of pointing out and exploring the weaknesses in any given position is partly his presentation of contrasting positions. Often, though not always, opposing points of view zero in on the unknowable truth.

Occasionally, as in the *Manciple's Tale*, Chaucer presents positions we are meant to recognize as almost totally wrong. It is in tales of this kind that Chaucer's technique is most strikingly modern — most near, that is, to the technique sometimes used by Vladimir Nabokov or André Gide, among others. In such tales the narrator is "unreliable," which makes art itself — or at any rate *that* narrator's art — unreliable. Only very recently, understandably perhaps, have such tales begun to be admired: such manifestly bad and demonstrably late works as the *Physician's Tale*, the *Prioress's Tale*, the *Canon's Yeoman's Tale*, and the *Manciple's Tale*. Nevertheless, in their artistic undercutting of art's very foundations, they show — as do the late short poems (*Scogan, Bukton, Complaint to His Purse,* and others) — that Chaucer finally carried the nominalist argument, that nothing can be known, to its conclusion. Jokingly he makes the same point made by such twentieth-century artists as Ezra Pound who in their last years fell silent: art, like everything else, is an illusion. Chaucer may himself have fallen silent, toward the end. So he claims in his letter to Scogan and elsewhere. But if Chaucer fell silent, his silence was serene, as Pound's was not. He never lost faith in the divine reasonableness beyond the reach of man's reason.

The following chapters will spell out, briefly, how these processes work in the *Canterbury Tales* by pointing out the argumentative function of the more important tales and links, for the most part ignoring all other aspects of Chaucer's art — the brilliant line-by-line play of wit, the echoes and symbols which weave the whole great work together, and so forth. I will try to show how, throughout the tales, Chaucer approaches truth and at the same time dramatizes the elusiveness of truth through analysis of the struggle of conflicting truths and, sometimes, falsehoods — in other words, how he suggests truth by study of that old cluttered jungle, multiplicity.

viii

Fragment I, from the *General Prologue* to the *Cook's Tale* ~~~~~~~~~~

O ONE WHO LOOKS AT THE *General Prologue to the Canterbury Tales*, especially if he's been reading more conventional medieval poetry, can fail to be struck by the freshness, the openness, the strangely modern ring of its imagery and concerns. That impression is quite right, though also, of course, wrong. The Pilgrims' chatter has the sound of real talk; their physical appearance and manners, their change-able moods and inclinations, make them seem not mere "vividly imagined types," like the allegorical figure "Glut-tony" in *Piers Plowman*, but real individuals Geoffrey Chaucer must have known — which indeed, as J. M. Manly showed, some of them were.[1] But for all their vitality, the Pilgrims serve — however uncomfortably — as figures in an allegory whose antique rigidity, designed to house cool, sublime abstractions, the Pilgrims by their calm, fierce, or boisterous individuality, threaten to bring crashing down.[2]

We've seen this artistic trick before, but how strange the transformation! We saw in the *Parliament of Birds* a serene and orderly "background poem" — a numerological and musi-cal structure invisible to the questing, realistic narrator — and we saw in the *House of Fame* Koonce's shadow poem on an orderly universe rising, unbeknownst to the clownish, realistic narrator, to the house of celestial fame. But in the *General Prologue* not just the Chaucer narrator but a whole company of people — each soon to become a narrator himself — bustles about unaware of the structure that controls them, or rather, tries to control them. Here, as if daunted by the fact that narrators have ganged up against it, the superstructure no longer stands stable and imperturbable, an ironic comment on the antics of those below. Except for a few pillars, the superstructure is as much a thing to be tested, perhaps discarded, as the views of, say, the Cook.

Since the *Canterbury Tales* is an incomplete work, no one can say what its total organization was to be; but Rodney Delasanta has pointed out that, at least in general terms, a controlling question for the work is "How shall a man be judged?" The poem opens, as did Dante's pilgrimage, in the sign of the Ram, a sign naturally provocative of pilgrimage, for astrologers, and near its close with the Parson's allusion to the sign of Libra, implying the scales of balance.[3] Throughout the pilgrimage, in their prologues and tales, characters angrily or lightheartedly judge one another, giving praise, blame, or forgiveness, and defend themselves, either openly, as in the prologues of the Wife and Pardoner, or more subtly in their tales. (It was once commonly believed that the real answer on how men are to be judged is spelled out in the *Parson's Tale* at the end of the pilgrimage, but that opinion will no longer stand. When we study the changes Chaucer made in his sources for the *Parson's Tale* we see that even the Parson is just one more human being, one more limited point of view, a mind enclosed in its own language and ideas.)[4] Given this major theme of judgment — man's judgment of his fellow man and God's final judgment — it was almost inevitable that Chaucer should open with a cluster of poems which explore the nature of justice.

§ 1

THE WHOLE FIRST FRAGMENT is allegorically ordered by the old Platonic (and Aristotelian) scheme of the tripartite soul — rational, irascible, concupiscent. This, as I said earlier, was the scheme Fabius Fulgentius found in the *Aeneid*,[5] and it became in the Middle Ages the most popular of all models for allegorical construction, governing poems as diverse as *Beowulf*, the *Divine Comedy*, and *Sir Gawain and the Green Knight*. The importance of the scheme for medieval thinkers probably needs no comment. In the *Republic* Plato had introduced the scheme as a way of clarifying the nature of justice in the individual and the state. The proper balance of the soul's three faculties — or of ruler, defender, and worker in the state — creates justice; imbalance creates injustice. Christian thinkers worked out refinements and new ornaments — relationships between the soul's three faculties and the Trinity in whose image man is created, a new treatment of Plato's image of the state as leviathan, and a more detailed account (which Plato would have disliked) of the relationship between the tripartite soul and matter, that is to say, earth, water, air, and fire. All these terms and categories are of course typically medieval: schematically brilliant, like tracery on a great church window, but occasionally stiff, difficult to make things fit into if one looks away from the scheme to the actual turtle one is trying to push into its place, or the actual stone, or Wife of Bath. (It was this difficulty that nominalism made apparent.) This queer tendency of things not to fit their philosophical boxes, this "recalcitrance of matter" in a sense Plotinus never meant, is one of the things Chaucer discovered in writing the poetry of his middle period — the *House of Fame*, the *Troilus*, the *Legend* — the poetry Roger Bacon would instantly have recognized as *poetry of authority (tradition) checked by experience*. By the time he began his *General Prologue* (sometime after 1385, when the nature of justice was an important question in Gloucester-ridden England), Chaucer was so sure of the harm done to particulars by vague universals, or, to put it another way, so familiar with the stubborn willfulness with which horses and bedbugs keep bending out the sides of the category *animalness*, or women like Criseyde, Thisbe, and Medea, keep blurring grand old notions of *womanness*, that he could lay out the problem in a few comic strokes.

Chaucer sets up his Neoplatonic allegory in the famous first lines of his *General Prologue*.

> Whan that Aprill with his shoures soote
> The droghte of March hath perced to the roote,
> > [drought; pierced]
> And bathed every veyne in swich licour
> Of which vertu engendred is the flour;
> Whan Zephirus eek with his sweete breeth
> Inspired hath in every holt and heeth   [breathed into]
> The tendre croppes, and the yonge sonne
> Hath in the Ram his halve cours yronne,
> > [i.e., the sign of the Ram]
> And smale fowles maken melodye,
> That slepen al the nyght with open ye
> (So priketh hem nature in hir corages);
> Thanne longen folk to goon on pilgrimages,
> And palmeres for to seken straunge strondes,
> > [pilgrims; strands]
> To ferne halwes, kowthe in sondry londes;
> > [distant holy shrines]
> And specially from every shires ende
> Of Engelond to Caunterbury they wende,
> The hooly blisful martir for to seke,   [seek]
> That hem hath holpen whan that they were seeke.
> > [helped; sick]
> > [CT, I, 1–18

The primary function of these magnificent lines, needless to say, is to catch and hold the listener with *tour-de-force* lyricism and to provide physical setting and motivation for the Canterbury pilgrimage. But the lines serve these functions in allegorical as well as literal ways. Arthur Hoffman long ago pointed out that two contrasting forces, Nature and Spirit, are brought together here to motivate the pilgrimage.[6] The opening lines focus on the four elements — *water* reawakening the parched *earth*, then *air* (Zephirus), then *fire* (the yonge sonne) — and gradually introduce lower, then higher life-forms: plants, birds, man, associated, respectively, with the three faculties of soul by Aristotle's system, the vegetative (seat of concupiscence), animal (seat of irascibility), and rational. Whereas plants have only the lowest faculty and animals only the lower two, man has, or ought to have, all three in balance, with the lower faculties ruled by reason.

Though it's an oversimplification to say, as critics have often said, that the Canterbury pilgrimage is, allegorically, from Nature to Spirit — from the enlightened pagan world summed up in the *Knight's Tale* to the world summed up in the *Parson's Tale* — it is nevertheless true that the motivation of the pilgrimage is not simply spiritual. Nature and spirit work together to urge Englishmen good and bad, ascetic and sensual, to the shrine at Canterbury and spiritual health. As we see more and more clearly as the pilgrimage unfolds, one of the forces prompting the pilgrimage is the individual natural complex of desire and will within each Pilgrim, the wish for prestige, gain, entertainment, sexual adventure, and the like. The lower, natural force says "Go"; the higher, spiritual force, symbolized by the martyr, calls "Come." Spring brings physical regeneration, as the phallicism of the opening lines hints; the martyr and all he represents brings — hopefully — another kind of regeneration.

The same concern with man's double nature informs Chaucer's handling of the portraits of the Pilgrims. He rings every possible change on the commonplace medieval idea of character as a combination of nature (set by astrological influences and revealed in physiognomy) and form, that which gives order and significance to nature and is discovered in individual lives by reason, or higher nature. The particular quality of the desires and passions of any given man are the effect of the stars at the time of his birth and shape his body through the humors, substances which make a man sanguine, bilious, phlegmatic, or melancholy; by means of a man's higher nature, each man controls his inclinations and finds his proper place in society and the cosmos, that is, the right and useful expression of his talents and special penchants, his *role,* or, in Chaucerian language, his place in the "commune profit" of family, society, the Church.

The usual medieval attitude is that a man ought to suppress his lower nature for the sake of his higher, in approximately the way a fencer or a ballet dancer suppresses his individuality for the formal steps and positions of his art. Read in the light of this traditional view of human character, the *General Prologue* is a comic critique of the traditional idea of man: insisting on particulars of the sort grand abstractions necessarily ignore, Chaucer introduces complications which throw the whole theory into question.

In the Knight, Clerk, Plowman, and Parson, among others, nature and role interpenetrate and cohere. In the Prioress and the Wife more or less divided natures lead, in different degrees, to confusion. A good deal might be said in favor of both aspects of the Prioress's nature and of both of the forms (roles) to which her divided nature inclines her: that of genteel courtly lady, associated with ennobling chivalric love, and that of nun, associated with holiness more direct. Both are admirable, but not in one person at the same time. As for the Wife, simultaneously Venerian and Martian (born under both Venus and Mars, love and war), everything must hang on her pleasure in the fact that, as she puts it, "I have had my world as in my tyme" — either a statement which condemns her as a wretched sinner mired in cupidity and willfulness, or the manifesto of the first modern woman in English literature. In the case of the Monk, nature seems to conflict with form. Formally committed to the contemplative life, he nevertheless, as a "manly man," inclines largely toward the life of action and scorns the old rules of his order. In such characters as the Friar, a theoretically worthwhile role and a revolting nature are brought together. In the Pardoner a role generally acknowledged by medieval writers to be corrupt and perverse is united with a crippled physical and spiritual nature. Chaucer might agree with the normal opinion of his age, that people confused in nature and role ought to mortify the flesh and look to divine love, but it is not always clear which role should be chosen or how corrupt natures can be overthrown — unless by the grace which may come at last (symbolically, at least) at Canterbury. It's even unclear, we discover later, whether corrupt natures like the Pardoner's are really as corrupt in the eyes of God as we proud mortals imagine.

For all the casual and colloquial presentation, Chaucer's organization of the portraits is at least loosely systematic, following the tripartite Platonic scheme relating human faculties and social roles. The one true aristocrat or leader of men present among the Pilgrims is the Knight, here seen only as lord of his small household. Outwardly and inwardly, the "condicioun" of the Knight is worthiness. He is a figure, in short, of the rational man. All his life, "fro the tyme that he first began / To riden out" (44–45), he has loved ideals — chivalry, truth, honor, freedom (selflessness), and courtesy. He has proved himself worthy in "his lordes werre [war] " (47) — apparently a pun since all the campaigns listed are from religious crusades; he somehow missed all skirmishes of the sort his son has engaged in, secular battles.

, The Squire, also a good man, on the whole (the point has been much debated), contrasts with his father the Knight as the Platonic man of silver contrasts with the man of gold. The Squire looks up not to abstract ideals (province of the rational soul) but to love and fighting (province of the concupiscent and irascible souls, respectively): his condition is that of "lovere" and "lusty bacheler" (i.e., soldier or aspirant to knighthood). This is of course why the description of the Squire verbally echoes the opening of the *General Prologue*, which spoke of lower natures, plants and birds.[7] His clothes are beflowered like a meadow (cf. the "tendre croppes") and he is as musical and sleepless as a nightingale. Because his nature is less rational than the Knight's, he is motivated not by abstract ideals but by a human embodiment of them, his lady: he fights for his lady's grace, not God's. He may never be the man his father is, but there's hope for him, through a Neoplatonic rise (such as Dante experienced) from sense to spirit. Whereas his father is humble and self-effacing, the buoyant young Squire is vain perhaps to the point of putting curlers in his hair (Chaucer only hints at this, but a comic writer's hints have special force). Nevertheless, the Squire is not to be laughed away. According to the chivalry books of the time, men who fight for a noble lady's grace are only slightly below men who fight for God's; and Chaucer makes it clear that he likes his Squire: he praises the young man's accomplishments and ends with a couplet proving the Squire's good manners and knowledge of his place.

Taken together with the portrait of the rational man and the portrait of the man more or less virtuous in will and desire but not yet mature in reason, the Knight's Yeoman is an obvious figure of healthy concupiscence alone. The portrait deals exclusively with the Yeoman's function and dress. By function, as guardian and bearer of the Knight's equipment, the Yeoman is associated with the concupiscent or vegetative soul "healthily achieving a right use of the things of this world," as Fulgentius would say.[8] The Yeoman's green garb and his love of woodcraft suggest a touch of personal vanity, since his work for the Knight must involve numerous tasks less romantic than forestry (such as getting the Knight lodging and cleaning up after him); but his green color and love of woodcraft suggest, too, a proper functioning of the lowest of man's three faculties or souls.

And now Chaucer begins to introduce complications. The next three portraits, of the Prioress, Monk, and Friar, form a second group which comments on the first, and again the progression develops the scheme of the tripartite soul. The Prioress, as a governess, should be identified, like the Knight, with the rational soul; but here something's gone amiss. Whether by nature or by reason of the limits of her convent education (most likely both) the Prioress is not very bright: her aristocratic bearing is, as a pun hints, counterfeit; it consists of a penchant for etiquette (courtesy as mere good manners), for hollow elegance of the kind represented by her funny name borrowed from courtly romance, not Church history, and so on. Though she does not seem to know it, her renunciation of the world is imperfect, as nothing shows better than the broach of gold which can be read in either a secular or a religious way — *Love conquers all.* Her worldiness is unwitting, of course: though she plays courtly lady and has many qualities of the stock courtly mistress, she means no harm. She's a sweet, somewhat overweight, childlike soul, all "conscience and tendre herte." Both her position as convent head and nun (married to Christ) and her affected role of courtly lady, Platonic model for some courtly lover, urge that she be an icon of Reasonable Virtue, but the two goods are mutually exclusive.[9]

The Monk, also delightfully dim-witted, is a figure of flawed — but not thoroughly corrupt — irascibility: he's a Platonic defender, or man of silver, like the Squire, but a man who, as a monk, has no business playing war games. He is worse than the Prioress in that his worldliness is willful: he boasts to Chaucer (as Chaucer merrily tells us, pretending to agree) of his lordly disregard for the stiff old rules of his Benedictine order. He would rather hunt than sweat away his life in a cloister, he says, and he defends his choice with arguments. Chaucer's imagery, as well as the Monk's own, throughout the portrait, comically undercuts the Monk's seeming good sense. The bells on the Monk's bridle jingle as loudly as the chapel bell he ought to attend to. The comparison of a monk out of his cloister and a fish out of water is based on a traditional symbol of the damned soul. The oyster image the Monk stumbles onto is a traditional symbol of the good Christian life (or, sometimes, the Church), humble on the outside but glorified within by the Pearl of Great Price. Chaucer's physical description of the Monk compares him to a stock Christian symbol of pride, the horse ("ful fat and in good poynt, / His eyen stepe, and rollynge in his heed" [201–2]; compare "proude Bayard" in *Troilus*, I, 218 et seq.). And just after saying that the Monk is not "pale as a forpyned goost" (205), i.e., pale as a tortured or suffering spirit (precisely what a proper monk ought to be in the medieval view), Chaucer says the Monk loved a fat swan best of any roast — the swan being another traditional symbol of the soul. Whereas the Prioress unwittingly behaves like a lady of the court, the Monk, partly through willfulness but mostly from a sort of harmless and in fact quite delightful stupidity, behaves like a knight. Hunting in Chaucer's time was a soldier's means of maintaining his military skill. As many a writer before Chaucer had complained, a monk's hunting, not aimed at later defense of right on the battlefield, and wasteful of those goods which a monastery ought to distribute among the poor, is silly self-gratification, needless slaughter, and sinful waste.

Both the Prioress and the Monk are unduly secular, but the Friar is worse. If the Prioress is dim-witted and the Monk both dim-witted and willful, the Friar is sinfully perverted by

base desires. The portrait is loaded with sexual puns. On the
innocent level, the Friar pays for the marriage of girls without
a dowry "at his owene cost" (213) because he's generous; but
puns suggest that he does so because he himself has gotten
them pregnant. As in the seventeenth century, "cost" may
have the sense of (to speak politely) ejaculation; at all events,
"Unto his ordre he was a noble post" (214) — a noble pillar.
He is "well beloved" and "familiar," both in a double sense,
with men as well as with women. But sex is not his only fault.
All he does, he does wrongly. He gives false confessions,
taking money instead of true repentance, which would be
shown, according to Chaucer's age, by tears; he makes himself
rich, though sworn to poverty by his mendicant oath; he avoids
the sick and poor he's supposed to serve, and when he does go
to some widow, he sings his *In principio* so prettily that,
whatever her poverty, he would "have a ferthyng, er he
wente" (255), but also a "fair thing," that is, sexual gratifica-
tion. His worldliness is complete, his nature thoroughly
corrupt.

At this point in the *General Prologue*, Chaucer expands his
ordering principle, the tripartite scheme: the Merchant, Clerk,
and Man of Law, as members of what we would call the
upper-middle class, are not quite lords in the old sense, but
they are nevertheless all three associated with the rational
faculty — all three are great reasoners — and in loose association with this group comes the thematically transitional
Franklin. The Merchant's arguments ("resons" [274]) all have
to do with the "increase of his winnings" (275); the Clerk, in
contrast, is genuinely concerned with truth, though he is
acquisitive of books; the Man of Law, Chaucer hints, seems
better than he is because "his wordes weren so wise" (313).
Clearly both the Merchant and the Man of Law are more
interested in getting things for themselves than in truth. One
worries about politics (276–77) because of his concern about
his own business, part of which is illegal, the selling of French
sheeldes, forbidden by statute. The other, the Man of Law, uses
his special knowledge as a lawyer to buy up foreclosed
property for practically nothing. It is usually thought that the
Clerk is entirely selfless, in Chaucer's view, and that may be

right; but his "Twenty bookes, clad in blak or reed" (294) seem slightly suspect. For a man who must borrow everything from friends, he has an extravagantly large library, by medieval standards; and it is a library of Aristotle, not what one would expect, perhaps, of a man too pious to accept any secular office. Furthermore, part of Aristotle's medieval reputation derived from his supposed mastery of alchemy — a point interesting in the light of Chaucer's joke on the Clerk as "philosophre" (297), which can mean alchemist; and there are curious parallels between this mature and stable Clerk and the lecherous young clerk in the *Miller's Tale*. But however the Miller may tease the Clerk, the Pilgrim Clerk loves knowledge and gladly shares it.[10]

The Franklin is a lord — just barely — by social position, and he too has his theories: he's "Epicurus owene sone" (336) and delights in food and drink. The portrait is one of Chaucer's finest. The comparison of the red-faced, white-bearded Franklin to the red and white English daisy is visually striking and has, in addition, delightful symbolic overtones. In the marguerite-daisy poems of Chaucer's age (including Chaucer's own *Legend of Good Women*) the daisy functions as an ambiguous earthly and/or heavenly love symbol. The Franklin's food-filled place in the country — his proof to himself and others that he has at last "arrived," is a kind of paradise, "true felicity" (see I, 338), an imitation, in fact, of the celestial banquet in heaven. In terms of medieval character theory, the Franklin is ruled entirely by willful aspiration and concupiscence, yet aside from the symbolic ironies, the Franklin portrait, like that of the Monk, feels favorable. The Franklin is, whatever else, a good neighbor, the "Seint Julian" of his country (patron saint of hospitality). He has served in various public offices, including Knight of the Shire, and Chaucer does not comically undercut that service. But the group portrait which immediately follows offers belated ironic comment. The Haberdasher, Carpenter, Weaver, Dyer, and Tapestry Maker are all men who have done well financially, have risen in their guilds, and because of their possessions (373), not because of any inner qualities, are fit to be guild aldermen. Their wives would not mind, Chaucer says slyly, for it is pleasant to be called "madame" and "goon to vigiles al bifore, / And have a mantel roialliche ybore" (377–78). Possessions, it seems, make positions. Social role, even in the case of those who rule, has nothing much to do, in fact, with reason.

The portraits of the Cook and Shipman provide further joking comment. The Cook is a man whose work greatly pleases the lordly guildsmen: he is an excellent chef and can make stew with the best. But he has an itchy, open sore on his shin, probably syphilitic. If he scratches, then tastes with the same fingers, as cooks do, his stew is more than it seems to those who eat it. And it is men like the Shipmen, cheerfully murderous, who bring wine from Bordeaux to men like the guildsmen — drawing off some on the way and replacing it with water.

In his portrait of the Physician, Chaucer presents a man whose whole concern, professional and personal, is with "lower nature," things physical. He is clearly a good medieval physician, grounding his practice on Fortune (as reflected by astrology) and Nature (in a limited sense: the humors which control the body). As Professor Curry pointed out, the Physician boasts of having read more books than were in fact available to him, engages in underhanded deals with druggists, and has in him a touch of the godless rationalist — "His studie was but litel on the Bible" (438). He's fond of gold, with perverse will goes after it, and rationalizes his greed by the argument that "gold in phisik is a cordial [medicine] " (443). The Physician, though in some ways virtuous, is thus both a specialist in, and an embodiment of, reason's misrule and perversion.

So is the Wife of Bath, much as Chaucer enjoys her. As D. W. Robertson, Jr., has pointed out, she can be associated with the woman Christ met beside the well ("bath") and accused of "adultery," a word early Church writers take in a spiritual as well as a physical sense (delight in the carnal rather than the spiritual). The Wife is certainly one who delights in lower nature and uses all her impressive intellect and wit to defend that delight. Everything she does shows her pride (a function of the irascible soul misgoverned by reason) and concupiscence. If someone goes before her to the offering, she's so cross at not being first that she'll give nothing. As for her concupiscence, she's had five husbands, "Withouten oother compaignye in youthe" (461) — a touchy subject Chaucer embarrassedly drops. She loves pilgrimages, and the reason is not entirely piety. Pilgrimages were frequently denounced, in the Middle Ages, because of the unholy sexual opportunities they afforded. The Wife is "gat-toothed," in fact, a physiognomic sign of strong sexual inclination; hence such double entendres as "She koude muchel of wandrynge by the weye" (467) and — the most obscene pun in all of Chaucer — "She hadde passed many a straunge strem [stream]" (464). Throughout this portrait Chaucer teases but refuses to judge (compare the jabs in the Physician portrait). Neither on the surface nor by allegorical hints does he explain his liking for Dame Alice, but one can guess the reason. She likes people — as the Monk and Prioress do — and in a Wyclifite scheme which reduces Christian doctrine to "Love God and your fellow man," the scheme Chaucer understood in his blood, liking people is a valuable start.

The rest of Chaucer's portraits are all of people of the lower class, Plato's men of iron as opposed to silver or gold, except that, in fact, the Parson and the Plowman are really lower-class men whose spiritual "gentilesse" makes them, in effect, aristocrats. As Plato and all who followed him agreed, a man need not be a philosopher-king to be just and governed by reason. In the Parson and the Plowman, Chaucer presents ideals of humility, one religious, one secular. The Parson works at his job with all his heart, does not rent out his pulpit and go live at ease in London (as many priests did), and does not preach one thing and live another, but "first he wroghte, and afterward he taughte" (497). When men do wrong he corrects them sharply — even if they're men of station, who might harm him. His brother the Plowman has the same integrity: works very hard, loves God, shows charity to all, pays his debts, and has no false pride (he "hadde ylad of dong ful many a fother" [530]).

The remainder of Chaucer's lower-class pilgrims are of course less exemplary: an iron-headed thieving miller, a manciple whose business cunning beats that of all the lawyers he serves, a reeve who gets rich by cheating the foolish young lord whose estate he manages, and two out-and-out villains, a summoner (one who calls people to trial at an ecclesiastical court) and a pardoner (a seller of indulgences and phony relics). Each portrait has, besides its realistic charm, its own way of bending and comically blurring the controlling scheme.[11]

At the Tabard Inn the Pilgrims meet Harry Bailey, Innkeeper, one of the most fascinating of all Chaucer's characters — a character so rich and fully rounded that he baffles all critical attempts to nail him down. His function is undoubtedly allegorical, at least in part. The Devil is sometimes pictured as an innkeeper in medieval visual art, and "Bailey" can suggest imprisoning walls, as in the bailey of a castle; the free supper he promises the best of the storytellers has sometimes been read as parodic of the celestial banquet, that is, as the traditional parodic banquet in hell. If we take "Host" as a pun — and no pun goes past Chaucer unnoticed — he's a parodic Christ; and Harry Bailey makes a point of the fact that he can penalize as well as reward. That the Devil, Christ's mimic, might be present among mortal men was a common notion in the Middle Ages — it's part of the plot of the *Canon's Yeoman's Tale* — and ominous touches toward the end of the pilgrimage become more ominous still if we think of the Devil as near at hand. I mean such touches as those Rodney Delasanta points out: the agonizingly short time left before night on the last day of the pilgrimage, and the death symbolism of Chaucer's lengthening shadow.[12] But Harry Bailey is by no means simply the Devil or even an essentially demonic man. As ruler of the company (or symbolic king), he serves the Pilgrims efficiently and, for the most part, kindly; he's solicitous of their welfare and shows sincere, charitable concern when he meets the Canon's Yeoman, whom in fact he "saves"; he has excellent credentials as a literary critic and has a first-rate imagination.[13] He's a man, in short: a crafty innkeeper, henpecked husband, joker, philosopher, tyrant, fair judge (except when the Pardoner and later "Chaucer" threaten his *machismo*. He has the doubleness — ambiguity —

of all things earthly, but he's the best man anyone could imagine for the job he takes on.[14]

The Pilgrims agree to Harry Bailey's proposal that each tell two tales on the way to Canterbury and two on the way back, and that the winner of the competition receive a free dinner at the Tabard. This plan — which calls for 120 tales and sets up monstrous problems of organization if the collection as a whole is to have profluence — was of course never completed by Chaucer. The Introduction to the Parson's Tale shows that Chaucer at some point decided on a plan of one tale per Pilgrim on the way to Canterbury and (probably) no tales for the return. (A return would of course change the symbolism.) Even this plan proved too ambitious. But when he abandoned his project, Chaucer had already found ways of dividing the whole huge collection into smaller thematic units. The same principle which gives a general kind of order to the *General Prologue* gives order to the remainder of Fragment I.

§ 2

AT THE END OF THE *General Prologue* the Pilgrims draw lots, and the first tale falls to the Knight. The detail is significant: it is the Knight's *fortune* to tell the first tale, and he uses his fortune well — for dramatic explanation of the right use of Fortune and the relationship of Fortune and that which controls it, God's Providence.[15] Perhaps the best way to explain — and then only very generally — how the allegory works is to run through the whole plot, pointing out the meaning of events. The poem is one worth dwelling over — by any standard, the best poem Chaucer ever wrote, simultaneously a send-up of the whole romance tradition[16] and a magnificent philosophical poem.

Chaucer's source for the *Knight's Tale* is Boccaccio's *Teseida*, but he works very freely, suppressing long passages, expanding others, developing his own theme.[17] The Knight begins with a very brief summary of Theseus' war with the Amazons and his marriage to their queen, Ypolita. Here as in other medieval allegories, Theseus (like Chaucer's Knight himself) is an embodiment of the ideal *human justice,* that is, *reason.*[18] In standard medieval Christian opinion, woman ought to be ruled by man, and a female ruler represents social disorder. Whereas Ypolita is "faire" and "hardy" (882) — reflections of the well-ordered concupiscent and irascible souls — Theseus is characterized by "wysdom" and "chivalrie" (865), right thought and action, and he rules the center of learning and justice, Athens. Having overthrown the disorderly "regne of Femenye" (866), Theseus starts home with his new wife. Near Athens, at the temple of Clemency, he meets a band of wailing women and learns of the cruel actions of the tyrant Creon, another embodiment of disorder. Creon has murdered the husbands of the Theban women, and now, to show his scorn, he leaves his fallen enemies to the dogs. Moved by the women, Theseus vows that he will help them and quickly does so.

Theseus' two wars — with the Amazons and with Creon — strike down two different kinds of social disorder or false rule: Amazon society is basically good but needs the rule of male rationality; Creon's dictatorship is worse because Creon's base lower nature ("Fulfild of ire and of iniquitee") has usurped the place of his reason. The two wars are significant in another way as well. In the standard medieval view (which Chaucer will later show he somewhat distrusts), they show the ideal knight's relationship with women. Theseus chastizes, then marries and rules Ypolita; he lends his strength to the women of Thebes who cannot help themselves; but at the same time women's tenderness, repeatedly moving Theseus to pity, completes Theseus' nature, much as the quality of mercy in God extends his essential quality, justice.

After the battle with Creon, Theseus returns the Theban dead to the women of Thebes for ceremonial burning and does "grete honour" to the women. Chaucer's Knight hastens over these ceremonies, just as he hastened over the feast at the wedding of Theseus and Ypolita; nevertheless, ceremony, or ritual, is one of the central concerns of the Knight's Tale. Ceremony is the outward sign, the expression, of human order: it is man's imitation of the order of the universe, or, to put it another way, man's demonstration that he submits himself to the larger good of which Theseus speaks at the end of the tale. It is by rituals that men, as Theseus says, "make a virtue of necessity." Man is free to defy God's Providence, but if he does so he will be mowed down by the universe: God's plan, man's necessity, refuses to swerve. On the other hand, man is also free to accept and promote the larger plan, the "commune profit." Ritual and pageantry (the kind of thing King Richard and his chief spokesman John of Gaunt set such store by) are the public expression of this choice.

After the destruction of Creon's forces, booty hunters find, in a pile of dead bodies, two young knights who are not quite dead. Because they are of royal blood, the two knights, Palamon and Arcite, are carried to Theseus, who decides against executing them — though that is the punishment they deserve, since in total violation of chivalric law they have followed a tyrant. Theseus puts them in prison for life, with no hope of ransom. Their misfortune seems absolute, but as we see again and again in this tale, Fortune is changeable.

The poem now becomes, superficially at least, a story of the rivalry of Palamon and Arcite. (The real central character remains Theseus, the icon of just rule Chaucer holds up to Richard and his advisors.) To tell the story, the Narrator-Knight switches (or pretends to switch) from the epic genre in which he has firmly lodged everything so far (the epic, that is, as the Middle Ages understood it) to patently trivial medieval genres, the chivalric romance and the *demande d'amor,* or love question, a form in which the audience — implicitly the ladies in the audience — are asked to determine which of two suitor knights is more worthy of a lady's favor. Usually this genre sets up clear rival claims — for instance, soldier versus poet — each of which has validity. Part of the Knight's humor throughout the tale is that neither of his lovers, Palamon and Arcite, is worthy at all. They begin as the medieval equivalent of the Nazi SS, they break the solemn oath they swore to each other, and they fight each other not like rational human beings but like wild animals.

So Palamon and Arcite are locked up in prison. Now Chaucer introduces one of the finest scenes he ever wrote

(1033–1186), a scene which is at the same time lyrical and elevated, on one hand, and arch, satirical, on the other. On a May morning, below the tower dungeon in which Palamon and Arcite are locked, Ypolita's sister Emelye comes to walk in the walled garden. Chaucer's description of Emelye is conventional, that is, it uses a medieval poetic convention of imagistic associations: the lady is like a flower, and so forth. But here, as in Chaucer's description of Criseyde, the convention has special force. Emelye, "that fairer was to sene / Than is the lylie upon his stalke grene" (1036), is emphatically a beautiful creature of nature, at one with the garden and the spirit of May; but like nature itself (or like Criseyde), she has a radiance which suggests something beyond nature. The flowers mentioned have both secular and religious significance: the lily may either represent purity of thought or the purity of the resurrected soul, and the rose may either represent sexual love or holy passion. The season, May, was in Chaucer's day powerfully associated both with sexual rites (May Day) and with Christ's resurrection. In the same way, Emelye suggests more than nature: "And as an aungel hevenysshly she soong" (1055). The whole description delicately sets up the question: How is one to take Emelye? How is one to understand any natural thing? or, What is the right use of the World? This is, of course, precisely the issue at the heart of the absurd argument between the young prisoners Palamon and Arcite (1074–1186).

To know the right use of the World, one must first know that all natural things exist in the realm of Fortune, where beauty can fade, power can decline, bad luck can turn good, and so on. All of the characters tied to nature, in the *Knight's Tale*, are puppet-like. Palamon, Arcite, and Emelye again and again "start up out of [their] sleep" (cf. lines 1044, 1080, and so forth). They have an appearance of freedom, but only an appearance. Inside her walled garden, Emelye "romed up and doun," we are repeatedly told (e.g., lines 1052, 1069, 1099); inside their literal and Boethian prison "thikke of many a barre / Of iren greet and square as any sparre," Palamon and Arcite do the same, "romynge to and fro" (1065, 1071). Intellectually, at least, the knights understand their position, though they do not understand that the mind can escape the chains of Fate binding lower nature. When Palamon sees Emelye and cries out, Arcite, misunderstanding the cry, gives him a lecture on stoic resignation to the will of the stars (1081 et seq.).

Of Emelye, Palamon says, "I noot wher she be womman or goddesse, / But Venus is it soothly, as I gesse" (1101-2). Though he speaks in hyperbole, he means it, in a way: he even prays to the girl. He has made a mistake, confusing a lower good and a higher, and his misdirected desire to serve her is, in theological language, a perversion of the concupiscent or desiring soul. Now Arcite sees her. Palamon reminds Arcite of the vow they've sworn, each to serve the other, and claims Emelye because he saw her first. Arcite answers, rightly, that Palamon's feeling is "affeccioun of hoolynesse, / And myn is love, as to a creature" (1158-59), and he justifies breaking his vow and any other law on the grounds that all's fair in love (1164 et seq.). He's made no mistake about Emelye's nature, but he has made a mistake about order. Giving all his loyalty to a woman, and turning his back upon the larger order, he falls into a perversion of the irascible soul, or will.

The comically senseless philosophical struggle of Palamon and Arcite continues, though neither knight has any hope of winning the lady. Then Arcite's fortune changes. Perotheus, a friend so loyal he will later seek Arcite in the house of Hades, comes to Theseus and wins Arcite's release. Theseus does not even demand ransom; he merely insists that Arcite shall never be found within Theseus' lands. What has changed Arcite's fortune is, in effect, Venus: Perotheus' love and Theseus' compassion give Arcite his freedom. But Arcite is not pleased. In a formal speech loaded with dramatic irony, he wishes he had never known Perotheus and envies Palamon the "paradise" of his prison near Emelye. As always, his thought can rise no higher than mere nature: "ther nys erthe, water, fir, ne eir," he says, "Ne creature that of hem maked is, / That may me helpe" (1246 et seq.). Forgetting — or denying — that above the four physical elements is spirit and the divine plan, Arcite falls in "wanhope," that is, the sin of despair — the belief that God is merciless. He rages against the stupidity of men like himself who complain against divine "purveiaunce" (Providence) and Fortune which in fact work things out better than men could do; he talks — borrowing the language of Neoplatonists like Macrobius — of how men are "dronke," an image Macrobius uses to explain the dulling of men's wits as they descend from spirit to mere matter; and in all this Arcite fails to see that he is now doing precisely what he did before — howling against Fortune.

Palamon meanwhile complains that Arcite is luckier than himself: being free, he says, Arcite can raise an army and overwhelm Theseus. Whereas Arcite spoke of man as animal-like ("dronke as a mous"), lamented the impotence of the four elements, and condemned man's stupidity, Palamon compares men to sheep cowering in the fold (cf. God's "sheep") and blames man's plight on the madness of the gods (1328 et seq.). Perverse of will, Arcite cannot appreciate the good he gets — Perotheus' love, Theseus' mercy. Perverse of desire, Palamon cannot believe that human will is of any use: "man is bounden to his observaunce, / For Goddes sake, to letten of his wille" (1316–17). At the end of Part I, Palamon is in a double sense imprisoned (locked in his misreading of the universe) and Arcite is in a double sense exiled (cut off, by his mistake, from the possibility of action). Which, the Knight slyly asks, is worse off?

Arcite sinks into lover's melancholy, believing, in his maniacal nearsightedness, that no man ever suffered or will suffer as he does. He grows hollow, grizzly, pale as ashes in his madness. At last Mercury, messenger of the gods, comes to him and orders him to Athens, saying, "Ther is thee shapen of thy wo an ende." (In Christian iconography, Mercury is often a devil figure; the "ende" is Arcite's death.) Arcite takes this as hopeful news, but the outcome is subtly foreshadowed in the Knight's brief allusion to Argus. Mercury is arrayed, Arcite notices, just as he was when Argus "took his sleep." In the background legend, Mercury went to the many-eyed Argus with a lyre and a sword, put the Argus to sleep with the lyre, then killed him with the sword. Given the patterns already established in the *Knight's Tale*, the lyre and sword are fitting instruments of Fortune's victory over man: one lulls desire, the other overmatches the sleeping will.

Looking in a mirror, Arcite sees that he is so changed that he will not be recognized in Athens, and so, humbly dressed, and "al allone, save oonly a squier," he returns. His condition, "al allone," is significant. The Narrator-Knight speaks again and again of the social "compaignye" — "Palamon, with ful greet compaignye" (2909), "Emelye, / The rewefulleste of al the compaignye" (2886), Theseus, always in accord with his parliament (e.g., 3076); and he speaks just as often of aloneness, the terrible alternative — e.g., "Allas, departynge of oure compaignye!" (2774), "Allone, withouten any compaignye" (2779), and so forth. The contrast is of course one between action for the common profit and action, willful or not, which isolates — the way of death. But Arcite proves worthy, happy in his position close to Emelye and ennobled by love, and Theseus and his company, unaware of his identity, take Arcite in as a fitting "charity" (1433).

Meanwhile, Palamon, still in prison, suffers daily "martirdom" (1460) for his goddess. But at last, whether by chance or destiny, the Knight says (1465), he escapes with the help of a friend (cf. Perotheus). The escape takes place in the seventh year, on the third night of May. All these details have numerological significance: seven is the number of man and of physical life (four elements, three aspects of spirit) and also signifies an end, preparation for a new beginning;[19] May 3 is commonly associated with resurrection. He flees to a grove, planning to wait for the following nightfall, then go to Thebes to raise an army against Theseus.

That same morning Arcite goes by chance to the same grove to do, as Emelye once did (1034 et seq.), his May "observaunce." There, seeking some "grene" for a garland, "he rometh up and doun," praising May, then suddenly sits down and, talking to himself, reveals his identity to Palamon, who is watching from the bushes. As Palamon did earlier, Arcite blames the gods for his misfortune.

Palamon leaps up and swears he'll kill Arcite for all his lawbreaking (the breaking of their oath as brothers, the double cross of Theseus, the "false" changing of his name). Arcite again claims that love is above law and says he'll bring weapons so that he and Palamon may duel tomorrow. Palamon agrees. In an aside, the Narrator-Knight laments the fact that neither love nor lordship will have any "felaweshipe" — both are absolute and tyrannical. He means, of course, selfish love and "lordship" like Creon's. Arcite gathers the promised weapons and other goods and then, "allone as he was born" (1633), returns to the grove. The two knights meet and fight like animals — like lions, tigers, bears, boars — and they dismiss all ceremony ("Ther nas no good day, ne no saluyng") except for the seemingly friendly action they cannot avoid: "Everich of hem heelp for to armen oother / As freendly as he were his owene brother" (1651–52).

Meanwhile, as destiny has designed, Theseus comes to the grove, hunting a great hart. He has already served Mars, the Knight says, and will now serve Diana (1681–82). Here as in the *Book of the Duchess*, *hart* (ME *hert*) puns on *heart*. The goddess Diane represents purity (or chastity); Theseus, the rational man, hopes to serve her by becoming the killer of the great heart; in other words, the desire of Wisdom is to subdue the heart "great" with pride. Though the allegory may seem strange to the modern reader, it reflects the same concern we have seen in Theseus throughout, in his battle with the Amazons and with Creon: he imposes the rule of reason on man's lower elements (whether healthy or perverse), desire and will, summed up in the fleshly heart.

He stops the duel and rebukes the knights for their abnegation of lawful ceremony — their fighting "Withouten juge or oother officere." Palamon tells all, demanding only that both of them be killed for their crimes, and Theseus swears by Mars that the wish shall be granted. But the women of the company weep and beg mercy for the knights, and Theseus is moved to compassion, or mercy, which goes beyond mere rational justice (1766 et seq.). It would be wrong, he says, to behave like a lion (cf. Palamon and Arcite) toward humble and repentant men. He jokes then about the "miracles" of the god of love and points out the chief absurdity in the knights' situation: Emelye "woot namoore of al this hoote fare, / By

God, than woot a cokkow or an hare!" (1809–10). But absurd
as the knights' behavior may be, Theseus understands it; he
himself was once a servant of love. And so he proposes an
alternative to lawless dueling — a formal tournament, with
each knight supported by a hundred men.

Part III of the *Knight's Tale* opens with the Narrator-
Knight's description of the theater for the tournament and the
theater's three altars, to Venus, Mars, and Diana. The
description of the altars is long and — quite properly — static.
They bring the misguided roamings up and down of Palamon
and Arcite to a full stop, replacing pointless rushing with
stately ceremony. Though Venus, Mars, and Diana can all be
forces either of good or evil, only their harmful aspects are
represented in the theater. The Knight turns next to description of the two bands of one hundred — Lycurgus and his men,
who come to support Palamon, and Emetreus and his men,
who support Arcite. The symbolic descriptions are compli-
cated, as recent scholarship has shown, but essentially Lycurgus is a Saturnalian figure and Emetreus a Martian figure.
Arcite will pray to Mars, and it is Saturn who will give the
ultimate victory to Palamon.

Now the Narrator-Knight presents the three prayers of
Palamon, Arcite, and Emelye. Palamon prays to Venus, asking
not that he win the battle or earn fame (relevant to the
irascible soul) but only that he somehow get Emelye, his
desire. He receives a sign that his wish is granted. Emelye
prays to Diana, asking that her chastity be preserved. If
possible, she prays, let both knights forget their love for her; if
that is not possible, let the knight who loves her most win her.
Though she admits the possibility that she may have to marry,
her fundamental wish is clear: "Noght wol I knowe compaignye of man," she says (2311); and at the end of her
prayer: "My maydenhede thou kepe and wel conserve, / And
whil I lyve, a mayde I wol thee serve" (2329–30). Diana, who
may represent either purity of heart or chastity, means simple
chastity to Emelye. In other words, Diana represents, to
Emelye, not reasonable rule of the irascible and concupiscent
elements but out-and-out rejection of them. The altar fires
behave strangely, foreshadowing the momentary victory, then

death of Arcite, and Diana appears to tell Emelye that finally she must marry. Arcite, in his turn, prays to Mars. He believes that only force can win Emelye's love (2400 et seq.) and asks the "strong god" to lend his power. In return, he promises to give Mars his hair which (like powerful Samson's) has never been touched by shears. Mars gives him a sign that he will win victory.

Immediately strife breaks out in the realm of the gods (or astrological forces) between Mars and Venus, and Jupiter cannot check it. It is Saturn, god (or planet) of misery and death, who resolves it, for he is old, wise, and mighty (2448–55). He tells Venus,

> Now weep namoore, I shal doon diligence
> That Palamon, that is thyn owene knyght,
> Shal have his lady, as thou hast him hight,
> Though Mars shal helpe his knyght, yet natheless.
> Bitwixe yow ther moot be som tyme pees,
> Al be ye noght of o compleccioun.
> That causeth al day swich divisioun.

[2470–76

Saturn's object, notice, is to harmonize individual will and common profit in heaven. The cosmic emblem of desire, Venus, and the emblem of will (or the irascible part), Mars, must be brought back into company through the agency of Saturn's dark wisdom.

Part IV opens with a brief (five line) treatment of the great feast in Athens on the day in May, a year after the duel in the grove, when all the people have gathered for the following day's tournament. On the day of the feast, people joust and dance "in Venus heigh servyse" (2487); but they retire early. Tomorrow, except insofar as they fight for their ladies (cf. lines 2111 et seq.), the company will serve Mars. The Narrator-Knight turns to description of the crowd just before the tournament—a magnificent description, full of splendor and noise and bustle, and shot through with echoes: as Emelye alone in the walled garden and the two knights alone in their prison roamed to and fro, up and down, so here

armorers are seen "prikynge to and fro" (2508) and the palace
is "ful of people up and doun" (2512). A crowd may be no
more free than an individual, but the quality of its excited, in
effect communal, movement makes a difference. And a crowd
has no more providential knowledge than one man — or one
drunken mouse — can have, but their communal "divining,"
even after the time for divination is over ("after the sonne gan
to sprynge") makes a difference.

With great ceremony, Theseus goes to his palace
window, and his herald reads the tourney rules: on reflection,
Theseus has decided that all weapons must be blunted. Then,
again with great ceremony, Theseus and all his company ride,
"oon and oother, after hir degree," to the tournament. (Social
degree, visible sign of society's order, is emphasized throughout the tale.) Arcite enters the theater through the western
gate devoted to Mars (and associated with sunset and death),
carrying a banner of Mars' red. Palamon enters through
Venus' gate, with a banner of white (Venus' usual color when
she is associated with spiritual love). The battle begins (2599
et seq.) and proceeds with superb imagery and rhetoric to the
capture of Palamon and Theseus' judgment that Arcite has
won.

The scene shifts to the realm of the gods. Mars' promise
to Arcite has been fulfilled, but Venus, "for wantynge of hir
wille" (2665) weeps (making it rain on the theater below).
But Saturn has arranged matters so that both Mars and Venus
shall win. A fury sent from Pluto, god of the underworld,
makes Arcite's horse shy, and Arcite falls. He is carried to
Theseus' palace, while Theseus with slow and dignified
ceremony leads the company back into Athens. He is
unwilling to spoil the pleasure of the whole company for one
man's mishap, especially since the mishap is not yet known to
be serious. But in Arcite, it turns out, "The vertu explusif, or
animal, / Fro thilke vertu cleped [called] natural / Ne may the
venym voyden ne expelle" (2749–51). In this antique medical
system, the virtue natural, physical correlative to the concupiscent soul, is poisoned, and the *vertu expulsif*, physical correlative to the irascible soul or active part, will, is ineffective.
Nature, in Arcite, has indeed lost its "dominacioun." "And

certeinly, ther Nature wol nat wirche, / Fare wel phisik! go ber the man to chirche!" (1760). As nature looses its hold on him, Arcite grows reasonable at last and recommends the love of Palamon to Emelye. Then he dies, all Athens mourns him, and Theseus' aged father Egeus gives his gloomy consolation. Fortune is ever changeable, he says, bringing "Joye after wo, and wo after gladnesse." Since all joy passes, sooner or later, "This world nys but a thurghfare ful of wo, / And we been pilgrymes, passinge to and fro" (2847–48).

Theseus arranges a great funeral for Arcite, one more ritual joining of men and the rolling of the universe, and in a long, high-style rhetorical figure (*occupatio* — a listing of the things one says one cannot take time to list), the Narrator-Knight describes it. After this, years pass; then Theseus calls a great parliament to work out alliances with various countries and to promote a marriage of Palamon and Emelye. He explains to them two Boethian doctrines — the fair chain of love and the principle of temporal succession. Everything that exists, "fyr, the eyr, the water, and the lond," has both its own nature and the "bounds" which prevent it from fleeing its place: the fair chain of love maintains order among things not of "o compleccioun," as Saturn put it earlier (2475). The Prime Mover himself is eternal and stable; but nature, having descended from perfection and stability is mutable, and so, just as there is order in space (all things keeping their place through the power of the fair chain), there must be order in time (generations taking their place in turn). Mutability is inescapable — even rocks wear away, even oak trees fall — and so succession is for man a necessity, a matter of Fate. "Thanne is it wysdom," Theseus concludes, "to maken vertu of necessitee" (3041–42). To deny the progress of time, to resist the movement in nature from a time of mourning to a time for marrying, would be "wilfulnesse"; and for Emelye to resist Palamon after all he has suffered for her would be a failure of charity (right desire; see lines 3041–89). And so they marry, and the Knight closes his tale.

Chaucer's use of the gods in this tale should by now need no comment. They obviously represent abstractions: good or bad power (Mars), good or bad love (Venus, sometimes

Cupid), good or bad purity (Diana). Jupiter, like Theseus, stands for rational rule (cf. line 3036); but just as Theseus is at times helped by the dark philosophy of his father ("Deeth is an ende of every worldly soore," 2849), so Jupiter is helped by the god of chaos and death, Saturn. Egeus comforts Theseus when the duke is undone by sorrow, freeing him to work on the funeral rites; Saturn is the death principle on which orderly succession depends. Rationality breaks down because not everything is known, but acceptance of the breakdown puts rationality back in business.

Though his vision is in fact as Christian as that of Boethius, the Knight's concern is with nature and Fortune, and he fittingly chooses a theology worked out in the age of natural law, prior to revelation. Like Virgil's *Aeneid* as medieval Christians read it, following Fulgentius, the *Knight's Tale* dramatizes the right ordering of the elements of the soul, of society, and of the cosmos. We may believe the Knight, because his theory of universal order is impressive; but if we ask how the Knight knows what he thinks he knows, we can only answer, "By old authority (pagan) and by reason (another kind of authority, men like Bacon would say)." The tales which follow in Fragment I — the tales of the Miller, Reeve, and Cook (this last tale unfinished) — develop baser theories on the same theme, that is different opinions. How these tales work as argument can be sketched in briefly.

§ 3

ALL THE COMPANY, especially the gentry, are pleased by the Knight's story, and Harry Bailey irreverently puns, "unbok-eled is the male," that is, "the poke (of stories) is opened" and also "the Knight has unbuckled his male — revealed (or exposed) himself." If class is to determine the order of the tales, the highborn Monk should come next. But the drunken Miller, ignoring his rightful place in the social order, defying both the secular and religious estates (the Knight and the Monk),[20] and without a trace of concern for Providence or

Fortune (the rule of Harry Bailey or the drawing of lots), obstreperously insists on telling the next tale, to "quite" — repay or get even with — the Knight. His oath, "By armes, and by blood and bones" (3125), sounds like a burlesque allusion to the opening line of Virgil's *Aeneid* — the noblest tale of all from the medieval point of view, and, as I've said, a tale regularly treated in the commentaries as a poem on the right use of the three faculties. The *Miller's Tale* is a far cry from either the *Aeneid* or the *Knight's Tale*, chiefly because it is largely not "ernest" but "game"; yet up to a point it comically and unwittingly (from the Miller's point of view) supports the Knight's opinions.[21] Finally, however, the Knight and the Miller do not agree about the universe. They are two different men, a nominalist would explain, and have a different life-experience. And even if one is entirely right and the other quite wrong, the nominalist would add, neither will ever be able to convince the other. Both agree that Providence rules the world, but whereas from the Knight's point of view the plan of the universe is merciful, granting to every man better than he deserves, from the Miller's point of view it gives a man what he has earned.

Chaucer used no known source for the *Miller's Tale*, but in outline (though not in its rich detail) it is one of the common earthly folktales or fabliaux. (The idea of a girl sticking her naked rump out the window to receive her unwanted lover's kiss comes from a Middle English bawdy song, "Old Hogan's Adventure.") The Miller tells of an old carpenter, John, who had a luscious young wife and, alas, a roomer, a young scholar named Nicholas. By means of his supposed knowledge of astrology, Nicholas is able to trick the carpenter into building tubs which are to save the three when a flood like that of Noah's day comes. The three tubs are suspended from the rooftree of the house, and while the carpenter sleeps in his tub, Nicholas and the young wife slip down to the bed below and revel there. The young wife, Alisoun, has another admirer, an effeminate, persnickety incense swinger at the church, Absolon, a man "squeamish of farting." Absolon comes to the bedroom window, asks for a kiss, and gets, instead, a dire humiliation which leads him to seek revenge. He returns with a hot iron — a sharpened plowshare (comic reversal of Christ's "Let your swords be beaten into plowshares")[22] — and when Nicholas repeats Alisoun's trick, jutting his buttocks out the window and adding to Alisoun's trick a mighty fart, Absolon brands him. Nicholas cries for water, the carpenter thinks the flood has come and cuts the rope suspending his tub, and down he crashes, whereupon Alisoun and Nicholas run howling into the street, revealing all. The neighbors laugh at the carpenter's explanation and call him mad. Thus all the characters get what they deserve: for all the carpenter's jealousy, his wife gets swyved; Nicholas gets a foretaste of hell's fiery torment, and in lines rich in comic echoes of the biblical Last Judgment, Absolon gets a whif of hellish stench (and somewhat more).

The tale is the funniest Chaucer ever wrote (as everyone agrees), partly because of Chaucer's use here of comic incongruity, partly because of his characterization, partly because of the incredible neatness of the tale's construction. By comic incongruity I mean things like:

> And prively he caughte hire by the queynte   [cunt]
> And seyde, "Ywis, but if ich have my wille,
> For deerne love of thee, lemman, I spille."
>   [die or, as a pun, spill]
>   [3276–78

Nicholas' action here (nothing could be more direct) makes totally incongruous his language of the courtly lover, nobly pining away for a lady far beyond his station. As for characterization, behold the magnificent presentation of Alisoun (lines 322–70), in which every detail identifies her with some joyful natural creature — all creatures traditionally identified (when the listener stops to think) with various kinds of wickedness, cunning, and delectable, nasty sin.[23] The whole description is full of high spirits, seemingly innocent praise — her body "gent and smal" as a weasel's, her singing "as loude and yerne [eager] / As any swalwe sittinge on a berne [barn]" — so that the listener, like Nicholas, is carried away, or as the Narrator-Miller himself is carried away. The same delightful farmer's-daughter innocence fills her response to Absolon's horror after her trick — " 'Tehee!' quod she, and clapte the wyndow to" (3740).

The handling of Nicholas is equally brilliant. The lascivious clerk has just enough in common with the sober, middle-aged Pilgrim Clerk to keep the framing story of competing Pilgrims alive; but what's best about Nicholas is his creative brilliance — as suitor, as schemer, as consummate actor (especially in his mad scene). Chaucer's emphasis on the rascal's creativity — here and in other tales — is something new in the Middle Ages, and a proof of the civility of Chaucer and his audience. A. Booker Thro has pointed out that, like Southwestern American humor, the old fabliau farce, from which Chaucer draws, emphasizes the fool's deflation and discomfiture. In Chaucer the emphasis is on the cunning of the trickster; and the fool, in this case Carpenter John, is treated with sympathy. Witness, for example, his genuine concern when he finds his boarder gone mad, or notice how, when he hears the world must end, his immediate thought is of his beloved young wife.[24] Compare Chaucer's sympathy for poor ridiculous Absolon when he realizes what it is he's kissed. In other words, all the characters in the *Miller's Tale* are fools, from a sober Christian point of view; but Chaucer treats them gently, joyfully, so that the tale is at once hilarious and touching and only on afterthought "moral." All this, of course, is more than mere tone. Insofar as the speaker's exuberance carries the listeners along, or, to put it another way, insofar as tone softens the audience's judgment, inclining the audience to make allowances, tone changes the argument.

The neatness of the tale goes far beyond appealing characterization and the comic inevitability of its plot. In the medieval view, Noah's flood came about because men had become carnal — they fell into promiscuity and perversion, thus violating God's only command to them in that age before the incarnation, "Go forth and cleanly multiply." The same sins bring on the comic catastrophe in the *Miller's Tale*, except that the burden is to some extent shifted from concupiscence to non-omniscience. Characters are caught in a cosmic plan they cannot see.

Each character's vocation is comically relevant to the plan of the whole tale, which they only understand when it collapses on them. Carpentry is relevant because it justifies old John's building of the tubs; because it was the carpenters' guild that normally staged the Noah play in the medieval mystery cycles; and because Noah was, in the standard exegetical view, an Old Testament prefiguration of Christ: as Noah built the ark and saved the best of his time, so Christ (a carpenter) founded the Church, which carries men to their spiritual salvation. The new destruction of the world (the second "flood") is Doomsday, scripturally spelled out in the Apocalypse of John — hence the carpenter's name. His comic knowledge of what is to come parodies the true knowledge of the biblical John.

Nicholas' vocation — scholarship and, especially, astrology — works in that it justifies his trick on old John, but the detail also involves more. Astrology is, in one common medieval view (not necessarily a view held by Chaucer),[25] a pursuit of "wrong reason" — an attempt to know more than man's business. The Miller is jokingly alluding to the idea that man should mind his own business, not God's, when he says in his Prologue, "An housbonde shal nat been inquisityf / Of Goddes pryvetee, nor of his wyf" (3163–64), and the same phrase, "Goddes pryvetee," comes up repeatedly in his tale (e.g., at 3454 and 3558). In studying or (at times) pretending to study the message of the stars, Nicholas oversteps himself and isolates himself from the common "compaignye," just as Arcite did in the *Knight's Tale*; and so, fittingly, the same phrase used of Arcite is used of Nicholas: he is "Allone, withouten any compaignye" (3204). Man's "pryvetee" and man's "purveiaunce" (providence) seek to replace God's. (See, for example, lines 3493 and 3566.) Ironically, the old carpenter's responses to Nicholas' usurpation of God's role are correct and orthodox: "What! Nicholay! what, how! what, looke *adoun!* / Awak, and thenk on Cristes passioun!" (3477–78; my italics), and "What! thynk on God, as we doon, men that swynke" (3491). But old John, being stupid, doesn't understand what he's saying. When he says "looke adoun" he means it literally (Nicholas has been staring at the ceiling); he does not mean, as he should, "keep your eyes on the business of man." And when he says "thenk on Cristes passioun!" he does not really understand that Christ's passion has saved man already from Doomsday extinction.

Nicholas' name, like old John's, is also significant. It may or may not be intended to recall the demonic Nikolatinae of the Apocalypse, but certainly in this tale full of theater allusions (the Noah play, which made famous the unwilling-ness of Noah's wife to enter the ark — lines 3538 et seq. — and the Herod play, in which Absolon plays the part of the ranting king), Nicholas the boarder recalls Saint Nicholas, the myste-rious guest in the numerous Saint Nicholas plays of the Middle Ages.[26] Whereas the Saint Nicholas of the plays thwarts his evil hosts and returns them good for evil, the Nicholas of the *Miller's Tale* gives evil for good. (I must leave to my reader the larger purpose of the theater imagery — man's action as mere role in a controlled universe, the "actual" as a farcical representation of the "real," and the reflection here of theater imagery — the tournament — in the *Knight's Tale*.)

Absolon's character and vocation as incense-swinger is equally relevant to the tale's large plan. Absolon is, as we've said, a man "squeamish of farting" (3337–38), one who scents his breath and person to make himself attractive; so his humiliation by Alisoun, then Nicholas, is comically appropri-ate. The incense he swings is, here as elsewhere in Chaucer, a traditional symbol of grace or good works, ironically appropri-ate since Absolon wants not God's grace but Alisoun's . In pursuit of her grace he sings at her window a song which, as Professor Kaske first pointed out, echoes the *Canticles*, tradi-tionally interpreted as songs of Christ the Bridegroom to His Church (see lines 3698 et seq.). His name, appropriately, is that of David's beloved and beautiful but disloyal son.

The *Miller's Tale*, like the *Knight's Tale*, deals, then, with order and disorder, justice and injustice, Providence and Fortune. All the characters are concupiscent, the men desiring Alisoun above all else, Alisoun desiring — merry animal that she is — nothing higher than a good sound swyving. They get just what their theology allows them. Forgetting about God, to whom one can appeal for mercy beyond one's merit, and hoping to work everything out for themselves by their own "providence," they slip neatly, unknowingly, into Fortune's larger pattern. All their individual plots backfire and, however ludicrously, God's order reasserts itself, making one plan of the characters' several schemes concocted "in privitee."

§4

THE ONLY PILGRIM who dislikes the *Miller's Tale*, apparently, is Oswald the Reeve, who, being the kind of man he is, takes it as a personal affront. He speaks pompously of the condition of old men like himself, incapable of doing much but as strong in will as ever. He mentions *will* repeatedly (3877, 3880, 3887) and claims for age the four common sins of will, "Avauntyng [boasting], liyng, anger, coveitise" (3884). Harry Bailey prods him to tell his tale and quit preaching, and Oswald says he will do so, strictly to get even with the Miller. He says, alluding to scripture, that the Miller can see the moat in another's eye but not the beam in his own (3919–20) — a passage treated in medieval biblical commentaries as a figure of irascibility overruling reason. Whereas the Miller has told a comic tale of concupiscence, the Reeve will tell (without fully understanding what he's doing) a comic tale of irascibility.[27] Like many of the tales, what the *Reeve's Tale* attempts is self-justification and a piece of "eye for an eye" revenge. Like the *Miller's Tale*, the story the Reeve tells backfires, comically discrediting him. What Chaucer ingeniously establishes, slyly playing games behind his narrator's back, "is a standard by which one law is measured by another — the old by the new, the Continental by the English, the private by the public, the Mosaic by the Christian." [28] Professor Baird points out in detail how this works. I will restrict myself here to more general comment.

The Reeve tells of a proud, dishonest miller who so cruelly cheats a certain college at Cambridge that eventually two scholars come for vengeance. The miller cheats them as he has cheated all others, but when they stay overnight in his house they get their revenge by lying with the miller's wife and daughter, then pummeling him.

The description of the miller makes him a very emblem of perverse irascibility. He is proud as a peacock (willfully rising above his station), a fierce wrestler, a thief, a man who walks about heavily armed. He has a wife who is the illegitimate daughter of the town parson, a matter of great pride to fierce Simkin the miller since it means she is of "noble" blood and has nunnery education. He also has a half-year-old baby (a "propre page") and a twenty-year-old daughter, fat, flat-nosed Molly, whom the miller and parson hope to marry off to nobility, using church money for her dowry.

Enter the two young scholars. With comic overconfidence (and a broad northern or Scots accent which heightens the comedy of their concern that they not be cheated), they try to watch the miller closely. But "for al the sleighte in her philosophye," the miller outfoxes them. He unties their horse, letting it run to the mares, and then, while the scholars are out chasing it, steals their grain. It's nightfall when the boys catch their horse, and they ask that the miller let them stay overnight. The miller agrees, scornfully teasing them as he does so: his house is small, he says, but since they are logicians, "Ye konne be argumentes make a place / A mile brood of twenty foot of space" (4122 et seq.). After much drinking, they all go to bed in the only bedroom available, and the miller's family goes loudly to sleep, snoring and farting.

The humor in the *Reeve's Tale* is less complex than that in the *Miller's Tale*, though there are some fine moments. One is fat Molly's tender speech of parting to the scholar who has been so kind as to swyve her (lines 4240 et seq.); another is the wife's cry of alarm when she imagines some goblin has fallen on her. (*"In manus tuas!"* is a common opening of prayers against the night goblin.) The end of the tale is a good deal more violent than the end of the *Miller's Tale*, and one reason is that the Reeve has a different definition of justice. In the *Knight's Tale* men get better than they deserve and in the *Miller's Tale* men get just what they deserve; in the *Reeve's*

Tale they get worse, which is to say that, where irascibility dominates, punishment becomes fierce vengeance. The structural key to the tale is John's legalistic remark "That gif a man in a [one] point be agreved, / That in another he sal [shall] be releved" (4181–82). When the miller releases the clerks' horse the clerks get "wet as a beest" in the rain (4107); the turn-about is that the miller gets so drunk (wet) he snorts like a horse. Similarly, as the miller steals the clerks' grain through his trickery, the clerks steal from the miller's household sexually. Verbal innuendos underscore the relationship of the two kinds of theft.[29] Aleyn and John talk of the grinding of their meal in covertly sexual terms. John says "right by the hopur wil I stande, / . . . and se howgates the corn gas in. / Yet saugh I nevere, by my fader kyn, / How that the hopur wagges til and fra" (4036–39). Grinding meal is common fourteenth-century slang for sexual intercourse. (Cf. the Wife of Bath's talk of bread and grinding in the Prologue to her tale, and compare, by the way, Bessie Smith's coffee-grinder imagery.)

The universe deduced from the Reeve's crabby nature seems about as bad as a universe can get, yet in the unfinished *Cook's Tale* it was apparently to get still worse. The tale was apparently to have dealt with total perversion of the tripartite human soul. The central character in the tale "haunteth dys [dice], riot, or paramour" (439). Wisdom as the Knight understood it (the right interpretation of Fortune and Providence) is reduced to blind dependence on chance (dice); irascibility is reduced to "riot" (beating people up for the fun of it); and concupiscence, good or bad, is reduced to whoring.

§ 5

TAKEN AS A WHOLE, the first fragment of the *Canterbury Tales* sets up and undermines a theory of Justice. The tales of the Knight, Miller, and Reeve (however the *Cook's Tale* might have worked) offer three points of view on order, one rational and valid, two irrational but tending to support the first — ex-

cept for one thing: each view is grounded on the character of
its proponent. The *Knight's Tale*, because of the kind of man
the Knight is, shows men working in cooperation with the
Prime Mover, reaffirming on earth, through ritual, the order of
Providence. The Miller, because of the kind of man he is,
shows unreasonable, concupiscent men working independ-
ently, each by his own plan, outfoxing themselves and
submitting perforce to order. But the Reeve, because of the
kind of man he is, shows men ruled by irascibility and shows
how such men come to a painful comeuppance, again despite
themselves. In each case, as Chaucer's audience understands, it
is God who brings justice; but that justice comes in different
ways to different kinds of men, and comes, when we stop to
think about it, in ways which leave human beings fairly
helpless. Life goes best for the reasonable man with a superior
philosophy, we see by inspection, but how are the Miller and
Reeve, with their inferior philosophies, to be turned into
reasonable men? and what authority has the Knight, in fact,
for his worldview? He sets his story in a pagan world of
experience and deduction, where some, like Theseus, learn by
reason and the influence of merciful women; where others,
like Arcite, learn by suffering; and still others, like Palamon
and Emelye, act properly by ducal command. If we ask
ourselves "Whence comes the command, finally, beyond ducal
opinion?" we get no answer, or none but the Christian
assumptions of the audience, God's revealed law; and that law
is foreign to both the Knight's pagan setting and, at least to
some extent, the experience and emotion of the Miller and
Reeve. "Yet surely it is true," Chaucer's audience might
exclaim, "that scriptural authority is answer enough — obedience to divinely established law!" "Perhaps," Chaucer answers, looking sly. And he begins Fragment II.

ix

Fragments II–V, from the *Man of Law's Tale*
to the *Franklin's Tale* ᕫᕫᕫᕫᕫᕫᕫᕫ
*"Authority" and "Experience" as
Principles of Government*

Y THE EARLY 1390s, KING RICHARD HAD taken firm control of his government, and was beginning to implement his absolutist theory of monarchy, much to the distress of some of his magnates. In Richard's view a king should be to his people a virtual god, and he did everything in his power to make himself just that. Like an oriental monarch, the chronicles report, he sat in a high throne sternly watching all those in attendance at court, and if anyone caught King Richard's eye the courtier was to genuflect at once. He brooked no interference from parliament and even demanded and received from his lords a judgment that any man caught inciting parliament to criticism of his household accounts was guilty of treason. Since, by his theory, his strength and wealth must be greater than that of any other lord in his kingdom, he seized men's lands on any pretext that might come to hand and, though a pacifist, built a huge and costly royal army. Under John of Gaunt's management (as Steward of England),

Richard's government prospered and criticism of the king's tyrannical ways was kept to a whisper. Nevertheless, any intelligent English public servant could see that there was trouble brewing. Some, like Chaucer's friend the poet John Gower, began to slip from loyalty to the king toward opposition and, eventually, revolt. Others, like Chaucer, remained staunchly loyal but criticized the king's ways.

Chaucer had finished, by the early nineties, several of his *Canterbury Tales*. His book included at this time (momentarily discounting short prologues and introductions) the *General Prologue*, the *Knight's Tale, Miller's Tale, Reeve's Tale, Man of Law's Tale* (the present tale of Melibeus), and the original *Wife of Bath's Tale* (the present *Shipman's Tale*). His book may have included certain other tales as well, such as the *Monk's Tale*, but we have no way of being sure. Watching King Richard's tyrannical behavior from the seclusion and semiretirement of his house in Greenwich, Chaucer decided to make a major change in his plan for the *Canterbury Tales*, decided, that is, to introduce a group of tales which would comment, discreetly and indirectly (for the most part), on Richard's ideas of proper government. He detached the Man of Law's prose tale of Melibeus from its introduction, gave the Man of Law a new tale, this one in verse (the present Man of Law's tale of Custance), wrote a new prologue and tale for the Wife of Bath, then added the further tales in fragments II–V of the Ellesmere manuscript, shifting the earlier Wife of Bath's tale to a new speaker, the Shipman.[1]

The inserted group of tales works in two ways at once. On one hand, it develops logically out of the first fragment, exploring the question raised by the disagreement of the Knight, Miller, and Reeve, namely, "What authority can we find for our beliefs?" and, on the other hand, it examines a new and, in Chaucer's England, urgent issue: "What is just government?" In this group of tales, fragments II–V, Chaucer considers the related problems of knowledge and justice in a new way, that is, in terms of what Roger Bacon saw as the competing bases of our knowledge of what is right, authority on one hand, experience on the other. Before examining the tales one by one, it will be useful to get an overview.

The theme of the *Man of Law's Tale* is *constancy* (constancy to revealed law on every level of the medieval hierarchy, to God, to king, to husband, and so forth), a term nearly interchangeable with another, to be introduced as a major element in the *Clerk's Tale, patience.* Constancy, as we will see, implies absolute submission, slavish obedience. Patience means much the same thing but assumes a less rigid relationship between lord and vassal, each of whom is required to be patient or, in a sense, passive in relation to the other: the lord does what is good for the vassal, not whatever he may please, and the vassal submits, or shows constancy. If the lord fails in his obligation, the vassal is required to be "patient" or "constant in adversity," praying that the lord will come to his senses. In other words, constancy — at least as the Man of Law uses the word — means obedience no matter what, on the grounds that the lord (or authority of any kind) is always right; but patience takes as its premise the notion that a certain kind of behavior should be expected of a lord (or of any authority) and that the lord may sometimes be wrong, so that one cannot be strictly "constant" (loyal to the absolute principles the lord ought to embody), one can only wait patiently for things to mend. Patience is a virtue conspicuously missing from the character of the Wife of Bath, who takes the view that when a lord (in this case a husband) is bad, the vassal's response (in this case the wife's) should be revolution. Though the Wife does not generally practice patience, the virtue is one she understands, as the end of her tale shows. For full development of the idea of patience, however, we must wait for the *Franklin's Tale*, the final tale in what G. L. Kittredge called the "marriage group" and the only Chaucerian work in which the concept of patience is spelled out. The Franklin says in his tale (and Chaucer says urgently to Richard and his court, despite his comic tone):

> Love wol not been constreyned by maistrye.
> Whan maistrie comth, the God of Love anon
> Beteth his wynges, the farewel, he is gon!
> Love is a thyng as any spirit free.
> Woomen, of kynde, desiren libertee,

And nat to been constreyned as a thral;
And so doon men, if I sooth seyen shal.
Looke who that is moost pacient in love,
He is at his avantage al above.
Pacience is an heigh vertu, certeyn,
For it venquysseth, as these clerkes seyn,
Thynges that rigour sholde nevere atteyne.
For every word men may nat chide or pleyne.
Lerneth to suffre, or elles, so moot I goon,
Ye shul it lerne, wher so ye wole or noon;
For in this world, certein, ther no wight is
That he ne dooth or seith somtym amys.

[v, 764–80

Obviously as Chaucer and his age use the word, *patience*
is not mere toleration of delay. It is a social virtue found in
relationships between persons of higher and lower station —
God and man, lord and vassal, master and servant, husband
and wife — and it is found, as Chaucer's lines suggest, only in
relationships characterized by consent, or, better, "love" rather
than "maistrye." In political discussions, *patience* contrasts with
agency, the one referring to government in which the ruler and
ruled are mutually responsible, the other referring to government in which the ruler is (as King Richard hoped to be)
absolute. To act with patience, in such a context, is to act
responsibly, in view of one's contract or position as voluntary
partner among free men. This usually means, of course, to
suffer with a sigh of resignation any misbehavior of the higher
or lower partner. Patience is faithfulness when the going is
rough.

Patience, or constancy in adverse times, is relevant to all
vassal-lord relationships: Church-Christ, state-king, wife-hus-
band, and so forth. It is not to be thought of, obviously, as a
tool of oppression (though it may become one in practice),
since it is grounded on the interdependence of all stations. On
all levels of the cosmic hierarchy, both lord and vassal freely
renounce their freedom for reciprocal obligation. The lord, in
fact, is ruled by his servant insofar as what the servant desires
is "lawful" both with respect to the individual and with respect
to the larger order. Since all forms of headship are analogous in

medieval thought, it is natural that Chaucer should see the good marriage as an earthly reflection of the ideal union to be found in heaven and as metaphorically equivalent to the well-ordered society: just as the courtly lover's service to his lady parallels religious devotion, the life together of husband and wife, or of king and state, parallels the union of God and man in the kingdom of heaven. The metaphor is, of course, traditional.[2]

It should hardly surprise us that every one of the tales in fragments II–V, written when Richard's near tyranny and the barons' disloyalty was on everyone's mind, is a tale which comments directly or indirectly on the interrelated ideas *constancy* and *patience*, introduced in the tale of Custance. Kittredge's identification of these tales as a marriage group was right; it merely missed the fact that the debate is uninterrupted (the Friar and Summoner speak on the same central point). To observe, as some critics since Kittredge have done, that other tales in the Canterbury collection also deal with marriage is to miss the point. What is central in the *Shipman's Tale*, for instance, is the power of social position and wealth; marriage is merely one vehicle of the discussion. In fragments II–V, the real subject is "headship" or proper authority, whether in the marriage of men and women, or in some other kind of marriage.

Let us turn now to the tales themselves.

The Introduction to the *Man of Law's Tale* was written for a tale in prose (almost certainly, as I've said, the *Melibee*, full of legal jargon) which was replaced by the present tale. The Introduction has a superficial relevance to what's gone before: from the *Knight's Tale* forward things have been going, philosophically at least, from bad to worse. Now the Host makes some ingenious calculations (calculations impossible even for a first-rate mathematician without instruments), discovers that time's awasting, jerks his horse around and asks for a tale from the Man of Law. The calculations look forward to those made by the Pilgrim Chaucer in the Parson's Prologue — calculations with dark symbolic overtones — and it was partly for the sake of this element of foreshadowing or linking that Chaucer kept the Man of Law's Introduction.

Both calculations make the same point: life passes quickly. But the Host's observation that time is passing and that lost time can never be recovered has also a nearer purpose in that it comments on the tale which is to follow. If the original Man of Law's tale was the tedious and endless tale of Melibeus, a time-waster if there ever was one (which is not to deny that the tale has also its delightful qualities), then the Host's urgent comment on time's swift passage sets up an ironic view of the long, dull tale. But the Host's remark on time takes on an even more interesting irony as a comment on the new Man of Law's tale of Custance. Unfailingly obedient to authority, Custance wastes (in a sense) her whole life. Pushed about by fate, in God's protection, she drifts for years from place to place, misses all but the first and last years of her marriage to her beloved husband Alla, misses almost totally what the Wife of Bath would call her world and time.

Though the Man of Law is perfectly serious in his praise of constancy, being by profession and inclination devoted to hierarchic Law and believing with all his soul in authority, authority does not in fact come off well in this tale. Though not in any sense comic, the tale is, like the *Physician's Tale* and several other late works, ironic. That fact has been missed by most critics of Chaucer, with the result that the tale has not been much admired. The usual argument is that in some respects Chaucer was medieval in his sentiments and therefore not at all like us; our proper response as readers is therefore to try to put ourselves in Chaucer's sober, medieval frame of mind and appreciate a work we would otherwise find unappealing. The argument has, of course, some validity. It is always a temptation, when we read older poetry, to delight in what seems modern, grossly distorting the poetry in the process—as Jan Kott, for example, distorts Shakespeare and the Greek tragedians, turning their plays into existential or absurdist works. But in fact no such distortion is involved in a reading of the Lawyer's tale as ironic. We come to Fragment II with the question, generated in Fragment I, "What authority can we find for our beliefs?" (or how can we resolve differences between such men as the Knight, Miller, and Reeve?), and in Fragment II we get a defense of authority which in fact does the defendant more harm than good.

Trevor Whittock calls the tale "decidedly inferior," [3] but little as Whittock likes the *Man of Law's Tale*, he is probably the critic who has best understood it. He points out that

> Chaucer, unlike Gower [Chaucer's source, along with Nicholas Trivet], goes out of his way to stress the incredibility of what happens in the tale. For example . . . Gower "explains" Constance's survival for three years on the ship by saying that it had been provisioned for five years. Chaucer asks how could she possibly have survived without meat and drink, and answers the question by referring to miracles in the Scriptures. With Gower it is relatively easy to suspend disbelief; with *The Man of Law's Tale* it is more difficult unless one accepts implicitly the authority of the Bible and the preachings of Christianity.[4]

Chaucer, as Whittock goes on to point out, alters his sources to introduce Christian antifeminism not required by the plot. "The effect," he says, "is to make the fair-minded reader pause and query the validity of the Christian picture." [5] And lest anyone argue that Chaucer, as a fourteenth-century Christian, expected his listeners to accept the tale in devout faith, Whittock notes that

> Christian belief in the late middle ages was by no means as monolithic as this, and arguments as sceptical as any today had wide currency. For example, there is the dispute between Siger of Brabant and Thomas Aquinas which has been described as the most important intellectual episode of the thirteenth century. Siger taught the supremacy of reason over faith. Religion was necessary for the masses, but not for educated people. Dogmas were beneficial for faith, but were often contrary to reason and then reason was to be followed. There was also Boetius of Dacia who taught that the greatest beatitude was to be found in the practice of the good and the cognition of the true. Man's intellect, he wrote, could guide him to these, for if there is anything divine in man then it is the intellect.[6]

So the *Man of Law's Tale* enters the debate as a means of giving authority to the Knight's ideas, but it is in fact merely one more human point of view. To quote Professor Whittock one more time, "Chaucer was quite deliberate in so shaping the Man of Law's Tale that it may evoke belief *or* skepticism." [7]

Custance, the Man of Law's saintly and allegorical heroine, is the spiritual antithesis of — as we later discover — the Wife of Bath. Custance teaches endurance in adversity and trust in God. She teaches, too, constancy to commitments and submission to Law, authority, for though she weeps she does not strive against lawful authority — the will of God, of parents, or of husband. When she must leave home, Custance says:

> "Allas! unto the Barbre nacioun
> I moste anoon, syn that it is youre wille;
> > [i.e., her father's]
> But Crist, that starf for our redempcioun   [died]
> So yeve me grace his heestes to fulfille!
> I, wrecche womman, no fors though I spille!
> *Wommen are born to thraldom and penance,*
> *And to been under mannes governance."*
> > [II, 281–87; my italics

That view of women, even when presented with scriptural echoes, is one that takes some proving, the Wife of Bath would say. We get in the tale no proof but flat assertion, on the grounds of revealed religion. And the validity of revelation and religious custom is undermined in various ways throughout the tale, for instance in Chaucer's treatment of the "wicked" sultan's mother. Chaucer writes:

> The mooder of the Sowdan, welle of vices,
> Espied hath hir sones pleyn entente,
> How he wol lete his olde sacrifices;   [quit]
> And right anon she for hir conseil sente,
> And they been come to knowe what she mente.
> And whan assembled was this folk in-feere,   [together]
> She sette hire doun, and seyde as ye shal heere.

"Lordes," quod she, "ye knowen everichon,
How that my sone in point is for to lete
The hooly lawes of our Alkaron,
Yeven by Goddes message Makomete.
But oon avow to grete God I heete,
The lyf shal rather out of my body sterte
Or Makometes lawe out of myn herte!

"What sholde us tyden of this newe lawe
But thraldom to oure bodies and penance,
And afterward in helle to be drawe,
For we reneyed Mahoun oure creance?
But, lordes, wol ye maken assurance,
As I shal seyn, assentynge to my loore,
And I shal make us sauf for everemoore."

[II, 323–43

Though the Man of Law may call her "welle of vices," the fact remains that the sultan's mother is a figure of constancy to the only law she knows, a law sent down by God through a messenger as convincing, in the eyes of the sultan's mother at least, as Jesus. By what authority, Chaucer asks, can we determine which of two revealed religions is the right one? (In a later tale a more sympathetic narrator, Chaucer's gentle Squire, will praise a pagan king, Cambyuskan, on the grounds that "Hym lakked noght that longeth to a kyng; / As of the secte of which that he was born / He kepte his lay [law, or religion], to which that he was sworn.")

The *Man of Law's Tale* is, then, an ironic work which undermines the very authority it means to celebrate. Indeed, the irony is so insistent that we may wonder if for any listener at all the tale is meant to evoke belief. The irony is clearly Chaucer's, however; the Man of Law intends nothing of the kind. For its argument — its contribution to the great debate which makes up the *Canterbury Tales* — let us look at the tale as the Man of Law means it.

The emphasis in the *Man of Law's Tale* is on the power and safety which comes with Christian constancy. As for what constancy entails, the Man of Law's position is supremely orthodox — constancy means steadfast devotion to God and all who rule by his will, and indifference to the World. The poem opens with a contrast of the wealth of this world — the wealth of merchants and sultans — and the wealth of spirit, summed up in the emblematic character of Custance, who lives in the seat of Christendom, Rome. The sultan in the *Man of Law's Tale* must die if he cannot have Custance, for, as Chaucer often says elsewhere (sometimes ironically, sometimes not), death invariably lays its claim on the unhappy courtly lover who, focusing on the bliss of this world, cannot endure.[8] Alla, the northern pagan whom Custance marries, is as dear to Custance as was Custance to the sultan, but Custance does not die of sorrow when she is widowed. Looking forward to the bliss of the next world, Christian constancy can tolerate grief, the cruelty of Fortune. Constancy can resist the temptations of the "serpent depe in helle" with whom the sultana and Donegild are linked (the mothers of the men who choose Custance as wife); and above all, the constant servant of God, like the old Hebrew nation (as the Man of Law repeatedly reminds us) can prevail, maintaining his lineage, the specific continuity of medieval order. The line of Custance and the converted Alla survives: the child, Maurice, becomes an emperor and does great honor to the Church, that is, he serves both secular and ecclesiastical order in this world. Maurice, it should be added, provides Custance with a reason for not having to remarry and fail in constancy to her first husband's memory: although it was "skile and right" once for her, like other wives, to "take *in pacience* at night / Swiche manere necessaries as been plesynges / To folk that han ywedded hem with rynges, / And leye a lite hir hoolynesse aside, / As for the tyme" (II, 710–14; my italics), the birth of Maurice has freed her of her obligation to God to "go forth and cleanly multiply," God's first commandment to his creatures, according to medieval Church writers.

The entire plot of the *Man of Law's Tale* is an orthodox illustration of the way constant loyalty to the higher good can save one from treacherous Fortune. When her father has given Custance to the sultan as bride, Custance starts on her journey under unlucky stars. (The whole tale, as Manly showed, is worked out astrologically, the movement of the stars serving as a sign of God's Providence.) Her groom-to-be is murdered, along with all his company, but Custance survives. She is equally unlucky in her dealings with the man she does manage to marry, Alla. Though he, like Custance, is willing to accept whatever Fortune sends, his wicked mother casts poor Custance and her child adrift; but again Custance emerges unscathed. When Fortune turns benevolent and she is reunited with her husband, the change is brief; but that, too, Christian obedience can tolerate.

Though some critics have argued that the *Man of Law's Tale* is not fully appropriate to the acquisitive and self-regarding Lawyer introduced in the *General Prologue* (a feeble argument, actually; such men are invariably among the first to speak of God), it is indeed a tale of Law in the widest medieval sense of the word: it defines the authoritarian basis of medieval Christian society. The order of this world, from the Lawyer's point of view, depends upon absolute Christian constancy in service to the order, or Law, of the cosmos. Participation in the total order means contempt for the world (in Saint Jerome's relatively mild sense), absolute submission to authority, willingness to suffer, and trust — in short, constancy. Directly or indirectly the *Man of Law's Tale* treats at least five kinds of "authority": God's Providence, that is Supernature's control of Nature through Time (the point of the tale's astrological machinery, miracles, and the like); the authority of divine revelation; the rule of temporal and ecclesiastical lords; the authority of male over female and father over child (age over youth); and the rule of right reason over the passions, desire, and will. These various kinds of authority make up, together, universal Law as the Pilgrim Lawyer understands it.

Though the Man of Law's scheme of order may have seemed right to King Richard and those of his advisors who supported his theory of monarchial absolutism and divine right, Chaucer's ironies in the tale make clear that the basis of the scheme is at best somewhat doubtful; moreover, the extreme suffering of Custance throughout the tale hints that the Lawyer's system is, right or wrong, terribly grim — certainly more grim than the worldview of the Knight. Only out of duty does Custance do what the Wife of Bath does best, or

anyway once did, the "olde daunce" of lovemaking. If all real
buoyancy, all physical joy must go, one may wonder whether
cosmic order is worth the cost. As far as the Wife is
concerned, it is not, and she instantly objects.[9] She has had
ample experience of suffering and her first words to the
Pilgrims reveal what she thinks of it:

> Experience, though noon auctoritee
> Were in this world, is right ynogh for me
> To speke of wo that is in marriage!
>
> [III, 1–3

Her prologue and tale will present a view directly opposed to
the Lawyer's.

In denying the over-grim orthodox (but by the fourteenth century somewhat old-fashioned) Christian position on
marriage — Custance's notion that "Wommen are born to
thraldom and penance, / And to been under mannes governance" — in opposing otherworldliness, and in advancing comfort and pleasure as the basis of order, Dame Alice strikes out
at the fundamental premises of medieval stability, and with fair
emotional justification. She does not exactly mean to attack
constancy. The end of her tale presents a wife who will indeed
be constant, but by choice, not because that is her "place."
Neither does the Wife really mean to be a Protestant. What
she trusts is "experience," as she says, but she is careful to
show as best she can that her views, though not based on
scripture and Church authority, can be made to square with
them. The fact remains, however, that from the medieval
viewpoint her argument is upside-down. She deduces the
divine plan from human need and desire. At least technically
her argument is heretical, and the Clerk will, in his sly, ironic
way tell her so; but it is not really her heresy that the Clerk
attacks. He makes a fool of her because on her own grounds
she goes too far. Denying that a woman's life ought to be one
of "thraldom and penance," she asserts that when a marriage
lacks love, the tyranny should rest with women, thraldom with
men. To put this another way, the Wife, who is really
thinking mainly of her own troubles, not those of the world,

rejects the unpleasant element of self-denial implicit in constancy and patience by denying the view of headship which makes them meaningful. If she turns the universe upside-down, she does it partly by accident.

The Prologue to the Wife's tale presents the experiential basis for the Wife's theories. She tells the lively story of her five marriages and how she got the upper hand with each of her husbands, including even the young one she loved. She satirically treats man as forever "preaching" and gets her revenge by presenting, in her Prologue, a neatly worked out sermon of her own (that is, the Prologue is cast in the strict form of a medieval "university" sermon). Everything in the Prologue reveals the Wife's quick wit and delight in life. For instance, in her buoyant defense of herself, she points out (59 et seq.) that God never expressly commanded virginity but merely counseled it. She elaborates, then concludes: "The dart is set up for virginitee: / Cacche whoso may, who runneth best lat see" (75–76). The "dart" here refers to the prize in a running contest, and the humor of the ending, "Cacche whoso may . . ." is in the fact that the Wife is rhetorically calling for a race she has every intention of losing if she can. At the same time, the dart which is "set up for virginitee" is inescapably phallic: win the race and lose the maidenhead. In short, the Wife, win or lose, must win.

At the end of the Wife's Prologue an argument breaks out between the Friar and the Summoner, and in one sense the headship debate is interrupted, Chaucer shifting his attention to another matter, setting up the ferocious rivalry to be developed later in the warring tales of the Friar and Summoner. But in another sense the interruption furthers the debate on government: the Summoner promises to humiliate the Friar with mocking tales, "For wel I woot thy *pacience* is gon" (III, 849; my italics). Harry Bailey interrupts the two angry men and by his authority as host to the Pilgrims gives the Wife her turn to speak. The Wife's response, though joking and ironic, is a model of patience: "Al redy, sire," quod she, "right as yow lest, / If I have licence of this worthy Frere" (III, 854–55). The Friar defers to her and to the Host, and the Wife tells her tale.

The Friar's little outbreak leads the Wife to begin with a harmless little joke at the expense of friars. In the old days of King Arthur, she says, there were elves and fairies everywhere, "as thikke as motes in the sonne-beem," but nowadays friars, with their endless blessing of "halles, chambres, kichenes, boures, / Citees, burghes, castels, hye toures, / Thropes, bernes, shipnes, dayeryes," have driven all the elves and fairies off. Creatures associated with the spirit of Nature have been replaced by friars, associated — wrongly, it turns out — with Spirit: "In every bussh or under every tree / Ther is noon oother incubus but he, / And he wol don hem [women] but dishonour," (III, 879–81). The joke presses no serious argument, but it conforms to the Wife's general way of thinking: piety is mostly a trick men play on women. Sex rules the world.

The Wife's story is of a young knight who rapes a girl and is taken to King Arthur's court, where he is sentenced to die. Persuaded by the ladies of the court to give them authority to judge the reprobate knight, King Arthur's queen commutes the sentence from death to a quest: The knight is to search the world for a year and a day for the answer to a question: What do women most desire? If the knight can find the answer he will be spared. After much travel he learns the answer from an ugly old hag, who makes him pay for it with a promise that he will marry her. When she has given him the answer at last (women desire sovereignty) and the court has acknowledged the answer correct, the marriage takes place, and a wonderfully comic scene ensues:

> Greet was the wo the knyght hadde in his thoght,
> Whan he was with his wyf abedde ybroght;
> He walweth and he turneth to and fro.
> His olde wyf lay smylynge evermo,
> And seyde, "O deere housbonde, benedicitee!
> Fareth every knyght thus with his wyf as ye?
> Is this the lawe of kyng Arthures hous?
> Is every knyght of his so dangerous?
> I am youre owene love and eek youre wyf;
> I am she which that saved hath youre lyf,
> And, certes, yet ne dide I yow nevere unright;

Why fare ye thus with me this firste nyght?
Ye faren lyk a man had lost his wit.
What is my gilt? For Goddes love, tel me it,
And it shal been amended, if I may."
    "Amended?" quod this knyght, "allas! nay, nay!
It wol nat been amended nevere mo.
Thou are so loothly, and so oold also,
And therto comen of so lough a kynde
That litel wonder is thogh I walwe and wynde.
So wolde God myn herte wolde breste!"

[III, 1083–1103

In a masterful parody of scholastic reasoning, the hag proves that the young knight ought to be happy with her. She quotes numerous authorities, including Scripture, and no medieval man in his right mind could possibly deny that all she says is — theoretically — right: there is nothing wrong with old age, poverty, outer ugliness, or lowly birth. Nevertheless, human feeling naturally cries out against marriage to an ugly old crone. Finally the hag offers the knight a choice: as his wife she will either be ugly and faithful or beautiful and — perhaps! — faithless. Helpless in the face of such miserable alternatives, the young knight leaves the choice to the hag, and, since sovereignty has been given her, she generously promises to be both beautiful and faithful.

The "carnality" of the Wife of Bath is of course blatant. She herself admits it, both explicitly and, at several points, more subtly. Near the end of his quest the rapist knight comes upon a dance of twenty-four ladies (992). When he approaches they vanish; he finds only the old hag. The dance is apparently the ancient dance of the hours, and the stock medieval Christian reading is that to involve oneself in the dance of time instead of the calm of eternity is to be left wasted and foul, like the hag. But the stock interpretation will not work in the Wife's tale. It is in Time that the knight's life is saved — in the experience of life and time that all of us come to wisdom and whatever happiness we achieve. The allusion to the Midas story (952 et seq.) is equally ironic: through Midas' bestiality, symbolized by the ass's ears, Midas' wife gains the power to destroy him. But the Wife does not, in the usual fashion, condemn Midas for his bestiality but instead makes that weakness the impetus to virtue in both Midas and his wife. He shares his secret with his wife and trusts her, and because Midas' wife has been given power over him — given her husband's complete trust — she resists her own nature as an inveterate gossip and whispers his secret not to a human being but to the water in a marsh.

In the *Wife of Bath's Tale* all forms of traditional headship are explicitly or subtly overthrown. Divine revelation — to which the hag appeals in her argument that a young knight should be happy with an ugly old wife, so long as she is virtuous — proves feeble enough against human experience, natural desire. And the authority of great men and old books proves equally vulnerable — the authority of Dante, Valerius, Seneca, and Boethius (cf. lines 1126, 1165, 1168). As for the authority of kings, the old hag motif comes from Ireland, where in songs still sung and stories still told today, the old hag is the spirit of Erin, resisting the cruel domination of England. (Richard, we may recall, was sympathetic to the Irish demand for partial self-government and equality, so that insofar as the tale gives political advice to King Richard — it is of course broader than that — it does so cunningly, playing Richard's Irish policy and sympathies against his absolutist theory.) So all authority fares in this tale. King Arthur submits to the rule of Guinevere, abandoning both his headship of the state and his headship of the family; the ladies of the court, instead of Arthur's knights, serve as justices; noble lineage gives way to "gentilesse," that is, natural nobility, whatever the person's class; eternity takes second place to natural time, that is, men learn by experience and, in particular, by experience with women. Finally, in the choice the hag offers, feeling takes precedence over reason. Her long sermon to the moaning knight is, as we've said, completely reasonable; nevertheless, both alternatives the hag offers are emotionally intolerable, even though one — the choice of an ugly but faithful wife — can be supported with elaborate arguments and even Christian revelation. The Wife has set the orthodox medieval hierarchy on its ears.

Both the *Friar's Tale* and the *Summoner's Tale* capitalize
on the Wife's inversion of values. The antagonism set up
earlier between the Friar and Summoner, which culminated
with the Summoner's promise that he will teach the Friar
patience, bursts into the open once more, and without respect
for the "yerde" of Harry Bailey, the Friar declares that he will
now tell his tale. The Host says:

> "A! sire, ye sholde be hende   [noble]
> And curteys, as a man of youre estaat;
> In compaignye we wol have no debaat.
> Telleth youre tale, and lat the Sumonour be."
>
> [III, 1286–89

The Host's remark shows the behavior and the language of a
prudent lord; and both prudence and an understanding of
interdependence are implicit (jokingly and ironically) in the
Host's calling the Friar, later, "my leeve maister deere" (III,
1300).

The *Friar's Tale* is one of upside-down headship of the
sort the Wife has recommended but in a sphere she did not
have in mind.[10] At the top of the hierarchy in the tale stands
the bishop (III, 1317), whose business is to instruct and correct
straying Christians, drawing them back into the fold with his
shepherd's crook. Next on the hierarchy stands a harsh
archdeacon who, in the upside-down world of the Friar, sets
out after sinners on his own, that is, puts them down in his
book before the bishop has heard of them. The wicked
summoner of the tale is supposedly a vassal "to his hond," but
he in fact works for his own gain, going after sinners before
even the archdeacon has heard of their misdeeds. And the
summoner has, in turn, his servants, "bawdes redy to his
hond," who identify sinners for a price. The devil whom the
summoner meets on the road is also a vassal, and also traveling
"for to reysen up a rente / That longerth to my lordes
duetee" — the soul of the wicked summoner. False to his
immediate lord the archdeacon and to his ultimate lord, God,
and false also to those toward whom he stands in a position of
authority, the people within his jurisdiction, the summoner

abnegates responsibility and must be overthrown by a more loyal servant at the top of the upside-down hierarchy — a fiend. Appropriately, the summoner who breaks both social and divine pacts is destroyed by a pact at once social (one "bailly" to another, as the summoner thinks) and divine.

The relationship between the summoner and the widow is another ironic inversion which in the end brings about a return to order. The summoner goes to the widow's door as a representative of the established Church which can bless or damn. But the old widow, both literally and symbolically, *is* the Church. She greets the summoner with the Church's blessing and in the end sends him to hell with her curse. The comic symbolism which identifies the widow as the Church is one of the tale's most delightful ornaments. A widow is of course a common emblem of the Church, Bride of the crucified Christ, but Chaucer ingeniously supports the stock emblem. The summoner calls the widow an "old rebekke," Middle English slang for any old woman (the rebekke was a small, somewhat squeaky bowed instrument), but the word puns on the name Rebecca, wife of Isaac, who, because his life was nearly sacrificed by his father Abraham, became for the exegetes a type of Christ. Seeking a wife for Isaac, Abraham at God's instigation sent servants to a well to find a woman (Rebecca) with a vessel. If the old woman is the Church, that is, the "New Rebecca," Chaucer's irreverent version of that vessel is the old woman's "newe panne."

To get even with the Friar for his tale of a wicked summoner, the Summoner now tells a tale of a wicked friar who tormented a sick man — a doubting "Thomas" — into giving a gift to the friar's convent:

> "Now thanne, put in thyn hand doun by
>   my bak,"
> Seyde this man, "and grope wel bihynde.
> Bynethe my buttok there shaltow fynde
> A thyng that I have hyd in pryvetee."
>   "A!" thoghte this frere, "that shal go
>   with me!"
> And doun his hand he launcheth to the clifte,

In hope for to fynde there a yifte.
And whan this sike man felte this frere
Aboute his tuwel grope there and heere,
Amydde his hand he leet the frere a fart,
Ther nys no capul, drawynge in a cart,
That myghte have lete a fart of swich a soun.

[III, 2140–51

The friar has solemnly vowed that he will distribute this gift — the sick man's fart — equally to the convent twelve. The tricked friar goes, in howling rage, to a great lord to complain, and the lord's meat-carver explains how the distribution may be managed.

The *Summoner's Tale* at once contributes to the conflict between the brilliant, malicious Summoner and the corrupt, stupid Friar of the pilgrimage and comically develops the Wife's upside-down order. The tale is organized around two major motifs, impurity, or the failure to subjugate the desires of the flesh (cf. the Man of Law's position and also the Wife of Bath's closing joke at the expense of reason) and wrath (antithetical to patience). Like the wicked summoner of the preceding tale, the friar of this tale is another false vassal. Preaching purity and patience, he is himself impure and wrathful. As God's wrath is aroused by Satan, the sick Thomas's wrath is roused by the friar: Thomas would like to see him "on-fire" (III, 2122). The *Pearl*-poet, among others, tells us that God's gift is freely and equally given to all His church, symbolized by the number *twelve*. Thomas gives his gift and asks that it be equally shared by the twelve of the convent. (Stench, as we've seen, is a stock figure of hell in medieval writing.) The Summoner has indeed taught the Friar his "office," that is, has revealed the obscenity of the convent's eucharist, as he warned he would do (III, 1297).[11]

Another organizing feature of the *Summoner's Tale* is the scheme of the tripartite soul, in this case the soul perverted. The friar preaches desire for higher things, but his own voracious appetite is for food and the things of this world; he preaches patience and self-control, healthy activities of the irascible soul, but he himself gives way to wrath; and he

preaches the virtues of the rational soul on its two levels, vision
and reason, but his own vision is fake, his glossing mere
sophistry. (The moral of the Eden story turns out to be that
husbands should listen to their wives — III, 1992.) In his
perversion he is, like the central character in the Friar's story,
a type of corrupt vassal, a man who, turning from the spiritual
to the carnal, lacks constancy. In this upside-down world
where exegesis is carnality, the neat slicing up of an intellectual difficulty (how to share the sick man's fart) is managed by
a carver of meat.

And now it is time for the Clerk's comment.

The Clerk's Prologue, focusing on the virtue and learning of Petrarch, the source of his tale, is a defense of clerks, the
class maligned in the Wife of Bath's Prologue; it is, in other
words, at least partly a defense of reason. But the Clerk does
not underestimate the importance of feeling in human experience. The tale he tells treats the whole range of, loosely, feudal
interrelationships, metaphysical, social, private. He tells of a
lord, Walter, who, consenting to marry at the desire of his
people, chose a peasant girl for his bride, then cruelly and
needlessly tested her to prove her worthiness.[12] What interests
the Clerk as he tells the story of patient Griselda, judging by
his asides to the Pilgrims, is the contrast between Griselda's
almost insufferable patience and Walter's sad deficiency in
that virtue.[13]

The Clerk focuses, in his opening lines, on the traditional
social values: lineage, responsibility, love. Because he loves his
"owene peple deere," who also love him, Walter voluntarily
relinquishes the freedom of bachelorhood to satisfy his people's
desire that his lineage go on, assuring order in the future. All
this is most explicit. After his people have implored him to take
a wife,

> Hir meeke preyere and hir pitous cheere
> Made the markys herte han pitee.
> "Ye wol," quod he, "myn owne peple deere,
> To that I nevere erst thoughte streyne me.
> I me rejoysed of my liberte,
> That seelde tyme is founde in mariage;

Ther I was free, I moot been in servage.
"But natheless I se youre trewe entente,
And truste upon youre wit, and have doon ay;
Wherfore *of my free wyl* I wole assente
To wedde me, as soone as evere I may."

[IV, 141–51; my italics

The people, in turn, must of their own free will lay aside the
right ever to complain against Walter's choice. Then, having
selected Griselda, Walter first asks the free consent of his
vassal, Griselda's father (again recognizing mutual obligation
as the right basis of social order), and afterward asks the free
consent of Griselda herself, once more demanding absolute
loyalty freely given. The beginnings are promising, but
Walter, alas, is arrogant (not unlike King Richard). Contrary
to the best interest of his people (it is because of Griselda that
there is no "discord, rancour, ne hevynesse"; indeed, "The
commune profit koude she redresse" [IV, 431–32]), and
contrary to the best interest of Griselda, not to mention her
children, Walter tests Griselda's patience. As a ruler Walter is
inconstant to his obligation to serve law; as a husband he is
inconstant to his duty of family headship for mutual benefit.

The tale invites allegorical interpretation as well as literal.
On this level it treats patience in the metaphysical scheme.
The persistent testing which marks overweening pride in a
mortal like Walter is legitimate in God. His test of his Church
(of which the wife may be a figure) is a test of that quality of
patience never perfectly embodied except in Christ, closely
anticipated in the patience of Job and in the Virgin Mary,[14]
with all of whom Griselda is obliquely identified. The tale's
allegory is much too complex for detailed discussion here, but a
few examples will show the Clerk's method. Griselda's birth is
associated with that of Christ, when "grace" was sent to "a
litel oxes stalle" in Jerusalem (IV, 207); like Christ she "kepte
her fadres lyf on-lofte / With everich obeisaunce and diligence / That child may doon to fadres reverence" (IV,
229–31); she keeps her father's sheep; and like Isaiah's lamb
led to slaughter, "as a lamb she sitteth meke and stille, / And
leet this crueel sergeant doon his wille" (IV, 538) when her

child is slain. Griselda tolerates all Walter's cruelties and in so doing brings about a happy conclusion. Thus the Clerk refutes the Wife of Bath, whose heretical "secte" (*sex*, but also *sect*) would substitute for masculine tyranny like Walter's the tyranny of women who would make men "care, and wepe, and wrynge, and waille!" (IV, 1212).

The argument is by no means that the oppressed ought not to complain or seek a better lot (the Clerk expressly disavows that view), and it is not that social oppression is a splendid thing, improving inferiors. By means of his ironic intrusions into his tale, the Clerk acknowledges the legitimacy of the Wife's objection to being tyrannized. The point of the Clerk's ironic argument is that society depends upon love and mutual fidelity, both the fidelity of those who are in power and that of those who are not. The Clerk makes his point very clear at the end, openly reaffirming the virtue celebrated by the Man of Law:

> This storie is seyd, nat for that wyves sholde
> Folwen Griselde as in humylitee,
> For it were inportable, though they wolde;
> But for that every wight, in his degree,
> Sholde be constant in adversitee.
>
> [IV, 1142–46

To make certain no one can misunderstand, the Clerk again and again alters his source to heighten Griselda's humanness. If we think of the story as merely a fairy tale, as in the Arabic original (behind Petrarch and others), a story which goes something like "Once there was a prince who married a peasant girl and decided to test her to see if she was worthy . . . ," then nothing in the plot is especially strange — no stranger, anyway, than the idea that Snow White should go live with seven men. By insisting on Griselda's humanness — giving her lifelike emotions and even breaking into his story to ask, "Why on earth would Walter *do* a thing like that?" (See, for example, lines 457 et seq.) — the Clerk forces our attention to how unpleasant the whole affair is for Griselda, or for any woman tyrannized. And that effect was perhaps even stronger for the original audience. To modern readers Griselda seems a mostly allegorical stick figure, despite her lifelike reactions to misery. But though her submissiveness is extreme, in fact "inportable," it did not seem to medieval listeners completely unrealistic. Like modern Chinese and Japanese wives, medieval wives tried, in general, for submissiveness not altogether unlike Griselda's, supporting and dutifully obeying their husbands.

Superb human beings like Queen Philippa, Queen Anne, and Princess Joan — to speak only of ladies of fourteenth-century England — all deeply valued that wifely ideal, though if it always worked in practice we would have no Chaucerian "marriage group." In short, the *Clerk's Tale* was far more realistic in its day than it seems to the modern reader. Submissiveness offered what seemed a valid solution, though no woman could carry it as far as did Griselda. It was expected, socially acceptable behavior, so that, to the Clerk at least, the obstreperous and uppity Dame Alice seemed a great threat. This is why the Clerk turns suddenly nasty and ironic in his Envoy. He understands the Wife's hatred of male tyranny, as his tale shows; but also he hates the threat to all order that the Wife, in his opinion, represents.

The Merchant, as Professor Stevens has pointed out, is a cheerful enough fellow, not as unhappily married, perhaps, as critics have imagined;[15] but despite his good-business exterior, he is inwardly — like too many merchants in any age — cynical, even nihilistic. With his bitterly scornful view of marriage (and everything else, though he smiles and smiles), he indirectly supports and expands the Clerk's point (though he may not exactly understand it) with a story of a foolish old husband and a deceitful young wife. The tale is another of Chaucer's best, certainly one of his funniest, so that the lack of serious critical attention it has received is surprising.[16] The husband in the tale is a "worthy knyght" — translate "stupid old fool" — who for sixty years has refused to set aside his liberty (cf. the *Clerk's Tale*) but finally does so, more in dotage than in holiness, we may be sure. The knight is convinced that "in this world it [marriage] is a paradys," and perhaps it can be, if one chooses to believe in the Custance and Alla of the

Man of Law's Tale. The Merchant emphatically does not. He expounds the beauties of marriage in terms perfectly orthodox but so bitterly, sneeringly ironic that we laugh exactly as we laugh at Samuel Beckett. The chief of those beauties (to the rich, decrepit knight — an Italian at that!, the merchant would add acidly)[17] is that in marriage a man can "engendren hym an heir." Bachelors, living like animals "In libertee, and under noon arreest," sow on barren ground and reap barrenness (see IV, 1263 et seq.), says the Merchant, mocking and mimicking the knight "that was so wys." In this mutable world, only lineage gives permanence; therefore:

> A wyf is Goddes yfte verraily;
> Alle othere manere yiftes hardily,
> As londes, rentes, pasture, or commune,
> Or moebles, alle been yiftes of Fortune,   [furniture]
> That passen as a shadwe upon a wal.
>
> [IV, 1311–15

Men ought to have little regard for the gifts of Fortune, ought to be otherworldly (like Custance, to whom Fortune is so cruel); but a wife is no gift of Fortune. The Merchant venditates the high-minded orthodox opinion, but the truth, he hints — setting up an important motif — is that a wife is no gift of Fortune because she's a present from the Devil. Marriage is a "snare" (IV, 1227), a traditional image of the Devil's trickery. There is order in the world, perhaps, but the stupidity of both men and women, their ridiculous lack of "gentilesse," [18] makes order pointless and Providence impotent. The tale is the proof.

Young men moan and groan with lust, playing the field, treasuring their liberty, achieving nothing, but at least they feel a little normal lust. What old January feels mostly is a sterile inclination to spout vapid philosophy. He speaks line after line — or rather the Merchant speaks for him, with superb showmanship borrowing the old fool's character and voice — on the benefits of marriage, quoting all the poets and philosophers he can think of (another Chaucerian parody of scholastic authority-marshaling), and then, like Job in the time of his troubles, the old man calls his friends together and *they* spout philosophy, giving him advice. Two argue at length, Placebo, who, as his name tells us, will agree with anything, and Justinus, who, as his name tells us, sticks to what the Merchant believes to be facts. The old knight does, of course, just as he pleases, shoos away Justinus, and decides to get married. And now he turns from sterile reasoning to sterile "heigh fantasye" (1577), passing the image of all the ladies of the city through his mind, awake or sleeping.

Parodying the plot of the Clerk's story, the Merchant has January choose a young girl of low degree, because women who've been around awhile (like the Wife of Bath) become clever as clerks (IV, 1421–28). He has one worry, he tells his friends: that since marriage is a "paradise," as he has claimed and as the Man of Law has claimed, perhaps he will have his heaven on earth and thus miss heaven above. "Have no fear on *that* score," Justinus tells him. "Paraunter she may be youre purgatorie!" (1670). So indeed she proves. The wedding reception is properly jolly, but the whole scene flickers with that subterranean light we see in medieval illustrations of the pranks of hell's imps. There are instruments and foods everywhere, such instruments as not even that visitor to hell, Orpheus, heard, nor the magical musician Amphioun, husband of Niobe; instruments reminiscent of the trumpet of Joab or the trumpets ordered blown (according to Statius) by the augurer Theodomas for the murderous attack on Thebes. Bacchus the reveler, one of the pagan gods commonly introduced into medieval pictures of hell, pours wine in plenty, and Venus, who has similar dark associations, laughs with (or at) the guests, carrying a firebrand. (On the literal level, she is, of course, a dancing masque entertainer.)

Of the splendid wedding-consummation scene nothing need be said here but this: though May may be to January "his paradys, his make" (1822), the imagery has all the grotesquery of medieval hell illustrations—the "thikke brustles of [January's] berd unsofte, / Lyk to the skyn of houndfyssh, sharp as brere," (1824–25), the picture of January:

> al coltissh, ful of ragerye,
> And ful of jargon as a flekked pye;
> [magpie — a witch's bird]

The slakke skyn about his nekke shaketh,
Whil that he sang, so chaunteth he and craketh.

[IV, 1847–50

None too surprisingly, in this ghastly situation, May takes a lover who seems about to die for want of her,[19] outwits her husband's attempts to imprison her, and couples with her lover in a pear tree, taking advantage of her hoary husband's blindness. When in righteous indignation Pluto, god of the underworld, gives January sight, young May, inspired by Pluto's troublesome, once-mortal wife, convinces the old man that nothing has happened and that it was she who kindly won back his vision for him.

The Merchant's contribution to the headship discussion of fragments II–V is that all headship is tyrannical, because people are no damn good, not even hell is run properly; sterility is all. (It is both funny and symbolically fitting that, seeing his wife swyved, January "yaf a roryng and a cry, / As dooth the mooder whan the child shal dye.") Nature's law may be the law of God, and man's concern with lineage may be fully in accord with Christian constancy, even with otherworldliness, for lineage has not only private and social value but also value in the sight of God. (Cf. Theseus' words on temporal succession in the *Knight's Tale*, I, lines 3017 et seq.) But from the Merchant's point of view, human beings — especially women — wreck the system. They make bachelors miserable with desire, they trick their poor stupid husbands, they confound and abuse the very Devil, or anyway, Pluto.

Since time began, there has been only one answer to nihilism (cheerful or otherwise) like the Merchant's: the beauty of the innocent, foolish young. Nihilism is impossible to answer because it poisons premises. One look at a young man full of hope and amusing overconfidence, and the premises are magically restored. That is, I think, all that need be said here about the *Squire's Tale*, at least for the present argument on how the tales work together. Vastly more *can* be said, of course, but I leave it to others, mentioning only this: the *Squire's Tale* seems to be another example of intentionally bad art.[20] Again and again the Squire echoes his father's language, invariably in trivial situations which turn ludicrous when we recall the original context of the mighty lines. For instance, when tenderhearted, simpleminded Canacee holds the lady bird in her skirt, sweetly weeping at the bird's griefs (cf. Skelton's *Philip Sparrow*), the bird pipes the Knight's line: "pitee renneth soone in gentil herte" (V, 479). And when the male falcon leaves, the lady falcon relates, "I made vertu of necessitee" (V, 593). So it goes throughout this splendid burlesque. What counts here, I think, is not so much the tale as the teller.[21] Though there may be problems in the Man of Law's ideal of submission to authority, it is patent that, at least as a storyteller, the Squire has none of his father's authority, if only because he lacks his father's experience of the world.

The Franklin's contributions to the argument is an acceptable restatement of the position implied by the Clerk and Wife of Bath (at the end of her tale). Interestingly, this acceptable restatement comes from a kind of fool. His comments in the link show that he has no true understanding of "gentilesse" — he confuses it with something his son might learn. And his humble apology about his lack of eloquence, in the Prologue to his tale, triggers an absurd piece of rhetorical bombast:

> I sleep nevere on the Mount of Pernaso,
> Ne lerned Marcus Tullius Scithero —
> Colours ne knowe I none, withouten drede,
> But swiche colours as growen in the mede.
>
> [V (F), 721–24

He tells the story of a lord, Arveragus, who so loves his lady, Dorigen, that he gives her sovereignty, which she, for love, returns to him. Arveragus goes away on business, and Dorigen, explicitly doubting God's Providence, worries about the rocks that might wreck his ship when he comes home. When a young squire, Aurelius, pleads for her love, she thoughtlessly, impatiently tells him she will grant it if he removes all the rocks. The squire gets the help of a magician who makes the rocks seem to disappear. Arveragus returns,

Dorigen woefully tells him what she's done, and he insists that
he keep her bad bargain, for one must not go back on one's
"trouthe." She obeys, but when she tells the squire her reason
for coming, he releases her, moved by her love for her husband
and by her husband's nobility (gentilesse). When the magician learns of Aurelius' generosity to Dorigen, he in turn, of
gentilesse, releases Aurelius from his debt.

Most of the themes and motifs introduced in the
preceding tales are here reintroduced and organized in support
of the orthodox position of the Man of Law as tempered by the
sensuality and worldliness of the Wife of Bath. The Franklin's
position on marriage is very close to that of the Wife of Bath
and sharply differs from that of the Man of Law in that it takes
a far less austere view of this world's joys. The marriage in this
tale is one of mutual consent and mutual obligation — like the
marriage set up in Walter's contract with Griselda, in the
Clerk's Tale, or the marriage of the hag and the young knight,
once they have reached their understanding, in the Wife's tale.
Because of Arveragus' "meke obeysaunce," Dorigen accepts
him as "hir housbonde and hir lord." Because the knight, as a
true lover, gives his wife absolute command, his wife

> thanked hym, and with ful greet humblesse
> She seyde, "Sire, sith of youre gentillesse
> Ye profre me to have so large a reyne,
> Ne wolde nevere God bitwixt us tweyne,
> As in my gilt, were outher werre or stryf,
> Sire, I wol be youre humble trewe wyf."

[v, 753–58

This is of course exactly the solution the Wife proposed in her
tale — though not quite the solution recommended in her
prologue. God himself, the Franklin says, is the model of
patient endurance. The otherworldliness of Custance and
Griselda is reflected in Arveragus' concern with "trouthe" and
the Franklin's own comically obsessive and unenlightened
concern with "gentilesse"; and the persistent appearance-real-
ity motif in the group of tales is introduced again through the
work of the magician of Orliens. If anything is sure or real,

says the Franklin — when even the stability of rocks can't be trusted — it is "gentilesse," that nobility of character which responds with justice, resignation, and compassion — with "trouthe," which is high-class language for "patience" or "constancy" — to all the tricks of Fortune.

The order of Arveragus' household is grounded not on mutual consent alone but on the mutual wish of husband and wife to do what is best for the other; yet the concept of headship has not been abandoned. Arveragus lays commands upon Dorigen, and he backs them with the phrase *up peyne of deeth.* Once love has been established as the foundation of order, it can be backed by legitimate power.[22] But while man does his best through constancy, it is finally God who makes things work out. Arveragus' idea of "trouthe" is in fact as hollow as the Franklin's idea of "gentilesse" in the prologue to his tale. Arveragus sends Dorigen to her sorrowful assignation because he is caught up in the letter of the law. Moreover, were he omniscient, like God, he would know that in fact the rocks have not been moved at all — the bargain has no reality. Arveragus does, simply, the best he can, and God makes the necessary repairs. By "aventure or grace," i.e., chance or grace (Fortune or — really — Providence), Dorigen happens to meet Aurelius not in their secret place of assignation but "Amydde the toun, right in the quykkest strete" (V, 1502), and because of that luck they talk rather than act at once. The Providence which saved Custance saves Dorigen.[23]

IN THIS SEQUENCE of tales, fragments II–V, Chaucer may be said to defend the orthodox medieval position on order, but the defense is not without significant qualifications and can find no sure authority to support it. If the Wife of Bath is heretical, every human being's experience must urge that she is also partly right. Ironically, the highly rational Clerk who answers her, recommending patience approaching that of Griselda, does so partly in anger, twitted by the Wife's animadversions on clerks. The final word in the argument — the wise resolution of the demands of orthodoxy and of medieval emotional experience — is given to a sort of buffoon, the social-climbing, slightly befuddled Franklin. We have come a long way from the reasonable Knight of Fragment I. We may still believe him, but the philosophical grounds of our belief are — God knows what.

X

Fragments VI and VII ✿✿✿✿✿✿✿

The Theme of Pride, and the Uses
of Unreliable Art

RAGMENT VI IS RELATED IN VARIOUS
ways to fragments II–V, though it has nothing
to do, except remotely, with English politics. For
one thing, the Physician and Pardoner who tell the
two tales in Fragment VI are both, in different
ways, illustrations of the principle that justice in the world
must come from God, since men are mentally or emotionally
limited. For another thing, the Physicians's foolish and
self-righteous hero, Virginius, is Chaucer's comment on the
simpleminded "trouthe" of Arveragus. The tales in Fragment
VI look forward, at the same time, to the series of tales on
human pride in Fragment VII, and (less directly) to the tales
which will close the collection. In a sense, Fragment VI is thus
a pivotal point in the collection. From the *Knight's Tale*
forward, Fortune has been the central concern, but from now
on Grace will be increasingly important. Professor Ruggiers
points out, after calling attention to the distinction in the
Parson's Tale between the gifts of Fortune and the gifts of
Grace, that the Host's interpretation of the *Physician's Tale*
makes it "the demonstration of evil resulting from the gifts of
fortune and nature," and that in the Pardoner's performance
the emphasis shifts (the point will need qualifying) to "an

[293]

abuse of the gifts of grace, with the consequent death of the soul." [1]

Like the *Man of Law's Tale* and the *Clerk's Tale*, the *Physician's Tale* is a moral allegory. [2] It is the story of a man who, to save his virtuous daughter from a wicked judge (Apius) and his henchman (Claudius), cuts off her head. The wicked judge hangs himself when thrown into prison, and his henchman is exiled through the father's mercy. The child, Virginia, represents Christian purity (virginity); the false judge, Apius, may be identified with impurity.

As a moral allegory, the tale lies in a tradition as highly venerated as any available to a poet of the fourteenth century. But the value of a tale must come in the telling. In the *Man of Law's Tale* (itself partly ironic), the conflict of good and evil is always, and explicitly, one between God and the Devil. Custance is consistently identified with that Christian constancy her name indicates. Her wealth is spiritual, directly contrasting with the wealth of merchants and sultans; her protector and defending knight is the protector and defender of the Hebrew nation of old. Those who seek to destroy her, on the other hand, are consistently identified with the power of Satan. In the more difficult and in some ways more interesting *Clerk's Tale*, the allegory is equally insistent. Griselda is treated both literally and allegorically, like Custance, but it serves the Clerk's ironic purpose to overemphasize the literal, heightening the disparity between reasonable husbandly behavior and that of proud Walter. Raising realistic questions about (in effect) fairy-tale characters, the Clerk forces his listeners to recoil from the suffering imposed on Griselda by her domineering husband just as they would recoil from the domineering female sect of the Wife of Bath (judged by her prologue). In short, the tales of the Man of Law and the Clerk are indeed, though in different ways, what Coleridge would call *tales*, works which ask for a suspension of disbelief, not realistic stories depending for their effect upon verisimilitude, or the overwhelming argument of detail. The narrative of the Physician is not a tale, though it ought to be, but a bad work of verisimilitude. Whereas the Clerk makes a point of the fact that Griselda is not to be thought a real woman, the

Physician insists that Virginia was an actual girl and that the whole grisly story is absolute fact. The *Physician's Tale* is another example of purposely bad art, in this case bad art which reveals the proud and empty character of the narrator and pleases only by its awfulness.

The Physician introduces Virginia in highly artificial terms, all excessively elegant and irreconcilable with realism. Dame Nature, a personified abstraction, speaks, and her style of unwittingly comic repetition of words and phrases insists on an image of Virginia not as a person but as a figurine. Engraving, painting, forging, and beating are mentioned again and again and again to the point of absurdity:

> Fair was this mayde in excellent beautee
> Aboven every wight that man may see;
> For Nature hath with sovereyn diligence
> Yformed hire in so greet excellence,
> As though she wolde seyn, "Lo! I, Nature,
> Thus kan I forme and peynte a creature,
> Whan that me list: who kan me contrefete?
> Pigmalion noght, though he ay forge and bete,
> Or grave, or peynte, for I dar wel seyn,
> Apelles, Zanzis, sholde werche in veyn
> Outher to grave, or peynte, or forge, or bete,
> If they presumed me to countrefete.
> For he that is the formere principal
> Hath maked me his vicaire general,
> To forme and peynten erthely creaturis
> Right as me list, and ech thyng in my cure is
> Under the moone, that may wane and waxe;
> And for my werk right no thyng wol I axe;
> My lord and I been ful of oon accord.
> I made hire to the worshipe of my lord;
> So do I alle myne othere creatures,
> What colour that they han, or what figures."
> Thus semeth me that Nature wolde seye.
>
> [VI, 7–29

Having accidentally done everything in his power to convince us that Virginia is pure fiction — having used all the "colors of rhetoric" he knows, because he really wants to win that supper — the Physician turns to realistic details (VI, 61–64) and pious generalizations. He speaks of what revels do to young ladies; then, in a long orbicular digression, he preaches clichés to governesses and parents, telling them how they can bring up little girls just like Virginia. (According to one theory, all this advice is meant for the household of John of Gaunt. A very dull theory.) Eventually he gets back to his tale, a tale we are not for a moment to take for fiction, according to the Physician. The criminal judge was Apius, he says:

> So was his name, for this is no fable,
> But knowen for historial thyng notable;
> The sentence of it sooth is, out of doute.
>
> [VI, 155–57

There is no suggestion, in the *Physician's Tale*, of allegorical intent. We do not even learn the emblematic name of the unfortunate girl until line 213, when the main action is almost over. The attempt at realism is disastrous for the pretentious Physician — though not for Chaucer. Whereas one may legitimately pit absolute good against unmitigated evil in an allegory or fairy tale, and may even get away with it in carefully documented realism, to present that opposition in what purports to be realism but is not is to set up the cheapest sort of melodrama. The Physician's story cannot help but ring false when we compare Virginia's sanctimonious notion — "Ther been two weyes, outher deeth or shame" — with the decision of Arveragus, who prefers that his beloved wife endure shame rather than commit suicide; and for all the Physician's righteousness, the tale ends in pious confusion. Apius slays himself in prison but his right-hand man, Claudius, is saved from hanging by the virtuous mercy of Virginius, the father — whereupon, we are ferociously told, the "remnant" (of whom we have heard almost nothing until now!) "were anhanged, moore and lesse, / That were consentant of this cursednesse!" (VI, 275–76). And the tale concludes with a moral that ludicrously undermines the tale, beware the "worm of conscience." [3]

Needless to say, the stupidity of Chaucer's Apius and Virginia story is not something Chaucer brought over from his sources. Livy's splendid version is realistic and carefully thought out, and in all important respects Jean de Meun, Pierre Bercuire, and John Gower — other sources for Chaucer — follow Livy closely. In Livy, the father's murder of his child is tragically inevitable, and every detail in the action gives emotional support to that conclusion. For one thing, Virginia is betrothed to a noble young hero, Icilius, a champion of the people; and it is partly the betrothal — solemnized by law and sanctified by religion — that motivates Virginia's rejection of Apius. (The Physician drops Icilius, drops the tyranny theme, and drops religion.) Again, whereas in the Physician's version we scarcely hear of Virginius' friends until, like a belated cavalry, they rush to support Virginius after his daughter's death, in Livy the populace supports Virginius all along and thus forces Apius to his machinations. In Livy, the father is away at war when Apius delivers his judgment, and the girl's friends demand a postponement; Icilius and the girl's great-uncle plead for her; and at last Virginius arrives to plead. His plea is cut short by Apius' hasty ruling, and when Virginius cries out against the false decree, he is accused, with Icilius, of sedition. Virginia is ordered to go with Marcus Claudius, and Virginius, seeing no alternative, asks permission to speak with her one last time, goes to her, and stabs her, saying, "Thus, my daughter, in the only way I can, I give you your freedom." Other versions differ slightly, but not in ways we need discuss.

There can be no doubt of Chaucer's purpose in retelling the story as he does. The Physician forgets all the motivation, yet insists that the thing is "historial"; Chaucer deliberately undermines the tale's probability, for instance by shifting the death scene from Livy's hectic court of Apius to the calm of Virginius' parlor; and he makes Virginius talk like a pompous fool.

The tale is bad art in almost every way possible. When the Physician introduces allusions, he does so clumsily, overreaching himself. The allusion to the Pygmalion story, for instance, detracts from the realism the Physician desires and perhaps also raises subliminal questions about the "naturalness" of Virginius' love for his daughter, whose character is in some measure his creation (cf. 72–103). The allusion to Jepthe (240) is hardly more fortunate. Jepthe's unconsidered promise to God that he would offer up the first creature that came to meet him led to his daughter's death, but whereas Virginia rejoices that she will die a virgin (248), Jepthe's daughter, like a proper Jewish maiden, grieved at her dying a virgin, unfulfilled.

Part of the ironic relationship between the *Physician's Tale* and the *Pardoner's Tale* is that both men are proud, self-loving dissemblers. But one of the two, the Pardoner, knows what he is, while the other, pompous and affected, does not. Both men, by virtue of their human limitations, add force to one of the central arguments in the *Franklin's Tale*. In support of his claim that every man must learn patience, the Franklin had remarked,

> For every word men may nat chide or pleyne.
> Lerneth to suffre, or elles, so moot I goon,
> Ye shul it lerne, wher so ye wole or noon;
> For in this world, certein, ther no wight is
> That he ne dooth or seith somtyme amys.
> Ire, siknesse, or constellacioun
> Wyn, wo, or chaungynge of complexioun
> Causeth ful ofte to doon amys or speken.
> On every wrong a man may not be wreken.
> [v, 776–84

The tale the Franklin tells, wherein both the hero and heroine, Arveragus and Dorigen, act foolishly despite their good intentions, gives ample evidence for the Franklin's judgment. And the self-righteous and pompous but stupid Physician is a further proof that we all do well to remember we sometimes "do or speak amiss." And the Pardoner, for all his intellectual brilliance, makes (because of his emotional defects), equally grave mistakes. Ultimately their human limitations, since they are storytellers, suggest limitations in art itself. The idea, grounded in nominalism, that art is futile — either wrong or incapable of communicating — will become increasingly important in the *Canterbury Tales*. This is not yet a serious concern in the *Physician's Tale*, where the narrator's faults are so obvious that the bad art he produces can be viewed simply as satire through self-revelation. But in the tales which follow, unreliable narrators one after another force us to face the question squarely, ultimately casting such doubt on art's validity as to bring on Chaucer's *Retraction*.

§ 2

THE PARDONER has not missed the affectation of the Physician. Neither has the Host. Nothing could be farther from the truth than the notion that (as one critic says) "the good-natured fellow is powerfully affected, his Englishman's sense of justice outraged." The Host has not been taken in for an instant by the Physician's literary trash. His pious exclamations are crafty mockery of the Physician's affectations. The Host shows off his knowledge of the technical language of medicine — managing to get most of it comically wrong — and is even naïve enough (or rather, sly enough) to call attention to his dubious skill. He asks the Physician, "Seyde I nat wel?" and then, with mock-humility, he adds, "I kan nat speke in terme" (see VI, 304–11). The remark ironically and intentionally echoes the Physician's praise of Virginia: "No countrefeted termes hadde she / To seme wys" (VI, 51–52). Harry Bailey also rejects the Physician's moral to the tale and substitutes one of his own: "That yiftes of Fortune and of Nature / Been cause of deeth to many a creature" (295–96). Fortune and Nature are the medieval physician's stock-in-trade: the stars and the humors.

From the Pardoner's point of view, a sanctimonious fool has told a cheaply pious story, a piece of literary filth, and the Host's reaction to the tale, ironic praise, is not really sufficient to ground the Pardoner's disgust. The pompous Physician is, the Host says, "lyk a prelat, by Seint Ronyan," and the Pardoner can well enjoy both the irony and the obscenity —

runian in the sense of *scrotum*. But then from the Pardoner the Host asks "som myrthe or japes," though preaching is part of the Pardoner's profession and the one thing in all the world he is most proud of. The Pardoner's reply is, "It shal be doon . . . by Seint Ronyon!" The Pardoner's echo of the Host's "Seint Ronyan" has in it some kind of insinuation, malicious or otherwise, perhaps indicating the Pardoner's irritation at hearing the Physician praised as "lyk a prelat" and then being asked himself for mere japes. Now, adding injury to insult, the company cries with one voice, "Nay, lat hym telle us of no ribaudye!" In terms of medieval physiognomy, as Professor Curry long ago pointed out, the Pardoner is a man of whom the worst may be expected.[4] Perhaps the Pardoner determines then and there to have his revenge on all his complacent, self-righteous tormenters, and decides to think his revenge out carefully — over a bottle. Or perhaps what happens is a trifle less sinister. But of this, more later.

In his Prologue the Pardoner frankly confesses that he is a fraud motivated by avarice, gives a delightful list of his confidence games, and admits, somewhat proudly, that he is guilty of all the seven deadly sins.[5] Then, to show the company how he cheats poor fools by stirring up their holy passions, he repeats for the Pilgrims the sermon he uses — the story of the three revelers. In plague time, three young men in a tavern hear that Death is abroad, and they go out to hunt him. They find an old man at a stile — perhaps Death, perhaps the Wandering Jew, perhaps someone else; a wonderfully gloomy mysterious figure. They ask if he is Death and threaten him with violence, then accept his word that Death is nearby, under a tree. They go to the tree and find there a fortune in gold. Each wants it for himself, and by trickery, each outsmarting himself, they kill each other.[6]

After the Pardoner has moved the Pilgrims to silence with a sermon not to be matched elsewhere in English literature, he ends with a benediction and a solemn reminder that, though the pardon he himself offers is fake, Christ's pardon is sure. Then — incredibly — he says, "But I forgot one thing," and, impish and shameless, he tries to sell a false pardon and some of his phony relics to the Host. The turnabout is startling, and critics have mused on it endlessly. G. G. Sedgewick, in "The Progress of Chaucer's Pardoner, 1880–1940," summarized the earlier musings and offered a theory of his own:

> Of course a benediction is partly a matter of traditional formula. But in it, if ever at any time, a Pardoner may be allowed to say something at once sincere and stripped of shamelessness. "I have not deceived you," he says in effect, "nor will I do so now. The false 'assoiling' I have just exhibited tends to destruction; but there *is* a cure for souls that is truly efficacious. I have proclaimed myself a charlatan, but I would not have you think me a heretic." In Chaucer's verse this is no paroxysm but a dignified and eloquent farewell. The teller of the Quest for Death knows what dignity is even if he does not put his knowledge into practice very often; and five centuries of listeners have never denied him eloquence. There is "some good" in the Pardoner, as two English editors say with commendable restraint. Tommorrow, perhaps, he will even be afraid and tremble "before that formidable power which he said he held in his hands and of which he has made a toy." [7]

For Sedgewick as for Kittredge, the Pardoner is capable of moral earnestness. His undoing, according to Sedgewick, is his "preacher's vanity." Having impressed the listeners, "he lets fling at the Pilgrims with his impudently ironic joke, all guards down."

Though more recent critics have strayed from the point, Sedgewick is right, or partly right; at least his theory accounts for what seems the Pardoner's odd reaction to the Host's "lyk a prelat." But rather more is involved. The Pardoner is a man instantly identifiable, by plain inspection, as "a gelding or a mare" — a eunuch or a homosexual. Whichever he really is, he plays, and brazenly, the role of homosexual. This is a standard observation in *Pardoner's Tale* criticism, but recent critics have leaped from the observation to a kind of stern moralizing that makes Chaucer a kind of man he simply was not. [8] No one would deny, not even the Pardoner, that the Pardoner is a bad man; but to call him "the one damned soul on the pilgrimage," as one critic does is foolishness. His social problem is considerably worse than his spiritual problem. As homosexuals sometimes do in a hostile society, he repeatedly and insistently calls attention to his condition, ironically telling the Wife of Bath he's been thinking of getting married (not, as some have thought, to hide his homosexuality, which is, as I've said, obvious at a glance, but to flaunt it) and now, after his sermon, turning to Harry Bailey with an obscene — and not serious — proposition. Asking for a tale, the Host addressed the Pardoner as "Thou beel amy," a term which can be used affectionately between close friends (as John of Gaunt used it in giving gifts to Chaucer) but which, in less intimate situations, has the effect of turning to a man and saying to him jokingly, "You, sweetie." The Pardoner responds merrily enough, echoing the Host's "Seint Ronyan," tossing out obscene puns on drinking and eating of a "cake" (*cah-keh*, shading toward *caw-keh*, "cock"), and tells his tale. While delivering his sermon he gives himself over to his role as priest; when the sermon ends, the Pardoner is merely a man again, self-conscious as ever (like any mortal preacher when he steps down from his pulpit), and being the kind of man he is, he covers as usual, by nasty jokes (on buying fraudulent relics and worthless pardons) and with his mock homosexual proposition, another echo of the Host (from I, 3115), "Unbokele anon thy purs" (VI, 945). (Since the medieval purse hung from the belt, in front, frequently under a man's outer clothing, the word was often given a sexual connotation.) The big, muscular Host, who prizes and jealously guards his manliness, as might many a burly bartender today, is outraged and flustered, though not quite as angry as the Pardoner becomes when his joke so horribly backfires. At the root of the anger on both sides is wounded pride. The Host cannot tolerate a homosexual threat and in the violence of his pride cruelly repulses it; but the Pardoner was not serious about the threat in the first place — not here in front of all these Pilgrims — and the unwarranted attack on him, a verbal castration and exposure of his chief point of vulnerability, leaves him speechless with pain and indignation. The Knight who, both by his character and by the nature of the tale he tells, stands as Chaucer's symbol of natural balance and proportion, steps between the two and directs them to kiss.

The kiss exchanged by the lusty Host and the effeminate Pardoner is comically ironic in more ways than one. The Pardoner, whose official role is to get men to call on God, through him, for forgiveness of their sins, is himself unmerciful — that is, unwilling to pardon. Part of his purpose in delivering his sermon was to take revenge on the Pilgrims for their outcry against him when he was asked for "myrthe or japes." Now, in the conflict between the Pardoner and the Host, pardon comes through the agency of the man who upholds not Christian doctrine (directly, anyway) but social order and the order of nature, the Knight. The Knight's kindness to the Pardoner is right, of course. He makes the people stop laughing at him and addresses the Pardoner as "thee," familiarly, saying "ye," more formally, to the Host. If the Pardoner is vicious, he is in fact not much worse than the self-righteous Physician (both of course take money unscrupulously); and as the Knight makes clear — both in language and action — the Pardoner is not so much vicious as he is a foolish, ill-behaved child. But though we need not consign the Pardoner to hell, the contrast between the *Physician's Tale* and the *Pardoner's Tale* raises an interesting aesthetic point. One makes bad art though his intentions are good; the other makes good art for mostly base reasons. Where such things are possible we can hardly accept the poet as "legislator for humanity," in Shelley's phrase — hardly accept the Aristotelian idea of the artist as imitator of universal moral process.

Fragment VII, springing from the opposition of the self-righteous Physician and the arrogant Pardoner in Fragment VI, presents a debate on the role of position and power in this world, one view tracing them to Fortune, the other tracing them to Grace, and both views having, oddly enough, their prideful streaks. The opening lines of the *Shipman's Tale*[9] establish the theme. The story will concern a rich merchant who has a certain authority over those around him because of his apparent wealth. He has also a wife who is "campaignable and revelous" (VII, 4), qualities which redound to the credit of the merchant but cost him dear, causing "more dispence [expense] / Than worth is al the chiere and reverence / That men hem doon at festes and at dances" (VII, 5–7). The glory the proud merchant gains from his outlay for his wife's wardrobe — the "salutaciouns and contenaunces" (VII, 8) which flatter his vanity — must pass; but if the joy is brief, the bills go on and on. Yet the merchant is not in a position to reject the expense. He must pay, because if he refuses then someone else will pay, and that, as the *Shipman's Tale* proves, is perilous.

The merchant has an acquaintance, a monk born in the same village, who calls the merchant "cousin." Actually there is no blood relationship, but the merchant accepts the cousinage (cozenage) because it flatters him, the monk being above the merchant's station. Others love the monk for other presents:

> Free was daun John, and namely of dispence,
> As in that hous, and ful of diligence
> To doon plesaunce, and also greet costage,
> He noght forgat to yeve the leeste page
> In al that hous; but after hir degree,
> He yaf the lord, and sitthe al his maynee,
>   [afterward; retinue]
> Whan that he cam, som manere honest thyng.
>   [VII, 42–48

By verbal echo Chaucer underscores the relationship of the monk's two kinds of gift. When the monk calls the merchant cousin, giving a gift of prestige, the merchant "was al glad therof as fowel of day" (VII, 38); when the monk brings presents to the household, "they were as glad of his com-yng / As fowel is fayn when that the sonne up riseth" (VII, 50–51). As the story unfolds, the thesis set up in the opening lines is borne out: the rich get richer and the less rich get cuckolded.

Now it is the Prioress's turn. She continues the debate on position and power and of course adds to the poem's treatment of the larger question, How is one to be judged? Whereas the

Shipman's story emphasizes the power of money and position and the weakness and vulnerability of those who lack them and must trust in prudence, the *Prioress's Tale* shows the power of the meek and poor who trust in Christ. A devoted and meek Christian lady (at least as she understands herself), she begins by offering a prayer to Christ and, especially, the Virgin, the gist of which is that since the Prioress is like a child, the Virgin must help with this story in her honor. In the tale the Prioress now tells, she sets up an opposition between Jews (in their traditional stereotype as people concerned wholly and solely with the power of this world, money) and other-worldly Christians. She insists from the start on the physical vulnerability of the Christian position. Their school is "litel," the children are repeatedly called "smale," or "litel." Even the book the little scholar in the tale reads is "litel." His mother is a widow, by implication poor and defenseless. But the seeming power of the Jews, who can accumulate money and kill little children, is overwhelmed by the Virgin's miracle and by those treasures of the spirit suggested by the pearl on the dead child's tongue and also introduced emblematically in the Prioress's imagery of precious stones: "This gemme of chastite, this emeraude, / And eek of martirdom the ruby bright" (VII, 609–10).

Everything in the tale enforces the contrast between the Prioress's position and that of the Shipman. The Christian child's gift to the Christ child — a song the little scholar does not even understand — contrasts with the gifts of the monk to the household he will dupe, and the focus on the Virgin, throughout the *Prioress's Tale*, clarifies the contrast between meekness and worldly power. The mother of the murdered child is a "new Rachel," her child implicitly a "new Joseph," for the exegetes an Old Testament prefiguration of Christ. Not, of course, that the *Prioress's Tale* is meant to be taken as Chaucer's serious, orthodox answer to the Shipman.

The Prioress's view that true power in the world lies in love of God is indeed orthodox, and there is no reason to doubt that Chaucer himself, up to a point, accepted it. But the presentation is ironic. The Prioress's own simplemindedness, not wholly excusable on the grounds that she has spent all her life in a convent, throws ironic light on the position she affirms.[10] Her violent hatred of Jews (historically, she cannot have known any) contrasts with her sentimental fondness for dogs and her pity for mice in traps; her too clever bit of science — the grain placed on the dead child's tongue (a commonly recommended but scientifically discredited cure for the loss of speech) — hints, like much in the *General Prologue*, at her vanity;[11] and her veneration of purity rings ironically against her scatological inclination. Having said that the Jews threw the dead child in a pit, she changes her mind and specifies a latrine where they were wont to empty their entrails (VII, 571 et seq.). Almost immediately afterward, Chaucer writes: "Now maystow syngen, folwynge evere in oon / The white Lamb celestial — quod she — " (VII, 580–81). Chaucer's "quod she" is no mere snatch at a rhyme. It recalls us the teller of the tale. The startling juxtaposition of images — a corpse in excrement, a pure white lamb in heaven — is the Prioress's own work. Innocence doesn't necessarily (as Henry James kept noticing) make virtue.

Standing alone, the *Shipman's Tale* expresses an attitude of irreligious but comfortable materialism which sophisticated middle-class people of Chaucer's day could not help but find fairly persuasive (though sinful of course); but in juxtaposition to the *Prioress's Tale*, the emotional sense of the *Shipman's Tale* shifts. Moreover, the *Shipman's Tale* has its own internal ironies. Whether one finds it in Chaucer or Balzac, the figure of the lecherous monk, even if the narrator approves of him, cannot help but comment on how monks really are "or elles oghte be," as the Prioress says. And in this case the outriding monk, Don John, seems obliquely to refer to the Monk of the pilgrimage, who has, judging by his appearance and pastimes, a similarly worldly outlook. It is partly the criticism implied by the Shipman's satirical portrait of the monk in his tale that provokes the Monk of the pilgrimage to the gloomy recitation of tragedies which at first glance seems to us so out of character for him. When the Host asks the Monk for a tale he first tries on him the name "daun John" (VII, 1929),[12] an allusion to the monk of the earlier tale (among other things);

he later changes his mind and calls the monk "daun Piers by youre name," alluding to that dreary, pious *Piers Plowman* (VII, 2792); and then he turns to the Nun's Priest and confidently addresses *him* as "sir John" (VII, 2810). As this linking suggests, the opposition of points of view set up in the juxtaposed tales of the Shipman and Prioress continues into the succeeding tales, a collection of parodies or, more precisely, pieces of intentionally unreliable art, each of which ironically qualifies those around it and complicates the theme. After the Prioress has told her tale in praise of childlike innocence, Bailey turns to the childlike mock-innocent Chaucer. The Host's merry words emphasize Chaucer's meek, childlike character: he is like a doll, elvish, a man for whom other, more impressive men must be asked to stand aside. Asked to tell a tale, "Chaucer" answers timidly: " 'Hooste,' quod I, 'ne beth nat yvele apayd, / For oother tale certes kan I noon, / But of a rym I lerned longe agoon.' " (707–9). That will suffice, the Host answers, and Chaucer begins.

In place of the Prioress's image of the miraculous pearl and her general concern with heavenly treasure, the sweet, dim-witted pilgrim "Chaucer" offers the story of a "gem" or "topaz" of a knight, a member of the merchant-born Flemish knighthood. The Prioress's concern with virginity, meekness, and innocence finds its reflection in the symbolic significance of the topaz as emblem of purity, in the comparison of the knight's pasty complexion with "payndemayn," a kind of bread which had once commonly been stamped with images of the Savior and Virgin. The unwitting affectation of the Prioress (especially clear in the *General Prologue* portrait) and the affectation theme in the *Shipman's Tale* find their reflection in the Flemish knight's ludicrous affectations. The description of Sir Thopas suggests a burgher; some of his activities, such as wrestling with a ram, are activities that would be more proper to a churl; his horsemanship is that of a city fellow; the plants in the forest where he boldly rides are herbs common in hearty lowlands cooking, and the "wild beasts" there are such creatures as the deer and rabbit. There are hints throughout that he is a homosexual or, perhaps, a

masturbator. One such hint is carried by the word *pricking,*
which normally means "galloping" but often has, in popular
verse, a sexual meaning:

> Sire Thopas fil in love-longynge,
> Al whan he herde the thrustel synge,
>   And pryked as he were wood.
> His faire steede in his prikynge
> So swatte that men myghte him wrynge;
>   His sydes were al blood.
>
> Sire Thopas eek so wery was
> For prikyng on the softe gras,
>   So fiers was his corage,
> That doun he leyde him in that plas
> To make his steede som solas,
>   And yaf hym good forage.
>
> "O seinte Marie, benedicite!
> What eyleth this love at me
>   To bynde me so soore?
> Me dremed al this nyght, pardee,
> An elf-queene shal my lemman be
>   And slepe under my goore.   [VII, 772–89

(The word *goore* is also a pun, apparently. On the literal level
it refers to a garment, but it can also mean as it did in Old
English, ugly spillings — blood or some other sort of mess.) Sir
Thopas is thus a burlesque innocent, a figure parodic of such
noble idealists as Thomas of Ereceldoun, who also had dealings
with the Land of Fayerye; Sir Gawain, whose dealings with an
elf and whose elaborate arming in *Sir Gawain and the Green
Knight* Chaucer parodies here; certain lesser heroes whom
Chaucer lists in haste, Horn child, Ypotys, Sir Bevis, Sir Guy
(of Warwick), Sir Lybeux, and Playndamour; even, at one
point, the young David who dared to meet Goliath, though
here the wrong contender has the slingshot. After stumbling
accidentally into a terrible giant in the Land of Fayerye,

> Sire Thopas drow abak ful faste;
> This geant at hym stones caste
> Out of a fel staf-slynge.

Whether or not the tale is, as Professor George Williams imagines, a lampoon against King Richard, who was often accused of homosexuality, Williams is right in identifying Sir Thopas as a caricature of the homosexual. Chaucer of course goes further. In his lisping, effeminate, overelegant bad verse, his *Gawain*-poet-like twitterings about the knight's dinner and lovely attire, in certain slyly suggestive innuendoes, as when he speaks, just before the poem is interrupted, of Sir Percival's being "worthy under wede," i.e., worthy under his clothes, Chaucer himself imitates an age-old homosexual style. The Host crossly stops Chaucer's drasty rhyming, and Chaucer meekly turns to the prose tale, *Melibee*.

Though some of Chaucer's contemporaries, like John Lydgate, admired this tale, as do some recent critics, Chaucer surely recognized that however serious the tale's purpose, the thing was comically long-winded (considerably longer than its French source: Chaucer added more proverbs). He therefore introduced "Chaucer's" long proof that since his only concern is the sentence or moral meaning of the tale he will tell, he must not be interrupted in his "litel tretys." The plot of the tale — a comically wooden allegory — is monstrously simple. A rich man, Melibee, has enemies who beat up and sorely wound his daughter. Wildly angry, Melibee decides to avenge himself, but his wife Prudence talks him into getting advice first, then convinces him that her own advice is best, talks him out of vengeance, and goes to reason with his enemies, who are easily persuaded that they were wrong. The tale is a popular medieval form: the quotation collection, with the quotations strung along a plot. Since the plot happens to be one involving fierce emotions and actions, the long-winded quotations are comically inappropriate, completely undermining the emotion (Melibee's wrath) that makes the plot move.

In *Melibee* the debate on power and position, sources of Pride, emerges as a question of man's most prudent attitude toward Fortune. The turning point of the tale comes when Dame Prudence, Melibee's wife, tells her husband: "Thy name is Melibee, this is to seyn, 'a man that drynketh hony [honey].' Thou hast ydronke so muchel hony of sweete temporeel richesses, and delices and honours of this world, that

thou are dronken, and hast forgeten Jhesu Crist thy creatour"
(1409). What this means, she goes on to explain, is that he has
been given good fortune, a thing God may at any time take
away. And since Fortune may change, she says, "I conseille
yow that ye bigynne no werre in trust of youre richesses, for
they ne suffisen noght werres to mayntene" (1649).

In the Prologue to the *Monk's Tale*, the Host reacts to the
Melibee with what amounts to a comment on what is wrong
with Prudence's position and, indeed, Chaucer's whole foolish
tale. The *Melibee* ignores the force of human passion — the
force Melibee talks about with such remarkable detachment,
for an angry man, and which the Host's wife Goodelief
embodies. After this, Chaucer introduces the Monk's series of
little tragedies, which report the gloomy news that all wealth
and position in the world are empty illusion, and nothing,
neither God nor human prudence, can prevent the fall of the
proud. The Monk sums up his theme in the introductory
stanza:

> For certein, whan that Fortune list to flee,
> Ther may no man the cours of hire withholde.
> Lat no man truste on blynd prosperitee.
>
> [VII, 1995–97

— exactly the point Dame Prudence made to Melibee. The
Monk then tells the stories of Lucifer, Adam, Samson,
Hercules, and so on — yet another example of intentional bad
art, though some of the tales are much better than the Monk
deserves. The Monk's whole position is oversimple, of course,
as the Nun's Priest will show and others have shown already.
As the *Franklin's Tale* revealed, and as Boethius taught,
Fortune destroys only those who can look no higher than
nature, for behind Fortune lies God's ruling Providence.[13]

The Knight eventually interrupts the Monk's long
recitation: a little of this gloom goes a long way, he says; he
would rather hear of people who rise from sorrow to joy. The
Host agrees and asks for some other sort of tale from the
Monk, but the Monk is stubborn — in fact proud — and at last
the Host turns to the Nun's Priest for a tale.

§ 3

THE NUN'S PRIEST brilliantly summarizes and resolves — or perhaps dissolves — the debate on power and position.[14] He opens with a description of the poor old widow who owns the noble cock, Chauntecleer, then turns to Chauntecleer, his glory and his problems. In a dream, Chauntecleer is frightened by a fox. When he tells his wife Pertelote of this, claiming that the dream forewarns of something about to happen, Pertelote scoffs and berates him for his timidity. He brilliantly defends himself, telling stories, quoting authorities, slyly mistranslating Latin, and so forth, and at last Pertelote is satisfied. Alas, the victorious Chauntecleer has now forgotten all about the fox. The fox arrives. He snatches Chauntecleer by means of a scornful trick appealing to the cock's pride (and implicitly scoffing at his alleged learning), and all the farm pursues the fox to the woods. But Chauntecleer escapes by his own wits, with a little help from God, using on the fox the same trick the fox used on Chauntecleer. When his tale is finished, the Nun's Priest hints that there is more here than meets the eye ("Ye that holden this tale a folye, / As of a fox, or of a cok and hen, / Taketh the moralite, goode men") and graciously withdraws.

The Nun's Priest's position is set up in his genially ironic attitude toward both the simple life and the life of the great. The widow represents one, the cock the other. As I've pointed out elsewhere, the whole opening description of the widow is built of carefully balanced ironies, lines which slyly mock both the rich and the poor, the high and the low. If the widow's life is spare, it is spare for a reason: she led a simple life *because* little was her chattel and her rent; i.e., she did not have much and it did not cost her much to get along. The implication is, it's easier for the poor to live the humble Christian life than for the rich, who have, like Chauntecleer, great responsibilities; but on the other hand, can we really take seriously the idea of great responsibilities in a chicken? — or even a human being?

Chauntecleer has great talents as well as grave responsibilities: "In al the land, of crowyng nas his peer," (2850) and "whan degrees fifteene weren ascended, / Thanne crew he, that it myghte nat been amended" (2857 et seq.). The cock's talent (crowing, and so forth) is obviously at least slightly absurd, however proud he may be of it (in Middle English, "crowing" can also mean boasting), and his responsibility, making sure the sun does not go back down in the morning, is less important to the coming of day than he thinks. His other responsibility, taking sexual care of his wives, that is, his sisters — an activity adorned with the language of courtly love — is equally ludicrous. Nevertheless, Chauntecleer is a prince of sorts, and even though human princes, like cocks, may overestimate their importance to the universe, they are, in fact, of some importance. The poor old widows of the world have no need or use for the things which occupy people in castles. (Chauntecleer lives in a yard "enclosed al aboute / With stikkes, and a drye dytch withoute" [2847–48]). But the rich have need and use for art, philosophy, and courtly show, the things which occupy Chauntecleer and Pertelote. As no one knew better than the people in attendance on King Richard II, lover of pageantry, symbolism, painting, music, poetry, astrology, and philosophy, such things can directly contribute to a ruler's power and prestige and can help him toward wisdom. Princes may easily overvalue such things, naturally, as Richard II did and as Chauntecleer does when the fox slyly begs, "Now syngeth, sire, for seinte charitee; / Lat se, konne ye youre fader countrefete?" (3520–21). But the finer things of life (as Mars learned in his *Complaint*) are not evil in themselves; it is their misuse that leads to misfortune. At the same time, when Fortune turns on them, the rich have the same recourse other men have, God's help ("as wys God helpe me") and their own wits.

Part of the Nun's Priest method in his lighthearted, comically inflated tale of human pride is, as E. Talbot Donaldson has pointed out, ironic identification of Chauntecleer with everything noble that he can think of. Pertelote is like "Hasdrubales wyf, / Whan that hir housbonde hadde lost his lyf, / And that the Romayns hadde brend Cartage" (VII,

3363–65); Chauntecleer's other wives cry like the senators' wives when Nero burned Rome. Chauntecleer is like King Priam, like Christ himself. This last comic hyperbole is worked out in some detail and comments throughout on Chauntecleer's exaggerated sense of his own importance. The first image we get of Chauntecleer among his wives is one which calls up the picture of Christ among his celestial brides, a picture common on cathedral transoms:

> And so bifel that in a dawenynge,
> As Chauntecleer among his wyves alle
> Sat on his perche, that was in the halle.
>
> [VII, 2882–84

The fox is, then, Judas Iscariot (3227), and "on a Friday fil al this meschaunce" — the black Friday of the crucifixion. The same ironic allegory is involved in the final lines of the brilliant climactic passage of the poem:

> This sely wydwe and eek hir doghtres two
> Herden thise hennes crie and maken wo,
> And out at dores stirten they anon,
> And syen the fox toward the grove gon,
> And bar upon his bak the cok away,
> And cryden, "Out! harrow! and weylaway!
> Ha! ha! the fox!" and after hym they ran,
> And eek with staves many another man.
> Ran Colle oure dogge, and Talbot and Gerland,
> And Malkyn, with a dystaf in hir hand;
> Ran cow and calf, and eek the verray hogges,
> So fered for the berkyng of the dogges
> And shoutyng of the men and wommen eeke,
> They ronne so hem thoughte hir herte breeke.
> They yolleden as feendes doon in helle;
> The dokes cryden as men wolde hem quelle;
> The gees for feere flowen over the trees;
> Out of the hyve cam the swarm of bees.
> So hydous was the noyse, a, *benedicitee!*
> Certes, he Jakke Straw and his meynee
> Ne made nevere shoutes half so shrille

Whan that they wolden any Flemyng kille,
As thilke day was maad upon the fox.
Of bras they broughten bemes, and of box,
Of horn, of boon, in whiche they blewe and powped,
And therwithal they skriked and they howped.
It semed as that hevene sholde falle.

[VII, 3375–3401

The ironic identification of Chauntecleer and Christ keeps us from taking Chauntecleer as seriously as he takes himself (should anyone be tempted); yet the tone is not simple farce. The brilliance of the passage just quoted is that it shows a perfect marriage of the two styles of life, epic and mundane, and that the marriage of life styles, like all marriages, forces a compromise: each must acknowledge both its virtues and its limits. The rhythmical energy, the drive of the imagery, the leaps of diction and metaphor, all come from what Chaucer knew of the epic manner: alter the subject and the lines would be Dante or Virgil. It is epic that the fox bears the chicken "upon his bak," epic that these country people cry "welaway!" like medieval courtly ladies or like Aeneas himself in Chaucer's burlesque translation of Virgil in the *House of Fame*. The catalogue of heroes is epic too: Colle and Talbot and Gerland and Malkin. The swarm of bees is out of Virgil and Dante, and so is the listing of weapons brought to the battle, though everything is also emphatically barnyard. But what Chaucer is doing is not mere burlesque; his poem is not merely, as we say for the sake of classification, a "beast epic." If the situation is exaggerated for comic effect — "art" transforming "reality" — the emotions are nevertheless real, the poet's eye precise and concerned. He provides a reason for the running of "the verray hogges," and, foolish or not, the running of the men and women is supported by details which make it as convincing as, say, Achilles' pursuit of Hector. They run so hard they're afraid they may have heart attacks. Jack Straw and his rabble (which Chaucer elevates with the word *meynee,* or retinue) may not seem epic material, but they force into mind the similarity between the outraged barnyard and larger social catastrophe. Thus the Nun's Priest's resolution of the debate on power and social position is partly stylistic: the aristocratic epic style by nature mocks the barnyard, but the vividly realized excitement of the barnyard earns for the barnyard the right to be taken seriously, even while we laugh. No one, rich or poor, can really foretell the future (a major theme in the tale), and no one, rich or poor, is any safer than his neighbor. We can only, so far as our stupidity permits, watch and wait, hope for grace, and when the moment arrives, act to the best of our ability. By feigned emotion (his pretended deep involvement in the woes of a chicken) and by stylistic distortion of reality, the Nun's Priest makes lying art creep up on truth.

xi

The Conclusion ᥉᥉᥉᥉᥉᥉᥉᥉᥉᥉

From the Second Nun's Tale to the Parson's Tale and Retraction

HE TALES WHICH CLOSE THE CANTER-
bury pilgrimage are all moralistic or explicitly
religious, though not necessarily serious or even
right. They offer, in various ways, orthodox answers
on how men are to be judged and how society can be ordered
when we can find no certainties; but the answers do not in fact
resolve much. The nominalist premise of the whole collection
becomes increasingly apparent and in the end at least partly
undermines the very making of the collection.

Both tales in Fragment VIII are ingeniously constructed
on principles of alchemy, one on "true" alchemy, the other on
"false." The *Second Nun's Prologue and Tale*, probably written
for the Clerk originally (he was jokingly called a "philosophre" in the *General Prologue*, 297, and the Second Nun calls
herself a "son of Eve," VIII, 62), treats the life of Saint Cecilie
as one of alchemistical purification. "True alchemy," in the
Middle Ages, was religious. Even for serious, practicing
chemists, the "purification" of metals was ultimately important
because analogous with purification of the soul, just as, for the
student of optics, the ultimate goal (in Robert Grosseteste's
theory anyway) was an understanding not of light but of the
soul's illumination, "light metaphysic."

[316]

The Prologue begins with four stanzas on the value of work and the danger of "ydelnesse" or sloth, then turns to eight stanzas of invocation to Mary. Through the purity of Mary, who is identified with the element fire ("sonne of excellence," 52, and "light," 71), God came into the "tryne compas," or realm of the elements earth, water, and air. The Nun asks that Mary's help and her own labor save her from the "contagioun / Of my body" and the "wighte [weight] of erthely lust and fals affeccioun" (72 et seq.). She is asking for purification in language which suggests alchemistical transmutation. Then the Prologue shifts to interpretation of the name Cecilie, a traditional interpretation which identified Cecilie with 1) heavenly purity, 2) a road for the blind, 3) a combination of heaven and the biblical Leah, the worker, and 4) heaven made visible to people. The last two stanzas elaborate the fourth point: just as men see the sun, moon, and stars in heaven, so they see faith, "magnanymytee," and the "cleernesse hool of sapience / And sondry werkes, brighte of excellence" (110 et seq.) in Saint Cecilie. And just as heaven is "swift and round and eek brennynge," so Cecilie is "Ful swift and bisy evere in good werkynge, / And round and hool in good perseverynge, / And brennynge evere in charite ful brighte" (116 et seq.). In true alchemy, the Philosopher's Stone is heaven or, alternatively, Christ (the temple, i.e., heaven). If heaven and Cecilie are metaphorically one, as the imagery here suggests, Cecilie is (or has the quality of) the Philosopher's Stone, that which can (figuratively, spiritually) transmute lead into gold.

In the Nun's tale, Cecilie proves her powers. She marries a good young pagan named Valerian, and, to preserve her chastity and closeness to God, she purifies and converts both Valerian and his brother, Tiburce. The pagan prefect, Almachius, demands that all men bow to Jupiter, and when Valerian and Tiburce refuse, he has them killed. An officer to Almachius, Maximus, who knows what the Christians believe and who sees their souls borne away by angels, tells the crowd what he has seen and converts many more. Almachius has him beaten to death, and Cecilie buries him with Tiburce and Valerian. Then Almachius has Cecilie brought in and questions her, demands that she bow to Jupiter, and at last — not without difficulty — kills her.

All this, too, is worked out alchemistically. Each character who gets purified ("purged") or saved is purified first in memory and sensation, then in will ("engyn," 339), then in intellect. The images of gold, fire, and stone control the entire tale — traditional emblems of, respectively, sapience, will, and substance, seat of memory and desire; in other words, gold, fire, and stone are associated with the rational, irascible, and concupiscent souls respectively, each of which must be transmuted as lead is changed to gold. The two crowns which an angel gives to Cecilie and Valerian, one of snow white lilies, the other of red roses, refer to the "white" purity of Cecilie's thought and to the red of the bloody martyr's passion, to which both Cecilie and Valerian come, desiring heaven and purity more than life on earth at any price.

The poem has other alchemistical devices. When Almachius questions Cecilie he "multiplies," as alchemists say — that is, like self-seeking, gold-hungry false alchemists, he complicates and confounds. For instance, " 'I axe thee,' quod he, 'though it thee greeve, / Of thy religioun and of thy bileeve' " (426–27). Cecilie says in answer, "Ye han bigonne youre questioun folily / . . . that wolden two answeres conclude / In o demande" (428–30). Again, Almachius asks the multiplied question, Will you choose to sacrifice to Juppiter, or will you choose to deny Christ? and Cecilie laughs at him and calls him insane.

Cecilie is the mystical stone burning in its alembic (or, in medieval English alchemistical writings, its "house"). Almachius

> weex wroth, and bad men sholde hir lede
> Hom til hir house, and "In hire hous," quod he,
> "Brenne hire right in a bath of flambes rede."

[513–15

She is burned night and day, but nothing happens; when men seek to chop off her head, three blows — the legal limit — will not suffice. She lives three days more, preaching and bleeding (cf. the two crowns), then finally dies, leaving her goods (the garnerings of her desiring faculty) to establish a church.

As this summary and brief explication should suggest, the *Second Nun's Tale* is an odd piece of writing. It's the most old-fashioned thing Chaucer ever wrote — virtually straight hagiography, the kind of thing Englishmen were writing in the ninth and tenth centuries — and the alchemistical ornamentation, like the mathematical punning Professor Grennen pointed out some years ago, attests to the care with which Chaucer worked. It will not do to claim, as critics used to claim about the *Man of Law's Tale*, that the tale is simply proof that Chaucer could be, among other things, a simple and devout man. If the *Man of Law's Tale* tends to raise doubts, as Trevor Whittock pointed out, the *Second Nun's Tale* flatly asserts the unthinkable. For instance:

> The longe nyght, and eek a day also,
> For al the fyr, and eek the bathes heete,
> She sat al coold, and feelede no wo.
> It made hire nat a drope for to sweete.
>
> [519–22

The explanation, I think, is that the *Second Nun's Tale* is what might be described as a piece of pure art, an ingeniously fabricated antique — not simply an imitation of an ancient form but an expressionist imitation designed to be more like the original than the original. Everything is heightened: the allegorical rigidity, the cool intellectuality, the sternness, the indifference to mere probability, above all, the quiet violence, the gore. It's as if a modern painter should do a series, on wood, on the agonies of Saint George. Such a series, if the painter were a master craftsman, would be supremely unmedieval precisely because the painter sees the Middle Ages, its ideas, emotions, and techniques, clearly, with full respect and absolute incredulity. Chaucer does not laugh, in the *Second Nun's Tale*, at the bogus authority of hagiographic tradition: he stares at it in artistic fascination, as a complete outsider, and "presents" it. The subject of the *Second Nun's Tale* is not the efficacy of faith and works (the ostensible theme) but the saint's-life genre itself. The poem is, I think, a further development of Chaucer's experiment with unreliable art. What stands as true art in one age can become in another a curiosity, an *object*. Isak Dinesen touches on this curious problem in her story *The Poet* when a character remarks,

> I have learned that it is not possible to paint any definite object, say, a rose, so that I, or any other intelligent critic, shall not be able to decide, within twenty years, at what period it was painted, or, more or less, at what place on the earth. The artist has meant to create either a picture of a rose in the abstract, or the portrait of a particular rose; it is never in the least his intention to give us a Chinese, Persian, or Dutch, or, according to the period, a rococo or a pure Empire rose. If I told him that this was what he had done, he would not understand me. He might be angry with me. He would say: "I have painted a rose." Still he cannot help it. I am thus so far superior to the artist that I can mete him with a measure of which he himself knows nothing. At the same time I could not paint, and hardly see or conceive, a rose myself. I might imitate any of their creations. I might say: "I will paint a rose in the Chinese or Dutch or in the rococo manner." But I should never have the courage to paint a rose as it looks. For how does a rose look? [1]

I can offer no very convincing argument that Chaucer, a fourteenth-century poet, could have entertained such a seemingly twentieth-century aesthetic question. He speaks in several places of how languages, manners, and styles change (see, e.g., *Troilus*, II, 22–35); he might have learned from the newly rigorous discipline of translation that an understanding of the usual and accepted style of a given period can often clarify the meaning of a text; and, having mimicked bad writing in various tales, he might well have come up with the idea of mimicking a once-admired but long-abandoned genre. But such arguments carry no weight, being merest speculation. The fact is that he did write this tale in an antique mode and did not, so far as I can see, undercut the form with ironies of the kind we discover in, say, the *Man of Law's Tale*. He cannot have expected the story to be believed by King Richard, John of Gaunt, Queen Anne, or Princess Joan — sophisticated people sympathetic to religious thinkers like Wyclif, who doubted even that wine can turn to blood. And so the *Second Nun's Tale* seems best understood as a comment on the limitations of art. At the same time, the tale has a virtue beyond ingenious imitation: it sets up the magnificent *Canon's Yeoman's Tale*.

Just as the *Second Nun's Tale* closes, two strangers gallop up to the pilgrimage and join it, a church canon and his servant, or yeoman, bringing with them, it turns out, one of the finest, most ingenious tales in the collection — another tale worth dwelling upon.

The Yeoman is a strange character, as Harry Bailey soon discovers, asking him questions. He is not at all what early critics thought him, a "stupid fellow." Rather, he's devious. His characteristic manner is wry, ironic, subtle: he hints at what he does not choose to say outright. Even at the start the Yeoman's manner is no mere matter of safety, one suspects. Speaking openly is against his nature. For one thing, he's congenitally sly: his very cleverness, the perversion of which is craftiness, is one reason for his admiration of the Canon, whose misuse of a good mind he laments. And for another thing, reality itself is ambiguous for the Canon's Yeoman.

The first hint of the Yeoman's disillusionment comes in his remark that his master "to ryden with you [the Pilgrims] is ful fayn / For his desport; he loveth daliaunce." Although *desport* and *daliaunce* may be innocent enough, their possible darker connotations accurately describe the Canon's activities, his play and trickery. Chaucer points up the irony in the Yeoman's private joke by means of the Host's response: "Freend, for thy warnyng God yeve thee good chance!" By *warnyng* the Host means the Yeoman's notification to his master that the Pilgrims have just passed on the road; but *warnyng* can also mean "word of caution," and that is in a sense what the Yeoman, in his wry, extremely guarded way, has just given. The reader passes over the word with only a momentary flicker of doubt about whether the word means only notification; but when he encounters the word again at the end of the next exchange his doubt reawakens. In the next exchange between Host and Yeoman, the Yeoman's hint becomes a shade more bold. The Host says innocently, "Can he oght telle a myrie tale or tweye, / With which he glade may this compaignye?" The Yeoman replies in his characteristic manner. Pretending to speak of his master's ability to "telle a myrie tale" but in fact speaking of his master's ability to trick his dupes into short-lived joy and also of his master's fake ability to turn base metal into gold or silver, the Yeoman says:

> "Who, sire? my lord? ye, ye, withouten lye,
> He kan of murthe and eek of jolitee
> Nat but ynough; also, sire, trusteth me,
> And ye hym knewe as wel as do I,
> Ye wolde wondre how wel and craftily
> He koude werke, and that in sondry wise.
> He hath take on hym many a greet emprise
> Which were ful hard for any that is here
> To brynge aboute, but they of hym it leere.
> As hoomly as he rit amonges yow,
> If ye hym knewe, it wolde be for youre prow.
> Ye wolde nat forgoon his aqueyntaunce
> For muchel good, I dar leye in balaunce
> Al that I have in my possessioun
> He is a man of heigh descrecioun."

And the Yeoman echoes the Host's inadvertent pun:

> "I *warne* you wel, he is a passyng man."
>
> [599–614

Irony plays throughout, in the hidden equation of storytelling and the alchemist's trickery, in the hidden comparison of the listener's pleasure with the dupe's pleasure, in the cynical bet that the company would pass up much good to know this evil one, in the penniless Yeoman's "Al that I have in my possessioun," and, finally, in the pun on *warne*. In fact, the Yeoman's "Who, sire? me lord?" suggests that the whole description really concerns not the Canon — or not exclusively the Canon — but also the Devil, who, as the Yeoman tells us later, has been the Yeoman's true master. The Host has not yet understood, and there is impatience in his next question:

> "Wel," quod oure Hoost, "I pray thee, tell me than,
> Is he a clerk, or noon? telle what he is."
>
> [615–16

And again the Yeoman speaks riddles:

> "I seye, my lord kan swich subtilitee —
> But al his craft ye may nat wite at me,
> And somewhat helpe I yet to his wirkyng —
> That al this ground on which we been ridyng,
> Til that we come to Caunterbury toun,
> He koude al clene turne it up-so-doun,
> And pave it al of silver and of gold."
>
> [620–26

Now at last the Host thinks he understands. The Canon is a man of marvelous "prudence," the Host says (line 630), ironically commenting on the Yeoman's reference earlier to "discrecioun" and his statement that knowing the Canon would be "for youre prow." The Yeoman continues to speak in riddles, each riddle more open than the last, and finally he goes so far as to hint that his master is a crook; or, anyway, he *lives among* crooks. The Yeoman is about to draw back, having said as much as he can bring himself to say. What makes him go on to a full exposé of these men too curious in study is, ironically enough, the curiosity of the Host.

The Canon's Yeoman has strong feelings about the occult activity in which for some time he has been engaged, and he sees the pursuit of alchemy as the Devil's work, not an honest occupation of right reason but a madness grounded on overweening pride. He turns alchemists into devils incarnate and identifies their dupes with poor Adam. If so extreme a view seems remarkable in Chaucer, we need not explain it by supposing (as critics used to do) that Chaucer was himself duped by some alchemist: the view is not Chaucer's but the Yeoman's. The tale is comic throughout, but comic despite the sustained indignation of the narrator: we detach ourselves from the melodramatic extravagance of the Yeoman (as from any extreme point of view in Chaucer's world), and thus we are able to see him as at once generally right and funny. But for the Yeoman the whole business is in dead earnest. At every point when we might be tempted to laugh at the duped priest in Part Two, the Yeoman forestalls our laughter as well as he can — by forcing us to identify with the dupe: "But therof wiste the preest nothyng, allas!" — by crying out against the alchemist in outrage: "the devil out of his skyn / Hym terve, I pray to God, for his falshede!" — or by moralizing: "Consider-eth, sires, how that, in ech estaat, / Bitwixe men and gold ther is debaat." Throughout the tale, in short, the humor has more to do with the teller than with the tale.

The sin of alchemists, the Yeoman says (conventionally enough) is intellectual pride, which can result in a substitution of reason for faith, the basis of the foolish priest's fall. He believes his merely mortal eyes, and, foolishly generalizing from a small evidence of the master alchemist's honesty, he comes to accept the alchemist's imperative: "Bileveth this as *siker as your Crede*" — belief in the Creed being, of course, a matter of faith.

In lines 962–65 the Yeoman sets up his symbolic extension of the tale:

> But al thyng which that shineth as the gold
> Nis nat gold, as that I have herd it told;
> Ne every appul that is fair at eye
> Ne is nat good, what so men clappe or crye. [claim]
>   [962–65

The expressions are proverbial, requiring in themselves no more than their obvious interpretation; but in their present context they are significant on a deeper level. Gold (or wealth in general) may be associated either with heaven or with concupiscence; and in medieval descriptions of the fall on its tropological level, to eat of the apple is to mistake the lower good for the higher.

The Yeoman claims that the master alchemist of whom he speaks is not his own canon but someone else. Critics have sometimes refused to believe him, preferring to think that the

Yeoman is being defensive and that indeed, he still partly believes in his master's art and cannot admit even to himself that his master is a fraud. The irony would be typically Chaucerian, but it's illusory here. The Canon is probably a charlatan, but he is also a passionate believer in his art. He has spent everything he ever had and everything the Yeoman ever had on his science; and the at once comic and pitiful result is:

> The pot tobreketh, and farewel, al is go!
> Thise metals been of so greet violence,
> Oure walles mowe nat make hem resistence,   [may]
> But if they weren wroght of lym and stoon;
> They percen so, thrugh the wal they goon.
> And somme of hem synken into the ground —
> Thus han we lost by tymes many a pound —
> And somme are scatered al the floor aboute;
> Somme lepe into the roof. Withouten doute,
> Though that the feend noght in oure sighte hym shewe,
> I trowe he with us be, that ilke shrewe!
> In helle, where that he lord is and sire,
> Nis ther moore wo, ne moore rancour ne ire.
>
> [907–19]

The Devil is with them, but alchemists like the Canon refuse to believe it. They struggle to explain the failure, and they go on and on until, penniless and hopeless and damned (according to the Yeoman), they die. And therefore — "Men may hem knowe by smel of brymstoon. / For al the world they stynken as a goot" (885–86) — the smell, that is, of the brimstone of hell, and a "goot" in contradistinction to God's chosen, the sheep.

Considering the Canon's devotion to his art, his delusion, and his sympathetic treatment at the hands of the Yeoman, there can be no question of the Canon's being anything but a man. A man possessed, perhaps, hence perhaps a devil's agent and thrall, but a man. The master alchemist of the tale is not. He is, on the literal level, a "chanoun" out of hell. The Yeoman says of him:

> There is a chanoun of religioun
> Amonges us, wolde infecte al a toun,

Though it as greet were as was Nynyvee,
Rome, Alisaundre, Troye, and othere three.
His sleightes and his infinite falsnesse
Ther koude no man writen, as I gesse,
Though that he myghte lyve a thousand yeer.
In al this world of falshede nis his peer;
For in his termes he wol hym so wynde,
And speke his wordes in so sly a kynde,
Whanne he commune shal with any wight,
That he wol make hym doten anonright,
But it a feend be, as hymselven is.
Ful many a man hath he bigiled er this,
And wole, if that he lyve may a while;
And yet men ride and goon ful many a mile
Hym for to seke and have his aqueyntaunce,
Noght knowynge of his false governaunce.

[972–89

Though he poses as a Canon, it is clear that the character
described here is the Devil — or, since fiends are legion, *a*
devil. He moves *amonges us* constantly — among all mankind
and among the Canterbury pilgrims, though invisible to them.
As he once infected Nineveh, so he would infect, if he had his
way, a city the size of Nineveh, Rome, Alexandria, Troy, and
three more rolled into one; his falseness is "infinite," not finite;
a thousand years would not suffice to chronicle his activity; he
has no peer for wickedness. The word *wynde*, referring to
involved and specious argument, faintly suggests a serpent
image which is subtly supported in the following line, "And
speke his wordes in so sly a kynde." Satan spoke to Eve in the
"kind" or nature of a snake (traditionally "sly"). The line
"But it a feend be . . ." explicitly identifies him as a devil.
And so on. The master alchemist is not an allegorical figure,
then, and not the Yeoman's Canon, but a fiend pure and
simple. If his identity is not obvious, that is because it has never
been obvious at a glance.

    If the canon of Part Two is on the literal level a fiend, the
priest is, on the literal level, a man. The fiend, we are told,
abides nowhere but is seen here and there throughout the
world; but the priest lives in London. On a second level,

however, the priest functions as a figure of Adam. He is an "innocent," we are repeatedly told, who does not need to "paye / For bord ne clothyng, wente he never so gaye." After his encounter with the fiend in disguise the priest becomes one who, like the fallen Adam, sweats. The deception of the priest thus becomes equivalent to the deception of Adam, or, to put it another way, equivalent to the deception of any innocent; and the temptation of the fires of the alchemist becomes for the Canon's Yeoman the temptation of the fires of hell, which man must, like the Canon's Yeoman, renounce. Not to renounce these fires, not to pursue right reason, is to become, oneself, a kind of fiend. This is the point artistically urged by the Yeoman's reversal of the order of his narrative and by his shifting identifications of the several persons in the tale.

The deluded priest, the Yeoman, and the Yeoman's Canon are treated in terms of a single set of images. The Yeoman's Canon dresses in rags, and the Yeoman says with heavy irony that the Canon dresses badly only to preserve himself from envious men. The Yeoman himself was once "wont to be right fressh and gay / Of clothyng and of oother good array" but "Now may . . . were an hose upon [his] heed." As for the priest in the tale, at the start he need "no thyng for to paye / For bord ne clothyng," and so forth, but ultimately he will lose all, as the Yeoman hints at lines 1376–78, when the priest says:

> "Yet hadde I levere spenden al the good
> Which that I have, and elles wexe I wood
> Than that ye sholden falle in swich mescheef."

(Cf. also "make his writtes thynne," line 740.) The priest, the Canon of Part One, and the Yeoman all sweat fiercely; and the Yeoman's emphasis on his own blowing of the fire (an image he sometimes goes out of his way to bring in, as at lines 923–24) parallels his emphasis of the priest's blowing of the fire (e.g., 1146). At the same time, the indignation the Yeoman feels when he speaks of his Canon in Part One parallels the indignation he feels when he speaks of the Canon of Part Two. If the Yeoman's Canon is the deluded priest, he is also, at another phase of this infinitely repetitive drama, the crooked canon of the tale (Part Two). In short, in Part Two of the *Canon's Yeoman's Tale* the identity of characters is ambiguous: the fiendish canon is at the same time a human canon and may once have been the human dupe; and in the same way the human Canon of the Prologue is sufficiently equivalent to the fiendish canon of Part Two that the Yeoman may speak of either as he would of the other, as the Yeoman does at 599 et seq., mentioned already.

Alchemy is the pursuit of a false heaven, as the Yeoman hints by a double-entendre at lines 870–76:

> But that good hope crepeth in oure herte,
> Supposynge evere, though we sore smerte,
> To be releeved by hym afterward.
> Swich supposyng and hope is sharp and hard;
> I warne yow wel, it is to seken evere.   [sigh]
> That futur temps hath maad men to dissevere,
> In trust therof, from al that evere they hadde.

Just as the good Christian suffers and gives up all his goods to buy the pearl of price, joy hereafter, so the alchemist suffers and gives up all his goods in hopes of being rewarded hereafter (but still in this world) by "him," the Philosopher's Stone.

At the end of the tale, Chaucer makes more of this. The Yeoman says (lines 1426 et seq.) that he will now tell what philosophers themselves have to say of the Stone. *True* philosophers, we must understand; that is, those philosophers who have been given, as Augustine says in the *City of God* (XXII, 23) "the true philosophy — this sole support against the miseries of this life — [which] has been given by heaven only to a few." Chaucer selects his first true philosopher with ingenuity: Arnald of Villa Nova — that is, Arnald of the New City (the New Jerusalem). And from old alchemistical writers Chaucer has the Yeoman choose not the book actually containing the incident to be recounted but instead a book with an appropriately religious title, the *Rosarie*. Hermes says, according to the Yeoman,

> the dragon, doutelees,
> Ne dyeth nat, but if that he be slayn

With his brother; and that is for to seyn,
By the dragon, Mercurie, and noon oother
He understood, and brymstoon by his brother,
That out of Sol and Luna were ydrawe.

[1435-40

In traditional Christian iconography, the dragon is the serpent,
the Devil, that first destroyer. Whereas, as the Yeoman tells us
earlier, "Sol gold is, and Luna silver we threpe [call],"
Mercury is quicksilver, identified in astrology with intellect
(cf. the theme of Part One of the tale) and in alchemy with
both the "philosopher's child" and the Devil or monster.

As the only two essential features of the alchemist's work,
mercury and brimstone may be taken to represent alchemy
itself; and as false Sol and Luna, they come to be (and alchemy
comes to be) associated with what Boethius calls turning away
from God or the reasonable. The alchemist, then, is a servant
of the Devil and the kingdom of hell. The anecdote continues,

"And therefore," seyde he, — taak heede to my sawe —
"Lat no man bisye hym this art for to seche,
But if that he th'entencioun and speche
Of philosophres understonde kan;
And if he do, he is a lewed man.
For this science and this konnyng," quod he,
"Is of the secree of secrees, pardee."

[1441-47

A man who truly understands the philosophers is "a lewed
man" because the philosophers' words, rightly understood,
lead not toward the laboratory but away from it. The true
philosophers' science is not the alchemistical Secret of Secrets
but the Christian mystery of salvation. Once upon a time a
disciple of Plato asked,

"Telle me the name of the privee stoon?"
    And Plato answered unto hym anoon,
"Take the stoon that Titanos men name."
    "Which is that?" quod he. "Magnasia is the same,"
Seyde Plato. "Ye, sire, and is it thus?

This is *ignotum per ignocious.*
   [the obscure explained by the more obscure]
What is Magnasia, good sire, I yow preye?"
  "It is a water that is maad, I seye,
Of elementes foure," quod Plato.
  "Telle me the roote, good sire," quod he tho,   [then]
"Of that water, if it be youre wil."

[1452–62

The *prima materia,* the essence of mercury, was mercury freed from the four elements earth, air, fire, and water. And that is of course one meaning of the Yeoman's lines. But an equally possible meaning — a meaning completely consistent throughout the passage and consistent with Chaucer's method elsewhere in this tale (as well as with the Yeoman's view of alchemy as a false religion) is that Magnasia (the Lodestone, equivalent here to Christ the Rock) combines the four elements as they would be combined in the Incarnate, that is, elemented, God, the "roote" of that water. The water is the ceaselessly flowing fountain of grace.

Asked to speak of the ultimate mystery, the Christian Secret of Secrets, God, Plato must draw back:

"Nay, nay," quod Plato, "certain, that I nyl.
The philosophres sworn were everychoon
That they sholden discovere it unto noon,
Ne in no book it write in no manere.
For unto Crist it is so lief and deere
That he wol nat that it discovered bee
But where it liketh to his deitee
   [i.e., in Scripture, in religious books, and so forth]
Men for t'enspire, and eek for to deffende
Whom that hym liketh; lo, this is the ende."

[1463–71

The philosophers sworn to secrecy are of course the pagan philosophers. *Since* the coming of the true Philosopher's Stone, writing about salvation is an excellent thing. (Chaucer substituted the name of Plato for that of Solomon in his source, since Solomon, according to the exegetes, frequently spoke of Christ's coming.)

But if this is the right interpretation of Plato's remarks, the Canon's Yeoman misses it. He says:

> Thanne conclude I thus, sith that god of hevene
> Ne wil nat that the philosophres nevene   [name]
> How that a man shal come unto this stoon,
> I rede, as for the beste, lete it goon.   [counsel]
>
> [1472–75

In short, the Yeoman has quoted the anecdote exactly, has misunderstood it, and has done precisely what he would have done if he understood it — turned away from alchemy to true religion. So much for miracles like Cecilie's. The Yeoman is saved not by purification, not by right understanding of the kind she can give, but by concern for his fellow man, that is, by his grief at what alchemy does to men like his Canon.

§ 2

SEEING THE COOK dead drunk and asleep on his horse, the Host wakes him and, as a joke, demands a tale. The Manciple offers to tell a tale instead and hurls abuse on the Cook, mainly jokes about the incredible stink of his breath. When the Cook grows wrathful, as well he might, and falls off his horse, so that the whole company must push and shove to get him mounted again, the Host reproves the Manciple, and the Manciple makes cynical and ironic peace by offering wine to the drunken, half-dead Cook. Though "Chaucer" himself dislikes the joke, Harry Bailey laughs and ironically blesses the great peacemaker Bacchus, giving him his due — giving nature its due — but no more than its due.

This little prologue is one of the fine moments in the collection, not only for its vividness but also for the way it pulls things together — an indication of how tight the whole work might have been if Chaucer had lived to finish it. The Manciple's Prologue recalls the drunkenness of the Miller at the beginning of the pilgrimage, recalls imagery from the tale the Reeve told, ironically recalls the Knight as well — the Manciple asks the Cook, "Now, sweete sire, wol ye justen [joust] at a fan?" that is, joust at the revolving bar in the roughneck game of quintain.² The prologue brings back, through Harry Bailey's exclamation "for cokkes bones," the cock imagery introduced in the *Shipman's Tale* and picked up throughout the seventh fragment, culminating in the image of Chauntecleeer. And the prologue does one thing still more interesting: by its insistent imagery of deathlike pallor, deathlike or hellish stench, and the leaden, unwieldly "corpse" of the Cook, it turns the essentially comic situation into something more ominous, something fully appropriate to this closing movement of the pilgrimage-of-life. That dark note is deepened by the strange malevolence of the Manciple. Though the Cook's drunkenness has reached a dangerous state, the Manciple cynically gives him, "on pain of death," more wine — and not just a swig or two — so that, however Harry Bailey may laugh, the pilgrim Chaucer cries out in alarm,

> Of this vessel the Cook drank faste, allas!
> What neded hym? he drank enogh biforn!
>
>   [ix, 88–89

And in response to Harry Bailey's reprimand:

> Manciple, in feith thou art to nyce,   [too critical]
> Thus openly repreve hym of his vice.
> Another day he wole, peraventure,
> Reclayme thee and bringe thee to lure —
>   [requite; bait for a falcon]
>   [69–72

the Manciple, with sudden, slimy piety, tells his tale on the theme *speak no evil*, a dreadful botch of a tale, artistically (another of Chaucer's purposely bad pieces), a tale in which a great Christian virtue is made of keeping people's secrets, that is, of never doing what the stern and noble country parson does, snib men he sees doing wrong.

The story is simple — a snow-white crow is turned black

for telling the god Phoebus about the sins of his wife and causing him to kill her — but the ostentatious Manciple's ornamentation turns the simple legend into something ludicrously overblown. He alludes to all sorts of classical lore, not all of it relevant; he stops his narration for prissy digressions on his way of narrating (e.g., 205 et seq.); and he piles up more or less pointless rhetorical devices. The moral he appends is, in terms of the tale's literary tradition (Ovid, and so forth), a stupid oversimplification, and in his remarkable last flurry of rhetoric (309–62), in which he tells in maudlin terms, endlessly repeating himself, of the good advice his mother used to give him — "don't talk" — his fawning hypocrisy becomes a kind of comic madness.

The Manciple's closing lines recall the end of the *Nun's Priest's Tale*:

> "Nay," quod the fox, "but God yeve hym meschaunce,
> That is so undiscreet of governaunce
> That jangleth whan he sholde holde his pees."
>
> [VII, 3433–35

And the *Manciple's Tale* has in common with the *Nun's Priest's Tale*, and with the earlier *Franklin's Tale*, a distrust of those opinions, words, and deeds of which human beings (also talking birds) are so foolishly proud. In the Franklin's view, God steps in and resolves difficulties when the well-intentioned actions of human beings are ill-considered. Though the Nun's Priest knows people (or chickens) behave foolishly, as when Chauntecleer eloquently defends his fear, then forgets all about the dream that frightened him, the Nun's Priest argues that with a little luck and grace, one can escape some evils if one uses one's wits. The Manciple sees no such hope in the world. All Nature is determined, in the Manciple's opinion, and all Nature is base. Phoebus is by nature a jealous husband who tries to cage his wife; he has no choice. And the wife and her lover are equally helpless. As the Manciple sees it, "God it woot, ther may no man embrace / As to destreyne a thyng which that nature / Hath natureely set in a creature" (IX, 160–62). He gives scornful examples of how Nature works:

Taak any bryd, and put it in a cage,
And do al thyn entente and thy corage
To fostre it tendrely with mete and drynke
Of alle deyntees that thou kanst bithynke,
And keep it al so clenly as thou may,
Although his cage of gold be never so gay,
Yet hath this brid, by twenty thousand foold,
Levere in a forest, that is rude and coold,
Goon ete wormes and swich wrecchednesse.
Fore evere this brid wol doon his bisynesse
To escape out of his cage, yif he may.
His libertee this brid desireth ay.
Lat take a cat, and fostre hym wel with milk
And tendre flessh, and make his couche of silk,
And lat hym seen a mous go by the wal,
Anon he weyveth milk and flessh and al,
And every deyntee that is in that hous,
Swich appetit hath he to ete a mous.
Lo, heere hath lust his dominacioun,
And appetit fleemeth discrecioun.
A she-wolf hath also a vileyns kynde.
The lewedeste wolf that she may fynde,
Or leest of reputacioun, wol she take,
In tyme whan hir lust to han a make.

[IX, 163–86

Human beings, he says, are just as bad, if that's how Nature happens to have shaped them, and though we may call human behavior one thing when we speak of aristocrats, another when we speak of commoners, it all comes, invariably, to the same thing:

I am a boystous man, right thus seye I,
Ther nys no difference, trewely,
Bitwixe a wyf that is of heigh degree,
If of hir body dishonest she bee,
And a povre wenche, oother than this —
If it so be they werke bothe amys —
But that the gentile, in estaat above,
She shal be cleped his lady, as in love;
And for that oother is a povre womman,

She shal be cleped his wenche or his lemman.
And, God it woot, myn owene deere brother.
Men leyn that oon as lowe as lith that oother.

[IX, 2 1 1–2 2

In a world so mechanically determined, there is no point in
warning or chastising, much less any point in reporting crimes,
the Manciple says; one can only keep silent, protecting one's
skin by refusing to get involved. The Manciple, arguing for
moral inertia, is, in fact, the moral equivalent of the dead-
drunk Cook of the prologue. And in the *tour-de-force* speech
arguing against speech, with which he closes the story, he in
effect cancels his whole tale — cancels all tales, withdrawing
into silence. After thirty-some lines on the importance of
keeping silent, he concludes:

". . . Reed David in his psalmes, reed Senekke.
My sone, spek nat, but with thyn heed thou bekke.
Dissimule as thou were deef, if that thou heere
A janglere speke of perilous mateere.
The Flemyng seith, and lerne it if thee leste,
That litel janglyng causeth muchel reste.
My sone, if thou no wikked word hast seyd,
Thee thar nat drede for to be biwreyd;
But he that hath mysseyd, I dar wel sayn,
He may by no wey clepe his word agayn.
Thyng that is seyd is seyd, and forth it gooth,
Though hym repente, or be hym nevere so looth.
He is his thral to whom that he hath sayd
A tale of which he is now yvele apayd.
My sone, be war, and be noon auctour newe
Of tidynges, wheither they been false or trewe.
Whereso thou come, amonges hye or lowe,
Kepe wel thy tonge, and thenk upon the crowe."

[IX, 345–62

When the *Manciple's Tale* is finished and night is not far
off, both literally and symbolically, Harry Bailey asks for a tale
from the Parson. The stern old man says they will get no
"fables and swich wrecchednesse" from him, nor will they get
poetry: "But trusteth wel, I am a Southren man, / I kan nat

geeste 'rum, ram, ruf,' by lettre, / Ne God woot, rym holde I but litel bettre" (43–45). The Host politely accepts whatever the priest will offer, and the tale begins. He speaks — far more grimly than Geoffrey Chaucer would speak, we may be sure — of how all life is a pilgrimage from this world to the next, and preaches on how man must release his hold on the things in this world to enter the place where all grief ends.

In arguing withdrawal from the sensual world, the Parson takes a position partly like that of the Manciple; but the Parson's position is not one of cowardice or inertia. Systematically he spells out the sins of commission and the sins of omission, using all the force medieval pulpit rhetoric could afford him, and ends with a compelling image of the goal of man's pilgrimage, heaven and immortality.

The tale is of course a fitting conclusion. Professor Finlayson has recently pointed out that the tale is keyed to the hardshell religion of the teller,[3] that its antifeminism, anti-Semitism, and so forth, ironically introduced by Chaucer, make the tale at least to some extent satirical, and thus no more absolute than any other mere human being's opinion; but on the whole the *Parson's Tale* is not a conclusion Geoffrey Chaucer would scorn. Though not a final answer to the poem's great questions — there can be no final answers — it is a right answer to the poem's dramatic movement. It provides an emotionally perfect close — or at any rate it once did. Hardly anyone reads it anymore, except Chaucer scholars, and that is perhaps as it should be. One knows the tale is there, knows the mood on which the huge poem closes, and that is, in a way, sufficient.

Then comes Chaucer's Retraction. Nearly everything he mentions among the books he revokes is, though secular, shot through with religious feeling. *Troilus and Criseyde*, the *Book of the Duchess*, and so forth. The question of just what to do with the Retraction has nagged Chaucer criticism for centuries,[4] but perhaps the answer is relatively simple. Obviously Chaucer was not making some sly joke when he wrote the Retraction, nor was he detached from his subject, as he was when he composed his sermon for the good but narrow-minded Parson. In the Retraction Chaucer lays aside all masks, lays aside his art (no mask, no art), the nominalist-inspired skepticism we discern throughout the *Canterbury Tales* giving way at last to a simple affirmation of faith: the poet abandons himself to Christ's mercy. No one, I think, can deny the Retraction's moral honesty, but this is the honesty of life, not art. "I am helpless, worthless," is the language not of a poet but of a man. Having noticed and enjoyed the limitations of art, Chaucer wrote the Retraction, first an assertion that all he had ever composed he intended "for oure doctrine," then a revocation of most of his best poetry on the chance that it might lead someone toward sin. As Ruggiers says, for the Christian poet (for *any* poet, he might have said) poetry is finally "insufficient." So is life, in a different way. When Chaucer wrote the Retraction, his friends were mostly dead. His sons were full of promise, but a man could guess in those evil times that the odds were against them, and in fact his line perished. Nothing survived but the poetry he doubted: not only survived but made the world more healthy, like sunlight or a man's clear memory of his youth, or an old civilization's clear memory of its childhood. He was right, of course, to doubt: beauty is only a poor cousin to truth, and the nominalists were right in thinking poetry no helpful weapon in the hunt for universals, if they exist. But despite Geoffrey Chaucer's doubts and scruples, never in six hundred years has his poetry done harm. We find in it only our first great English poet's celebration of vicious souls and blockheads, gentle souls and villains, self-righteous, ridiculous, confused sad clowns like ourselves, talking and shuffling toward darkness or, possibly, light.

Notes

Index

NOTES

þ

Introduction

1   C. G. Osgood, ed., *Boccaccio on Poetry* (New York: Library of Liberal Arts, 1930), p. xviii.

2   Ibid., p. 65.

3   See Petrarch, *Invective Against the Physician*, III. Osgood, in *Boccaccio on Poetry*, notes that Boccaccio's *"Life* [of Dante], XXII, 12, 42, shows that theology is naught but the poetry of God" (p. 167, n. 5). Elsewhere (p. 46) Boccaccio says, "Aristotle, to be sure . . . asserts that the first poets were theologians, by that meaning Greeks." Osgood finds the same idea in Petrarch and Augustine (p. 163, n. 19). The identification of poet and theologian is made easier by the common medieval mistake of identifying Moses and Musaeus. See also Osgood's note 17, p. 172.

4   See Lactantius, *The Divine Institutes*, I, 5, and Petrarch, *Invective*, III.
Lactantius finds pagan poets, philosophers, prophets, Sibyls, and oracles recognizing only one god. An interesting discussion of some aspects of the taming of the pagans in the Middle Ages is that of Katherine Lever, "The Christian Classicist's Dilemma," *Classical Journal*, 58 (1963), 356–61. On the allegorizing of Virgil, see, for instance, Domenico Comparetti, *Virgil in the Middle Ages*, trans. E. F. M. Benecke (London: S. Sonnenschein, 1895); and on Ovid see, for instance, Lester K. Born, "Ovid and Allegory," *Speculum*, 10 (1934), 362–79.

5   See C. S. Lewis, "What Chaucer Really Did to *Il Filostrato*," *Essays and Studies by Members of the English Association*, 17 (1932), 57–58.

6   All reasonable critics now read *Beowulf* as a Christian poem, a reshaping of pagan elements. See, for instance, Lewis E. Nicholson, "The Literal Meaning and Symbolic Structure of *Beowulf*," *Classica et Mediaevalia*, 25 (1964), 151–201.

7   The passage reads: "But the Lord granted them good fortune in war, the Weather-Geatish people, comfort and help that they should overcome their foe through the power of one man, through his sole strength. The truth has been made known that Mighty God has always ruled mankind."

8   *The Didascalicon of Hugh of St. Victor: A Medieval Guide to the Arts*, trans. Jerome Taylor (New York: Columbia University Press, 1961), pp. 144–45 (VI, 5).

9   "The Wound and the Comforter: The Consolations of Geoffrey Chaucer," *Papers on Language and Literature*, 3 (1967), 14–27.

10 Neoplatonism was old and familiar by Chaucer's time, and Oxford's activity in the retranslation and study of classical texts made for a reappraisal of Neoplatonic ideas. Chaucer may have learned the Neoplatonic approach in conversation with Oxford thinkers like his friend and neighbor Ralph Strode, but we know very little about what such men thought. (Nothing of Strode's has survived.) And we're not on much surer ground when we turn to Chaucer's reading. For all Chaucer's fondness for alluding to his sources, critics have sometimes found it hard to make out what he got from them or even whether or not he had really read the writer to whom he alludes. Macrobius' *Commentary on the Dream of Scipio* — though I think no Chaucerian seriously doubts that Chaucer did indeed read it — is a prime example.

Macrobius' *Commentary* has been described as second only to Chalcidius' *Commentary* as a source of Platonism in the Latin West. His eighth chapter, containing his classification of the virtues and elaborating the hint in Cicero that the work of military leaders and statesmen gratifies the Ruler of the Universe, cites Plotinus' treatise, *On the Virtues*, and seems nearer than anything in Cicero to Chaucer's concern with "common profit" in the *Parliament of Birds*. The next six chapters, the core of the *Commentary*, all have as their underlying purpose support for the belief of Plato and Cicero that there is a life beyond the grave. These chapters were cherished and widely quoted in the Middle Ages, and many ideas to be found here can be found in Chaucer — the distinction between the Many and the One, the image of corporeal life as drunkenness, the Milky Way as boundary of the corporeal. The condemnation of suicide in the thirteenth chapter has echoes in Chaucer (e.g., *Book of the Duchess*, 721–39). The cosmographical section of the *Commentary* was, for the Middle Ages, a primary source of classical ideas on astronomy and was frequently bound separately; it seems unthinkable that the author of the *Astrolabe*, and perhaps two other astronomical works, would not have known this book.

All Chaucer's poetry suggests that he knew Macrobius very well indeed, but as far as technical proof is concerned, it is impossible to be certain that Chaucer really knew the *Commentary* at first hand, or if he did, when he read it. At times, some critics have pointed out (slightly exaggerating the difficulty, perhaps), Chaucer seems not to be aware that Macrobius was the author only of the *Commentary*, while Cicero wrote *Scipio's Dream*, and that Scipio was, at least technically, not a king but a king's favorite general. (Some medieval poets do sometimes use *king* in a broader sense — for instance the author of the *Alliterative Morte Arthure*.)

In the opening lines of the *Romaunt of the Rose*, Macrobius, not Cicero, seems to be taken as the author of the *Dream*, and in the *Book of the Duchess* (284–87) Chaucer speaks of "Macrobius / He that wrot al th' avysyoun / That he mette [dreamed], kyng Scipioun." In the *House of Fame* (916), Scipio is "kyng, Daun Scipio," and in the *Nun's Priest's Tale* (VII, 3123–25) *Scipio's Dream* is again credited to Macrobius. Yet in the relatively early *Parliament of Birds* Chaucer apparently understands that Cicero wrote the *Dream* (31) and that Macrobius wrote the *Commentary* (111).

It's entirely unlikely that the solution of this real or imagined difficulty lies in the chronology of the poems. (See Martha Shackford, "The Date of Chaucer's *House of Fame*," *Modern Language Notes*, 31 [1916], 507–8. Cf. Robert A. Pratt, "Chaucer Borrowing from Himself," *Modern Language Quarterly*, 7 [1946], 264. Pratt agrees with Shackford in finding the *House of Fame* earlier than *Parliament*. But see my arguments in chapter 5, below.) But it is clear that Chaucer knew the *Dream* itself when he wrote the *Parliament*, and also very likely that by the time of the *Parliament* Chaucer knew the whole *Commentary* as well. As E. P. Anderson points out, Chaucer would not have required "al the day" (*Parliament*, 28), to read the 228-line dream in what was for Chaucer easy Latin. (Anderson, "Some Notes on Chaucer's Treatment of the *Somnium Scipionis*," *Proceedings of the American Philological Association*, 33 [1902], xcviii–xcix. Cf. *Macrobius' Commentary on the Dream of Scipio*, trans. William H. Stahl [New York: Columbia University Press, 1952], pp. 53–55.) But we cannot be certain that the image of the knowledge-hungry poet bent over his book "the longe day ful faste" (*Parliament*, 21) is not merely a comic fiction, or that Chaucer was not simply alluding to a standard, though erroneous, title for the whole manuscript. There are striking parallels of thought and language between Macrobius and Chaucer, so that most critics agree with John Livingston Lowes' opinion that among those books which most profoundly influenced Chaucer's thought we must include, second only to Boethius' *Consolation*, Macrobius' *Commentary*. (Lowes, *Geoffrey Chaucer and the Development of his Genius* [Boston and New York: Houghton Mifflin Company, 1934], 112–13.) But we have no proof. In dealing with any medieval writer we must be wary of tracing much-quoted and frequently restated ideas to any one source. Professor Lowes himself granted that some lines from Chaucer which seem to echo the *Commentary* have also a resemblance to material in Servius and might be traced to still another source, Albericus, who drew from Macrobius and Servius as well as from, perhaps, Donatus and others. But though it is impossible to prove that Chaucer knew all or part of Macrobius' *Commentary*, it *is* clear that he knew some writer or group of writers familiar with at least some of Macrobius' ideas. Macrobius is one of the most frequently cited classical authors in Petrarch's works, some of which were known to Chaucer; and Dante, Chaucer's greatest model, was certainly familiar with the *Commentary*. We know that the influence of Macrobius on medieval philosophy was considerable and that his work was one of the few classical works available to medieval scholastics.

We encounter the same difficulty when we try to prove that Chaucer understood the Neoplatonic strain in the thought of Augustine (in *De Trinitate* especially), John of Salisbury, Robert Grosseteste, Cassiodorus, and others; for though Chaucer sometimes mentions and seems to reproduce the thought of such writers, we can never be sure he's not simply following the medieval fashion of borrowing a source encountered at second or third hand in his reading. And it's equally difficult to know for sure where Chaucer found the Neoplatonic view of love as an ennobling force, which we so often discover in his poetry (e.g., *Troilus*, III, 1772 et seq.). The idea that a man may be improved by the love of a noble woman is stock in the French and Italian poetry Chaucer knew (including of course Dante), but he might as easily have found it in books on chivalry, in scholastic writing, in books on music (as a branch of philosophy), or in English verse. To further complicate matters, there are signs that Chaucer, either on his own or through the influence of other writers (probably on his own), often combined rather different attitudes toward love into a single idea. The idea that a man's imitation of his beloved may improve his character has intrinsically nothing to do with the Boethian idea of providential love, yet both ideas are involved in Chaucer's statement about Troilus' love, "That Love is he that alle thing may bynde, / For may no man fordon the lawe of kynde" (I, 237–38). By nature Troilus must love the beautiful Criseyde and will be improved by his love for what, rightly or wrongly, he imagines her to be; yet his love is also an instance of that controlling providence which binds or "knits" lower natures, establishing order and relationship in the universe.

Chapter 1

1   See Bradford B. Broughton, "Chaucer's *Book of the Duchess*: Did John
     Love Blanche?" in *Twenty-Seven to One: A Potpourri of Humanistic
Material Presented to Donald Gale Stillman*, ed. Bradford B. Broughton
(Oldenburg, N.Y.: Ryan Press, 1970), pp. 71–84. Gaunt held elaborate
anniversary ceremonies in memory of Blanche until his own death in 1399.
See Sidney Armitage-Smith, *John of Gaunt* (London: Constable &
Company, 1964), p. 77. According to D. W. Robertson, Jr. (in "The
Historical Setting of Chaucer's *Book of the Duchess*," in *Medieval Studies in
Honor of Urban Tigner Holmes, Jr.*, ed. J. Mahoney and J. E. Keller
[Chapel Hill: University of North Carolina Press, 1966] pp. 169–95), the
Black Knight in the poem is not Gaunt. He elsewhere treats the poem as a
debate between desire and reason. Cf., for even stranger notions, Edward I.
Condren, "The Historical Context of the *Book of the Duchess*: A New
Hypothesis," *Chaucer Review*, 5 (1974), 195–212.

2   One group of critics has pointed out that the poem is a *tour de force* of
    allusion, and has sometimes surprisingly concluded, in effect, that the
poem has itself no particular meaning. For instance, F. N. Robinson says
(pp. 266–67): "To fulfill the double purpose of the poem Chaucer had the
happy idea of adapting a love-vision of the familiar kind to the uses of an
elegy. Therein lies the chief originality of the work. . . . For most modern
readers the artificial conventions undoubtedly impair the effect of the story;
and the young poet had not yet much thought to contribute or great
mastery in expressing it" (*The Works of Geoffrey Chaucer*, 2nd ed. [Boston:
Houghton Mifflin Company, 1957]). Other critics have pointed out
exegetical symbolism and have concluded that the surface is a ruse of sorts,
the true meaning lying in the allegorical subsurface, awaiting discovery by
right-thinking Christians. See D. W. Robertson, Jr., *A Preface to Chaucer:
Studies in Medieval Perspectives* (Princeton, N.J.: Princeton University
Press, 1962), pp. 463–65, and B. F. Huppé and D. W. Robertson, Jr.,
Fruyt and Chaf: Studies in Chaucer's Allegories (Princeton, N.J.: Princeton
University Press, 1966), pp. 32–100. G. L. Kittredge read the poem, more
convincingly, as a well-made dramatic narrative, purposely baffling at
certain points because of its psychological realism. As sometimes happens in
dreams, Kittredge says, the narrator both knows and does not know what
he's about. See Kittredge's *Chaucer and His Poetry* (Cambridge: Harvard
University Press, 1915) pp. 52 ff. Most of these interpretations take it for
granted that the narrator is an unhappy lover, but this point, too, has been
debated. J. Burke Severs argues that the narrator is the standard Chaucer
narrator, a man entirely inexperienced in love. See "Chaucer's Self-Portrait
in the *Book of the Duchess*," *Philological Quarterly*, 43 (1964), 27–39. Other
wrong opinions are that the narrator suffers from the war-veteran's
insomnia (Andrew Lang, *History of English Literature* [New York:
Longmans, Green, 1921]), p. 84; that he suffers as henpecked husband
(F. G. Fleay, *Guide to Chaucer and Spenser* [London: R. West, 1877], pp.
36–37); and that his problem is social, that is, that he's "a relatively
unsophisticated, socially naive, would-be courtier who, however, has social
pretensions and tries very earnestly to appear very courtly and sophisticated" (James Neil Brown, "Narrative Focus and Function in the *Book of
the Duchess*," *Massachusetts Studies in English*, 2 [1970], 71–79). I don't
take time to answer these arguments in detail in this chapter. Some
provided advances in our understanding once but are now outmoded; some
are plain wrong. There's a great deal of plain stupidity in Chaucer
criticism. To take just one example, James Neil Brown, claiming that the
narrator's melancholy is revealed as a pose by his unwitting assertion of a
basic contentment and optimistic view of life in "Al is ylyche good to me"
(line 9), has inexplicably misunderstood that line. "Al is ylyche good" to
the narrator because *nothing* is good. Later echoes of that line say that all is
equally good in heaven (where everything is wonderful) and in hell (where
everything is terrible). Though the narrator's misery is comic, it's real.
One of the best studies of the poem to date, though it ignores the humor, is

Russell A. Peck's "Theme and Number in Chaucer's *Book of the Duchess*," in *Silent Poetry: Essays in Numerological Analysis*, ed. Alastair Fowler (New York: Barnes & Noble, 1970), pp. 73–115. Another study sometimes interesting, though I reject the overall interpretation, is that of Edward E. Foster, "Allegorical Consolation in the *Book of the Duchess*," *Ball State Forum*, 11 (1971), 14–20.

3   There has been a great, exceedingly peculiar fad for argument that "courtly love" never existed, either in poetry or life. At its most outrageous this argument can become — as in Henry Ansgar Kelly's "Clandestine Marriage and Chaucer's *Troilus*," *Viator: Medieval and Renaissance Studies*, 4 (1973), 435–58 — that *Troilus and Criseyde* is not a story of illicit love but of "licit love," a disguised marriage. All this nonsense was begun by E. Talbot Donaldson, "The Myth of Courtly Love," *Ventures: Magazine of the Yale Graduate School*, 5 (Fall 1965), 16–23, rpt. in *Speaking of Chaucer* (London: Athlone Press, 1970). It has been refuted by Francis L. Utley in "Must We Abandon the Concept of Courtly Love?" *Medievalia et Humanistica*, 3 (1972), 299–324. Professor Utley points out that "there is not one courtly love but twenty or thirty of them, warring with theories of divine love and with popular reductions, such as those few which seem at times to condone adultery" (p. 322). I make in this book no fine distinctions between the twenty or thirty kinds, since I speak here of only plain and obvious things: Troilus loves Criseyde, and it seems to them necessary to sneak around.

4   For the change brought about by the fall, see *The Mind's Road to God* (*Itinerarium Mentis ad Deum*), trans. George Boas (New York: Liberal Arts Press, 1953), p. 9; or the *Breviloquium*, trans. José de Vinck, in *The Works* (Paterson, N.J.: Saint Anthony Guild Press, 1963), pp. 101–3 (II, 11). On the two books see, e.g., *Breviloquium*, p. 81 (II, 5). On Chaucer's use here of the law of nature, see Lynn V. Sadler, "Chaucer's the *Book of the Duchess* and the 'Law of Kinde,'" *Annuales Mediaevale*, 11 (1970), 51–64.

5   On Christian readings of pagan material see Jean Seznec, *The Survival of the Pagan Gods: The Mythological Tradition and Its Place in Renaissance Humanism and Art*, trans. B. F. Sessions (New York: Pantheon Books, 1953), pp. 84–103. On allegory in Ovid see, especially, Lester K. Born, "Ovid and Allegory," *Speculum*, 9 (1934), 362–79.

6   Severs, "Chaucer's Self-Portrait," pp. 30–32.

7   Kemp Malone, *Chapters on Chaucer* (Baltimore: Johns Hopkins University Press, 1951), pp. 22–24.

8   See Wolfgang Clemen's discussion of the *House of Fame* in *Chaucer's*

Early Poetry, trans. C. A. M. Sym (New York: Barnes & Noble, 1964), pp. 70 ff.

9   Robert Burton, *The Anatomy of Melancholy*, ed. Floyd Dell and Paul Jordon-Smith (New York: Farrar & Rinehart, 1955), pp. 485 ff. Burton also recommends music and poetry (pp. 478 ff.) and talk with a friend (p. 471) — both obviously relevant to the *Book of the Duchess*.

10   Huppé and Robertson, *Fruyt and Chaf*, p. 46.

11   Ibid., p. 49.

12   For a narrow but complementary medical reading of "heart-hunting" see Joseph E. Grennen, "Hert-huntyng in the *Book of the Duchess*," *Modern Language Quarterly*, 25 (1964), 131–39. Medieval "psychiatrists" worked like confessors, probing for deep problems, trying to revive emotion.

13   The identification of narrator and hart is parallel to the identification (pointed out by Bronson) of narrator and Black Knight in what I would call the second hunt. Since Chaucer does not insist on the narrator's metamorphosis (in either case), our best course is to notice the structural parallels without worrying much over what *pictures* the action calls up, a matter for individual interpretation.

14   *Romaunt*, 1449–1538. The narrator is caught in the same way, 1543–1648.

15   Consider the "fallow doe" in the familiar ballad, "The Three Ravens."

16   The hound "koude no good," contrasting with the lady as she is presented at 998 and 1012. (The hound is also compared and contrasted with other characters, of course.) The image "heres" is echoed at 855 in connection with the lady. The hound leads to the garden or at any rate a flowery place associated with the lady (400–409 and 820–26). The hound's flight and the initial rejection by the lady are parallel elements of the flight or withdrawal motif working throughout the poem.

17   B. H. Bronson, "The *Book of the Duchess* Re-Opened," *Publications of the Modern Language Association*, 67 (1952), 870–71.

18   "King" may have reference to the chess game the Knight has played with Fortune, though I'm not fully convinced. For a not very careful study of the chess game metaphor, see Johnye E. Mathews, "The Black Knight as King of the Castle in the *Book of the Duchess*," *South Central Bulletin*, 31 (1971), 200–201.

19 See Huppé and Robertson, *Fruyt and Chaf*, p. 92. Cf. the use of twelves in the *Pearl*, lines 992, 993, 1022, 1030, and so forth.

20 For discussion of this theme in the *House of Fame*, see Barry Sanders, "Love's Crack-up: The *House of Fame*," *Papers on Language and Literature*, 3 (1967), 3–13.

21 Dorothy Everett commented on repetitions of "reste" and other key words in "Some Reflections on Chaucer's 'Art Poetical,' " *Proceedings of the British Academy*, 36 (1950), 131–54.

22 Elaborate verbal repetition may be found in such poets as Raimbaut d'Orange, Piere Vidal, Raimon de Miraval, Lanfranc Cigala. The disparity between the theory of the rhetoricians and the practice of medieval poets was discussed by Margaret Louise Switten, in "*Repetitio* in Theory and Practice: A Problem of Medieval Poetics" (Paper delivered at the December 1965 meeting of the MLA at Chicago).

23 On this theme see J. A. W. Bennett, *The Parlement of Foules: An Interpretation* (London: Oxford University Press, 1957).

24 Nicolai Von Kreisler shows that right love of the lady is compared, by means of repeated allusions, to right love of Christ. See his "A Recurrent Expression of Devotion in Chaucer's *Book of the Duchess, Parliament of Fowles*, and *Knight's Tale*," *Modern Philology*, 68 (1970), 62–65.

25 The *Pearl*-poet treats souls of the blessed as "pearls" in the crown or garland of the New Jerusalem. He speaks of the Virgin as the Phoenix of Araby (430), and his emphasis is, like Chaucer's, on the lady's uniqueness. Chaucer's line, "For wher-so men had pleyd or waked" may involve a play on the idea of resurrection.

26 Other passages in which the love-religion borrows church language are 911 et seq. and 961 et seq., where the lady is "lyght" to the lover; indeed, she is

> lyk to a torche bryght
> That every man may take of lyght
> Ynogh, and hyt hath never the lesse.

A striking and original application of church notions to the love-religion occurs at 890, where among the ladies' lovers "The formest was always behynde" — cf. the conclusion of the Parable of the Vineyard. (The torch image, the phrase "never the lesse," and the Parable of the Vineyard all occur in *Pearl*.)

27 In his allegorical treatment of the Dead Sea as a figure of hell, the
Purity-poet mentions the impossibility of either living or dying in that
sea.

28 Cf. Robert O. Payne, in *The Key of Remembrance: A Study of
Chaucer's Poetics* (New Haven: Yale University Press, for the
University of Cincinnati, 1963), p. 46: "Poetry as an art must remain, as
long as the framework of medieval belief stood, a process of favorable
responses to a fittingly dignified statement of pre-existing truths. At least
those were the only terms in which its theoricians could discuss it. Thus
inventio, if it remains in the discussion at all, becomes a process of verbal
ingenuity or a search for a theme." (And cf. pp. 45–51.)

29 My summaries and comments here depend on work done for me by
Karen Tyrrel, awesome graduate student.

30 Albert I. Dickerson, Jr., "Chaucer's *Book of the Duchess*: A Critical
Edition with Introduction, Variants, Notes, and Glossary," *Dissertation Abstracts,* 29 (1969), 2256A.

Chapter 2

1 Kemp Malone, *Chapters on Chaucer* (Baltimore: Johns Hopkins
University Press, 1951), p. 64.

2 See David Chamberlain, "The Music of the Spheres and the
Parliament of Foules," *Chaucer Review,* 5 (1970), 32–56.

3 Ibid. Several detailed interpretations of the *Parliament of Birds* have
been published. Some of the best, besides those already mentioned, are
J. A. W. Bennett, *The "Parlement of Foules": An Interpretation* (London:
Oxford University Press, 1957); *The Parlement of Foulys,* ed. D. S. Brewer
(New York: Barnes & Noble, 1960); B. F. Huppé and D. W. Robertson,
Jr., in *Fruyt and Chaf: Studies in Chaucer's Allegories* (Princeton, N.J.:
Princeton University Press, 1966); Donald C. Baker, "The Poet of Love
and the *Parlement of Foules,*" *University of Mississippi Studies in English,* 2
(1961), 79–110; Rhoda H. Selvin, "Shades of Love in the *Parlement of
Foules,*" *Studia Neophilologica,* 37 (1965), 146–60; R. M. Lumiansky,
"Chaucer's *Parlement of Foules*: A Philosophical Interpretation," *Review of
English Studies,* 24 (1948), 81–89; and B. H. Bronson, "In Appreciation of
Chaucer's *Parlement of Foules,*" *University of California Publications in
English,* 3 (1935), 193–224; and Wolfgang Clemen, *Chaucer's Early
Poetry,* trans. C. A. M. Sym (New York: Barnes & Noble, 1964), pp.
122–69.

4 Chamberlain, "The Music of the Spheres," p. 33.

5 Mary Giffin, *Studies in Chaucer's Audience* (Hull, P.Q.: Editions L'Eclair, 1956), p. 64.

6 Chamberlain, "The Music of the Spheres," pp. 49–50.

7 Ibid., pp. 48–49.

8 John P. McCall, "The Harmony of Chaucer's *Parliament*," *Chaucer Review*, 5 (1970), 22–31.

9 On the role of the poet, see Clemen, *Chaucer's Early Poetry*, pp. 126–28, and also Dorothy Everett, *Essays on Middle English Literature*, ed. Patricia Kean (Oxford: At the Clarendon Press, 1955), p. 111.

10 On playful ironic intrusions, see B. H. Bronson, "The *Parlement of Foules* Revisited," *English Literary History*, 15 (1948), 260.

11 This continual shifting of tone is one of the chief reasons critics have had difficulty finding unity in the poem. Muscatine, among others, has viewed the shifting itself as a unifying principle (Charles Muscatine, *Chaucer and the French Tradition* [Berkeley and Los Angeles: University of California Press, 1957], p. 116). Other studies of the poem's unity or disunity include Bronson's "Appreciation"; R. C. Goffin, "Heaven and Earth in the *Parlement of Foules*," *Modern Language Review*, 31 (1936), 493–99; R. E. Thackaberry, "Chaucer's *Parlement of Foules*: A Reinterpretation," *Wilson Dissertations*, listings for 1937, p. 87; Lumiansky, "Chaucer's *Parlement of Foules*"; G. Stillwell, "Unity and Comedy in Chaucer's *Parlement of Foules*," *Journal of English and Germanic Philology*, 49 (1950), 470–95; D. Bethurum, "The Center of the *Parlement of Foules*," *Essays in Honor of Walter Clyde Curry*, ed. Richmond C. Beatty et al. (Nashville, Tenn.: Vanderbilt University Press, 1954), pp. 39–50; Charles O. McDonald, "An Interpretation of Chaucer's *Parlement of Foules*," *Speculum*, 30 (1955), 444–57; Robert Worth Frank, Jr., "Structure and Meaning in the *Parlement of Foules*," *Publications of the Modern Language Association*, 71 (1956), 530–39.

12 Muscatine, *Chaucer and the French Tradition*, p. 116.

13 Malone, Clemen, Muscatine, Bronson, and others have pointed out the striking change in style and tone at this point. For defense of the shift, see Frank, "Structure and Meaning in the *Parlement of Foules*."

14 See, for example, Muscatine, *Chaucer and the French Tradition*, pp. 115–16, and Clemen, *Chaucer's Early Poetry*, pp. 128–32. On the

"baffling" structure, Clemen writes: "Thus, long introductions are typical of all Chaucer's allegorical dream-poems. It is as though we were being led by devious routes towards the principal room in a house. The trend of the period in regard to style was not towards simplification, but baffling complexity and intricacy. Ornamental and decorative elements were not confined to any recognizable external zone surrounding the core; they covered the whole, and sometimes constituted the essence of the work itself. In literature as in other arts, there was frequently no clear line between essential expression and additional ornament" (p. 129).

15 See the articles previously cited — Goffin, "Heaven and Earth in the *Parlement of Foules*"; and Lumiansky, "Chaucer's *Parlement of Foules*"; and pp. 101–48 in Huppé and Robertson, *Fruyt and Chaf*.

16 Muscatine, *Chaucer and the French Tradition*, pp. 122–23.

17 Huppé and Robertson, in *Fruyt and Chaf*, rightly point out (pp. 102–3) that Chaucer is echoing Boethius, 2, prose 3, but their interpretation of the echo is wrong. Chaucer's meaning is that he had from the book what he did not want and could not find in the book what he thought he would find. The contempt for the world found in Scipio's dream cannot be identified with "the possession of earthly goods." Chaucer has ironically inverted Boethius: the book's talk about the detachment which ought to make man tranquil turns out to make Chaucer nervous.

18 McDonald, in "An Interpretation of Chaucer's *Parlement of Foules*," says: "The poet is telling us that all the elements of courtly love allegory are present in this garden, but he makes them generally as unattractive as possible by allowing them few qualifying adjectives with which he was so lavish in listing the trees," and so forth (p. 444).

19 Bennett, *The Parlement of Foules*, p. 178.

20 On carnality in this extended sense, see D. W. Robertson, Jr., *A Preface to Chaucer: Studies in Medieval Perspectives* (Princeton, N.J.: Princeton University Press, 1962), pp. 70 ff. With the sanction of tradition, Chaucer has turned both sides of the Boethian opposition — "love" and "nature" or self-will — into forms of love, that is, good love and bad. Love becomes (as for Boethius, in a sense) a metaphor for everything.

21 On the music of the spheres, see (besides Boethius, *De Musica*) Macrobius, 2, 1–4 (*Macrobius' Commentary on the Dream of Scipio*, trans. William H. Stahl [New York: Columbia University Press, 1952], pp. 185–200). Macrobius says that the numbers whose relationships are responsible for the harmony of the spheres are masculine (odd) and feminine (even). "Since the uneven numbers are considered masculine and

the even feminine, God willed that the soul which was to give birth to the universe should be born from the even and uneven, that is from the male and the female." (See 1, 6.) He also speaks of the union of one and seven, representing God and the Pallas Athene or, alternatively, soul and body.

22   In Petrarch's *Africa*, as in all commentaries on Scipio, Scipio is the emblem of the political hero, keeper of the "political virtues" of which Macrobius speaks (1, 8).

23   In political discussions, *patience* refers to forms of government in which ruler and ruled stand in a relation of mutual interdependence; *agency* refers to government in which the ruler acts as agent for the ruled and without their consent. Cf. Chaucer's remarks on patience in love in the *Franklin's Tale* (V, 761 et seq.) and see my discussion of the "marriage group" in the *Canterbury Tales*.

24   F. L. Ganshof, *Feudalism*, trans. Philip Grierson (New York: Harper & Row, 1961).

25   See John Gardner, "Theme and Irony in the Wakefield *Mactatio Abel*," *Publications of the Modern Language Society*, 80 (1965), 516–21; and cf. my commentary on *Patience* in *The Complete Works of the Gawin-poet* (Chicago: University of Chicago Press, 1965).

26   See Dante, "On Monarchy," in *Medieval Political Philosophy: A Sourcebook*, ed. Ralph Lerner and Muhsin Mahdi (New York: Free Press of Glencoe, 1963), pp. 432–35.

27   On Chaucer's use of his sources, see Bennet, *The Parlement of Foules*, and cf. F. N. Robinson's notes in *The Works of Geoffrey Chaucer*, 2nd ed. (Boston: Houghton Mifflin Company, 1957).

28   Or perhaps of art generally. At all events, the emphasis is on the conventionality and artificiality of everything seen.

29   Huppé and Robertson, *Fruyt and Chaf*, p. 145.

30   Chamberlain, "The Music of the Spheres," p. 47.

Chapter 3

1   Frank T. Zbozny, "The Metrical Structure of Chaucer's *ABC*," *Dissertation Abstracts*, 31 (1970), 2359A.

2 See F. N. Robinson's note to line 27, p. 861. (*The Works of Geoffrey Chaucer*, 2nd ed. [Boston: Houghton Mifflin Company, 1957]).

3 Lines from the *Prima Pastorum* are quoted from the edition of A. C. Cawley, *The Wakefield Pageants in the Towneley Cycle* (Manchester: Manchester University Press, 1958), p. 31. I discuss the play's punning technique in *The Construction of the Wakefield Cycle* (Carbondale: Southern Illinois University Press, 1974).

4 Frank John Chiarenza, "Chaucer and the Medieval Amorous Complaint," *Dissertation Abstracts*, 31 (1970), 2337A.

5 Robinson, *The Works of Geoffrey Chaucer*, p. 304.

6 James I. Wimsatt, "*Anelida and Arcite:* A Narrative of Complaint and Comfort," *Chaucer Review*, 5 (1970), 1–8.

7 For a less convincing theory but some valuable insights along the way, see Michael D. Cherniss, "Chaucer's *Anelida and Arcite:* Some Conjectures," *Chaucer Review*, 5 (1970), 9–21.

8 Wimsatt, "*Anelida and Arcite*," p. 8.

9 Cherniss, "Chaucer's *Anelida and Arcite*," p. 16.

10 George Williams has a theory that the *Complaint of Mars* tells in disguised fashion a story of how one time Chaucer helped John of Gaunt and Katheryn Swynford in their love affair. Because of vicious gossip, Katheryn (Venus) fled from the house of Gaunt (Mars) to the Chaucers' house, where Geoffrey (Mercury) took care of her. All this Williams supports with great ingenuity (*A New View of Chaucer* [Durham, N.C.: Duke University Press, 1965], pp. 56–65), but no one, so far as I know, has been persuaded. Edgar S. Laird's interpretation of the poem, in "Astrology and Irony in Chaucer's *Complaint of Mars*," *Chaucer Review*, 6 (1972), 229–31, would destroy Williams' reading in that Laird argues, plausibly, that when Venus is with Mercury generous Mercury goes to bed with her, as hopefully Chaucer did not do with Katheryn. (Their astrological relationship is, in the language of the Trinity College, Cambridge, MS. which continues Chaucer's *Astrolabe*, one of "a privy and secret benevolens." Laird denies opposition in the MS. between "amity and love," on one hand, and "frenship" and "benevolens" on the other. On several grounds I disagree.) But even if Laird is wrong, as I think he is, Williams' theory is pretty crazy. What poet in his right mind would compliment his friend by reminding him of the time "you'd've had it, old boy, if it wasn't for you-know-who!"

11   See Edmund Reiss, "Dusting Off the Cobwebs: A Look at Chaucer's Lyrics," *Chaucer Review*, 1 (1966), 57–62.

12   *On the Sacraments of the Christian Faith*, trans. Roy J. Deferrari (Cambridge, Mass.: Mediaeval Academy of America, 1951), p. 125.

13   Quoted by D. W. Robertson, Jr., *A Preface to Chaucer: Studies in Medieval Perspectives* (Princeton, N.J.: Princeton University Press, 1962), pp. 71–72.

14   J. S. P. Tatlock, *The Mind and Art of Chaucer* (Syracuse, N.Y.: Syracuse University Press, 1950), pp. 83–84.

15   Cf. *Pearl*, lines 649–60.

Chapter 4

1   See Hamilton B. Smyser, "A View of Chaucer's Astronomy," *Speculum*, 20 (1945), 359–73. On Gower's comparative ignorance, see p. 362.

2   *Astrolabe*, Part I, line 92; Part I, conclusion 17, line 21.

3   See *The Equitorie of the Planetis*, edited from Peterhouse MS. 75. I, by Derek J. Price, with a linguistic analysis by R. M. Wilson (London: Cambridge University Press, 1955).

4   On Chaucer's serious concern with astrological powers see Smyser, "A View of Chaucer's Astronomy," and Chauncey Wood, *Chaucer and the Country of the Stars: Poetic Uses of Astrological Imagery* (Princeton, N.J.: Princeton University Press, 1970). Charles A. Owen, Jr., argues — rightly, I think — that in Chaucer's later work (that is, the later parts of the *Canterbury Tales*), Chaucer grows less and less interested in astrological concerns and increasingly interested in character — finally character independent even of the controlling author. See "The Problem of Free Will in Chaucer's Narratives," *Philological Quarterly*, 46 (1967), 433–56. Chaucer's use of astrological devices of course goes far beyond mere astrology. For instance, though Venus functions as an astrological force in the *Troilus*, Chaucer's presentation of Venus in the Proem to Book III calls up all the major traditions and associations established by two centuries of courtly-love poetry. See Dorothy Bethurum Loomis, "The Venus of Alanus de Insulis and the Venus of Chaucer," *Monographs*, 37 (1970), 182–95.

5 On the Platonic contrast of "the many" and "the one" see Thomas
Aquinas' *Summa Theologica*, especially Part I, Q3, Q11 (articles 2–4);
Part II, Q27, Q36, Q39, Q42; Part III, Q44, Q45 (articles 7–8), Q47,
Q48; Part VI, Q75, Q76. And see note 19 below.

6 Russell A. Peck, "Numerology and Chaucer's *Troilus and Criseyde*,"
Mosaic, 5 (1972), 1–29.

7 I think no one has exactly pinned down the narrative technique in this
poem, though every reader intuits it. (I make my own try at pinning
it down at the end of this chapter.) For some interesting attempts see
Murray F. Markland, "*Troilus and Criseyde*: The Inviolability of the
Ending," *Modern Language Quarterly*, 31 (1970), 147–59 (an argument
that the narrator is not Chaucer, that the disorder Chaucer "intentionally
creates" in the poem is meant to characterize the narrator, a man whose
wisdom may be sound but does not derive from the story); Allen C.
Koretsky, "Chaucer's use of Apostrophe in *Troilus and Criseyde*," *Chaucer
Review*, 4 (1970), 242–66 (the narrator is "highly ambiguous"); Joseph E.
Gallagher, "Theology and Intention in the *Troilus*," *Chaucer Review*, 7
(1972), 44–66 (an argument that Chaucer himself is narrator and that he
attempts to evade the strictest terms of medieval religion — which is
certainly true, though I think true in ways Gallagher oversimplifies);
Willene P. Taylor, "Supposed Antifeminism in Chaucer's *Troilus and
Criseyde* and its Retraction in the *Legend of Good Women*," *Xavier
University Studies*, 8–9 (1969–70), 1–19 (an oversimplified poet-versus-
persona argument); and Ann Chalmers Watts, "Chaucerian Selves — Especially Two Serious Ones," *Chaucer Review*, 4 (1970), 229–41. Other
writers on this subject I mention in other connections later.

8 See, for early examples of this approach, Bernard L. Jefferson, *Chaucer
and the "Consolation of Philosophy" of Boethius* (Princeton, N.J.:
Princeton University Press, 1917), pp. 120 ff.; Howard R. Patch, "Troilus
on Determinism" *Speculum*, 6 (1931), 225–43; Theodore A. Stroud,
"Boethius' Influence on Chaucer's Troilus," *Modern Philology*, 49 (1951–
52), 1–9; Charles A. Owen, Jr., "The Significance of Chaucer's Revisions
of *Troilus and Criseyde*," *Modern Philology*, 55 (1957–58), 1–5. (Cf.
Robertson, "Chaucerian Tragedy," cited in note 10 below.) More recent
studies of Boethian influence are in general concerned, properly, with the
interpenetration of philosophy and dramatic event in the poem. Ida L.
Gordon argues, unconvincingly (in *The Double Sorrow of Troilus: A Study
of Ambiguities in "Troilus and Criseyde"* (London: Oxford University
Press, 1970), that the love between Troilus and Criseyde is "idolatrous in
him and unstable in her, but in presenting that love, Chaucer simultaneously [by means of narrator and event ironies] censures it and uses it to
praise the possible beauty and power that it might have attained if it were
properly directed" (p. 39), as in Boethius' vision of divine love. (On

Gordon's weaknesses, see Joseph E. Gallagher's review in *Medium AEvum*, 41 [1972], 39–46.)

In three important articles, Robert ap Roberts clears up some of the usual confusions about the poem's use of Boethian thought. He points out in "The Boethian God and the Audience of the *Troilus*," *Journal of English and Germanic Philology*, 69 (1970), 425–36, that when Troilus and Criseyde part, in Book IV, their intentions are noble and their choices are free, so that to judge them harshly is to resist the plain evidence of the poem. Given their virtue and nobility, if they could know the providential plan, they would behave differently. The audience, granted a providential overview, understands the short, merely human view and also the long view unattainable by mere mortals. Ap Roberts further elaborates the irony of Criseyde's faith and the audience's sense of the inevitability of her fate in his article "Love in the *Filostrato*," *Chaucer Review*, 7 (1972), 1–26, and in "Criseyde's Infidelity and the Moral of the *Troilus*," *Speculum*, 44 (1969), 383–402. John W. Conlee gives ap Roberts brilliant support in "The Meaning of Troilus' Ascension to the Eighth Sphere," *Chaucer Review*, 7 (1972), 44–66, showing that the three stanzas at the end are not there to reveal Troilus' ultimate fate but to "emphasize the Boethian concept of the discrepancy between man's limited perception while in this world and his vastly expanded perception after his release from this world" (p. 27). He shows that the lines suggest a "synthesis of pagan and Christian concepts of immortality . . . reinforced by the meanings of the number *eight* in traditional medieval number symbolism" (pp. 27–28), which he analyzes in detail. With the readings of ap Roberts and Conlee compare Charles Moorman's excellent analysis, " 'Once More Unto the Breach': The Meaning of *Troilus and Criseyde*," *Studies in the Literary Imagination*, 4 (1971), 61–71, and Stephen A. Barney's fine essay, "Troilus Bound," *Speculum*, 47 (1972), 445–58. See also Joseph J. Morgan, Jr., "Free Will and Determinism in Chaucer's *Troilus and Criseyde*," *Western Studies in Language and Literature*, 2 (1969), 131–60, and Richard A. Lanham, "Opaque Style and its Uses in *Troilus and Criseyde*," *Studies in Medieval Culture*, 3 (1970), 169–76. The most complete available analysis of the poem's Boethian element is John M. Steadman's *Disembodied Laughter: Troilus and the Apotheosis Tradition* (Berkeley and Los Angeles: University of California Press, 1972).

9 For scholarly opinion on the poem's reflection of courtly love, see W. G. Dodd, *Courtly Love in Chaucer and Gower* (Boston and London: Ginn and Company, 1913), pp. 154–78; G. L. Kittredge, *Chaucer and His Poetry* (Cambridge: Harvard University Press, 1915), pp. 126–36; K. Young, "Aspects of the Story of Troilus and Criseyde," *University of Wisconsin Studies in Language and Literature*, 2 (1918), 379–94, and "Chaucer's *Troilus and Criseyde* as Romance," *Publications of the Modern Language Association*, 53 (1938), 49, 51–56; C. S. Lewis, *The Allegory of Love* (London: Oxford University Press, 1936), pp. 182–90, et passim;

Howard Rollin Patch, *On Rereading Chaucer* (Cambridge: Harvard University Press, 1939), pp. 74–83; T. A. Kirby, *Chaucer's Troilus: A Study of Courtly Love* (Baton Rouge: Louisiana State University Press, 1940), pp. 192–238; J. S. P. Tatlock, "The People in Chaucer's *Troilus,*" *Publications of the Modern Language Association,* 56 (1941), 96–102; John Speirs, "Chaucer (I) *Troilus and Criseyde,*" *Scrutiny,* 11 (1942), 84–108; Laurens J. Mills, *One Soul in Bodies Twain: Friendship in Tudor Literature and Stuart Drama* (Bloomington, Ind.: Principia Press, 1937), pp. 60–63, et passim; and Robert Reilly, "The Narrator and His Audience: A Study of Chaucer's *Troilus,*" *University of Portland Review,* 21 (1961), 23–36. As I've mentioned, it has been much debated whether courtly love ever really existed outside poetry and whether the concept of courtly love helps us understand the *Troilus.* See Francis L. Utley, "Must We Abandon the Concept of Courtly Love?" *Medievalia et Humanistica,* 3 (1972), 299–324.

10 Kittredge, in his *Chaucer and His Poetry,* viewed the conclusion of the *Troilus,* especially V, 1835–48, as Chaucer's repudiation of courtly love in favor of Christian love (p. 143). James Lyndon Shanley, in "The *Troilus* and Christian Love," *English Literary History,* 6 (1939), 271–81, rightly argued that both courtly love and Christian love are viewed as good in this poem, though one is transitory and thus ultimately unsatisfactory. According to Father Alexander J. Denomy, in "The Two Moralities of Chaucer's *Troilus and Criseyde,*" *Transactions of the Royal Society of Canada,* 44 (series 3, section 2 [June 1950]), 35–46, "Chaucer not only rejects, disapproves of and condemns, he repudiates Courtly Love as vain, ephemeral, and fallacious, the blind effect of passion, and that not only in the Palinode but within the very fabric of the story itself" (p. 43). See also D. W. Robertson, Jr., "Chaucerian Tragedy," *English Literary History,* 19 (1952), 1–37, later included in modified form in Robertson's *A Preface to Chaucer: Studies in Medieval Perspectives* (Princeton, N.J.: Princeton University Press, 1962), pp. 472 ff. In the *Troilus,* in Robertson's opinion, "The three stages of tragic development — subject to Fortune, enjoyment of Fortune's favor, and denial of providence — correspond to the three stages in the tropological fall of Adam, the temptation of the senses, the corruption of the lower reason in pleasurable thought, and the final corruption of the higher reason" ("Chaucerian Tragedy," p. 13). Judging by more recent criticism, such views as Robertson's and Father Denomy's have been generally abandoned. See Markland, and Gallagher (cited in note 7 above); Moorman, and ap Roberts (cited in note 8 above); and Rodney Delasanta, "Chaucer and the Exegetes," *Studies in the Literary Imagination,* 4 (1971), 1–10.

The trouble with earlier exegetical, or "historical," criticism is of course partly that it oversimplifies medieval Christianity. The Christianity of Chaucer was mellowed not only by the ideas of men like Wyclif and the practice of Christian laymen like Henry of Lancaster but also by Eastern and Neoplatonic influence coming through, for instance, the School of

Chartres, which gave Chaucer an optimistic worldview wherein Augustine's *cupiditas* and *caritas* are not norms but extremes. For detail see Terrance A. Hipolito, "Chaucer and the School of Chartres," *Dissertation Abstracts International*, 31 (1971), 6551A.

Whether or not the *Troilus* is an authentic "tragedy" is a question much worried by Chaucerians. The question is merely semantic, finally, but those who have raised it have sometimes made important contributions to our understanding of the poem. See especially Samuel L. Macey, "Dramatic Elements in Chaucer's *Troilus*," *Texas Studies in Literature and Language*, 12 (1970), 301–23, finally a fairly convincing argument that Chaucer, like Shakespeare, provides "a drama of real life, a drama giving not merely aesthetic pleasure because of the alignment of structure with content, but a drama also from which may be drawn a message that is fleshly or spiritual, local or universal, in accordance with the eye of the beholder or the perspective of the critic" (p. 323).

11 Professor Meech's attempt at resolution of the problem is typical of earlier scholarship: "Until the Epilog, the oppositions which Chaucer effects are oblique rather than polar whether between virtues and defects in individuals, between persons, or between the endeavors of these mortals and what is celestially decreed for them. We can be amused by his Diomede and charmed by Criseyde while recognizing the heartlessness of the one and the halfheartedness of the other; grant Troilus' worldly merits, yet smile at the absurdities in which the plots of his friends involve him; appreciate the latter's motives in procuring for the prince without being put off by his joviality from condemning them; and savor the delight which he won for his master with the help of a storm, though we must anticipate that destiny so impressively evidenced in this phenomenon will overwhelm them both. And even the polar opposition in the Epilog of heavenly to mundane affection cannot obliterate our memories of the fine if soon withered fruits which the latter yielded to the hero. Our zest unspoiled by the finale, we begin the poem again and again, which as its author prayed with some worldliness has been spared the ravages of time" (Sanford B. Meech, *Design in Chaucer's "Troilus"* [Syracuse, N.Y.: Syracuse University Press, 1959], p. 427).

For a more recent, in some ways more subtle reading, see Anthony E. Farnham, "Chaucerian Irony and the Ending of the *Troilus*," *Chaucer Review*, 1 (1967), 207–16 — an argument that, although at the end of the third book the love of Troilus and Criseyde imitates celestial love, two forces combine to doom that love, namely their own imperfections, which make them freely choose wrongly (answered by ap Roberts), and the power of Fortune. See also ap Roberts's articles (cited in note 8 above); and Markland, and also Gallagher (cited in note 7 above). Benjamin R. Bessent, "The Puzzling Chronology of Chaucer's *Troilus*," *Studia Neophilologica*, 41 (1969), 99–111, provides another approach to Chaucer's justification of Criseyde, one which closely ties her actions to the "destinal forces" of the poem and the narrator's role as sorrowing historian. See also Steadman, *Disembodied Laughter.*

12 See especially ap Roberts's articles (cited in note 8 above). The contrary view, that Troilus and Criseyde are miserable sinners, was fashionable in the 1950s and sixties and still has adherents. It's true, admittedly, that most of Chaucer's more obvious sources took a hardshell stand on human love. Even the *Roman de la Rose*, which used to be read as a vision of the joys of earthly love, has been shown to be another hardshell allegory on cupidity. (For this demonstration and for comment on other of Chaucer's main sources, see Charles R. Dahlberg, "Macrobius and the Unity of the *Roman de la Rose*," *Studies in Philology*, 58 (1961), 573–82.

13 See Donald R. Howard, "Literature and Sexuality: Book III of Chaucer's *Troilus*," *Massachusetts Review*, 8 (1967), 442–56.

14 See Charles A. Owen, Jr., "Mimetic Form in the Central Love Scene of *Troilus and Criseyde*," *Modern Philology*, 67 (1969), 125–32.

15 *Dissertation Abstracts*, 23 (1964), 3352. Though Sister Costello is the first (I think) to state the point explicitly, others have come close, notably Meech, *Design in Chaucer's "Troilus,"* pp. 262–70.

16 On the plan of the action see John P. McCall, "Five-Book Structure in Chaucer's *Troilus and Criseyde*," *Modern Language Quarterly*, 23 (1962), 297–308, and Meech, *Design in Chaucer's "Troilus,"* pp. 3–22. Readings of the *Troilus* as five-act tragedy are common. See Willard Farnham, *The Medieval Heritage of Elizabethan Tragedy* (Berkeley: University of California Press, 1939), pp. 137–60. In "Destiny in Chaucer's *Troilus*," *Publications of the Modern Language Association*, 45 (1930), 164, Walter Clyde Curry says the poem "occupies a sort of middle ground artistically between the ancient Greek tragedy and the modern tragedy of Shakespeare." Professor Root calls the poem "a tragedy in the medieval sense of the term" but acknowledges its effect not really tragic. See *The Book of Troilus and Criseyde*, ed. R. K. Root (Princeton, N.J.: Princeton University Press, 1926), pp. xlix–l.

17 Charles Muscatine, *Chaucer and the French Tradition* (Berkeley and Los Angeles: University of California Press, 1957), pp. 164–65.

18 Biblical and patristic allusion in the *Troilus* has not yet been treated in the detail it deserves. For beginnings, see R. E. Kaske, "The Aube in Chaucer's *Troilus*," in *Chaucer Criticism*, vol. 2, ed. Richard J. Schoeck and Jerome Taylor (Notre Dame, Ind.: University of Notre Dame, 1961), p. 177, and Robertson, "Chaucerian Tragedy." (Other works treating such allusions are mentioned in other notes to this chapter.)

19 There's a brief discussion of Neoplatonic thought as related to Augustine, Aquinas, and other church writers in Etienne Gilson's *A History of Christian Philosophy in the Middle Ages* (New York: Random House, 1955), especially pp. 20–39. Cf. Gordon Leff, *Medieval Thought* (London: Penguin Books, 1958); David Knowles, *The Evolution of Medieval Thought* (Baltimore: Halicon Press, 1962), pp. 22 ff.

20 Macrobius generally reflects Plotinus' views, which Chaucer's orthodox inclinations would perhaps modify in the general direction of Aquinas' arguments in the *Summa*, somewhat enshadowed in Chaucer's day but still widely influential. I'll summarize relevant sections of the Plotinus-Macrobius line of thought and merely allude in passing to Aquinas' main points of disagreement. (A convenient English translation of Macrobius is that by William H. Stahl, with introduction and notes, *Macrobius' Commentary on the Dream of Scipio* [New York: Columbia University Press, 1952].)

For both Plotinus and Macrobius, as for Aquinas, and so forth, the One is the first cause. Aquinas and later Christian writers of course deny Plotinus' opinion that the One is not a being (because, Plotinus says, we can attach no categories to it) but agree, with reservations, that it is indescribable to man. Late Christian writers of course reject, too, Plotinus' opinion that the One cannot think (see Aquinas' *Summa*, Part I, Q14). Thinking suggests to Plotinus a dualism between the thinker and the thought-upon, thus destroying unity (the same mistake Jean Paul Sartre makes). But Christian writers agree that the One contemplates itself. The productiveness of this contemplation reaches such a fullness that the One overflows and through this "emanation" forms the second level, which is, for Macrobius and Plotinus, spirit, and which contemplates the totality of Forms. Spirit (God's being) overflows in its contemplation and forms the World Soul. Thus the One is connected with the Many: the One is, for Macrobius and Plotinus, the World Soul which touches every level of being. (Aquinas of course strenuously disagrees. See *Summa*, Part III, Q44.)

In Plotinus the *essence* of the One is found in its unity and permanence, while plurality and variability belong only to the *workings* of the One. (For greater detail, see W. Windelband, *A History of Philosophy* [New York: Macmillan, 1901], p. 244.) Aquinas agrees (*Summa*, Part I, Q3 and Q4, Part III, Q44–47). For Plotinus and Macrobius, matter is a purely negative concept. Matter devoid of qualities is the evil in Plotinus' system. It is absolute want, absolute negation of the One and of being. Thus evil is not something existent, but a deficiency, a lack of the good. Following Parmenides' dictum, "What is not is not," Plotinus thinks evil not a positive part of the system and, ergo, that it needn't be justified. (This has an obvious influence on Augustine, as can be seen in his handling of the Manichean affair, and on Aquinas later. See Windelband, *A History of Philosophy*, pp. 247–48.) The corrupting process in which the world proceeds from the divine principles in an eternal and necessary downward flow, Plotinus and Macrobius say, is the reason for the constant need for purification and reversal of the flow. The soul has an inclination toward what is void and vain, thus is drawn into the sensuous body, a kind of death (as Macrobius and Chaucer say). Once cast into the body, its job is to estrange itself from the body and purify itself once again from its new home. After this process is complete, the soul may travel back up the stages emanating from the deity, and thus return to God. (For Aquinas' distantly related view, see Part III, Q47, article 2.)

Means of purifying the soul, for Plotinus and Macrobius, include civic and political virtue — by which man asserts himself as a rationally formative force in the phenomenal world (see Windelband, *A History of Philosophy*, pp. 249–50) — and also the virtue of knowledge, which results from the turning inward of the soul to its own spiritual life. To aid in attaining this virtue, Plotinus suggests contemplating the beautiful, much in the manner Plato suggested — first being stimulated by sensuous beauty, then, in overcoming the inclination toward matter, moving from the sensuously beautiful to the spiritually beautiful. (Compare Bonaventura's opening section of *The Mind's Road to God* and Boethius' ideas on the value of music, in *De Musica*.) Even this step is only preliminary to the phase in which the individual loses all consciousness and unifies himself with the "ground of the world." The sinking into the all-one is "the salvation and blessedness of the individual." Porphyry — also Bonaventura — stresses the assistance given the individual by religion and acts of worship — a point with which Macrobius agrees.

Macrobius depends on numerous Neoplatonists, not just Plotinus (see Stahl's introduction), so that his system is finally not exactly like anyone else's; but his *Commentary* has all the main Neoplatonic features: how souls descend from the celestial or "fixed" sphere into mortal bodies, what all this has to do with music, astronomy, geography, numerology, and so on. Most important, for our present purpose, he expresses the Neoplatonic view of the universe as a ladder, every rung of which contains in some measure "the Supreme God even to the bottommost dregs of the universe" (p. 145), or, to put it another way, the view that God's light "suffuses all below with life, and since this is the one splendor lighting up everything and visible in all, like a countenance reflected in many mirrors arranged in a row" (p. 145), contemplation of anything can lead heavenward.

21 See Meech, *Design in Chaucer's "Troilus,"* pp. 379–83.

22 For abundant evidence of a significant parallel between the love religion and Christian religion in *Troilus*, see Meech, *Design in Chaucer's "Troilus,"* pp. 264–70.

23 See Gareth W. Dunleavy, "Natural Law as Chaucer's Ethical Absolute," *Transactions of the Wisconsin Academy of Sciences, Arts, and*

Letters, 52 (1963), 177–87, and Thomas A. Van, "Imprisoning and Ensnarement in *Troilus* and the *Knight's Tale*," *Papers on Language and Literature*, 7 (1971), 2–12.

24 Jefferson, *Chaucer and the "Consolation of Philosophy,"* pp. 65–66.

25 Patch, "Troilus on Determinism," p. 240.

26 On the larger implications of this departure from Boccaccio, see P. M. Kean, *Chaucer and the Making of English Poetry* (London: Routledge & Kegan Paul, 1972).

27 On the world as phantom see, for instance, Augustine's discussion of numbers in Boethius, *De Musica*, Book VI; on the deceptive nature of "fantasie," see Jehan le Bel, *Li ars d'amour*, ed. J. Petit (Brussels: V. Devaux, 1867–69), vol. 1, pp. 201–3. For a Freudian reading of the dreams in *Troilus*, see Helen A. Corsa, "Dreams in *Troilus and Criseyde*," *American Imago*, 27 (1970), 52–65.

28 Boethius, *Consolation*, Book 4, prose 6, 41–139, et passim. Cf. Macrobius, *Commentary*, I, 22.

29 Stahl translation, p. 135.

30 Ibid., p. 145.

31 Ibid., pp. 121–22.

32 Ibid, p. 145.

33 Meech, in his *Design in Chaucer's "Troilus,"* points out and discusses religious and feudal diction in connection with the central characters, pp. 262–89. Very little of this diction, Meech shows, is borrowed from Boccaccio.

34 The love-friendship metaphor is examined by Leah F. Friewald, "Swich Love of Frendes: Pandarus and Troilus," *Chaucer Review*, 6 (1971), 120–29.

35 That is, the *aubé* within which, as Professor Kaske pointed out, Criseyde is clearly characterized as timid and a trifle selfish, and within which, also, Troilus defies Phoebus, binding his doom to Troy's.

36 Criseyde's plea to Hector occurs in Boccaccio's *Il Filostrato*, I, 12–13. But Chaucer invents all the remainder of the Criseyde-Hector friendship — Hector's esteem for her (*Troilus*, II, 1450–56), his attempt to

persuade the Trojan parliament not to make the exchange of Criseyde for Antenor (IV, 174–82), and so forth.

37 On this point see ap Roberts, "The Boethian God and the Audience of the *Troilus*," pp. 427–29.

38 On Zanzis, see Donald K. Fry, "Chaucer's Zanzis and a Possible Source for *Troilus and Criseyde*, IV, 407–413," *English Language Notes*, 9 (1971), 81–85.

39 Cf. the Black Knight's refusal to repent of love worship, *Book of the Duchess*, 1115 et seq.

40 See Meech, *Design in Chaucer's "Troilus,"* pp. 271 ff.

41 In the introduction to my book, *The Complete Works of the Gawain-poet* (Chicago: University of Chicago Press, 1965), I have tried to show that Middle English *courtesy* was sometimes used in an extended, metaphorical sense. Cf. *Pearl*, 459–68, and *Legend of Good Women*, 342.

42 On Pandarus as devil, see Robertson, *A Preface to Chaucer*, pp. 479 ff. Cf. Alan Gaylord, "Uncle Pandarus as Lady Philosophy," *Papers of the Michigan Academy of Science, Arts, and Letters*, 46 (1961), 571–95.

43 See Muscatine, *Chaucer and the French Tradition*, pp. 137 ff.

44 Cf. Bonaventura, *The Mind's Road to God*; Macrobius, *Commentary*, I, xii et passim. Cf. Boethius' imagery of night and day throughout the *Consolation*, and Chaucer's "blinde world," *Troilus*, I, 211; "blynde lust," V, 1824; and so forth.

45 "Distance in *Troilus and Criseyde*," *Publications of the Modern Language Association*, 72 (1957), 16–17; and Benjamin R. Bessent, "The Puzzling Chronology of Chaucer's *Troilus*."

46 "The Dual Time-Scheme in Chaucer's *Troilus*," *Modern Language Notes*, 56 (1941), 94–100.

47 Bloomfield, "Distance in *Troilus and Criseyde*," p. 17. And see William George Provost, "The Structure of Chaucer's *Troilus and Criseyde*," *Dissertation Abstracts*, 31 (1970), 400A. Bloomfield further elaborates one traditional aspect of the space-mutability idea as it is carried in Troilus' address to a door (V, 519–602), in "Troilus' Paraclausithyron and Its Setting," *Neuphilologische Mitteilungen*, 73 (1972), 15–24.

48 See Curry, "Destiny in Chaucer's *Troilus*," p. 144.

49 On Bracton's interpretation of "the King's pleasure," see Ewert
     Lewis, "King Above Law? 'Quod Principi Placuit' in Bracton,"
Speculum, 39 (1964), 240–69.

50 On the love versus power debate, see my "Theme and Irony in the
     Wakefield *Mactacio Abel*," *Publications of the Modern Language
Association*, 80 (1965), 515–21. For more detail on the complementary
nature of Troilus and Criseyde — also Troilus and Pandarus, and so
forth — see Ann I. Haskell, "The Doppelgängers in Chaucer's *Troilus*,"
Neuphilologische Mitteilungen, 72 (1971), 723–34. The mirror and echo
effects Haskell points out throughout *Troilus and Criseyde* would seem to
support my thesis that the many and the one are crucial to the poem's
structure and meaning.

51 See Curry, "Destiny in Chaucer's *Troilus*," pp. 139–43. Curry goes
     wrong in his interpretation of the narrator's remark that Venus "nas
nat al a fo" to Troilus. She was *one* of the influences at his birth, perhaps.

52 See Howard Rollin Patch, "Troilus on Predestination," *Journal of
     English and Germanic Philology* 17 (1918), 399–422.

53 Ibid., pp. 413 ff. The oppositions I've mentioned, along with some
     others, have been treated by Meech, *Design in Chaucer's "Troilus*,"
especially in chapters 2 and 3, pp. 141–366.

54 This is approximately Robert Reilly's point ("The Narrator and His
     Audience"), though I do not agree with Reilly that at the end of the
poem Chaucer himself steps in to resolve "the ambiguity." What is
involved is not ambiguity at all but partisanship. Cf. Laila Gross, "Time
and the Narrator in Chaucer's *Troilus and Criseyde*," *McNeese Review*, 19
(1968), 16–26.

55 For a fine analysis of the concluding stanzas — one which I hope
     accords with mine, though not specifically involved with the *persona*
problem — see Francis L. Utley, "Stylistic Ambivalence in Chaucer, Yeats,
and Lucretius — The Cresting Wave and its Undertow," *University
Review*, 37 (1971), 174–98, especially pp. 181–92. The style of the
concluding stanzas is of course *not simply* a reflection of "Chaucer's"
whirling and gradually settling emotions; it also reflects his serious
intention of evading simpleminded clarity which might tend to nail down
the "meaning" of the poem, reducing it from art to sermon. See E. Talbot
Donaldson, "Chaucer and the Elusion of Clarity," *Essays and Studies*, 24
(1972), 23–44.

Chapter 5

1 No definite topical allusions have been found. Rudolf Imelmann
    argued in 1912 that the ending was to concern the arrival in England
of Anne of Bohemia ("Chaucers *Haus der Fame*," *Englische Studien*, 45
[1912], 397–431), and his argument, though weak, was revived by Aage
Brusendorff in *The Chaucer Tradition* (London: Oxford University Press,
1925), p. 165. It was answered by B. H. Bronson ("Chaucer's *Hous of
Fame*: Another Hypothesis," *University of California Publications in
English*, 3 [1934], 186–87), who argues for less sober-minded tidings.
Everyone now agrees with Bronson except B. G. Koonce (*Chaucer and the
Tradition of Fame: Symbolism in the "House of Fame"* [Princeton, N.J.:
Princeton University Press, 1966]), who imagines the tidings to be brought
at the end of the poem are the good news of salvation, the authority being
Jesus himself. (Cf. also F. C. Riedel, "Chaucer's *House of Fame*," *Journal of
English and Germanic Philology*, 27 [1928], 441–69.) Interpretations of the
poem as private allegory have all broken down or died for want of takers.
For a summary of such interpretations, see W. O. Sypherd, *Studies in
Chaucer's "Hous of Fame"* (Chaucer Society, 1906; rpt. New York: Haskell
House, 1965), pp. 156 ff. Stylistic tests — crude and subjective so
far — have proved inconclusive means of dating the poem. The tetrameter
line looks back to the *Book of the Duchess*, but Chaucer's heavy dependence
on Dante, Ovid, and so forth, removes the *House of Fame* from the
so-called French period; and despite Sypherd's labors, the poem is generally
agreed to have at least as much in common with epic tradition as with the
love-vision, so that it may easily be associated with the period in which
Chaucer wrote the *Troilus*.

Chaucer's claim that he dreamed his wonderful dream on December
10 has intensified the confusion. Ten Brink tried to argue that the poem's
references to Jupiter suggest that December 10 was a Thursday and
worked out his date of composition from this. Skeat, on the theory that
Chaucer imitated Dante's device of naming the day on which he started his
poem, argued that December 10 was the date on which Chaucer started
work, an opinion obviously conjectural at best. It's not impossible, for
instance, that the date is pure whimsey or a piece of comic realism aimed at
giving a false impression of verisimilitude which is to be exploded by the
rest of the poem. A more interesting theory is that of Koonce (*Chaucer and
the Tradition of Fame*, pp. 57 ff.), who argues that December 10, among
other things, makes the poem an advent vision. For answer to this, see John
Leyerle, "Chaucer's Windy Eagle," *University of Toronto Quarterly*, 40
(1971), 247–65, especially pp. 249–50 (the most convincing astronomical
explanation so far, though I disagree with Leyerle about the poem's date of
composition, Chaucer's birthdate, and other matters); and see also D. M.
Bevington, "The Obtuse Narrator in Chaucer's *House of Fame*," *Speculum*,

36 (1961), 291–92. Ten Brink's dating of the poem, 1383 or 84, is probably not far wrong. It's impossible to dismiss the similarity between the discussions of dream-lore in the *House of Fame* and *Troilus* (*HF*, 1 et seq.; *T*, V, 358–85), both strikingly different, especially in their skepticism, from the dream discussion in the *Parliament* and the assumptions underlying the *Book of the Duchess*. If in metrical form the comic epic looks back to the *Book of the Duchess*, it may as readily be said to look forward to the "drasty rymyng" of *Sir Thopas*, for, as various critics have pointed out, the *House of Fame* is mock-heroic. (See Wolfgang Clemen, *Chaucer's Early Poetry*, trans. C. A. M. Sym [New York: Barnes & Noble, 1964], pp. 70 ff.; Alfred David, "Literary Satire in the *House of Fame*," *Publications of the Modern Language Association*, 85 [1960], 333–39); William S. Wilson, "Exegetical Grammar in the House of Fame," *English Language Notes*, 1 [1964], 244–48; and Laurence Eldridge, "Chaucer's *Hous of Fame* and the *Via Moderna*," *Neuphilologische Mitteilungen*, 71 [1970], 111–12.) Chaucer's bad writing, especially in the "translation" of Virgil and Ovid (*HF*, 143–467) is intentional. Though we may agree with F. N. Robinson that Dante "would very naturally have been the first Italian author to engage [Chaucer's] attention" (*The Works of Geoffrey Chaucer*, 2nd ed. [Boston: Houghton Mifflin Company, 1957], p. 280), there is no evidence that this was the case. The *Parliament*, which preceded *Troilus*, shows relatively little influence of Dante, considerable influence of Boccaccio and Petrarch, while the *Troilus* leans heavily on Dante throughout. For summary of further arguments bearing on the date of the poem, see H. Lloyd Jones, Jr., "The Date of Chaucer's *House of Fame*," *Delaware Notes*, 19th series (1946), 47–55.

2   See Robinson's notes to lines 240 et seq. and line 379 (*The Works of Geoffrey Chaucer*). CF. E. F. Shannon, *Chaucer and the Roman Poets* (Cambridge: Harvard University Press, 1929), pp. 48 ff.

3   On the influence of Boethius, see Paul G. Ruggiers, "The Unity of Chaucer's *House of Fame*," *Studies in Philology*, 50 (1953), 16–29, and G. Stilwell, "Chaucer's 'O Sentence' in the *House of Fame*," *English Studies*, 37 (1956), 149–57. The extent of Dante's influence on the poem has been debated at length, but all recent critics agree that it's enormous. See especially Koonce, *Chaucer and the Tradition of Fame*, 73–279.

4   Numerous borrowings from French poetry have been pointed out (see Robinson's notes, in *The Works of Geoffrey Chaucer*, and cf. Sypherd, *Studies in Chaucer's "Hous of Fame,"* pp. 11–20 et passim, but a large share of these are really from Chaucer's own earlier work — for instance the invocation to Morpheus, *House of Fame*, 69 et seq., drawn from *Book of the Duchess*, 155 et seq., and the imitations of the *Roman de la Rose*, which go back to Chaucer's translation. As Koonce and J. A. W. Bennett both show, in the *House of Fame*, borrowings from secular poetry are mainly from

Italian and Latin. (See Bennett, *Chaucer's Book of Fame: An Exposition of the "House of Fame"* [London: Oxford University Press, 1968].)

5   On this verbal pattern in the *House of Fame*, see Barry Sanders, "Love's Crack-up: The *"House of Fame,"* Papers on Language and Literature*, 3 (1967), 5–6, and cf. *Knight's Tale*, lines 1052–69, and so forth.

6   According to Robert O. Payne, in *The Key of Remembrance: A Study of Chaucer's Poetics* (New Haven: Yale University Press, for the University of Cincinnati, 1963), proof by experience is a central theme throughout the poetry of Chaucer. Certainly the Wife of Bath has much to say on the subject; but I find the theme not central (if present at all) in *Book of the Duchess* and *Parliament*.

7   G. L. Kittredge, *Chaucer and His Poetry* (Cambridge: Harvard University Press, 1915), p. 76.

8   Koonce, *Chaucer and the Tradition of Fame*, pp. 15–16.

9   Ibid., p. 23.

10   Ibid., p. 64.

11   Ibid., p. 65.

12   Roger Bacon, *Opus Majus*, trans. Robert Belle Burke (Philadelphia: University of Pennsylvania Press, 1928), vol. 1, p. xi.

13   Ibid., p. 5.

14   Ibid., vol. 2, pp. 605–6.

15   Ibid., p. 618.

16   For bibliography of fourteenth-century thought in this area, see Eldridge's note 1, p. 107 ("Chaucer's *Hous of Fame* and the *Via Moderna*").

17   Ibid., p. 109.

18   (Chicago: University of Chicago Press, 1972.) Cf. J. F. McNamara, "Responses to Ockhamist Theology in the Poetry of the *Pearl*-poet Langland, and Chaucer," *Dissertation Abstracts*, 69 (1968), 04491, and William B. Joyner, " 'Craft' and 'Sentence' in Chaucer's *House of Fame*," *Dissertation Abstracts International*, 32 (1971), 3255A.

19   Eldridge, "Chaucer's *Hous of Fame* and the *Via moderna*," p. 110.

20 See Delany, 'Chaucer's *"House of Fame,"* pp. 48–57.

21 Eldridge, "Chaucer's *Hous of Fame* and the Via Moderna," p. 112.

22 Ibid., p. 113.

23 Ibid., p. 119.

24 Bennett, *Chaucer's Book of Fame*, p. x.

25 Clemen, *Chaucer's Early Poetry*, p. 97.

26 Leyerle, "Chaucer's Windy Eagle," p. 247. On the comic eagle, see also Joseph E. Grennen, "Science and Poetry in Chaucer's *House of Fame*," *Annuale Medievale*, 8 (1967), 38–45. Grennen shows that the eagle's attack parallels an attack of apoplexy. See also Mahmoud Manzalaoui, "English Analogues to the *Liber Scalae*," *Medium AEvum*, 34 (1965), 31–33.

27 Leyerle, "Chaucer's Windy Eagle," pp. 253–54. He goes on to give further evidence that eagle lecterns were used in this queer way.

28 Quoted by Leyerle, "Chaucer's Windy Eagle," pp. 251–52.

28 Ibid., pp. 254–55. Leyerle goes on to show that the joke comes from Chaucer's source, the *Speculum Naturale* by Vincent of Beauvais.

30 Payne, *The Key of Remembrance*, p. 133.

31 J. A. W. Bennett, though his main concern is scholarly commentary on Chaucer's adaption of sources, finds some kind of coherence (which I fail to understand) in the ambivalent mixture of true and false throughout the poem and in the progression from Venus (man's passion, he says) to Fame (man's renown), to Rumor (man's love of story). Leyerle sees the eagle as the connector. Eldridge, in his "Chaucer's *Hous of Fame* and the *Via Moderna*," if I understand him, finds confusion itself the poem's principle of order. If I've misrepresented his position I apologize, but this sentence is his and, I think, a true one: "And in such a world [a welter of individual instances] the only thing that a man of authority, even a man of great authority, can say is that it does not make very much sense" (p. 119).

32 A. C. Cawley, *The Wakefield Pageants in the Towneley Cycle* (Manchester: Manchester University Press, 1958), p. 10.

33 Leyerle, "Chaucer's Windy Eagle," p. 258.

34 "The Place of the Poet in Chaucer's *House of Fame*," *Modern Language Quarterly*, 27 (1966), 125–35.

35 The nature of Geffrey's quest has been debated. See W. O. Sypherd, "The Completeness of Chaucer's *House of Fame*," *Modern Language Notes*, 30 (1915), 67.

36 William S. Wilson, "The Eagle's Speech in Chaucer's *House of Fame*," *Quarterly Journal of Speech*, 50 (1964), p. 153.

37 Wilson, "Exegetical Grammar in the *House of Fame*," pp. 244–48.

38 John of Salisbury, *The Metalogicon of John of Salisbury*, trans. Daniel D. McGarry (Berkeley: University of California Press, 1962), p. 102.

39 Ibid., p. 79.

40 On sources of the fiction, the temple of Fame, see Sypherd, *Studies in Chaucer's "Hous of Fame,"* pp. 103–38.

41 John of Salisbury, *Metalogicon* p. 83.

42 See David, "Literary Satire in the *House of Fame*."

43 Clemen, *Chaucer's Early Poetry* pp. 99–100.

44 Ibid., cf. p. 100, n. 1.

45 Such modern views as those of Collingwood and Croce, for whom art is a means of "discovering" or "expressing" reality. The prevailing classical view was similar (as Payne, in *The Key of Remembrance*, notes). Plato's *Ion* suggests that poetry expresses divine truth, the poet serving as a kind of "mad" if not brainless conductor, and the poetry Plato admits into his Republic is that which expresses the ideal nobility of the State, and so forth. Aristotle, in answer to Plato's question, "What does the poet imitate as a carpenter imitates the ideal chair?" says (in effect) that the poet imitates process, or action, that is, reveals for the listener the causality of things. Most modern writers are Aristotelean; Henry James, for example. Poe stands with Plato, claiming that the poet "conveys impressions."

46 Payne, *The Key of Remembrance*, p. 45.

47 Ibid., p. 46.

48 See Boccaccio's remarks on poetry as a "veil," in C. G. Osgood, ed., *Boccaccio on Poetry* (New York: Library of Liberal Arts, 1930), passim.

49 Augustine speaks repeatedly of the "stupidity" of mistaking the letter for the spirit. Chaucer sometimes agrees, as when he makes fun of the "glossing" of the stupid friar in the *Summoner's Tale.*

50 Professor Smith's suggestion that the basis of the allusion may be *Roman de la Rose*, 243 et seq. (see Robinson's note, in *The Works of Geoffrey Chaucer*, to *HF*, 1117), may be right but seems not too helpful. I think Chaucer is talking, with comic literal-mindedness, about something he's actually seen in Spain. On the tradition of mountain symbolism, see Koonce, *Chaucer and the Tradition of Fame*, pp. 184 ff.

51 Dante, *De Vulgari Eloquentia*, in *Tutte le opere di Dante Alighieri*, ed. E. Moore (London: Oxford University Press, 1894); Eustache Deschamps, *Oeuvres Complètes de Eustache Deschamps*, vol. 7, ed. Gaston Raynaud (Paris: Firmin Didot, 1891), pp. 266–92.

52 For general discussion of exegetical grammar and poetic theory, and for comment on imitation and translation, see Eugene Vinaver's introduction to *The Works of Sir Thomas Malory* (London: Oxford University Press, 1947). On the moral value of old books and thus of "imitation" of older writers, see Payne, *The Key of Remembrance*, pp. 64 ff. I deal with this some in my discussion of the *Legend of Good Women*, below.

53 On moralizing as one of the functions of the poet retelling an old story, see Wilson, "Exegetical Grammar in the *House of Fame*," p. 247.

54 See John of Salisbury on "nature" and "art," i.e., craft, in *Metalogicon*, I, viii–xi, pp. 28–36 et passim.

55 Cf. B. F. Huppé and D. W. Robertson, Jr., *Fruyt and Chaf: Studies in Chaucer's Allegories* (Princeton, N.J.: Princeton University Press, 1966), p. 113.

56 A student, Maria Lattimore, has pointed out to me that the parallels between the eagle and Christ are numerous.

57 A standard identification in the lapidaries. Cf. Chaucer, *Prioress's Tale*, line 610.

58 See for instance Augustine's commentary on the *Canticles.*

59 Gawain, similarly, is introduced to a false paradise with the words from the castle's porter, "yea, Peter!" i.e., "yea, by Saint Peter!"

60　See Haldeen Braddy's note on symbolic colors in Chaucer, in *Geoffrey Chaucer: Literary and Historical Studies* (Port Washington, N.Y.: Kennikat Press, 1971), pp. 76–78.

61　*Satires*, IV, 23–24. The lines are quoted by John of Salisbury, *Metalogicon*, Prologue (p. 3). Chaucer's self-justification in Book III is to a man "at his back," whom Koonce identifies as maybe Satan.

62　"Chaucer's *The House of Fame*," *English Literary History*, 8 (1941), 255.

63　So far as I can remember, I've never run across a suggestion that the voice which cries "Awak!" is the voice of an employer or patron who is jokingly treated here as a slave driver, but it seems inevitable that eventually some clown will offer it, especially 1) since Gaunt sometimes used the eagle as his sign, 2) since the eagle was emblematic of Saint John, with whom Gaunt is punningly associated at the end of the *Book of the Duchess*, 3) since in the early eighties Gaunt was riding high and was probably responsible for Chaucer's court favor (including the tedious customs job), and 4) since Chaucer did in fact move, in the mid-eighties, to more pleasant work. In this case the phrase "oon I koude nevene" looks forward to the line on the man of great authority, whom Chaucer says "y nevene nat ne kan" (if the Skeat-Koch-Robinson reading is right), and the stranger is Gaunt, the poem a begging poem.

64　See Francis X. Newman, "*House of Fame*, 7–12," *English Language Notes*, 6 (1968), 5–12.

Chapter 6

1　On the *Legend*'s popularity in Chaucer's own time and on down to the nineteenth century, its decline in popularity after the critical comments of W. W. Skeat and Thomas R. Lounsbury, and its further decline in recent years, see Robert Worth Frank, Jr., *Chaucer and the "Legend of Good Women"* (Cambridge: Harvard University Press, 1972), pp. 189–210. Frank himself argues, more or less convincingly, that the *Legend* is the work in which Chaucer freed himself from medieval conventions and learned the art of narrative for its own sake. To Frank the poem is not bad at all, considering. His position is supported (or rather anticipated) in Eleanor Jane Winsor's "A Study in the Sources and Rhetoric of Chaucer's *Legend of Good Women* and Ovid's *Heroides*," *Dissertation Abstracts*, 28 (1968), 3161–62A. Winsor shows how much Chaucer learned about parody and other kinds of literary trickery from Ovid. Virginia A. Shea, in "Not Every Vessel Al of Gold: Studies in

Chaucer's *Legend of Good Women*," *Dissertation Abstracts*, 32 (1972), 6394A, praises the poem's irony, its exploration of the feminine psyche, and so forth. Mary Patricia Smagola, in " 'Spek Wel of Love': The Role of Women in Chaucer's *Legend of Good Women*," *Dissertation Abstracts International*, 33 (1972), 1696A, finds the poem "a masterpiece of comic irony," and so forth, and so forth. Roy A. Battenhouse, in *Shakesperean Tragedy: Its Art and Its Christian Premises* (Bloomington: Indiana University Press, 1969), finds more to say of the *Legend*. The tide, obviously, is turning.

2 So far as I know, no living Chaucerian believes that Prologue G. was written earlier than Prologue F. See F. N. Robinson, *The Works of Geoffrey Chaucer*, 2nd ed. (Boston: Houghton Mifflin Company, 1957), p. 839.

3 J. S. P. Tatlock, *The Mind and Art of Chaucer* (Syracuse, N.Y.: Syracuse University Press, 1950), p. 75 et passim. Cf. J. R. Hulbert, "A Note on the Prologues to the *Legend of Good Women*," *Modern Language Notes*, 65 (1950), 534–46. Hulbert argues that Chaucer's changes are designed to withdraw the poet and dreamer from any close connection with the "queen" who accompanies Cupid and from the cult of the Flower. Robert M. Estrich presents a related view in "Chaucer's Maturing Art in the Prologues to the *Legend of Good Women*," *Journal of English and Germanic Philology*, 36 (1937), 326–37. Estrich says Chaucer cuts conventional courtly love material and heightens the amused, ironic comedy of the prologue at the expense of the god of love and perhaps also at the expense of certain members of his audience who may have been shocked by the *Troilus*. All of these views focus — rightly, up to a point — on the first prologue's obvious function as a court piece.

4 For Kemp Malone's opinion, see *Chapters on Chaucer* (Baltimore: Johns Hopkins University Press, 1951). On p. 99 Malone admits frankly that he cannot say why Chaucer bothers at all to revise the prologue of *Legend of Good Women*; however, he does study the changes for clues to Chaucer's developing sense of style and craftsmanship. Cf. Malone, "A Poet at Work: Chaucer Revising His Verses," in *English Studies Today*, ed. C. L. Wrenn and G. Bullough (London: Oxford University Press, 1951), pp. 98–103. Here Malone takes less tentatively the view that Chaucer is "polishing." According to D. D. Griffith, in "An Interpretation of Chaucer's *Legend of Good Women*," *Manly Anniversary Studies* (Chicago: University of Chicago Press, 1923), p. 40, the revision was undertaken to remove "the obvious use of the Christian service," because "it seems tenable that Chaucer in his maturer life became more formally religious and regarded the analogies between the service of the Roman church and the service of Cupid as blasphemous."

5   *Unlust* is a standard Middle English word for *sloth*, and *lust* might conceivably occur in the special sense, "assiduous pursuit of the good." But this is farfetched here.

6   Cf. Chaucer's shift from *trowen* to *leven*, *Book of the Duchess*, 1046–48.

7   See Malone, *Chapters on Chaucer*, pp. 86–96.

8   For example, see Augustine's "Second Discourse on Psalm 32" in *St. Augustine on the Psalms*, trans. Dame Scholastica Hebgin and Dame Felicitas Corrigan (Westminster, Md.: Newman Press, 1961), vol. 2, pp. 105–7.

9   See B. F. Huppé on the May morning, in B. F. Huppé and D. W. Robertson, Jr., *Fruyt and Chaf: Studies in Chaucer's Allegories* (Princeton, N.J.: Princeton University Press, 1966), p. 45 et passim.

10   See, for instance, Saint Augustine's *Confessions*, Book 4, ch. 12: "Furthermore, it was through me that the serpent spoke to Alypius himself, weaving and laying in his path, by means of my tongue, pleasant snares, whereby his honorable and free feet might be entangled. For when he was surprised that I, for whom he had no little respect, stuck so firmly in the birdlime of that pleasure," and so forth (my translation).

11   On the Devil's envy see, for instance, Augustine's *City of God*, XIV, 27.

12   See D. W. Robertson, Jr., *A Preface to Chaucer: Studies in Medieval Perspectives* (Princeton, N.J.: Princeton University Press, 1962), pp. 72–75.

13   For argument that the *House of Fame* and the *Legend of Good Women* were written somewhere near the same time, perhaps just before and just after the *Troilus*, see chapter 5 above.

14   I assume here the reading of J. A. W. Bennett, *The "Parlement of Foules": An Interpretation* (Oxford: Clarendon Press, 1957) as modified in chapter 2 above.

15   Professor Frank's study does make some points worth repeating here — and a few mistakes misleading enough to need correcting. Chaucer's invention of the pentameter couplet (used in the *Knight's Tale* and the *Legend of Good Women*) was an important advance. It gave him flexibility and the means of achieving the colloquial tone necessary for straight narrative. As innumerable English poets have recognized, the

NOTES TO PAGES 217–22

rhymed tetrameter line is too symmetrically musical and swings in rhymes too often to allow any impression of ordinary speech. Rhymed pentameter, with enjambments and shifting caesurae, can hover beautifully between poetry and talk. Professor Frank is right, too, in arguing that in the *Legend of Good Women* Chaucer learned — possibly by noticing how Ovid had learned before him — the all-important art of abbreviation. In the early dream visions and *Troilus*, he'd been concerned mainly with amplification. In the *Knight's Tale*, and more drastically in the *Legend of Good Women*, what he had to do was cut. In his commentary on the legends, Frank now and then shows just how Chaucer did this cutting and what effects he achieved thereby. That alone (and much else that's good) makes Frank's book useful.

But he does also err. He finds the prologue a ruse, Chaucer's claim that he means to deal with courtly love when in fact he intends nothing of the kind. This comes from Frank's too narrow understanding of courtly love. Frank's sharp distinction between poetry Chaucer wrote before the *Legend of Good Women* and poetry he wrote after is mostly imaginary, and most of the things Frank claims Chaucer learned by writing the *Legend* (Frank, *Chaucer and the "Legend of Good Women,"* pp. 169–87), Chaucer had actually known for some time.

Chapter 7

1   Trevor Whittock, *A Reading of the "Canterbury Tales"* (Cambridge: Cambridge University Press, 1968), p. 37.

2   See Eugene Vinaver's remarks in his edition, *The Works of Sir Thomas Malory* (London: Oxford University Press, 1947), vol. 1, pp. xli–lxxxv, and also his "Form and Meaning in Medieval Romance," *The Presidential Address of the Modern Humanities Research Association* [Cambridge, England, 1966, 24 pp.].

3   The unity or disunity of Malory's work has been much debated, Vinaver on one side, everyone else on the other. Key contributions to the debate are Vinaver's introduction to *The Works of Sir Thomas Malory*; R. M. Lumiansky's "The Question of Unity in Malory's *Morte D'Arthur*," *Tulane Studies in English*, 5 (1955), 29–39; and Charles Moorman's *The Book of Kyng Arthur: The Unity of Malory's "Morte Darthur"* (Lexington: University of Kentucky Press, 1965).

4   I do not use the word *realism* in the overrefined, confusing way most scholars would approve. Morton W. Bloomfield has an elaborate analysis of differences between various kinds of "realism" ("Authenticating Realism and the Realism of Chaucer," *Thought*, 39 [1964], 335–58). Since

his article, critics have gotten stuffier and stuffier on the matter. In describing Malory and Chaucer as "realists" I don't mean that they regularly strive for verisimilitude (authenticating realism), though they often do, or that their apparent realism is not in large measure a matter of medieval realistic *convention*, though it sometimes is. I mean only that to a large extent they include life experience in their books, however influenced that experience may be by their experience of art. Realism is a long stretch on the continuum running from realism to artifice. A realist may sometimes write pure artifice, as when Chaucer wrote the *Second Nun's Tale*, and a thoroughly artificial writer may sometimes enliven his artifice by exactly describing some gesture used by his wife.

5   I don't mean to exaggerate here the unity of the *Canterbury Tales*.

Professor Kean is surely right in observing that "Chaucer would never have allowed the *Canterbury Tales* to develop the kind of schematization which is reached either by giving all the parts a uniformity which arises directly out of the nature of the frame or by a development of the frame which would render it completely independent of the tales and so allow complete freedom to introduce stories of any kind without any thematic interconnection. What he has arrived at, it seems to me, is a method by which frame and tales grow together, as the characters of the tellers reveal themselves increasingly through the frame and as the tales, in their turn, continue the revelation or arise naturally from one another, as Miller 'quites' Knight" (P. M. Kean, *Chaucer and the Making of English Poetry* [London: Routledge & Kegan Paul, 1972], vol. 2, p. 75.) A structure of this kind allows for unlimited expansion, especially when we add the possibility of unconnected tales like that of the Canon's Yeoman. But though the overall theme of the collection is so general that the poem can contain almost anything, much as an art museum can contain almost anything, it is nevertheless true, most critics agree, that the tales work in groups and that the groups explore a few basic, interrelated themes. (Cf. Kean, *Chaucer and the Making of English Poetry*, vol. 2, pp. 110–85, and Paul G. Ruggiers, *The Art of the "Canterbury Tales"* [Madison: University of Wisconsin Press, 1965], pp. xiii–xvi, 3–15, et passim.)

Critical focus on the unity or disunity of the tales began in earnest with Ralph Baldwin's monograph, "The Unity of the *Canterbury Tales*," published in *Anglistica*, 5 (1955), and anthologized by Richard J. Schoeck and Jerome Taylor in *Chaucer Criticism. The "Canterbury Tales": An Anthology* (Notre Dame, Ind.: University of Notre Dame Press, 1960), pp. 14–51, wherein Baldwin tried to link the Pilgrims and their tales to the sins denounced in the *Parson's Tale*. The unity Baldwin finds is an illusion — the whole approach is much too sober-minded (as is even my approach, I suspect from time to time) — but Baldwin's impulse in looking for unity is right. Robert M. Jordan's *Chaucer and the Shape of Creation: The Aesthetic Possibilities of Inorganic Structure* (Cambridge: Harvard University Press, 1967), denies that the collection has unity, arguing (unpopularly at the time his book came out) that our conventional attitudes toward the tales are wrong, especially the standard concept of the tales' dramatic structure, the assumption of a close relationship of tale to teller, of purposefully developed characterization, and the significance of the narrator and the nature of his audience. Like D. W. Robertson, Jr., Jordan is a man who can be brilliantly informative on certain matters yet infallibly wrong about tone and intention. He points out what is antique and static or "inorganic" in the tales and behaves as though there were nothing else. But the tales *are* keyed to their tellers, as a hundred sensible critics have shown repeatedly and as most of Chaucer's editors have recognized. The fad of pointing out that a few are not is mere obstreperousness, or perhaps simplemindedness, or desperate publication for promotion. The tales of the Shipman, Second Nun, and Man of Law are not, perhaps, well keyed to their tellers, but this is because Chaucer changed his mind while he was working. (For detail on how he changed it, see John Gardner, "The Case Against the 'Bradshaw Shift'; or, the Mystery of the Manuscript in the Trunk," *Papers on Language and Literature*, 3 [1967], 80–106.) Only pedantic cowardice denies that the *Shipman's Tale* was originally for the Wife of Bath, the *Second Nun's Tale* originally for the Clerk (see my comments on the tale), and the present *Man of Law's Tale* a substitution for his original story, the *Melebee*.

For all their cool allegory, the tales have perfectly obvious dramatic structure and purposefully developed characterization. (See for instance Charles Muscatine's "The *Canterbury Tales*: Style of the Man and Style of the Work," in *Chaucer and Chaucerians: Critical Studies in Middle English Literature*, ed. D. S. Brewer [University: University of Alabama Press, 1966], pp. 88–113; Donald R. Howard's "Chaucer the Man," *Publications of the Modern Language Society*, 70 [1965], 337–43; or Ruggiers, *The Art of the "Canterbury Tales*," cited above.) One of the proofs of Chaucer's concern for organic unity is the collection's wealth of internal echoes and its repetition of a few basic symbols and other devices throughout. For demonstration of this see Jim W. Evers, "Some Implications of Chaucer's Use of Astrology in the *Canterbury Tales*," *Dissertation Abstracts International*, 32 (1972), 4561A; Jeanette Richardson, *Blameth Nat Me: A Study of Imagery in Chaucer's Fabliaux* (The Hague: Mouton, 1970); and (for symbolic and imagistic continuity in the tales), Ann S. Haskell's "The Golden Ambiguity of the *Canterbury Tales*," *Erasmus Review*, 2 (1971), 1–9. For a moving and solid defense of one character as a real human being (at any rate, no mere type), see Britton J. Harwood, "The Wife of Bath and the Dream of Innocence," *Modern Language Quarterly*, 33 (1972), 257–73. See also, on the same Pilgrim, Joseph F. Mogan, Jr., "Chaucer and the *Bona Matrimonii*," *Chaucer Review*, 4 (1970), 123–41.

In the light of all this, I need not too strenuously apologize for finding the collection tightly unified, each tale coming at exactly the right point (in the Ellesmere arrangement), the end mirroring the beginning, and so on. But Chaucer had clearly not made all his corrections and clearly planned to add many more tales (and finish those unfinished), as we might assume from the fact that he apparently had tales by other people (the "tale of Ganymede," for instance) in with his manuscript. Which is to say that the unity we discern in the collection was provisional in Chaucer's own mind. But it was there.

6 For translations of, and commentary on, most of the debates mentioned here, see John Gardner, *The "Alliterative Morte Arthure," The "Owl and the Nightingale," and Five Other Middle English Poems* (Carbondale: Southern Illinois University Press, 1971).

Chapter 8

1 I have mentioned (ch. 7, n. 4) the fad of denying that Chaucer is a realist. On the non-realism of his *Prologue* portraits, see J. Lawrence Badendyck, "Chaucer's Portrait Technique and the Dream Vision Tradition," *English Record*, 21 (1970), 113–24.

2 On the allegorical superstructure, see Robert M. Jordan, *Chaucer and the Shape of Creation: The Aesthetic Possibilities of Inorganic Structure* (Cambridge: Harvard University Press, 1967).

3 See Rodney Delasanta, "The Theme of Judgment in the *Canterbury Tales*," *Modern Language Quarterly*, 31 (1970), 298–307. Delasanta overstates his case, but he's right in general.

4 See John Finlayson, "The Satiric Mode and the *Parson's Tale*," *Chaucer Review*, 6 (1971), 94–116. On the mind's limitations as a central concern in the tales, see Raymond P. Tripp, Jr., "The *Knight's Tale* and the Limitations of Language (The Boundaries Which Words Are)," *Rendezvous*, 6 (1971), 23–28.

5 See *Fulgentius the Mythographer*, trans. Leslie George Whitbread (Columbus: Ohio State University Press, 1971).

6 Arthur W. Hoffman, "Chaucer's Prologue to Pilgrimage: The Two Voices," *Publications of the Modern Language Association*, 64 (1949), 823–28.

7 Several scholars have pointed out that the Squire portrait is not as favorable as readers used to imagine. Chauncey Wood, for instance (in "The Significance of Jousting and Dancing as Attributes of Chaucer's Squire," *English Studies*, 52 [1971], 116–18), shows how Chaucer's alterations of one of his sources, the *Roman de la Rose*, and his probable indebtedness to Henry Lancaster's *Livre de Seyntz Medicines* make jousting and dancing the inspiration of lechery, not bad in themselves but easily abused and therefore dangerous. I cannot go as far as Professor Wood goes in finding fault with the Knight's merry son, but it is certainly true that he is not set up as an absolute ideal. He has, along with virtues, at least potential defects, and maybe slightly worse.

8   See *Fulgentius the Mythographer*, trans. Leslie George Whitbread, p. 124.

9   Biblical allusions heighten the irony of Chaucer's presentation of the Prioress. For instance, the seemingly literal description of the Prioress's table manners (133–35) and the matter-of-fact description of her kindness to her dogs (145–50) are considerably broadened by Chaucer's indirect allusions to Matthew 23:25–26 and 15:26–28 respectively. For comment on all this see U. C. Knoepflmacher, "Irony through Scriptural Allusion: A Note on Chaucer's Prioress," *Chaucer Review*, 4 (1970), 180–83.

10   Chaucer's Clerk was probably modeled on some real Oxford logician whom Chaucer admired. See Huling Ussery, "Fourteenth-Century English Logicians: Possible Models for Chaucer's Clerk," *Tennessee Studies in English*, 18 (1970), 1–15.

11   The tripartite-soul scheme I've pointed out is supported by others, for instance an astrological scheme (see William Spencer, "Are Chaucer's Pilgrims Keyed to the Zodiac?" *Chaucer Review*, 4 [1970], 141–70); a minor scheme involving higher and lower loves (see George R. Adams, "Sex and Clergy in Chaucer's *General Prologue*," *Literature and Psychology*, 18 [1968], 215–22, and cf. Ruth Nevo, "Chaucer: Motive and Mask in the *General Prologue*," *Modern Language Quarterly*, 24 [1963], 227–36); the several organizing ideas pointed out by Donald R. Howard, including the use of idealized portraits to divide the "realistic" *Prologue* figures — by class and by companionship — into groups of seven (see Howard's "The *Canterbury Tales*: Memory and Form," *English Literary History*, 38 [1971], 319–28); and perhaps a musical scheme (see David L. Higdon, "Diverse Melodies in Chaucer's *General Prologue*," *Criticism*, 14 [1972], 97–108).

12   Delasanta, "The Theme of Judgment," pp. 303–4.

13   For recent critical comment on the Host, see William Keen, " 'To Doon Yow Ese': A Study of the Host in the *General Prologue* to the *Canterbury Tales*," *Topic*, 17 (1969), 5–18, and Barbara Page, "Concerning the Host," *Chaucer Review*, 4 (1970), 1–13.

14   I've said nothing here of the most important Pilgrim of all, "Chaucer."

See Paul G. Ruggiers, *The Art of the "Canterbury Tales"* (Madison: University of Wisconsin Press, 1965), pp. 17–41.

15 A few of the more important critical discussions of the *Knight's Tale* are: Charles Muscatine, "Form, Texture, and Meaning in Chaucer's *Knight's Tale*," *Publications of the Modern Language Association*, 65 (1950), 911–29; James Westlund, "The *Knight's Tale* as an Impetus for Pilgrimage," *Philological Quarterly*, 63 (1964), 526–37; F. Elaine Penninger, "Chaucer's *Knight's Tale* and the Theme of Appearance and Reality in the *Canterbury Tales*," *South Atlantic Quarterly*, 63 (1964), 398–405; David V. Harrington, "Rhetoric and Meaning in Chaucer's *Knight's Tale*," *Papers on Language and Literature*, 3 (1967), 71–179; Peter H. Elbow, "How Chaucer Transcends Oppositions in the *Knight's Tale*," *Chaucer Review*, 7 (1972), 97–112; Rodney Delasanta, "Uncommon Commonplaces in the *Knight's Tale*," *Neuphilologische Mitteilungen*, 70 (1969), 683–90; Thomas A. Van, "Theseus and the 'Right Way' of the *Knight's Tale*," *Studies in the Literary Imagination*, 4 (1971), 83–100; Jeffrey Helterman, "The Dehumanizing Metamorphoses of the *Knight's Tale*," *English Literary History*, 38 (1971), 493–511. Elements of the tripartite system I describe in the tale were first pointed out to me by Thomas J. Hatton, who got parts of it from Paul Olson. The reading has since become standard in many quarters, though a few critics plod on with the old argument that one of the young knights is "better" or "more central" than the other, e.g., A. V. C. Schmidt, "The Tragedy of Arcite: A Reconsideration of the *Knight's Tale*," *Essays in Criticism*, 19 (1969), 107–16 — an interesting article despite its wrong emphasis.

16 See Paul T. Thurston, *Artistic Ambivalence in Chaucer's Knight's Tale* (Gainesville: University of Florida Press, 1968). A useful book but not one to cherish.

17 On Chaucer's changes and his reasons for making them, see P. M. Kean, "The Knight's Tale," in *Chaucer and the Making of English Poetry* (London: Routledge & Kegan Paul, 1972), vol. 2, pp. 1052. There are numerous books which offer fairly detailed readings of the *Canterbury Tales*. One of the most trustworthy and generally pleasant is Ruggiers, *The Art of the "Canterbury Tales,"* cited earlier. There are also good things — to mention only more recent books — in D. S. Brewer's *Chaucer and Chaucerians* and Jill Mann's *Chaucer and Medieval Estates Satire: The Literature of Social Classes and the "General Prologue" to the "Canterbury Tales"* (London: Cambridge University Press, 1973).

18 This is not to say Theseus is, as some have thought, a stick figure. His character grows and develops as the tale progresses. See especially Van, "Theseus and the 'Right Way' of the *Knight's Tale*," pp. 99–100.

19   Russell A. Peck demonstrates how sevens and eights (among other things) work in the *Troilus*, if one can only believe him (and on the whole I do). See his "Numerology in Chaucer's *Troilus and Criseyde*," in *Chaos and Form: History and Literature, Ideas and Relationships*, ed. Kenneth McRobie (Winnipeg: University of Manitoba Press, 1972), pp. 7–36.

20   On the *Miller's Tale* as Estates literature, see Robert P. Miller, "The *Miller's Tale* as a Complaint," *Chaucer Review*, 5 (1970), 147–60.

21   My understanding of the *Miller's Tale* depends heavily on Paul A. Olson's "Poetic Justice in the *Miller's Tale*," *Modern Language Quarterly*, 24 (1963), 227–36, and Thomas J. Hatton's "Absolon, Taste, and Order in the *Miller's Tale*," *Papers on Language and Literature*, 7 (1971), 72–75.

22   See Edmund Reiss's delightful article on the demonic blacksmith who arms silly Absolon, "Daun Gerveys in the *Miller's Tale*," *Papers on Language and Literature*, 6 (1970), 115–24.

23   On this tradition see Beryl Rowland, *Blind Beasts: Chaucer's Animal World* (Kent, Ohio: Kent State University Press, 1971). Rowland is another of those excellent scholars who for lack of sensitivity occasionally messes up the poetry. For instance he insinuates, though he doesn't state it flatly, that Chaucer hates dogs. (This is an important matter, reader.) Rowland speaks of how Bartholomew the Englishman "devotes a chapter to the 'unclene and lecherous' propensities of the dog, and attributes to Aristotle the idea which is also expressed by Chaucer's Parson that 'houndes bothe male and female use lychery as longe as they ben alyue, and yeue them to vnclennesse of lechry, that they take noo dyuersyte bytwene mother and sister, and other bytches, towchynge the dede of lechery' (xxvii). But he also praises the dog's courage and loyalty, qualities which Chaucer chooses to ingore." (Rowland, *Blind Beasts*, p. 165.) Surely it is the grim old Parson who ignores those qualities, and untrue that Chaucer "is not interested in the animal for its own sake." According to Rowland, when Chaucer uses the dog "for purposes of illustration he applies conventional ideas which are almost wholly pejorative. He enhances the impact of the stereotype by skilfully adapting his knowledge of current practices to the situation immediately before him. The effect is to startle the reader with a brief but unsparing reflection of man's depravity or lack of dignity." What's askew here is that while Chaucer *does* use conventional pulpit notions of animals (even of our faithful friend the dog), he undercuts the stern conventions by his communication of his sympathetic feeling for animals. The dog in the *Book of the Duchess* — the subject of Rowland's discussion — is a lovable puppy the narrator wants to catch (as he wants to catch his lady and roll in the grass with her). He takes the same delight in the swallow singing on the barn. And when he's *not* writing "for purposes of illustration," his affection for animals is wholehearted, as in that famous chase in the *Nun's Priest's Tale*:

> Ran Colle oure dogge, and Talbot and Gerland,
> And Malkyn, with a dystaf in hir hand;
> Ran cow and calf, and eek the verray hogges,
> So fered for the berkyng of the dogges.
>
> [VII, 3883–86

It is of course true that some people, throughout history, have not been fond of dogs. But it is impossible to be a truly great poet and not feel affectionate toward dogs and also cats and, in some cases, ducks.

24 See A. Brooker Thro, "Chaucer's Creative Comedy: A Study of the *Miller's Tale* and the *Shipman's Tale*," *Chaucer Review*, 5 (1970), 97–111.

25 On Chaucer's attitude toward astrology (and thus for the meaning of his numerous astrological allusions), see Chauncey Wood, *Chaucer and the Country of the Stars: Poetic Uses of Astrological Imagery* (Princeton, N.J.: Princeton University Press, 1970).

26 The theater devices are more complicated than I can detail here. For slightly more discussion — though the study is by no means exhaustive — see Beryl Rowland, "The Play of the *Miller's Tale*: A Game Within a Game," *Chaucer Review*, 5 (1970), 140–46.

27 Some of what I say about the *Reeve's Tale* comes from Paul A. Olson, "The *Reeve's Tale*: Chaucer's *Measure for Measure*," *Studies in Philology*, 59 (1962), 1–17; Joseph L. Baird, "Law and the *Reeve's Tale*," *Neuphilologische Mitteilungen*, 70 (1969), 679–83; Ian Lancashire, "Sexual Innuendo in the *Reeve's Tale*, *Chaucer Review*, 6 (1972), 159–70; and Derek Brewer, "The *Reeve's Tale* and the King's Hall, Cambridge," *Chaucer Review*, 5 (1971), 311–17.

28 Baird, "Law and the *Reeve's Tale*," p. 680.

29 See Ian Lancashire, "Sexual Innuendo in the *Reeve's Tale*."

Chapter 9

1 Kittredge's observation that Chaucer was inclined to work with groups of tales rather than with individual pieces raises questions when we examine the sequence of tales in fragments II–V. The first question, of course, is whether the sequence is a sequence at all — whether the

Ellesmere (or group *a*) arrangement, followed by F. N. Robinson, is right and not some such arrangement as that chosen by Skeat in his Oxford edition. The second question is whether any principle of thematic unity or progression can be found in the group. I accept the Ellesmere arrangement, for reasons I've sketched here and presented in detail elsewhere ("The Case Against the 'Bradshaw Shift'; or, the Mystery of the Manuscript in the Trunk," *Papers on Language and Literature*, 3 [1967], 80–106), but perhaps no vitally important argument need hang on this. The sequence works better — and so does Fragment VII, self-contained in manuscript tradition — if the Wife speaks directly in answer to the Man of Law. But to reject this arrangement is merely to say (rather stupidly) that the Wife introduces the subject of the sequence (the same subject introduced by the Man of Law) without provocation.

2   On the "marriage theme" in this expanded sense, see Michael Wilks, "Chaucer and the Mystical Marriage in Medieval Political Thought," *Bulletin of the John Rylands Library*, 64 (1961), 489–530.

3   Trevor Whittock, *A Reading of the "Canterbury Tales"* (Cambridge: Cambridge University Press, 1968), p. 34.

4   Ibid., p. 113.

5   Ibid., p. 116.

6   Ibid., p. 114.

7   Ibid., p. 115.

8   As political flattery, the sultan episode of course suggests the infidel's need for the true Christian faith and thus praises Richard's dream of an Eastern crusade. The whole group of fragments, II–V, has a good deal to do, I think, with English politics in the 1390s.

9   For a long time the Wife of Bath was one of Chaucer's most popular and most frequently lauded characters, quite rightly. Lately critics have maliciously delighted in finding fault with her. To mention only some of the more recent libels or, anyway, unfriendly views, see James Finn Cotter, in "The Wife of Bath's Lenten Observance," *Papers on Language and Literature*, 7 (1971), 293–97, who argues (correctly) that in her Lenten capture of Jankyn, the Wife, "unwittingly or not . . . portrays herself as a follower of the god of love and Venus in her search for 'grace.' The favor of man and not of God is her aim" (p. 295). Judson B. Allen and Patrick Gallacher, in "Alisoun Through the Looking Glass: Or Every Man His Own Midas," *Chaucer Review*, 4 (1970), 99–105, argue that the Wife misapplies her Midas story (which is true) and irrationally, even sinfully,

asks the reader to be a bad judge like Midas. Nicholas Kiessling, in *"The Wife of Bath's Tale*: D878–881," *Chaucer Review*, 7 (1972), 113–17, goes so far as to argue that the Friar and the Wife are as close to being kindred spirits as any two people on the pilgrimage. David S. Reid, in "Crocodilian Humor: A Discussion of Chaucer's Wife of Bath," *Chaucer Review*, 4 (1970), 73–89, claims that we need to understand the Wife in terms of pantomime and farce, that she's a type, not an individual, that she's a vulgar convention and has only the liveliness of pantomime, and so forth. Bernard S. Levy, in "The Wife of Bath's *Queynte Fantasye*," *Chaucer Review*, 4 (1970), 106–22, argues that the Wife makes hay on "illusion caused by sin"; and Robert F. Fleissner, in "The Wife of Bath's Five," *Chaucer Review*, 8 (1974), 128–32, shows that Chaucer's use of pentad tradition and the stock numerological associations of *five* condemns the Wife's carnality. Beryl Rowland claims, in "The Wife of Bath's 'Unlawful Philtrum,' " *Neophilologus*, 51 (1972), 200–206, that the Wife takes God's law "Go and multiply" to mean "Get many husbands," and that she in effect practices "unnatural magic."

It is of course perfectly true that the Wife has faults from a medieval Christian point of view, and that Chaucer does partly satirize her; but to dismiss her as simply a sinner and standard type is foolish. For more favorable views of the Wife, see Michael D. Cherniss, "The *Clerk's Tale* and *Envoy*, The Wife of Bath's Purgatory, and the *Merchant's Tale*," *Chaucer Review*, 6 (1972), 235–54; David Parker, "Can We Trust the Wife of Bath?" *Chaucer Review*, 4 (1970), 90–98; Gloria K. Shapiro, "Dame Alice as Deceptive Narrator," *Chaucer Review*, 6 (1971), 130–41; and Beryl Rowland, "Chaucer's Dame Alice: Critics in Blunderland?" *Neuphilologische Mitteilungen*, 73 (1972), 381–95.

10 A few important relatively recent studies of the *Friar's Tale* are Paul E. Beichner's "Baiting the Summoner," *Modern Language Quarterly*, 22 (1961), 367–76; Adrien Bonjour, "Aspects of Chaucer's Irony in the *Friar's Tale*," *Essays in Criticism*, 11 (1961), 121–27; Earle Birney, *"After His Ymage* — The Central Ironies of the *Friar's Tale*," *Medieval Studies*, 21 (1959), 17–35; Joseph L. Baird, "The Devil's Privetee," *Neuphilologische Mitteilungen*, 70 (1969), 104–6; R. T. Lenaghen, "The Irony of the *Friar's Tale*," *Chaucer Review*, 7 (1973), 281–94; and Hugh L. Hennedy, "The Friar's Summoner's Dilemma," *Chaucer Review*, 5 (1971), 213–17.

11 The comic fart image has wider implications. See Alan Levitan, "The Parody of Pentecost in Chaucer's *Summoner's Tale*," *University of Toronto Quarterly*, 40 (1971), 236–46.

12 Richard's coronation had slyly undermined the whole theory of consent in England, and Richard's divine-right argument, one of the bases of his absolutist theory, flatly denied the doctrine of consent. Chaucer obviously — and openly — disagrees.

13   The best recent studies of the *Clerk's Tale* are, I think, Francis L. Utley's "Five Genres in the *Clerk's Tale*," *Chaucer Review*, 6 (1972), 198–228; Joseph E. Grennen's "Science and Sensibility in Chaucer's Clerk," *Chaucer Review*, 6 (1971), 81–93; John McNamara, "Chaucer's Use of the Epistle of St. James in the *Clerk's Tale*," *Chaucer Review*, 7 (1973), 184–93; and Delores W. Frese, "Chaucer's *Clerk's Tale*: The Monsters and the Critics Reconsidered," *Chaucer Review*, 8 (1974), 133–46. There's been a movement lately — completely wrongheaded — to give the Envoy at the end of the *Clerk's Tale* to some speaker other than the Clerk. See for instance Sister Francis Dolores Corella, "The Speaker of the Wife of Bath Stanza and Envoy," *Chaucer Review*, 4 (1970), 267–83.

14   On Griselda and Job see Donald H. Reiman, "The Real *Clerk's Tale*; or, Patient Griselda Explained," *Texas Studies in Language and Literature*, 5 (1963), 356–73. On Griselda and the Virgin, see Utley, "Five Genres in the *Clerk's Tale*."

15   Martin Stevens, "And Venus Laugheth": An Interpretation of the *Merchant's Tale*," *Chaucer Review*, 7 (1972), 118–31. According to Stevens the *Merchant's Tale* is not at all a "repugnant and bitter satire" as all other critics (he imagines) have supposed, because the Merchant is really a more or less nice man and the rules that govern the world of fabliau allow no such dark interpretation. "Repugnant" certainly the tale is not, and the point on the Merchant's personality is well taken. But the most casual inspection shows a comic bitterness in the *Merchant's Tale* that does not appear in the *Miller's Tale* or, say, the *Shipman's*. To deny it is to resist some of the tale's finest humor — the crabby-old-man humor we sometimes encounter in Al Capp, or the glory of Dickens' Scrooge, the humor of unreasonable testiness, satire without bite because the satirist has no teeth. The Merchant is of course not as decrepit or as henpecked as he pretends for the sake of his fiction; he's playing a character and playing it to the hilt, trying with all his competitive soul to win that supper. But the nihilism he lets slip out is real.

16   A few fairly interesting recent articles on the *Merchant's Tale* are Nicolai von Kreisler, "An Aesopic Allusion in the *Merchant's Tale*," *Chaucer Review*, 6 (1971), 30–37; Peter G. Beidler, "The Climax in the *Merchant's Tale*," *Chaucer Review*, 6 (1971), 38–43; Emerson Brown, Jr., "*Hortus Inconclusus*: The Significance of Priapus and Pyramus and Thisbe in the *Merchant's Tale*," *Chaucer Review*, 4 (1970), 31–40; Bruce A. Rosenberg, "The 'Cherry-Tree Carol' and the *Merchant's Tale*," *Chaucer Review*, 5 (1971), 264–76; Mary C. Schroeder, "Fantasy in the *Merchant's Tale*," *Criticism*, 12 (1970), 167–79; and Norman T. Harrington, "Chaucer's *Merchant's Tale*: Another Swing of the Pendulum," *Publications of the Modern Language Association*, 86 (1971), 25–31.

17 The knight of the tale was a man from Lombardy, born in Pavia. Emerson J. Brown shows, in "The *Merchant's Tale*: Why was January Born 'of Pavye'?" *Neuphilologische Mitteilungen*, 71 (1970), 654–58, that Lombardy and Pavia were commonly associated with, respectively, usurious wealth and sensuality. Cf. Peter G. Beidler, "January, Knight of Lombardy," *Neuphilologische Mitteilungen*, 72 (1971), 735–38.

18 On gentilesse in the *Merchant's Tale*, see P. M. Kean, *Chaucer and the Making of English Poetry* (London: Routledge & Kegan Paul, 1972), vol. 2, pp. 157–64.

19 On natural propriety as developed in the Merchant's and Miller's tales see Janet Boothman, " 'Who Hath No Wyf, He is No Cokewold': A Study of John and January in Chaucer's Miller's and Merchant's Tales," *Troth*, 4 (1963), 3–14. Cf. Karl P. Wentersdorf, "Theme and Structure in the *Merchant's Tale*: The Function of the Pluto Episode," *Publications of the Modern Language Association*, 80 (1965), 522–27.

20 On the Squire's ineptitude, see, among others, Stanley J. Karhle, "Chaucer's *Squire's Tale* and the Decline of Chivalry," *Chaucer Review*, 7 (1973), 184–93.

21 It has grown fashionable lately to argue that the *Squire's Tale* is complete — interrupted by the Franklin. Some of those who make this strange claim are Charles F. Duncan, in " 'Straw for Youre Gentilesse': The Gentle Franklin's Interruption of the Squire," *Chaucer Review*, 5 (1970), 161–64, and Joyce E. Peterson, "The Finished Fragment: A Reassessment of the *Squire's Tale*," *Chaucer Review*, 5 (1970), 62–74. For rebuttal see John W. Clark, "*Does* the Franklin Interrupt the Squire?" *Chaucer Review*, 7 (1972), 160–61.

22 On this point see A. M. Kearney, "Truth and Illusion in the Franklin's Tale," *Essays in Criticism*, 19 (1969), 245–53. Kearney seems a touch more male chauvinist than Chaucer, but the basic point is sound enough.

23 For more detail, see Gerhard Joseph, "The *Franklin's Tale*: Chaucer's Theodicy," *Chaucer Review*, 1 (1966), 20–32.

Chapter 10

1 Paul G. Ruggiers, *The Art of the "Canterbury Tales"* (Madison: University of Wisconsin Press, 1965), p. 123.

2   On the *Physician's Tale*, see Thomas B. Hanson, "Chaucer's Physician as Storyteller and Moralizer," *Chaucer Review*, 7 (1972), 132–39; and Lee C. Ramsey, " 'The Sentence of it Sooth Is': Chaucer's *Physician's Tale*," *Chaucer Review*, 6 (1972), 185–97.

3   On the *Physician's Tale* see Lee C. Ramsey and Thomas B. Hanson, cited in note 2 above; also Geraldine S. Branca, "Experience Versus Authority: Chaucer's Physician and Fourteenth-Century Science," *Dissertation Abstracts*, 32 (1972), 5731A; Richard L. Hoffman, "Jepthah's Daughter and Chaucer's Virginia," *Chaucer Review*, 2 (1967), 20–31; and Robert Longsworth, "The Doctor's Dilemma: A Comic View of the *Physician's Tale*," *Criticism*, 13 (1971), 223–33.

4   Walter Clyde Curry, *Chaucer and the Medieval Sciences* (New York: Barnes & Noble, 1960).

5   For more elaborate analysis of the *Pardoner's Prologue and Tale*, see Penelope Curtis, "The Pardoner's 'Jape,' " *Critical Review*, 11 (1968), 15–31.

6   The identity of the old man in the tale has been debated, some critics arguing that he really is Death, some that he is the Wandering Jew, and some that he is merely an old man. There's evidence for all three readings, but deciding the point is probably wrongheaded. He is all of them and none, a dark, mysterious figure, suited to the Pardoner's dark legend. An interesting recent view of the old man is that of Stephen A. Khinoy, "Inside Chaucer's Pardoner," *Chaucer Review*, 6 (1972), 255–67.

7   G. G. Sedgewick, "The Progress of Chaucer's Pardoner, 1880–1940," *Modern Language Quarterly*, 1 (1940), 431–58.

8   See for instance Robert P. Miller, "Chaucer's Pardoner, the Scriptural Eunuch, and the *Pardoner's Tale*," *Speculum*, 30 (1955), 180–99; Garland Ethel, "Chaucer's Worste Shrewe: The Pardoner," *Modern Language Quarterly*, 20 (1959), 211–27; and Clarence H. Miller and Roberta Bux Bosse, "Chaucer's Pardoner and the Mass," *Chaucer Review*, 6 (1972), 185–97. A defense of the Pardoner is offered by Edmund Reiss, "The Final Irony in the *Pardoner's Tale*," *College English*, 25 (1963), 260–66. See also John Halverson, "Chaucer's Pardoner and the Progress of Criticism," *Chaucer Review*, 4 (1970), 184–202 (an argument that both the character of the Pardoner and the tale he tells dramatize the human impulse toward death) and P. S. Tritt, "Harry Bailey and the Pardoner's Relics," *Studia Neophilologica*, 41 (1969), 112–14.

9   Not much of importance has been done on the *Shipman's Tale* except for those discussions which show it was originally for the Wife of

Bath, of which I here say nothing. One interesting piece on the tale itself is Michael W. McClintock's "Games and the Players of Games: Old French Fabliaux and the *Shipman's Tale*," *Chaucer Review*, 5 (1970), 112–36.

10 See Alan Gaylord, "The Unconquered Tale of the Prioress," *Papers of the Michigan Academy of Sciences, Arts, and Letters*, 46 (1961), 571–95.

11 On this cure see Ynez Viole O'Neill, "A Speculation Concerning the Grain in Chaucer's *Prioress's Tale*," *Medievalia et Humanistica*, 12 (1968), 185–90.

12 See Armand E. Singer, "Chaucer and Don Juan," *West Virginia University Philological Papers*, 13 (1962), 25–30.

13 On the development of Chaucer's understanding of tragedy, see Paul G. Ruggiers, "Towards a Theory of Tragedy in Chaucer," *Chaucer Review*, 8 (1973), 89–99. For praise of the *Monk's Tale*, see Estelle W. Taylor, "Chaucer's *Monk's Tale*: An Apology," *College Language Association Journal*, 13 (1969), 172–82. I have discussed one or two of the Monk's tragedies in my book, *The Life and Times of Chaucer* (New York: Knopf, 1977).

14 The *Nun's Priest's Tale* has been endlessly discussed, rightly. A few of the more interesting recent pieces are Richard J. Schroder's "Chaunticleer, the Mermaid, and Daun Burnel," *Chaucer Review*, 4 (1970), 284–90; D. E. Myers' "Focus and 'Moralite' in the *Nun's Priest's Tale*," *Chaucer Review*, 7 (1973), 210–19; Corine E. Kauffman, "Dame Pertelote's Parlous Parle," *Chaucer Review*, 4 (1970), 41–48; Peter Meredith, "Chauntecleer and the Mermaids," *Neophilologus*, 54 (1970), 81–83; and Constance B. Hieatt, "The Moral of the *Nun's Priest's Tale*," *Studia Neophilologica*, 42 (1970), 3–8.

Chapter 11

1 Isak Dinesen, *Seven Gothic Tales* (New York: Random House, 1934; Knopf, Vintage Books, 1972).

2 On pallor, the horse imagery, and so forth, see Alexander H. Brodie, "Hodge of Ware and Geber's Cook," *Neuphilologische Mitteilungen*, 72 (1971), 62–68.

3 John Finlayson, "The Satiric Mode and the *Parson's Tale*," *Chaucer Review*, 6 (1971), 94–116. On the Parson's orthodoxy see Siegfried

Wenzel, "The Source for the 'Remedia' of the *Parson's Tale*," *Traditio: Studies in Ancient and Medieval History, Thought, and Religion*, 27 (1971), 433–53.

4 An interesting recent argument is that of Olive Sayce, "The Conclusion of the *Canterbury Tales* and its Place in Literary Tradition," *Medium AEvum*, 40 (1971), 230–48.

INDEX

ABC, 65, 66, 70
Abel, 138
Abraham, 280
Absolon: analyzed, 254–56 passim, 258; mentioned, 380n22
Absolute, 137
Achilles, 57, 143, 314
Adam: fall of, 68, 87, 154; Troilus compared to, 137; mentioned, 83, 118, 133, 157, 323, 327, 357n10
Adam: in the *Monk's Tale*, 310
Adam the Scrivener, 194
Adjunctio, 24
"Advent poem": *House of Fame* as, 151
Aeneas: typic of Christ, xxviii, 170; Virgil's view of, 158; in *House of Fame*, 166; mentioned, 314
Aeneid: Fulgentius' treatment of, xxviii; in *House of Fame*, 158, 181; mentioned, 168, 170, 174, 229, 253, 254
Affectation: theme of, 299, 307
Affrycan, 49, 50–55 passim, 63
Africa, 50, 352n22
"Against Women Unconstant," 66, 183
Alanus de Insulis, xxii, 62
Albericus, 343n10
Alceste, 191, 200, 207, 208, 210, 212, 214
Alchemistic transmutation, 317
Alchemy: principles of, 316; in the *Canon's Yeoman's Tale*, 328, 330, 331; mentioned, 237
Alcyone, 4, 13, 17, 28–30 passim, 33, 49

Alcyone story: analyzed, 11, 12
Aldgate, 148, 149
Alexander, 39
Alexandria, 326
Alice in Wonderland, 192
Alisoun: analyzed, 254–56; mentioned, 258
Alla, 268, 272, 273, 285
Allegory: four levels of, xxviii; Chaucer's methods of in *Book of the Duchess*, 9; in *House of Fame*, 174, 175, 189; in *Canterbury Tales*, 216, 283, 309, 319; the *Knight's Tale*, 227, 229, 241; mentioned, 81. *See also* Poetic technique
Alliterative Morte Arthure, 31, 342n10
Almachius, 317, 318
Amazons, 241, 242, 248
Amor cortois: in *Parlement of the Birds*, 62; in *Legend of Good Women*, 208; in *Book of the Duchess*, 331. *See also* Courtly love
Amoretti, xviii, xix
Amorous complaint: Chaucer's use of, 73, 77, 81
Amorous cults, 207
Amphioun, 287
Anagram: Machault's use of, 37, 39
Anatomy of Melancholy, 11
Anderson, E. P., 343n10
Anelida: contrasted with Theseus, 74; analyzed, 76–78; mentioned, 73
Anelida and Arcite: date of discussed, 72; as a transitional work,

[389]